THE FOUNDATION
OF AUSTRALIA

(1786-1800)

A Study in English Criminal Practice and Penal
Colonization in the Eighteenth Century

by

ERIS O'BRIEN, M.A., Ph.D.

Fellow of the Royal Historical Society (London); Fellow
of the Royal Australian Historical Society

With a foreword by

JOHN M. WARD, M.A., LL.B.

Challis Professor of History, University of Sydney.

GREENWOOD PRESS, PUBLISHERS
WESTPORT, CONNECTICUT

Originally published in 1937
by Sheed and Ward

First Greenwood Reprinting 1970

SBN 8371-2968-0

PRINTED IN UNITED STATES OF AMERICA

FOREWORD

IT was with great pleasure that I heard of the decision to reprint Dr Eris O'Brien's *The Foundation of Australia*. Originally published in 1937, Dr O'Brien's book has won an unexcelled reputation in Australian historical scholarship. Succeeding authors have confirmed the accuracy of his judgments and have been glad to work within the general framework of his interpretation. There is no doubt that *The Foundation of Australia* will remain the standard work in its period for a considerable time to come.

It is altogether fitting that Dr O'Brien's scholarly work should make its reappearance at the present time when Australian historical studies are expanding so rapidly. The reprinting of the book is a source of special gratification to all students of Australian history in the universities. This work, so eminently readable, is regarded by students as a model of historical scholarship in the Australian field. I feel sure that the reprint of this book will be widely welcomed and desire to congratulate Dr O'Brien on its appearance.

JOHN M. WARD,
Challis Professor of History.

The University of Sydney,
5 *May* 1950.

AUTHOR'S PREFACE

THIS book, *The Foundation of Australia*, was first published in London, originally as a private issue for a university thesis in 1936, and later as a public edition in 1937.

For some years that edition has been exhausted. But, because the book has been in constant use as a reference work for university classes, it was suggested that a new edition should be brought out for the convenience of students.

Some alterations in the text have been made, where necessary. A new chapter has been written on the inter-regnum period of less than three years, during which the Lieutenant-Governors administered the Settlement for better and for worse, in order to indicate the extent of the political, economic and social changes which then occurred.

I have also provided brief outlines of two important matters which, when I was using the book as a text for students, I thought had been insufficiently discussed in it. One deals with the problems arising out of the defective original grant of Civil Jurisdiction and the unsatisfactory nature of the machinery provided to implement the Criminal Jurisdiction. This subject is now discussed in Appendix F. The other summarizes some recently published research into the growth of Trade and Commerce at the Settlement prior to 1800 and its relationship to the prerogatives of the East India Company. It is Appendix G. The bibliography has been extended and notices works published since 1937, which deal with the period here surveyed.

I thank Professor John M. Ward, Challis Professor of History at the University of Sydney, for the gracious Foreword which he has written for this edition. I am grateful also to the Officers of the Mitchell Library for their courtesy and generosity in facilitating my researches.

ERIS O'BRIEN

Sydney,
6 *March* 1950.

CONTENTS

PART II

THE BEGINNING OF TRANSPORTATION
TO AUSTRALIA

ABBREVIATIONS USED IN THE TEXT

Adm.   Admiralty Papers in the P.R.O.

B.M. Add MSS.   British Museum, additional manuscripts.

Chatham Papers.   The collection of MSS. in the P.R.O., relating to the Pitt family.

Dropmore Papers.   The MSS. of J. B. Fortescue, Esq.

C.H.B.E.   Cambridge History of the British Empire, vol. vii. Part I.

C.J.   Journals of the House of Commons.

C.O.   Papers of the Colonial Office at the P.R.O.

D.N.B.   Dictionary of National Biography.

H.O.   Papers of the Home Office at the P.R.O.

H.R.A.   Historical Records of Australia.

H.R.N.S.W.   Historical Records of New South Wales.

L.J.   Journals of the House of Lords.

P.C.   Papers of the Privy Council at the P.R.O.

P.H.   Parliamentary History.

P.P.   British Parliamentary Papers.

P.R.   Parliamentary Register.

P.R.O.   The Public Record Office, London.

INTRODUCTION

AN OUTLINE OF THE TRANSPORTATION SYSTEM

On August 18, 1786, after years of fruitless searching for a suitable base to take the place of the one lost by the American Revolt, Lord Sydney informed the Lords Commissioners of the Treasury that the Government had decided to dump its surplus felons on the territory discovered by Captain Cook sixteen years previously. In January 1788 approximately a thousand people were landed at Port Jackson; but of this number about 730 were transported prisoners. Such was the inauspicious beginning of the Australian Commonwealth.

Since the beginning the Australian population has increased to 7,579,358, of whom 99·5 per cent are of British nationality and 90·2 per cent are native born (Cf. Census June 30, 1947). The more recent changes that are being made through mass immigration schemes are noticed elsewhere I. Although the greater proportion of this native-born element was from Australian parentage the ultimate origin of all the present population has been due to migration, whether compulsory or free. With scarcely any interruption prisoners were transported annually from 1787 to 1840, when the practice ceased in New South Wales; but, with varying incidence, it was continued to other parts of Australia until the final abolition of the system in 1867. In all, about 160,000 prisoners were sent to Australia. The immigration of free men, however, has made the greatest contribution to Australian population. This immigration commenced almost at the beginning of the settlement and continued spasmodically until it began to receive encouragement after the Napoleonic wars. From 1830 it became a recognized and subsidized system, and after 1850, at the time of the gold discoveries, developed into a veritable flood, submerging the unpleasant relics of the earlier foundation and considerably modifying the trend of national development. From that time until the recent economic crisis, when the system was temporarily abandoned, successive Australian Governments have followed the policy of encouraging and subsidizing free immigration.

In the general histories of Australia the subject of transportation has necessarily occupied an important place, but, apart from a few works restricted to certain periods and phases of it, no recent

examination of the subject has been made.* The subject is not attractive. It would seem that historians have felt that they should either defend or apologise for the system. At the beginning of his career Dr. Lang strongly condemned it, but in later years regarded it as the only system by which the colony of Australia could be adequately populated by British people.[2] Rusden believed that Pitt's motive in transporting felons to Australia was patriotic and intended primarily to forestall occupation by the French.[3] Pitt's biographer, however, described Pitt's part in the matter as "prosaic" and placed the "discredit" of suggesting this colonization scheme on the shoulders of Lord Sydney.[4] Other writers have attempted to palliate the system by describing it as "the spirit of the age",[5] and from a different point of view it has been argued that as the convicts were merely victims of the brutal English penal laws of those days, they were pioneers of whom Australians might be justly proud.[6] Probably the more reasonable way to look at the subject is to accept it as an unpleasant fact, from which, fortunately, all evil effects have long been obliterated in Australia. It did, however, prevent the French occupation of Australia, and the *Cambridge History of the British Empire* expresses some satisfaction in the fact that although the first colonists had to be such as they were they had "the priceless advantage that they were British".[7] It would be futile to compare British convicts with free Frenchmen, but if the French designs upon Australia during the early nineteenth century were penal in character, the comparison would become interesting.† As, however, the transportation system had little or no influence upon the later development of Australia, the average Australian's interest in it is as slight as the average Englishman's in the Norman Conquest.

Yet it is evident that this system, which dominated more than half Australia's history, cannot be treated in any summary way, particularly since during most of that period it was a governing factor in the political and industrial development of the colony. The history of Australian penal colonization may conveniently be divided into six parts. The first embraced the period between the discontinuance of American transportation in 1776 and the decision to recommence the system in New South Wales ten years

* A detailed and well documented work, published in 1935 by W. D. Forsyth, is devoted exclusively to transportation. However, this work is confined to the administration of Governor Arthur, and the system is described only with reference to Van Diemen's Land, in the period 1824 to 1836.

† In a memorandum of Secret Intelligence from Paris in 1825, now among the Bathurst MSS., it was stated that "France intends to form a colony to which criminals who have hitherto been condemned to the galleys may be sent. Several places have been under consideration at which to establish it, but the general opinion has been favourable to New Holland, both as regards the climate and the little opposition that is to (be) apprehended from the natives. ——'s opinion is asked as to the probability of England making any objections. Only a very small part of the country is occupied by England; and there is space enough for every state to send colonies without their interfering with each other." (30. xi. 1825, Bathurst MSS., p. 595, 76th Report of Historical MSS. Commission.)

later. The second period extended from the foundation of the settlement in 1788 to 1800, during which the penal colonization procedure was first established under difficulties and then rendered ineffective as a means of convict reformation during the absence of a governor at the settlement. The convict colonization system really broke up before that time, but the year 1800 has been selected as a date when an abortive attempt was made to restore order under Governor King. The third division extended from 1800 to approximately 1812, when it was found impossible to exercise a proper control of the settlement which had completely fallen under the sway of the free settlers. From 1812 to 1821 control reverted to the governor after a parliamentary investigation in 1812; but in this fourth period British policy was negatived in the settlement and discontent resulted from the autocratic methods of Governor Macquarie and his attempts to establish ex-convicts as a dominant class. To this date the transportation system had been experimental, loosely controlled and scarcely understood in England. In 1819-21 the investigations which had been conducted by J. T. Bigge in the colony provided a basis for a more scientific control in the future. The fifth period, providing for a penal settlement alongside, and distinct from, a free colony began soon after 1821 and continued until the condemnation of the transportation system by the Parliamentary Committee of 1838 and the abolition of transportation to New South Wales in 1840. The sixth period omitted New South Wales and was confined to a procedure, sometimes well and sometimes badly regulated, in Norfolk Island, Tasmania and West Australia. It comprised various attempts to revive transportation as a colonizing method until the final abolition in West Australia in 1868, but at this late date the independent status of the Australian colonies had so much increased that within Australia itself a strong curbing influence was able to be exerted against the system.

When this study in penal colonization was begun, it was hoped to confine the experimental period, from 1786 to 1821, within one volume. It became evident, however, that if the real significance of British criminal transportation was to be shown the history of this system would have to begin much earlier than 1786, the year in which Australia was determined as the place to which criminals would in future be sent. Australia, or New Holland or New South Wales as this practically unknown continent was then called, was a make-shift to take the place of the North American colonies which had proclaimed their independence and to placate public opinion which was vehemently opposed to a penal settlement in Africa. Hence, the system by which Australia was settled was no new thing, although it had been modified in many respects

from the transportation practices hitherto prevailing. It might be said that the history of the new transportation system began in 1776, when the Hulks were instituted for confining prisoners.

Though it was but a small step ten years later to determine Australia as an enlargement of the hulks system, the development of penological procedure in those years was intricate and covered a wide field of thought and experiment. This had an essential bearing on the Australian system. Moreover, apart from showing the trend of English opinion and the plans for emptying criminals from overcrowded gaols, it is equally important that the criminal problem from the point of view of the criminals themselves should be described, so that their place as pioneers of Australia might be determined with some degree of accuracy. It would not be sufficient to accept them merely as criminals. The nefarious criminal code and the judicial procedure under which they were convicted and punished in such large numbers must be understood in all its amazing significance, if the criminal colonization of Australia is to be appreciated at its true value. But even more important than these considerations is the right understanding of the political and social conditions which existed in England and Ireland during the eighteenth century. The political conditions explain the code of laws; the social conditions explain, at least to an appreciable extent, the criminality of the lower classes. Then, too, a true estimate must be made of English public opinion concerning all these matters, for it would be wrong to hold the English public responsible absolutely for the inglorious and callous system which was applied to Australia in 1786. The English public had many great thinkers, reformers and humanitarians who were far in advance of the self-interested politicians of the time, and who were much opposed to the penal procedure adopted in England. Accordingly, in this volume an attempt is made to sketch the general background of English conditions and opinions. To omit these conditions from a history of the Australian transportation system would be like attempting to follow the sequence of a tragedy without having viewed its first and essential act.

As even the briefest exposition of so many factors in the transportation system must occupy a considerable space, the scope of this general study has had to be confined to the first three divisions which we have made in the history of transportation—from 1776 to 1800.* For convenience's sake the narrative is continued until the end of Governor Hunter's administration, who, though dismissed ignominiously as a failure in 1799, continued to act as Governor until succeeded by P. G. King in September 1800.

* In a subsequent volume the history of the experimenta period to 1821 will be completed

It is difficult to disentangle Australian penal history from the general history, political and economic. By transportation the colony was begun; from it came the first settlers and in the following years hundreds of others followed their example. Free settlers had meanwhile established themselves on the land or in commerce. Hence, as the numbers of the freemen and their industry increased economic and political problems naturally arose. It was the era of vain attempts to co-ordinate the penal and the colonial working of the settlement, which rapidly advanced beyond the intentions of its original foundation. Consequently, the system of control brought out with the First Fleet was not adapted or adaptable to the changing conditions. As the economic and constitutional problems arising from this conflict have already been described in special treatises, this volume will consider only their general significance as corollaries or developments of the penal colonization system.* The interesting and humane policy pursued by Governor Phillip in his dealings with the aborigines will not be noticed in this study.

Many varied problems arose out of the transportation system, some of which cannot be noticed in this volume, but others may be discussed briefly in this introductory chapter, as they are essential to a right understanding of the subject. The question of a heriditary "taint" which was raised by Lord Bryce, who considered that the "convict stain" was capable of being "washed out" in the third generation, cannot be discussed with any finality in this work, which treats of only thirteen years of the convict settlement.[8]† Discussion of it depends on an analysis of the numbers sent to Australia, the numbers who remained, their fertility and the submergence of this element by free immigration. This interesting problem has been treated by R. C. Mills and Sir T. A. Coghlan.[9] However, certain considerations arising from the discussion of that problem are pertinent to any history of the criminals transported to Australia. Were they hereditary criminals or victims of environment? What proportion of them were criminals in the real meaning of that word? The causation of criminality among the population is largely a question for the psychologist. The Lombrosian School, with Havelock Ellis, taught that criminality was derived from heredity alone. The opponents of this school

---

* Cf. S. H. Roberts: *History of Australian Land Settlement*; E. G. Shann: *An Economic History of Australia*; Sibella MacArthur-Onslow: *Some Early Records of the MacArthurs of Camden* (for the rise of the Wool Industry); A. C. V. Melbourne: *Early Constitutional Development in Australia*; G. Mackaness: *Life of Vice-Admiral Bligh* (for the deposition of an English Governor); in general, *The Cambridge History of the British Empire*, Vol. VII, Part I. For the Constitutional Problem see p. 272 *post*

† Cf. also Paul Leroy-Beaulieu: *De la Colonisation chez les Peuples Modernes* (ed. 4th, p. 624): "il ne seriat pas raisonnable d'espérer qu'une société fondée en grande partie sur la déportation devînt immédiatement une société modèle; on doit s'attendre à ce qu'une colonie qui a reçu dans son sein plus de 75,000 criminels en conserve longtemps la trace et à ce qu'il y ait sur elle, pendant une ou deux générations, une certaine flétrissure."

went to the opposite extreme, teaching that it was developed by environment. Dr Charles Mercier, a recognized modern authority on the subject, accepts both factors in the making of a criminal. He writes: "Crime is due to temptation or opportunity, the environmental factor or stress, acting upon the predisposition of the offender, the inherent or constitutional factor. The more potent the one factor, the less of the other will be needed to bring about the result."[10]

The necessity, therefore, of investigating the condition of those who were transported is evident. Sydney Smith was one of the first to call attention to "the different degrees and species of guilt among the convicts". Writing in the *Edinburgh Review* in 1823 he enlarged upon the argument which he had first made twenty years previously. Under the word "convict" crimes of varying degrees are comprehended, he wrote, and then in characteristic vein distinguished among the prisoners murderers, Irish political offenders, poachers, and men who had been transported for stealing a pot of sausages.[11] He could have extended his list sufficiently to fill a volume with such ludicrous "crimes" for which men had been made to suffer the severe penalty of transportation. In modern times it is easy to ascertain the offences for which criminals are sentenced, but in the early transportation period the crimes for which men were transported were not usually attached to the papers sent with them to the colony. The date and place of trial and the term of sentence comprised the information, and in the case of the Irish convicts even these essential particulars were generally lacking. In the "Alphabetical List of Convicts" which Governor Macquarie sent from the colony in later years, the crimes are not disclosed.[12] However, estimates of their criminality have been attempted, based naturally on the severity of the English penal laws and on whatever criminal statistics were available, and also, perhaps less conclusively, on the great predominance of seven years' sentences above those of fourteen years and life duration.

The basic principles in the transportation system were defined in the following way by Commissioner J. T. Bigge.[13] The Act of 1718, adopting the policy of the time of Charles II, had specified the classes of criminals who could be transported to the colonies. "The first class consisted of persons who, having been convicted of felony without benefit of clergy, were liable to be whipped or burned in the hand, or had been ordered to any workhouse"; the second class embraced those who should be "thereafter convicted of grand and petit larceny" although entitled by the law to the benefit of clergy; the third class was of those who, having been capitally convicted, had received the King's pardon on condition of being transported for a certain term. The last class included

the receivers of stolen goods. By several statutes passed after 1718, transportation was specifically appointed as a penalty for certain new offences. Apart from this last category, it was held that the serving of the required term of transportation had the effect of removing all disabilities from the criminal. Bigge stated that the leading principle in the statutory legislation specifically nominating transportation as a punishment was to make the sentence a severe one and to proportion the term of the sentence to the crime. By this means it was sought to recognize degrees of guilt among those transported.

Estimates of the degree of guilt among members of the First Fleet have been made by Dr F. Watson and Professor Wood. Dr Watson observed that the females then transported were part of a greater number of sentenced women whose combined thefts had averaged only 18s. 5½d. in value. Moreover, in a return of convicts on this fleet, it is recorded that only thirty-six were sentenced for life, twenty for fourteen years, 639 for the usual short term of seven years, and two for shorter periods. Because so large a proportion were sentenced for the short term Dr. Watson contended that about 83 per cent of the first convict colonists "were guilty of offences against the law for which in modern times they would be dealt with by the summary jurisdiction of a police court, or pardoned possibly under a First Offenders' Act". "Does this not largely falsify", he wrote, "the illiberal reproaches cast on the beginnings of a nation, unmerited odium given birth to in the eighteenth century and thriving still at the end of the nineteenth?"[14] With these statistics in mind Professor Wood was disposed to raise the level of comparatively innocent men and women on the First Fleet to 92 per cent. *The Cambridge History of the British Empire* appears to subscribe to Dr Watson's opinion.[15] The statistics on which these conclusions were based referred only to the First Fleet and are contained in the list of convicts which was compiled as an appendix to *The Voyage of Governor Phillip to Botany Bay*, published in 1789. This list, however, gives particulars for only 697 convicts out of a total of 778 embarked, but among these the proportion of seven years sentences is over 90 per cent. However, for the First Fleet there is also available a "Register of all convicts embarked", in which the crimes of 214 of the prisoners are entered.[16] It has to be remarked that these include a fair proportion of graver offences.*

Care should be taken not to make the statistics of the First

* Of the convicts particularized, twenty were being transported for highway robbery, nineteen for returning from transportation, nine for killing or stealing sheep, thirty-two for burglary, eleven for housebreaking, six for horse-stealing, five for receiving stolen goods, three for stealing cows, three for stealing woollens or clothing, and one each for robbery, shoplifting, forgery, and obtaining money by false pretences. It might be said that scarcely any one of these crimes merited the severe punishment of transportation, and the disproportion of the punishment is further seen in the fact that among the specified sentences seventy-eight were for grand larceny (stealing above the value of one shilling), and nineteen for petty larceny (stealing below the value of one shilling).

Fleet applicable to the whole history of transportation, though throughout the first thirty years of the system it does seem that the seven years sentence fairly constantly indicates a low degree of criminality among the prisoners. It is essential, however, to regard the varying terms of sentence in the colony not as original sentences, but in many cases as commutations from the death penalty and reductions from longer terms. Thus, the crime of a man undergoing a seven years' term would not necessarily be such as that to which the seven years' sentence would have been originally applied according to the English criminal law. Moreover, the English criminal law provisions were constantly evaded by sympathetic juries. Hence, the criminal who arrived in Australia was frequently the final residue of various eliminations, one of a small proportion who remained after acquittals by magistrates and judges and after pardons and commutations and selective processes adopted after conviction.

In the period just prior to the Australian system the method of procedure is worth noting, but it should be observed that the convictions and executions were then much higher than in later years. A synopsis of the Criminal Sessions at the Old Bailey between 1749 and 1771 reveals that 1121 persons were capitally convicted, and that as many as 678 of these were executed; the remainder were pardoned on condition of being transported. In the same period 5199 people were transported by direct sentence. Of the 1121 capital convictions of that period* only 104 were respited to transportation. Crime in the early part of this period was of a more serious nature and executions more brutal than in later years.[17] In 1773 and 1774 the commutation of death sentences into transportation was becoming more marked. In the cases specially referred to the Home Office a general survey indicates that practically all the death sentences were commuted to transportation for fourteen or seven years; one-third of those originally sentenced to transportation were pardoned, and, with few exceptions, the transportation sentences were reduced—life to fourteen years, and fourteen years to seven.[18]

The condition of affairs after the cessation of transportation to America is vividly described in a petition from the Lord Mayor and Aldermen of London to the King in 1786, in which they begged for a better disposal of criminals in order to stop the prevalent crime. Crime, they said, had greatly increased in the last ten years, and particularly in the last three years. Burglary had become a menace to civil life. In the ten years prior to 1776 about 6000 had been transported, but in the interval since that date there had been no adequate means of punishment, and, the Corporation thought,

* These included 208 cases of burglary and 362 cases of highway robbery.

about 4000 criminals had been released too expeditiously upon
society. This "dreadful accumulation" of criminals compelled
the Aldermen to petition His Majesty to direct such measures to
be taken as would provide "a speedy and due execution of the
law, both as to capital punishment and transportation".[19] The
remedy was applied when the decision to resume transportation
was made in that year. The petition of this responsible body
indicates that criminality in this critical year was of such a kind
as to call for stern repression.

To show how inconsistent the procedure was in every respect
some facts relative to the following years may be quoted. It will
be seen that the sentences were not only grossly disproportionate
to the crime, but also unequally executed. From the Newgate
Calendar of 1791 we have selected a couple of pages that may
be regarded as a fair sample of the period.[20] The sentence of death
is recorded in four instances, all for burglary; twice it is commuted
to life transportation, once to military service, and once to six
months' gaol. In the seventeen instances of transportation for
seven years, the offence is always larceny; in each case the goods
stolen are specified, and include a watch, a petticoat, a gown, a
looking-glass and soap. Two were sentenced for stealing a pocket-
handkerchief—one a boy of sixteen; a boy of fourteen was sentenced
for stealing sugar, and another of fifteen had stolen shoe-buckles;
another was sentenced to transportation on "suspicion of stealing
a trunk". Nevertheless, in the same sessions a man convicted of
manslaughter was fined 1s. and sentenced to a year in Newgate,
and another who had "stabbed a man in the face with intent to
rob" was sentenced to a year in gaol. The idiosyncrasies were
largely due to the influence that could be brought to bear on juries
by defendants, and also to the fact that petty crimes were well-
defined in the Statute Law and the greater crimes often defined
so loosely that technicalities could easily defeat conviction or alter
the nature of the crime. Records of the Old Bailey for the year
1793-94 show that among 1060 people committed for trial, 588
were acquitted or respited.[21*]

In 1795 among 1895 persons committed for trial in England†
998, or more than 50 per cent were for cases of petty larceny.
It would, therefore, seem that the lack of real crime among so-called
criminals is immediately apparent. However, the procedure again
makes it difficult to draw a conclusion. Out of 1895 commitments
made in that year 845 acquittals were recorded. Of the 949 people

---

* Those executed numbered only sixty-eight; the number punished in England was 235, and
those transported numbered 169. All these were transported for seven years.

† Forty-six were murder cases, twenty-nine for manslaughter, sixteen and seventeen for coining
and forgery, 159 for burglary and robbery, 108 for cattle- or horse-stealing, and 315 for felony.

convicted 218 were executed, 540 were imprisoned or punished in England, and only 169 were sentenced to be transported, all except two for a seven years' term.[22] The conclusion thus tends to be that the petty offenders were either acquitted or punished in England, and the fact that seven years was general among the transportations shows either that the penalty of seven years was regarded as sufficiently severe for the greater offences, or that the authorities more reasonably regarded the bulk of the offences as being too small to warrant a longer punishment. Colquhoun, who was a magistrate in this period, emphasized these points, remarking that among 2000 to 2500 prisoners tried annually in the metropolis, it generally happened that about two-thirds were charged with larceny, petty offences and vagrancy. He also observed that the greater part of these were either acquitted or released upon society after whipping or short imprisonment.[23] The same procedure was followed after 1800.[24]*

In Ireland a similar harsh penal code existed and the majority of those committed for trial and convicted were guilty of comparatively small offences, quite disproportioned to the punishments imposed. But the judicial processes of Ireland were inferior to those of England, where rules and procedure were usually strictly adhered to and juries and judges often intervened for the sake of justice and mercy. The Irish procedure raised a difficult situation many years later. It was the practice in Ireland for grand juries merely to read over the records of the magistrate's examination, after which without any further hearing of witnesses they found or rejected a bill of indictment against the accused. As Romilly remarked, this illegal procedure negatived the function of the grand juries. When Parliament attempted to rectify the results of this practice, Peel suggested that the reform should be made by an Enacting Bill rather than a Declaratory Bill, "because it would be dangerous to give the countenance of Parliament to a notion that such important proceedings, which have taken place for such a length of time, had all been illegal".[25] Under such a system and according to a repressive code hundreds of petty offenders were sentenced to transportation.†

---

* In an analysis of capital convictions in England between 1805 and 1818, it is shown that in 8430 cases only 12 per cent were executed. Here also the commutations of capital sentences into transportation must be appreciated. Summarizing the period 1749 to 1818 in convenient seven year intervals, the gradual decrease of executions among capital convictions is evident from these percentages: 66, 60, 50, 50, 50, 50, 26, 17, 13, 11½ (cf. *P.P.*, 23/3/1818). Between 1810 and 1825 larceny charges rose by 300 per cent and comprised 90 per cent of the crimes. The commitment figures in that period for all England numbered 168,759; but of this number only 110,793 were convicted. Of those convicted 14,452 were sentenced to death, but only 1326 were executed. Those sentenced to imprisonment in England numbered 70,862, of whom about 74 per cent were sentenced for less than six months. The number sentenced to transportation was 21,952, and of these only 1497 were sentenced for life, 2135 sentences were for fourteen years, but 18,320 were for seven years. (*P.P.* 1827, 534; 22/6/1827, pp. 66-70.)

† In Ireland, prior to 1800, and apart from the sedition charges, crime in the majority of cases was of the more trivial kind. For example, in the Monaghan gaols after the Lent Assizes of 1797, ight out of ten sentences were imposed for "felony", one for burglary and one for assault. All

The selection of prisoners for transportation was a complicated matter. As we have seen, prior to 1787 it had been the custom to remit part of the original terms of sentence and to transport most of the reprieved capital offenders for terms of fourteen and seven years. The seven years' term, predominant as it was over most of the period of transportation, has, therefore, to be regarded as an amended sentence—a commutation of the death sentence in some cases, and of the life and fourteen years' terms in most other cases. This statement may be generally applied to the English system, but not so generally to the Irish. In the First Fleet we may accept the seven years' term as being about 90 per cent of the total. From 1789 to 1792 the seven years men were about 82 per cent of all those transported from England.* However, in 1793, when the cost of transporting and maintenance was believed to be about £80 per head,²⁶ Ministers were feeling inclined to discontinue transportation altogether because of the expense. It was suggested, therefore, that "no convicts shall be sent out but those whose sentence is for life". Those with sentences of fourteen years were to be imprisoned "for twelve months in Newgate or the Compter", and those sentenced for seven years were to be kept in custody for three months.²⁷

In the following seven years, 1793 to 1799, the proportion of life sentences among the transported became much greater, but the total number of transportees was considerably reduced, being only 1248 English.† The longer sentences had risen to about 34 per cent of the total.²⁸ But this was only a temporary lull, and at the end of the century the crowded state of English gaols necessitated the sending out of greater numbers, and the seven years term continued in a much larger proportion.

Nevertheless, it is evident that those transported were men on whom a longer sentence had originally been imposed. The Report of the 1798 Committee on Finance makes this clear. It was found that among those who had been thus sentenced up to June 1798, a total of 1864 could not be transported, because, in the existing uncultivated state of the penal colony, it was thought inexpedient to send out larger numbers than could be readily absorbed. Within recent years, it was stated, transportation had

---

these, however, were transportation sentences. (Rebellion Papers, 85, 620/36.) In the six years 1815-20, the Irish statistics show: committed for trial, 67,426; convicted, 27,219; sentences of death, 1640; executions, 611; recorded commutations of death penalty to life transportation, 397; absolute pardons recorded, 40; transportation sentences: 120 for life, 238 for fourteen years, and 3069 for seven years; actually transported from this class and from commuted capital sentences, 3061; imprisonments: 1957 for less than three years, and 16,429 for six months and less; whipped, 418; fined, 2768; pilloried, 79; burned in the hand, 385; and respited and pardoned, 107 (cf. *P.P.* (1821) XX, 159-187). Of those transported in the same period from Ireland 1626 were for larceny, 309 for rioting and sedition. Nearly all of these were sentenced to seven years (*P.P.* (1821) XX, 164, 165).

* 3222 out of 3942.

† These are the figures of the 1810 Returns: in Appendix B the total is estimated at 1334. In that period there were 417 for life, 99 for fourteen years and 732 for seven years.

been regulated according to the capacity of the colony to receive convicts. Hence, in 1798 there remained in English and Scotch gaols 1449, and in the hulks 415 people who should have been transported. Nevertheless, among those who had been transported the Committee observed that the period of "seven years is by far the most common term of transportation, so much so that, without any material error it may be taken as the only one".[29]

In the Report from the Select Committee on Transportation in 1812, the procedure of selecting convicts for transportation is described. The Committee first called attention to the disadvantages under which governors were placed in having no records of the crimes committed by the transportees: "With the dispatches from Government a list of the convicts is generally sent, but this list has for the most part been very deficient in particularizing the offences of which they have been convicted; and in distributing them upon their arrival, the Governor has no clue to guide him in giving to them more or less advantageous situations".[30] The Committee recommended that this practice should be amended, but Governor Macquarie objected to such an amendment. The Committee's summing up of the system of selection of convicts for transportation from England was that when the hulks were filled a ship was chartered: the first selected were all those male convicts under fifty years of age who had been sentenced for life or fourteen years; the deficiency in the cargo was then made up from those seven years men who were "the most unruly" or had been guilty of "the most atrocious crimes". But among the females the only limitation for selection was that they should be below the age of forty-five years.[31] In evidence, J. H. Capper, superintendent of the hulks, stated that among the seven years prisoners "those guilty of atrocious crimes and insubordination" were chosen, in order to maintain the safety of the county gaols and hulks.[32] Insubordination among these after sentence, rather than their relative guilt, seems to have been a chief basis of selection.

Irish transportation must be considered separately. The system had long been practised, but, as in England, it had been hampered by the American revolt. The Irish Government did not at first join with the English-Australian system, begun in 1786, though in that year the Government took the precaution of copying the English Enabling Act and passed legislation authorizing the transportation of criminals to America or to such places outside Europe as might be determined. The history of this decision is given in the chapter dealing with the resumption of transportation.[33] Accordingly, in March 1791 a number of prisoners were sent from Dublin to Cork to join the transport, *Queen*, for Botany Bay.[34]

In Ireland the only prisons were county gaols and hulks, and

from 1791 the deficiency in gaol accommodation was made up by the system of transportation, which continued until 1835, when penal servitude within Ireland was authorized. Although transportation was made in English vessels the details of the system and the expenditure incurred remained a matter for Dublin Castle. The transportation accounts of 1791, submitted to the English Government, make a distinction between English and Irish expenditure, and from official papers still existing in Dublin Castle it is evident that even provisioning contracts were let to Irish contractors.[35]

Irish methods of selecting convicts for transportation differed considerably from the English. Unlike the English prisoners their sentences did not commence until the date of their embarkation, and as many of these had been kept prisoners for a great length of time before being embarked, a complaint was made in 1795 that they were undergoing a "superaddition of punishment". One man had been kept in prison for four years before being sent away; the same fact is borne out in numerous letters from Generals Dundas and Rose to Castlereagh during the rebellion period of 1798, when complaints were made that the gaols were full to overflowing, particularly with military prisoners and with rebels whose sentences had been commuted from death to life transportation.[36] The unsatisfactory state of Irish prisons continued, and difficulty was always experienced in obtaining papers relative to the sentences imposed and the terms which men would have to serve in Australia. After unsuccessful attempts to obtain these particulars governors sometimes felt themselves obliged to restore convicts to liberty, feeling certain that the original term of sentence had more than been completed. In a memorandum submitted to the Committee of 1812, Foster Archer, the Inspector-General of Irish prisons, described the procedure in selecting convicts for transportation and the methods adopted to solve the problem of insufficient Irish gaols. Reports on the condition and conduct of all prisoners were sent to the Lord-Lieutenant, who sent them back to the judges who had tried them, in order to ascertain whether mitigations might be sanctioned. Men and women of previous good character were often pardoned, and the industrious were occasionally sent to Irish penitentiaries. But those whose death sentences had been commuted were "universally" transported for life; of those primarily sentenced to life transportation a few were sent out for fourteen years, but the majority of all transportees were for seven years. The proportion of those transported to those retained in penitentiaries was about $2\frac{1}{4}$ to 1. After medical examination the selected convicts were transported in shiploads from Cork about twice in every three years.[37] Owing to the destruction in 1922 of the

Transportation Papers preserved in the Public Record Office in Dublin, it has not been possible to obtain full particulars of the early years of Irish transportation.

The majority of the English prisoners were transported for a seven years term.* The selection procedure, however, was not carried out in any scientific way. The heinousness of the crime was relative, according as it was viewed by reactionary legislators or by experienced criminologists like Bentham, H. G. Bennet or Governor Macquarie. Thirty years after the system had begun Bennet declared that "for the most trivial offences persons of both sexes are sentenced to seven years transportation; many have actually been transported for first offences, the crime being the theft of something valued at tenpence". Governor Macquarie regarded the seven years term as indicative of only "a trifling offence". The inconsistencies in the system are revealed particularly in the transportation of children and aged people. In the early years some were seventy years of age, others permanent invalids, and others boys and girls of twelve and thirteen years. However, these were few in that period; but between 1812 and 1815 there were 396 boys and 109 girls transported, two of whom were eleven years of age.[38]

The political prisoners swelled the totals of non-criminal convicts in Australia. The Irish were the more numerous and the greater part of them arrived in the colony during the period treated in this volume. Their expulsion from Ireland and the political leaven introduced into the colony after their arrival will be discussed in later chapters, where, also, the fate of the few political transportees from Great Britain will be recorded.†

These general facts relative to the transportation system will make it easier for the reader to follow the narrative of events in the following chapters. But before entering upon a discussion of the system in operation it is essential to describe how the political and social conditions of Great Britain and Ireland created such crime and punishment as have been described in this introductory chapter.

* In the First Fleet, among the 697 whose sentences were recorded in Phillip's *Voyage*, 92 per cent were for seven years, 3 per cent for fourteen, and 5 per cent for life. From 1789 to 1800 the percentages are: 76 for seven years, 7 for fourteen, 17 for life. In the period 1789 to 1810: 69.2 for seven years, 7.5 for fourteen, and 23.3 for life. (Cf *P.P.* 1810 (45), xiv, 487.)

† Cf. Part II, Ch. V, Section (a). Irish transportations began in 1791, when 155 were sent from Ireland. After that date to 1802, 2086 prisoners were sent from Ireland, many of whom were political prisoners. But they should be distinguished into two groups, allowing for a percentage of prisoners whose offences were not seditious, but criminal. Governor King estimated that more than 600 were to be regarded as "United Irishmen". Between 1815 and 1820 309 Irish prisoners were transported from Ireland for rioting and sedition; after the Famine Revolts in 1848 a few defined political prisoners were exiled but indirectly arising out of the famine the average annual transportation of Irish prisoners to all penal colonies increased from 681, prior to 1847, to 2658 in the following three years (cf. Grey's *Colonial Policy*, II, 30, 31). The defined political transportees from Great Britain were not numerous: five only came before 1800; about 215 of the Luddites were transported up to 1822; at least 450, and possibly 600 ,were transported after the Labourers' Revolt, and in the following years the "Tolpuddle Martyrs", Chartists and political agitators transported appear to have numbered about seventy-eight.

PART I

THE POLITICAL, SOCIAL AND LEGAL BACKGROUNDS OF THE TRANSPORTATION SYSTEM IN GREAT BRITAIN AND IRELAND

POLITICAL, SOCIAL AND ECONOMIC CONDITIONS

(a) The Political Background

AFTER having written seven volumes on the history of England during the eighteenth century Lecky declared it was "pre-eminently a century of good sense", in which throughout Europe sobriety of thought and action, growing toleration and humanity were manifested. Nevertheless, he conceded that it was more remarkable for intellectual than for high moral achievements and that the "strong conflicting passions aroused by the French Revolution somewhat altered its character". In England particularly, he remarked on the presence of a "free and temperate government", "a constantly increasing respect for law" and an absence of class warfare and great political and religious convulsions.[1] At first sight it would seem impossible to reconcile this encomium with the events which this study purposes to describe. But if the century is regarded only from the standpoint of the ruling classes in that period, and particularly if a comparison is made with the century that preceded it, Lecky's estimate is not exaggerated. The century was sober, but too sober; it manifested a reforming spirit, but, as Lecky himself remarked, that spirit was weak and philanthropy was only beginning. The century in England marked the development from the monarchical regime of the seventeenth century towards that system of government by the people which is only a recent phenomenon; but in this transition period government was assumed and carried on soberly by the aristocracy in the interests of the aristocracy. It saw the beginning and the growth of the great agrarian and industrial upheavals, which created new problems, arising from the policy of the government as well as from a rapidly increasing population. These problems necessitated changes in the antiquated machinery of public control. In justice to Lecky's favourable estimate of the period it must be conceded that not a few reforms were made, and considerably more would have followed at the end of the century, had not the events of the French Revolution precipitated the aristocracy into believing that political and social reforms were a national menace. Consequently the century, which had promised well, ended in excesses of oppression which were continued for twenty-five years until the reforming epoch of the nineteenth century.

The reigns of the first three Georges (1714-27, 1727-60, 1760-1820) cover the period in which we are interested. The political tenets of 1688, as expounded by Locke, had been firmly accepted as the basis of free government, and the eighteenth century simply settled down to work them out under the new system in which a secret committee of politicians, known as the Cabinet, excluding the royal and popular voices, largely appropriated to themselves the right of governing the nation.[2]

Eighteenth century government was founded upon landed proprietorship. Blackstone defined the House of Lords as an assembly of landowners and the House of Commons as those landowners who had not a seat in the House of Lords. The new monied class, the manufacturers, bought land in order to become eligible to enter, or at least to facilitate the entry of their descendants into, the ranks of the governing aristocracy. Hence this worship of wealth, and the acceptance of it as the norm of respectability and power, tended for unity. It was natural for the worshippers to obey the wealthy, to oppose the dividing of land among a fixed peasantry, and to stand solidly together to maintain the satisfactory *status quo* inherited from the settlement of 1688. Because it was based on property, this type of government was continuous and not subject to change, and accordingly, became a national institution.[3] Moreover, the phenomenon noted by Lecky of "a constantly increasing respect for law and order" is what we should naturally expect in such an aristocratic state, just as we should be surprised had he discovered a similar increasing respect for justice.

The defects in the parliamentary representation of this period are too well known to warrant our repeating them here; but they should be borne in mind when considering the criminal law and punishment of the time. Not only were the people unable to make their voice heard in the legislature, except by direct action, such as processions or petitions, but under the system of patronage in parliamentary elections, only a few men of reforming ideas managed to enter the Commons. The distinction between Whigs and Tories mattered little in practice, for politics were a personal rather than a class matter. "The political history of England . . . is very largely that of the quarrels and alliances of various aristocratic factions or family connections. The names Whig and Tory are quite misleading as explanations of party conflicts", wrote Turberville in his survey of the *House of Lords in the Eighteenth Century*.[4] As a result of the close affinity between the two parties the favour of landowners often veered from one to the other for purely personal reasons, and to avoid expenses the number of elections that came to a poll was small.[5] Nevertheless, it might be said that the Tories relied on the support of the country gentry, and generally were more popular

with the unenfranchised. The Whigs, professing and occasionally practising zeal for constitutional principles, were more aristocratic than the Tories, being dominated by groups of noble families and not oblivious of the interests of the mercantile classes. Hence, during the long régime of the Elder Pitt and of the succeeding composite ministries, domestic policy was subordinated to the preservation of the balance of trade and the consolidation of English interests in America and India. In the end, the American Colonies rebelled against this policy of coercion in the interests of English wealth; the Declaration of Independence was made in 1776, and after a vain struggle against France and the colonists Great Britain recognized the sovereignty of the United States by the Treaty of Versailles in 1783. At that date it became certain that English criminals could not be sent again systematically to America.

In view of the failure of parliamentary policy, it became evident that constitutional reforms must be made. Various proposals were made to increase the franchise, though little of importance was effected. However, in an atmosphere more favourable to reform than ever before, the reins of government were handed over to the younger Pitt and the Tories. Power remained with this party for most of the succeeding half-century, well beyond the period with which this study is concerned. Though Pitt was not unfavourable to reform, and even attempted it for a brief moment, the oligarchic control of the landowners continued. When opposing a Bill for a limited extension of the franchise, Lord North expressed not only his personal opinions, but those of the whole class which governed England. The constitution was "the work of infinite wisdom . . . the most beautiful fabric that had ever existed since the beginning of time", he said, and suggested that "the bulk and weight" of the legislative power ought to be "in the hands of the country gentlemen, the best and most respectable objects of the confidence of the people".[6] This attitude of reverence for a supposedly perfect and infallible constitution was also the chief stumbling-block of the penal reform movement during these years.

It is essential, also, to remember the troubled history of Ireland from 1688 to 1782—an era which Professor Holland Rose regards as "painful to contemplate".[7] We refer here only in the most general terms to the long incidence of "the ruffianly enactments of the Irish penal code": the systematic attempts made to rob the nation of its religion, education and opportunities for material subsistence, whether due to the English parliamentary overlordship or to the control of an equally unrepresentative Irish legislature or to resident or absentee landlords; and the peasantry starved and naked and degraded. All these facts, to describe which we have merely conglomerated a few of the graphic phrases deliberately used by

authoritative writers from Burke to Holland Rose, explain the course of subsequent events in Ireland, and to some extent in Australia also.

In this work we are more concerned with criminal procedure and the crimes of the people than with the general penal laws, which savoured particularly of religious and political oppression. However, as Lecky observed, the long train of penal enactments had naturally left the people but little amenable to law.[8] Irish "crime" was frequently mere rebellion against oppression, and therefore had a political rather than a really criminal significance. "Its great ebullitions may usually be traced either to the pressure of extreme poverty, or to disputes about the possession or the occupancy of land." The property of Ireland was held by the title of comparatively recent, and, therefore, memorable confiscations. To protect this new ownership not only were special penal laws enacted, but also the general common law was considerably extended, and put into execution with the balance of judicial favour always on the side of property. When considering Irish crime throughout this century and well into the next, it is important that the attitude of the two classes of people in Ireland should be clearly differentiated. "This fact lies at the very root of the social and political history of Ireland."[9] The discontented factions of England and Scotland during the same period differed considerably from those in Ireland. In Scotland the land remained with its original owners, and in England, despite the extent of the depredations made against the smaller farmers by enclosures, the land did not pass to an alien race. But in Ireland, where there was no compensatory development of manufacturing industry, the foreign landholders became necessarily the most potent force in the country and the law of the land was directed towards their security of tenure. Hence, allowing for the fact that the Irish were but human and as prone to violence and injustice as most other races, it is clear that a large proportion of those arraigned on criminal charges were the victims of an uncontrolled oligarchy of landlords, who in the country districts constantly disregarded the law.[10] At least, it should be conceded that in these breaches of the law the element of provocation must have been frequently present.

Another fact to be noticed is the growth of population in Ireland, increasing from just over a million at the beginning of the century to more than four millions in 1788, and adding another million in the next ten or fifteen years. This happened despite a vast emigration to America—more than 200,000 crossing the Atlantic in the first half of the century.[11] Along with the national revival in trade during a dozen or so years after the grant

of Irish parliamentary independence in 1782, distress and discontent continued to prevail among the masses of the people. The secret political societies that sprang up after the American Revolution manifested renewed religious frenzy, the rise of the "Peep o' day Boys" of the Protestant North forcing the Catholic South to band together as "Defenders". Grattan's motion for a parliamentary enquiry was rejected, and instead, the Insurrection Bill of 1787 was passed and was "followed by the usual crop of transportations and executions; after which, instead of improving, matters became worse than before".[12]

In the Introduction reference was made to the commencement of Irish transportation to New South Wales in 1791. From this date, however, Irish criminality tended more and more to be identified with political agitation and insurrection. Ireland was on the verge of radical political changes under the direct influences of French Revolutionary ideas and the repressive measures which the English party took to check insurrection. In 1791 Wolfe Tone founded his "United Irishmen" at Belfast, and from that date there was a rapid increase in the numbers of the *disaffected*, eventually bringing in the Catholics of Southern Ireland and ending with the insurrections of 1798.

In Scotland transportations directly for political offences were not so frequent as in Ireland, but the indirect effects of revolutionary teachings upon the Scottish people must be kept in mind. A year after the foundation of the "United Irishmen", the Scottish "Society of the Friends of the People" was formed.

As the subject of this study is the problem of crime and the methods adopted to punish criminals, it is well to keep in mind the vast gulf separating the common people of England and Ireland from the aristocracy that ruled them in the eighteenth century. We have, therefore, to regard the system of government primarily from the point of view of the masses whose criminality was always thrown into high relief, and only secondarily from the point of view of the legislators whose attitude towards the reform of social evils makes them, at least indirectly, interested parties in the transportation system.

(b) The Effect of Enclosures on Agricultural Employment

The economic and social problems of England during the eighteenth and nineteenth centuries are familiar to most people and a plentiful literature has been written around them. For several reasons it is certain that these problems had a not inconsiderable influence on the transportation system. The changing conditions of employment in England unsettled an agricultural

B

people, the town populations increased and poverty became an unmanageable burden. As the mentality and the machinery of government were unsuited and inadequate to cope with such problems, it might have been expected that the changed labour conditions would tend to create insubordination and that the poverty-stricken and thickly-populated areas would become favourable breeding grounds for crime and criminals. However, in so far as these social and economic facts are adduced to explain the origins and existence of English crime, it should be observed that they became urgent problems only in the second half of the eighteenth century. Generally speaking, it might be said, despite the earlier beginnings of commerce and industry and the enclosures of land, that the old industrial system continued in England until about 1760. The application of the great mechanical inventions to industry and the systematic enclosure policy followed that date. After 1760 the economic and social conditions must be considered as causes of crime.

The first matter of fundamental importance to note is the great increase of population. There were no official returns before 1801, the census proposal of 1753 having been rejected as "subversive of the last remains of English liberty", but Toynbee's estimate of 5,134,000 as the population of England and Wales in 1700 may be accepted. During the first half of the century it increased by less than a million, or between 17 and 18 per cent; but in the second half of the century the increase was more than three millions, the population rising in 1801 to 9,187,176, 52 per cent above that of 1750.[13] To this phenomenon there must be joined the more disturbing facts of the simultaneous decline in agricultural opportunities, the creation of vast new industrial towns in the northern counties, and the concentration of population in the crowded slum districts of London.

In the changes brought about in England we shall emphasize only two general features, first, the disappearance of the yeoman farmer and the driving of the agricultural labourers into the towns, which created social conditions favourable to the growth of crime; and second, the attitude of the aristocracy who, to safeguard their property interests against increasing crime, strengthened their position by all the machinery of Parliament which was at their disposal.

At the beginning of the eighteenth century much of England was still unenclosed; the land about a village was divided into small parcels of from one quarter to half an acre, of which a man might own one or more non-contiguous plots. Some plots were given over to wheat or other cereals, and others remained fallow; cattle grazed on the common. This system, with its manorial

element, provided for various classes—yeoman freeholders, great and small, copyholders, tenant-farmers, cottagers, squatters and farm labourers. They cultivated their strips of land communally, possessing rights in common to the waste lands, and even the labourers had rights by which their children worked for a master and lived in his house until they were able to build cottages for themselves. "The most important social fact about this system," according to the recognized authorities, Mr and Mrs Hammond, "is that it provided opportunities for the humblest and poorest labourer to rise in the village", and despite the disadvantages of the system "it formed a world in which the villagers lived their own lives and cultivated the soil on a basis of independence".[14]

Enclosure was not a new idea, but it might be said that the disappearance of the small yeoman farmer began to be marked from the first general Enclosure Act of 1710. The process of extinction, however, was more manifest in the second half of the century than in the first.[15]*

Justification of the policy has usually been sought by pointing to the necessity for scientific farming, which could not be achieved under the old primitive conditions. Also, it has been claimed that under the new system agriculture flourished to such an extent that England developed into a wheat exporting country until the end of the century, and that under the new conditions any "man of enterprise" who had been ousted from his holding could still find ample opportunities. Unfortunately, however, the bulk of the dispossessed were not men of enterprise; they grew poorer, and became either beggars in the towns or provided cheap labour for the new factories; the rich grew richer on the proceeds of their spoils, while the village sank into the state bewailed by Goldsmith. While arguments attributing the increase of production to the enclosure system tended to mark the new landlords as patriots of the highest merit and almost concealed the direct inspiration of self-interest, there was a much deeper significance in the policy, for the motives are to be found equally in the political and the economic spheres.[16] The concentration of land ownership assured the continuous supremacy of the country gentry both in Parliament and in local administration, and enabled them to perpetuate the system of oligarchical control. "Land, being the foundation of social and political influence, was eagerly sought after," particularly because the *parvenu* merchants and manufacturers could attain political power or the social prestige of "gentleman" for themselves or their children only with the backing of land. The

---

* Between 1700 and 1761, 152 Enclosure Acts covering 237,845 acres of common fields and some waste land were passed, as well as fifty-two Acts referring to 74,518 acres of waste; from 1761 to 1801 the numbers were tremendously increased, 1479 Acts affecting the ownership of 2,428,721 acres of common, and 521 Acts relating to 752,150 acres of waste land being passed.

policy of buying up freeholds and confiscating wastes and commons not only created a new class of unemployed but also a new class of industrial lords with property qualifications, to fortify the landed interests in Parliament. This fact had considerable bearing on the multiplication of new statutes to protect property rights against the depredations of the poor.

By the changes in land-tenure two classes were mainly affected, the yeoman-farmer and the agricultural labourer. The yeomen were small farmers, employers of labour on their own account, whose title-deeds were quite sound; but they were forced to sell to the big landowners because they could not afford to fence or improve their land, because the wholesale enclosures destroyed the villages which had been their markets and because of the decay of cottage industries. It is not necessary here to discuss whether the yeomen farmers would have eventually disappeared under the pressure of changing economic conditions, but it is important to note the rapidity of their disappearance once their ranks had been thinned and the survivors were unable to maintain an isolated existence. In 1700 there had been about 180,000 freeholders in England, but by 1800 Arthur Young was able to state that the small freeholders had practically disappeared. Toynbee remarked expressively that a person ignorant of our history might surmise that in the course of the century a bloody and internecine war had transferred this property from one class to another. It was progress won at the cost of much injustice, which was not inevitable and could have been avoided.[17]

The status of the agricultural labourer, however, was somewhat different. Generally speaking, it may be said that his position improved until near the end of the century. At the beginning of the century, when the price of corn was 38s. 2d., the average daily wage was 10½d. By 1760, when corn had dropped to 32s., the wage had increased to 1s. Adam Smith attributed the improvement to the general prosperity resulting from scientific farming and the beginning of industrial opportunities; other economists have assigned it to the slow rate of population increase before that date. The middle of the century might be regarded as the labourers' best period; but towards the end of the century, when prices had increased out of all proportion to the purchasing power of wages, a period of great economic distress ensued. Moreover, in this period the greatest numbers of enclosures were registered, and in 1775 the Elizabethan Act providing for a definite amount of land to be attached to each cottage was repealed, although it had long been a dead-letter. While admitting that enclosures did stimulate agriculture and absorbed considerable labour, it should be recognized that the displacements had serious consequences.

The yeomen had disappeared as a class, the villages had changed and were inhabited by labourers working for tenant-farmers at inadequate wages, supplemented by poor-relief. Others among the sturdy country folk drifted to the towns, where they furnished employers with that cheap and mobile labour that was destined to make England the world's workshop. Simultaneously, there appeared those vast numbers who could not be absorbed by industry, who created problems of poverty and crime which proved insoluble under the existing policy of the government.

This is, therefore, a period in which the agricultural community was taken to pieces and reconstructed in the manner in which a dictator reconstructs a free government. The metaphor is that of the Hammonds, who also saw in the policy the express determination of the landed gentry to rid themselves of all responsibility for the well-being of the lower classes of society. Philanthropy and social ideals are, therefore, not to be expected among this body generally, but only in those individual members of it who rose superior to the system.

(c) The New Industrial System

It would be incorrect to attribute to the Industrial Revolution any large share of responsibility for the foundation of the Australian penal settlement, for the real beginning of the factory system has been placed as late as 1780, although some have preferred a date ten years earlier. Nevertheless, in 1788 industrial conditions were frequently appalling, and before the end of the century the problems of poverty and crime had many direct connexions with industrialism.

Previously the farmer had combined agriculture with hand industry in his home. In 1724 Defoe described "houses full of lusty fellows, some at the dye-vat, some at the looms, others dressing the cloths; the women and children carding or spinning; being all employed from the youngest to the oldest. . . . Not a beggar to be seen or an idle person".[18] The scene thus depicted contrasts vividly with Arthur Young's later description of organized mills employing hundreds of men, women and children.[19] We need not trace the growth of the large employer from the time when he merely collected the work done privately by labourers and others with material supplied by themselves or by the employer, through the various stages of combined labour until, after the application of mechanical inventions, the workers became known as "hands" in well-organized industrial undertakings. For the changes being made a variety of causes may be cited, including particularly the concentration of wealth in the hands of a few capitalists, the

impetus given to commerce by the teachings of Adam Smith favouring the opening of foreign markets, the scientific outlook in agriculture, the mechanical inventions progressing from hand power to water power and then to steam, by which mass production was made possible, and also, the provisions made for cheap and rapid transport on the new canals and waterways. This sweeping advance made it impossible for the poorer classes to hold their own. Open markets and expanding industry necessarily induced intensive competition, and while the increasing population, the disinherited agriculturists and the defective poor law system provided a glut of workers, it was natural that economies should be effected by lowering employment standards. The lowered standard was to be seen more in the conditions of work than in wages, which actually increased, though ineffectively because of a concurrent increase in prices. We shall have to notice the excessive length of the working-day, the unhygienic factory conditions, and the employment of women and children.

In the coal industry the advance was remarkable in methods of working, transport and trade. Although the wages of the collier were higher than those of others after 1775 and mechanical appliances reduced the severity of his work, the general conditions were such that he remained almost uncivilized. Until the Acts of 1775 and 1779 forbade the selling of miners the Scottish miner was a serf, who was bought and sold with the mine and wore a collar round his neck.[20] The employment of women in this industry decreased after 1780, but an increase was registered in the employment of children in mines, who began working at the age of six or seven years for anything from fourteen to eighteen hours a day. In the iron industry, which absorbed large numbers of men, conditions were better. Cotton, which was to become so important a feature of the new industrial system, became a factory industry after 1770, and in 1784 employed 80,000 people either in factories or in homes working for factories. During the century the annual exports of cotton manufactures rose from £23,000 to over £7,000,000.[21] Conditions of employment in this highly-capitalized industry varied considerably; in some factories education and social welfare were encouraged, but in others conditions were atrocious. Child labour was general in the industry; the elder Peel employed over a thousand children, but was one of the first to suggest legislation for their protection. The horrors of child labour in the cotton industry, whether in the factories under the cruel supervision of overseers or in private homes under that of equally merciless parents, make a revolting story of conditions that were too often responsible for all kinds of immorality, loathsome diseases and legalized slavery.[22] The employment capacity of the

industry, however, fluctuated, with wages generally above those of farm labourers, who accordingly drifted into the mills in times of prosperity. During trade depressions, which were frequent, the Irish and ex-farm workers were willing to accept lower wages and standards, to the detriment of the other operatives.

Prior to 1776 the industrial changes had already begun, and before the end of the century "fluctuations in trade brought trouble to the employer" and "ruin to the worker", so that the loss of a week's work reduced him to extreme penury. In the unskilled trades the abundant supply of Irish immigrants and dispossessed English yoemen made it almost impossible for the domestic worker to compete with factory-produced goods.

There is, however, one aspect of general labour conditions throughout the early stages of the Industrial Revolution which must have predisposed tremendous numbers of people towards a life of crime. The employment of children in mines and factories has already been referred to, but only generally. There is not space in this synopsis of the social condition of England to describe the subject as it deserves, but its importance should be emphasized from two points of view: first, because of the evil influence it must have exerted on the thousands of people who at any time had been subjected to it, and on the many more who were directly associated with them; and second, because of the reluctance manifested by Parliament to abolish such evidently inhumane conditions in industry.

The significance of child labour conditions in predisposing youth towards crime appears to have been much neglected. One need not go further than the Hammonds' graphic chapters, the eighth and ninth of *The Town Labourer*, to realize that the system must be regarded as a social cause of crime. In these chapters a clear distinction is made between the children employed in home industry and the children employed at a later period in the factories. The factory children developed out of apprentices or were driven to their doom by pauper parents. Before 1766 it was estimated that the annual mortality of London parish-children was between 60 and 70 per cent. In that year Jonas Hanway succeeded in having an Act passed to board out at the expense of the parish such of these children as were under six years of age; one result of this was, according to Hanway, that "a deficiency of 2100 burials a year" occurred, but a further result was that the parishes found themselves hard pressed to provide for the increased numbers of children who were no longer dying in the workhouses. Moreover, it was a condition of granting poor-relief in London that the parishes should have the right of disposing of all the children of those receiving such aid. Hence, to relieve the burden of the workhouses, the new

cotton factories "made available a system of transportation for poor children, which was cheaper and more effective than the transportation system that brought relief to the London prisons."[23] The details of this commerce and the story of their lives, from the ages of seven to twenty-one, spent between the mills and the adjoining "prentice-houses", are so well known that they need not be repeated here. The Factory Act of 1802, resulting from the efforts of a millowner turned reformer, affected apprentices in textile mills only, but even with this limitation it applied to 20,000 children. In 1815 a Parliamentary Committee declared it was impossible to estimate the number of parish apprentices in such conditions throughout England, and proposed that no children should be sent more than forty miles from London. The proposal was rejected by the Lords, but in 1816 it passed both Houses, whereupon "the carts ceased to dump their living freights at the mill doors".

In the nineteenth century the practice of indigent parents selling their children's labour increased, and children, usually of seven, occasionally of four or five, became wage-earners, working from five or six in the morning until seven or eight at night, under a system of most repressive regulations, injurious both to physical and to moral well-being. In 1802 it was stated that the position of these children was no better than that of the apprentices, but not until 1815 were any steps taken to reform their conditions. By 1819 reform had so far progressed, after laborious efforts in Parliament, as to confine factory work to children over nine years, and the daily hours of work for them to not more than thirteen and a half. The reforms for children working in mines were far slower in arriving. The Report of the 1842 Royal Commission referred to the prevalence at the commencement of the century, and the continuance at the later date in 1842, of the employment of children of six years and under as trappers in the coal-mines: "a girdle is put round the naked waist to which a chain from the carriage is hooked and passed between the legs, and the boys crawl on their hands and knees, drawing the carriage after them".[24] Children had to work from twelve to fifteen hours a day, often in total darkness, and in the case of workhouse children "if they will not do" the work, "they take them to the magistrates, who commit them to prison". Girls and women, too, were in the earlier periods often employed in mines, and in 1842 one witness described his experience of fifty years before that date, when children, having graduated from trappers to pit-boys, often worked in harness from 2 a.m. until 8 or 10 p.m. on every day except Saturday, and in busy periods did not see daylight from Sunday to Saturday afternoon. Beside child-labour in mines and factories the Hammonds

take particular notice of children working as chimney-sweeps. The numbers affected were smaller in this calling than in the greater industries, being approximately a thousand in a given period, but the ghastly conditions of work, the fearful risks to life and health and the brutal callousness of the trade in these little boys, made it singularly repulsive. An Act of 1778 which sought to reform the practice by limiting it to children over eight years, proved a dead-letter; and a mild proposal in 1804 to require the licensing of such children was rejected by the Lords on July 19, in a House of twenty-five peers, among whom were six bishops.[25] In 1819 the Lords thwarted a further attempt to limit the age of chimney-sweepers to ten years, one of their number declaring that "if the legislature attempted to lay down a moral code for the people, there was always a danger that every feeling of benevolence would be extirpated".[26] Real reform was not achieved until 1840.

It is reasonable to assume that this state of abject misery must have predisposed the poor towards a life of crime and particularly to offences against property. But the prominence of child-labour as a regular part of the industrial machine seems to be the most important consideration. From the ranks of this forlorn body the criminals of future generations arose. In this period the foundations of modern capitalism were laid and the labouring population were being converted into a proletariat, whose main function was to provide labour at a cheap cost.

(d) The Poor Laws as a Social Cause of Crime

Poverty and crime were not new phenomena in England. They were interrelated problems centuries old, which were complicated and aggravated by the industrial changes that were taking place in the eighteenth century. Many reasons might be assigned for the acuteness of poverty in the period. The natural causes of idleness, sickness, old age and normal unemployment may first be taken for granted, and in the later years of the century the rapid increase of population and the rise in the prices of foodstuffs above the level of wages are the chief economic causes. But the enclosure movement must not be lightly dismissed as a contributory factor. At the end of the century, when Sir Frederick Eden examined *The State of the Poor*, it was established that not only had eviction become general, but that pauperism was greatest where enclosures had taken place. As a contributory cause of poverty the very laws intended to relieve it must also be cited, together with the attitude displayed by the landowners in ridding themselves of all personal obligations to the poor in their districts. Under the manorial system the local squire had helped to maintain his unemployed

within his own demesne; he now repudiated this liability, preferring to pay heavy poor-rates towards the support of the poor in workhouses.

The regulations regarding poverty that obtained in England during the eighteenth century were based on an Elizabethan statute that made the care of the impotent poor a charge upon the people by compulsory levies collected by overseers in parishes. Moreover, at the same time a distinction had been drawn between the impotent, to whom aid was to be given, and the able-bodied poor, who, if adults, were to be set to work on materials provided by the State, and if children or orphans, were to be apprenticed. This distribution of relief was not a simple process, but was converted into an almost unmanageable system by various Settlement Laws that were founded on an Act of 1662. Theoretically, every person had a settlement in one parish, outside which he was not entitled to receive poor relief. Originally, settlement in new parishes could be acquired in various ways, but in the eighteenth century the legal procedure was for a travelling workman to get a certificate from his parish, which allowed him to remain in another parish as long as he did not become chargeable to it. Once he became destitute, the parish to which he originally belonged was bound to effect his return and pay the expenses of so doing. The system was adopted to prevent the over-burdening of the poor-rates; but by robbing a migrant of his chief protection against starvation, it tended to prevent him from approaching districts where work was available or more suitable. Though it did not succeed in completely stopping this flow of labour, it nevertheless "regulated labour in the interests of the employing class", and lowered the standard of wages by providing labourers who were faced with accepting the alternatives of starvation or work for a miserable pittance. These regulations continued until 1795 when it was decided that the parish in which the pauper was actually settled became responsible for his removal. The procedure to our minds appears futile, but it had far-reaching consequences throughout a century. It was part of a definite policy to prevent certificated unemployed from settling in a parish; to such migrants the obtaining of work was made difficult, the poor were maintained at the lowest possible cost, and every effort was made to hire them, at any price, or to apprentice their children, at any work, to any employer beyond the confines of the parish. By every means, without consideration for the economic or moral welfare of the poor, the parochial rates were to be maintained at the lowest possible level.[27] Landlords refused to build cottages, and in 1771, wrote Arthur Young, "landlords often pulled down cottages that they may never become the nests, as they were called, of beggars'

brats".[28] Eden wrote that the worst grievance of the poor was the impossibility of finding habitations, and Adam Smith declared, "There is scarce a poor man in England of forty years of age . . . who has not in some part of his life felt himself most cruelly oppressed by this ill-contrived law of settlements."[29]

An Act of 1722 limited the scope of the poor-law by providing that relief should be withheld from those who refused to enter the workhouse. This "test" of willingness to work was sound, but, despite certain successes, it is admitted that the system proved a dismal failure in practice. We need not discuss the reasons therefor, except to indicate the conflict of jurisdictions between overseers and justices in applying relief and the popular view of workhouses rather as gaols or factories than as asylums or means of providing employment. Under the rigours of the system prior to 1770, the poor-rates naturally decreased, giving satisfaction to landowners, but a great many thinking men were realizing that the economies had been effected at the cost of the further impoverishment of the poor.

In an age that allowed degradation of the poor and sanctioned the exploitation of women and children it is amazing to find a large body of genuinely interested humanitarians and a mass of literature published in the cause of social reform. For our purpose, however, it is more interesting to note that much of this solicitude for the poor was excited by the phenomenon of increasing crime —which explains the numerous parliamentary proposals and the various enactments directed against vagrants and able-bodied poor from 1744 onwards. Writers like Massie and Burn and Young and Hanway, all of whom were social reformers, realized that the problems of crime and poverty were very closely related. Jonas Hanway is best remembered for his exposure of the shocking infant mortality in London and for his part in the passing of the Acts of 1761 and 1766 to safeguard child life and to regulate apprenticeship, but his numerous pamphlets and letters relating to crime among the poor are attempts to deal with the same problem from the different angle of criminal supervision.

The writings of the two celebrated London magistrates, the brothers Fielding, are among the most valuable records of crime in this earlier period. In Henry Fielding's *Enquiry into the causes of the late increase of robbers*, published in 1751, the stark facts are occasionally liable to obscure the very causes of crime which he set himself to investigate, as, for example, his description of a medium-sized room of a London brothel in which fifty-eight persons of both sexes lodged promiscuously, or of two little houses from which seventy persons were ejected. Men and women of this kind helped to make up the numbers transported to America.

Referring to the second case cited above Fielding wrote: "If one considers the destruction of all morality . . . the whoredom and drunkenness which is eternally carrying on in these houses, on the one hand, and the excessive poverty and misery of most of the inhabitants on the other, it seems doubtful whether they are more the objects of detestation or compassion." Such was the poverty of these seventy people that on being searched the money found on them did not amount to one shilling, "and I have been credibly informed", he wrote, "that a single loaf hath supplied a whole family for a week". If any of these unfortunates fall sick, "and it is almost a miracle that stench, vermin and want should ever suffer them to be well", they are turned out into the street, "where unless some parish officer of extraordinary charity relieves them, they are surely miserably to perish, with the addition of cold and hunger to their disease. The conditions of life among the masses", he wrote, "were very little known, especially to those of the better sort". He did not hesitate to ascribe to such wretched conditions the great and recent increase of crime. "The wonder in fact is", he wrote, "that we have not a thousand more robbers than we have; indeed, that all these wretches are not thieves, must give us either a very high idea of their honesty or a very mean one of their capacity and courage." In 1753 Henry Fielding wrote a pamphlet directly attacking the poor-law system and proposing that the able-bodied poor should be trained for manufacturing work and that the impotent poor should be supported solely by voluntary charity. Although the scheme was impracticable and overestimated the numbers that could be absorbed by industry, his statement that the inadequacy of the laws for providing for the poor or for restraining their vices was reprehended by "the universal voice of the nation", is significant. "It is questionable", he wrote, "who are the more dissatisfied, the rich who have to raise 'a million yearly' for the support of the poor, or the poor themselves, many of whom are starved, or found begging or pilfering in the streets of to-day and to-morrow are locked up in gaols and bridewells."[30] Henry Fielding's brother, Sir John, also a magistrate with special opportunities for understanding the criminal poor, was no less zealous a reformer. Although in his *Plan for preventing robberies*, published in 1755, he made no attempt to assess the actual influence of poverty on crime, in his evidence before the Parliamentary Committee of 1770 he stated that the present increase of crime among youth was due to their being sons of unfortunate people without trade, who begin as pickpockets and develop into robbers.[31]

We emphasize these views of such authorities as the Fieldings because the chief activities of the reformers, particularly towards the close of the century, become more and more concerned with

the problem of crime and do not stress its association with poverty. After 1776, when the transportation of criminals to America became impossible, the interests of Howard, Blackstone, Eden and Bentham were concentrated either on the penal code or the problem of gaol accommodation. The phenomenon of increasing and un-manageable crime tended to become an obsession, and the evident failure of the expensive poor-law system to cope with poverty was largely attributed to the crimes of the people, while the complementary fact that the poor laws helped in creating a state of endemic crime was not often appreciated outside the ranks of the Humanitarians. Henry Fielding had noted this fact in 1755, declaring that "the sufferings of the poor are indeed less observed than their misdeeds; not from any want of compassion, but because they are less known; and this is the true reason why we hear them so often mentioned with abhorrence and so seldom with pity. They starve and freeze and rot among themselves; but they beg and steal and rob among their betters".[32]

It is evident, however, that the twin problems of increasing crime and increasing poverty were manifested simultaneously, and that, with such a degree of intensity in both, their influence on each other must have been considerable. In 1775 a Committee appointed to examine the laws regarding poverty and vagrancy submitted two Reports. The first Report declared that the poor laws had failed to achieve the purposes originally intended, had produced unwarranted litigation, had proved burdensome in its public levies and had failed to find employment for the people. Recommendations were made to increase the parochial relief districts to county size, to allow the poor the right of access to any place to seek employment,[33] and to build houses of correction quite separate from the poorhouses.[34] The efforts of the Social Reformers elicited some response in Parliament, but apart from infant and apprentice reforms all the worth-while proposals were rejected. However, as a result of an Act of 1776 returns were made which revealed that approximately £1,850,000 was raised in England and Wales every year for the maintenance of the poor, of which about £1,600,000 was spent in poor-relief and expenses of organization, and £35,000 was wasted in litigation costs.[35] In 1782 Thomas Gilbert succeeded in having two of his bills passed by Parliament as temporary measures to deal with the urgent situation. One clause providing that the village poor-houses might be supplanted by central workhouses built by a Union of parishes was reasonable and would have proved beneficial if the plan had been widely adopted, but the clause which removed from the able-bodied labourer the necessity of submitting to a "workhouse test", before receiving relief was a fundamental

mistake. It was foolishly assumed that work would be found by the guardians, and provision was made to supplement poor relief and wages at the discretion of justices. The withdrawal of the distinction between the able-bodied and the impotent poor, enabling all to receive relief indiscriminately in such conditions of crime as then existed, made the Act "a landmark in the growth of laxity". Poor relief became more burdensome still, and the problem of crime more acute under conditions of subsidized idleness. In 1784 Gilbert's returns show the annual cost of poor relief as £2,000,000, having risen to that great sum from about £600,000 in 1742. At a parliamentary enquiry in 1786 it was revealed that the expectations of systematic relief by united parishes had been illusory. In some towns several workhouses existed, but in the county of Berkshire there was not one. In London some parishes hired their paupers to contractors at 3s. 6d. or 4s. each weekly, in other parishes the paupers worked for the benefit of the rates or for private employers.[36]

Shortly after this date the political and social outlook of England underwent a violent change as a result of the French Revolution. Parliament had been progressing slowly, though ineffectively, towards a realization of the social problem of poverty. With the example of France before its eyes it slammed the door against reform for the next thirty years. From that date also a change was manifested in a section of the proletariat. Under the influence of Tom Paine's writings and of new societies established for the political education of the working classes they began to demand rights which hitherto they had allowed to be disregarded. Their demands and activities were regarded as seditious and were refused or repressed as such. This phenomenon of sedition will be discussed in a later chapter,* but, in order to preserve continuity, the present section may conveniently be extended to describe economic and social conditions to the end of the century. Poor relief continued to follow slavishly along the principles of Gilbert's Act, acquiesced in by vast multitudes of the poor who thereby lost all ambition for self-support and, in the great towns, developed into idle vagrants; others, demanding work and sufficient wages, regarded this dole as "bribery of the people into passiveness" during an era when all established institutions were being shaken to their foundations.

In industry, where wages were admittedly insufficient for maintenance, the workers appealed to the remnants of their guild rights for the fixing of more adequate wages, and the employers demanded free contracts and the "healthy rivalry" of competition. The appeals of the framework knitters, whose wages had sunk to 6s. a week, were typical, but Parliament was more moved by the

* Cf. Part II, Ch. V, Section (a).

employers' arguments and resolved that *laissez-faire* must prevail in industry in view of the danger of Continental competition. Consequently an era of strikes, riots and machine-breaking ensued on the one side, and on the other a constant whittling away of the ancient rights by which workmen could claim the protection of the law. The Spitalfields Acts, empowering the magistrates to fix the wages of the silk-weavers, were repealed, and the ancient laws of apprenticeship joined them in the limbo of lost things. By the Combination Laws, which purported to protect employer and employee alike, the hands of the working man were so effectively tied that his slightest attempt to improve his lot became a punishable offence. Combinations of workmen to raise wages were illegal, but, as Adam Smith remarked, there was no such disadvantage against the employers who, by restricting employment, could bring masses of the people to starvation level within a few weeks. In these years when war had begun with France and property owners lived in constant dread of the spread of revolutionary doctrines, it was easy to mistake proletarian wage claims for sedition.

The sufferings of the people came to a crisis in 1795, a year of great distress in the agricultural districts, when food riots, largely organized by the wives of impoverished workers, broke out in many places in England.[37] The demonstrations were orderly, and when the produce was seized a reasonable price was paid for it. These activities, and those of a less orderly nature which followed until 1800, were protests against the exportation of corn and the monopolies of agents by which the price of wheat had risen to 115s. 11d. a quarter and a quartern loaf cost 1s. 10½d. The corresponding rise in wages, even when wages were available, was far below the cost of living. An interesting feature of the rioting was the attitude manifested outside the ranks of the labourers: in one case when a jury refused to bring in a verdict for a monopolist plaintiff, the judge congratulated them on a patriotic action.*

The most significant aspect of the riotings was the warning which they gave to the governing classes, for if a proletariat were left to starve they might eventually rise up and seize the goods of "those who lived on the spoils and sinecures of the State". "Fear and pity", wrote the Hammonds, "united to sharpen the wits of the rich and to turn their minds to the distresses of the poor."[39] Hence, there was to be seen in the governing classes a changed mentality regarding the poor, expressing itself occasionally in highly-developed social proposals which never became law, and

---

* Malthus remarked how "in the late dearth half of the gentlemen and clergymen in the Kingdom richly deserved to have been prosecuted for sedition. After inflaming the minds of the common people against the farmers and corn-dealers by the manner in which they talked or preached about them, it was a feeble antidote to the poison which they had infused, coldly to observe that however the poor might be oppressed or cheated it was their duty to keep the peace" *Essay on Population*, 7th ed., p. 438.)

in a system of bounties which defeated its own end. In 1795 the decision of the Berkshire justices, assembled at the Pelican Inn at Speenhamland, immediately to adjust the amount of poor relief so as to provide a living wage for all labourers, began the fatal Speenhamland system which lasted forty years. Having laid down a minimum wage for the support of a man, his wife and family, they decided that if wages fell short of it they would make them up, in proportion to the number of children in the family, from the poor-rates. Their motives were praiseworthy, but the consequences of the action, because of its inherent fallacies and general adoption throughout the country, were demoralizing in the extreme. It virtually stabilized the insufficient wage by supplementing it from the funds, and although the employers had to meet the increase in the rates, it permanently lowered the wage level. It tended to pauperize the labourers, causing them insolently to demand subsidies as their due, to use threats to enforce such payments and to become a body of men who with considerable truth were described as mutinous, lazy, unprofitable and criminally disposed. "The whole character of the people was lowered by the admission that they had a right to relief independent of work."

In Parliament the reaction was similar. Whitbread's Bill, introduced in December 1795, proposed to allow justices of the peace to fix a minimum wage for husbandry. In his celebrated speech on the second reading Pitt admitted the defects in the existing Poor Law system and supported the insurance schemes which had been favourably received during late years; but rather than fix wages he recommended a legalized general scale of supplementary poor-relief to be apportioned according to the number of children in the worker's family. The granting of such emoluments, he said, would tend to increase the size of families and was therefore to be regarded as "a matter of right and honour, instead of a ground for opprobrium and contempt". But, as a true disciple of Adam Smith, he looked askance at any interference by the State in regulating the wages to be paid by industry. "Trade, industry and barter", he said, "will always find their own level and will be impeded by regulations which violate their natural operation and derange their proper effect."[40] When Whitbread's Bill was negatived, Pitt undertook to introduce a Bill to reform the whole system, and in 1796 produced the elaborate "Heads of a Bill for the better support and maintenance of the Poor",[61] according to which the rates might be used to supplement wages and schools of industry should be founded for children, whose labour, he admitted, had supplied an incalculable portion of the national wealth. More than humanitarian motives had inspired Pitt's interest in larger families; it reflected the national views on a supposedly

decreasing population, which Malthus was to disprove three years later, and had one eye on cannon fodder for the French wars. As a piece of social legislation Pitt's proposal was undoubtedly sympathetic to the poor. But it was defective from the economic point of view and was "a cure suitable to the homes of Arcady" rather than the homes of England. In the face of the vehement opposition it aroused, the Bill was dropped, and a few months later an Act repealing the existing settlement laws was passed, by which the principle of Speenhamland became the recognized system of poor-relief.

In the following years economists examined the question from many novel points of view. Avoiding always the only rational solution of compelling industry to pay a reasonable wage and hoping to find a way to reduce the enormous cost of poor-relief, it was seriously contended, even by such humanitarians as Sir Frederick Eden, that the labouring poor should reduce that low standard of living which they were then being compelled to endure. Treatises and reports on diets were prepared, and the rich were amazed to find that "the poorer the labourer grew the more stubbornly did he insist on wheaten bread". In Parliament the attempts to bring about reform received scant attention. When Whitbread raised the matter again in 1800, Pitt laid particular emphasis on the desirability of keeping industry free from state interference and expressed the opinion that wages would naturally find their own level—an attitude which has been aptly described as that of "a statesman paying himself with soothing phrases in the midst of a cyclone".[42] Scarcely any changes of importance were made in the condition of the poorer classes, so that again in the years after 1810 there were riots and machine-breaking, and as late as 1821 Cobbett was able to declare that "every labourer who has children is now regularly and constantly a pauper".[43]

It must, however, be admitted that depravity had become deep-rooted among the masses. In his day Locke had ascribed the increasing poverty to "the relaxation of discipline and the corruption of manners" and had suggested enforcing the vagrancy laws.[44] A century later and after the most exhaustive examination of the poor laws, Sir F. Eden reached a similar conclusion. While there were thousands of deserving poor who were entitled to employment, he wrote, "there are more idle who do not call less loudly for compulsion to force them to labour";[45] nevertheless, he was not blind to the defects in the system. The rigours of the poorhouses made a mother unwilling to enter it herself, but it encouraged her debauchery by accepting her children. She could be certain that the child would be better fed there than she could feed it herself.[46] Eden, being an economist as well as a humanitarian

was inclined to solve the problem of poverty at the cost of the worker without interfering with the employer. The worker's inability to purchase food arose, he thought, from his unthriftiness and his adherence to "ancient improvident systems in diet and dress". He proposed that the southern labourers might copy the ways of the northerners who were able to concoct appetizing dishes out of oatmeal, salt and water, and believed that the Reformers might "better serve the cause of the industrious peasant and the manufacturer by pointing out the best means of reducing these expenses".[47] It would be unfair to judge Eden solely by these excerpts from his voluminous writings; he was one of the foremost humanitarians of his age. Howlett, too, writing in 1788 on the same subject, adduced four causes: the faulty execution of the poor laws, the engrossing of farms, and the great number of ale-houses and "the growing profligacy of the poor". This was the verdict of a genuine sympathizer, who had not scrupled to describe the labour done in the workhouses as state income "squeezed out of the flesh and blood of the poor".

The most important witness, however, to the prevalence of crime and its relationship to poverty is the benevolent London stipendiary magistrate, Patrick Colquhoun, whose *Police of the Metropolis*, published in 1795, attempted to right the wrongs of the past hundred years and point the way for more rational methods during the next century. Colquhoun was at the end of the eighteenth century what the Fieldings had been a generation before. As a police magistrate he had an extensive knowledge of the conditions of crime in the metropolis; as a Reformer under the influence of Bentham he was interested in the theory and practice of punishment, but he went beyond the more limited field of the Utilitarian Philosophers, and sought the actual economic causes of crime.[48] "Indigence in the present state of society", he wrote, "may be considered as a principal cause of crimes." He believed that the system of public management prevailing in the metropolis was not the least considerable cause of the corruption of morals in that class known as the "Casual Poor". Particularly was this the case with the numerous families who gravitated into the "Wen" from Ireland in search of work. "If these people have been 'virtuously brought up in the country', they are seized by despondency when their funds are exhausted in a vain search for work; they pawn their belongings; and having come from too great a distance to be legally transferred back to their parishes, they are thrown upon the mercy of the parish officers, who treat them with contumely. Although willing to labour, they have no one to aid them, consequently, not a few of them actually perish for want or contract diseases which terminate in premature death." Such,

Colquhoun stated, was the position of the decent labouring people who came to London to seek employment. The more profligate, however, joined up with thieves and rogues when they came to the end of their resources and could still find no work. The males went to swell the "phalanx of delinquents" and the young females "too often" became prostitutes. He stated that this "mass of indigence", in London, more poignant and extensive than perhaps in any other part of the world, "embraced all ranks of society; but, though sometimes resulting from unavoidable misfortune, it was more frequently generated by idleness and neglect of business". Nevertheless, he realized the heavy handicap placed particularly on the children born in such circumstances. "It is in the progress to the adult state", he wrote, "that the infants of parents broken down by misfortune, invariably learn, from the pressure of extreme poverty, to resort to devices which early corrupt their morals and mar their future success and utility in life." Under these influences girls "who in other circumstances might have been an ornament to their sex" became prostitutes, and the boys turned into what the twentieth century calls "public enemies". Familiarized in infancy to the pawnbroker's shop and to other even less respectable means of obtaining temporary subsistence, "they too soon become adepts in falsehood and deceit. Imperious necessity has given an early spring to their ingenuity". Their resourcefulness could have made them useful to society, but in youth their minds "have acquired a wrong bias, and they are reared insensibly in the walks of vice, without knowing in many instances that they are at all engaged in such pursuits".

He was emphatic, however, that "from indigence is to be traced the great origin and the progress of crimes", and deplored the fact that one million poverty-stricken people existed in a total population estimated at approximately nine millions.* The system of poor-relief had proved radically wrong in its execution; if this were not so it would be "impossible that there could exist in the Metropolis such an inconceivable portion of human misery". The distress of the poor had not arisen from the lack of funds, but from the failure to apply the funds beneficially. In the two parishes of St Giles-in-the-Fields and St George-the-Martyr, for instance, there were "1200 poor natives of Ireland", on whom £2000 was spent in 1796. An Act of 1792 had stipulated that all vagrants should be "publicly whipt", and as these unfortunates were "on the brink of vagrancy" the magistrates permitted them to remain a burden on the parishes, for they were loth to whip or imprison "poor

* The 1801 census showed that the population had risen to these figures: England and Wales, 8,892,536; Scotland, 1,608,420. For Ireland 5,216,331 (cf. John Ashton's *The Dawn of the Nineteenth Century in England*, pp. 30, 31). Toynbee, op. cit., presents the figure of 9,187,176 as the population of England in 1801.

miserable wretches whose indigence have [*sic*] rendered relief necessary". In the administration of poor-relief generally no steps had been taken to "restore the pauper to a capacity of earning his own livelihood", no effort made to redeem their pawned clothing, no enquiry instituted as to their fitness for work and nothing done to procure work for those willing but unable to find it. "Hence it is that poverty, under such circumstances, contributes in no small degree to the multiplication of crimes. The profligate thus partly supported, too often resorts to pilfering pursuits to fill up the chasm, and habits of idleness being once obtained, labour soon becomes irksome." We need not concern ourselves with the solutions proposed by Colquhoun to eliminate the worthless, to assist the deserving to obtain work, and to check crime by efficient policing. His reasoned exposition of the status of the poor in the community has a particular interest, largely because it was unusual in that age and was intended to enlighten those who were "apt to form erroneous views" of the poor man's proper place in society. He divides the poor into five classes; including the " 'useful poor', who are able and willing to work, and who should be regarded as pillars of the State, meriting the attention of Government to prevent their falling into indigence, and when indigent should 'be propped up' by the State; and the 'vagrant poor', who, though able to find employment are unwilling to work, or cannot be employed because of their bad characters. When these are aided by the State, the State not only suffers indirectly by the loss of their labour but also directly by the contributions made to perpetuate their indigence. Such vagrants should be turned to industry when possible, or refused aid when they are unwilling to co-operate, and their crimes should be punished". The three remaining classes include the "incapable, of whom the sick deserve to be restored to their former position, and the aged and infirm deserve such treatment at least as will prevent their being associated with criminal poor in workhouses; but the infant children reared in workhouses have special claims. The child asylum should be better conducted than the profligate homes of the poor, but in the present circumstances the children of the State are reared in such surroundings of profligacy that children become 'depraved in their progress to maturity'; hence it is that the rising generation enter upon life with wicked and dangerous propensities."

Colquhoun stated that this most difficult problem of the poor had been given scant attention in its management, having generally been entrusted to the care of the least competent. The system of Poor Law control had been criticized over a long period. Chief Justice Hale had long ago complained that it had been responsible for filling the gaols with malefactors and the country with idlers

who "will daily increase even to a desolation in time", and Sir Frederick Eden had recently confirmed the truth of this prophecy.

Such, then, were the connexions between poverty and crime, as known and described by contemporaries. Colquhoun, while supporting all other witnesses regarding the criminality of the poor, emphatically defined the social conditions of the poor as the chief cause of their crime. It is but just that this fact should be taken into consideration when we pass judgment on the men, women and children who were transported as criminals to Australia. But for the ill-regulated Poor Law system the numbers would not have been so great; it is not unreasonable to suppose that under more efficient control the problem of inadequate prison accommodation would never have arisen in England, in which case the foundation of Australia would have been considerably deferred. The opinions of the Fieldings illustrate the conditions under which criminals became a problem prior to 1786. Colquhoun fulfils the same office for those who followed until 1800, and after that time, for he did not change one word of his verdict in the later editions of his book. Even a generation later Peel, moving for the appointment of a committee to examine the cause of the increase of crime in 1828, thought that "the far stronger cause of crime" was the state and operation of the Poor Laws in some of the counties. The wage-level, which was so low as to require subsidy from parish funds, he considered as tending "to destroy that independence of mind which is the foundation of moral character", and he believed that the committee would find this cause of crime "of much more extensive operation than many of those which it was usual to assign".[49]

We may make one more deduction from the state of the poor in England, and apply it to Australian conditions. It will help us to understand the English criticism that was regularly levelled against the transportation system from its inception to its abolition. Even before the Australian system commenced it had been argued that transportation was not an effective punishment, and it was seriously maintained that by being transported the criminal improved his condition of life and his standard of living above what had been his normal lot in England. This argument was put forward by the Select Committee of 1798, and during the following years with increasing persistence until it was decided in 1819 to 1821 to add further horrors to the system. In 1836 one of the two purposes of Dr Ullathorne's mission and writings in England was to persuade the labouring classes of England that their condition of life would not be improved, as they had imagined, by their deliberate entry into the convict ranks in Australia. From the foregoing description of the state of the poor in England it is

possible to understand both the government dissatisfaction with transportation as an effective deterrent against crime, and why it was often welcomed by the impoverished criminal as an escape from hopeless misery. The opportunities offered in New South Wales to the transportee between 1800 and 1821, if he liked to avail himself of them and was strong enough to rise above the immorality prevalent in the settlement, frequently more than compensated for the loss of whatever rights and opportunities had been available to him as an impoverished citizen in England.*

(e) The Attitude of the Ruling Classes

When A. V. Dicey set himself to describe *The Relations between Law and Public Opinion in England during the Nineteenth Century*, he divided that century into three periods, the first of which extended from 1800 to 1830, and was designated "The period of Old Toryism or Legislative Quiescence".[50] The title was appropriate for the legacy of "Blackstonian optimism" left by the previous century. In fact, it might be said that the period of legislative quiescence had begun after the settlement of 1688 and endured, unchanged, until the theories of Bentham and his disciples gained practical recognition after 1825. From the date of Bentham's first criticism of the English system in 1776 until 1821 the changes made in the law were inconsiderable, and "such as were made were, as often as not, in the wrong direction". "During the first forty years of the reign of George III", Sir R. K. Wilson wrote in his review of English criminal law, "it would be hard to point out a single statute, within the domain of private law, which with our present lights we can unhesitatingly set down as an improvement; very few indeed of which it can be said that they were even honestly intended by their authors to promote the well-being of the people at large as distinguished from the immediate interest of the Government of the day, or, at most, of the limited class which alone had an appreciable share of political power."[51]

Accordingly, Parliament refused to support Pitt's modest proposals for parliamentary reform and consistently and vehemently opposed

---

* It is interesting to note how few expirees among the convicts, after Governor Macquarie's arrival, chose to return to England. In that administration, 1810-1821, the emancipists were treated with extreme liberality, but between 1792 and 1800 those who returned were more numerous. Throughout the period in which transportation continued in Australia the British Government opposed the repatriation of ex-convicts. In his *Report on the State of Agriculture and Trade in N.S.W.* (page 82) Commissioner Bigge stated that from 1810 to the end of 1820 only 389 persons had returned to Europe. 247 men and thirty-one women returned after expiry of sentence. Eighty-seven men and twenty-four women returned after free pardons. In 1820 he remarked that the time had passed for "getting rich quick"; much industry had then become necessary. But considerable opportunities did exist for English immigrants. There were few people of long residence in the country who were not suffering from earlier embarrassments, and their homes had little of the comfort that marked the houses of the middle classes in England. But Bigge did not remark that even these small comforts were better than those existing among the impoverished classes in England, from whose ranks the prisoners had come.

such obvious and comparatively innocuous reforms as the abolition of child labour and the slave trade, because vested interests were at stake.* The *laissez-faire* teachings of Adam Smith went beyond the economic and invaded the political field, but though Parliament refused to restrict the rights of the individual by too much legislation, it did not hesitate to make new laws to ensure the security of property. Such laws did not affect those who had no need to steal. Even the more liberal-minded statesmen, who dissented from the extreme harshness of the penal code, were against any course that placed obstacles in the path of industrialism. Burke opposed the artificial raising of wages, holding that wages and prices should be allowed to find their own level, and in his *Thoughts on Scarcity* argued against "an overdoing of any sort of administration, and more especially against this most momentous of all meddling on the part of authority, the meddling with the subsistence of the people". The Radicals themselves, such as Price and Godwin, subscribed to the same principle, though they demanded that Government should interfere "to suppress injustice".

It is possible, of course, to point to several reforms made in the eighteenth century, but many of them were abortive, and all were long overdue. The Factory Act of 1802, by which it is claimed that a breach was made in the policy of non-interference, granted only small concessions. The motive behind the government policy was not, as the patriots maintained, the traditional love of the Englishman for the constitution but a conscious effort to make the old régime, that had functioned so well in an agricultural nation, endure in the new industrial age. The effort succeeded for a time with the aid of additional penal statutes, which coerced the masses into submission or hopeless revolt.

England in the late eighteenth century was a country of glaring contrasts, with the polished and cultured aristocracy at the top, securely resting on their landed property, and a verminous and illiterate mob at the bottom, living in the gin-shops and gutters of the great cities and ports, especially London. In between came an infinite gradation of *parvenu* Indian nabobs vulgarly displaying their novel opulence; hard-working country squires, the backbone of the country's local administration and the saviours of the English aristocracy from the moral decadence that befell the *seigneurie* of France; industrious middle-class manufacturers and shop-keepers; a multitude of tenant farmers, agricultural labourers and other hangers-on of the great estates, men who worked and toiled that rakes like the Prince of Wales, Wilkes and Fox might drink and

* Between 1783 and 1793 it was estimated that England transported about 38,000 African negroes annually. Of 814,000 slaves sent to the West Indies in eleven years, half were carried in British ships, and from this trade the merchants of Liverpool made an annual profit of nearly £300,000. (Cf. Lecky, *History of England in the Eighteenth Century*, Vol. VII, 366.)

gamble and bet and debauch themselves in Hogarthian surroundings. There were even a few yeomen farmers left, where the tentacles of industrialism and the greedy spread of the new towns had allowed them to remain.

One class, however, that plays a very important part in modern life was absent from eighteenth century England. The salariat or professional class existed only in the most rudimentary form, and apart from a few lawyers and apothecaries who were still on a commercial basis, the Churches, and in particular the established Church, were the only considerable body of unpropertied educated men outside politics. The Church, like the Civil Service, was at this time a mere "out-relief department of the British aristocracy". Christian it was in name, but in practice the clergy departed very far from Christian tenets. Too many of them lived the lives of country gentlemen, farming their glebes, riding to hounds, dining and wining with the neighbouring aristocracy, sitting on the county bench, and altogether neglecting their proper work. Absenteeism was endemic, while incumbents sipped the waters of Tunbridge and Bath, and bishoprics and advowsons changed hands like counters in the game of political intrigue. The universities were educational institutions only in name and served chiefly to provide comfortable billets and plenty of port for the superannuated clergy of the Established Church.

Unfortunately the Church of England brought to Australia too many of its vices and too few of its scanty virtues. For thirty years it had practically a spiritual monopoly in the settlement, with all the rights, privileges and endowments of an Established Church, which it illegally claimed to be. For the first six years of the settlement, the only official representative of Christianity in New South Wales was a Moravian Methodist, functioning as the representative of the Church of England and appointed through the influence of Wilberforce; "a just, pious and inoffensive man", as Hunter described him, sincere and hard-working, but quite incapable of grappling with the Herculean task of giving a Christian basis to the life of a settlement composed mainly of debauched convicts and self-seeking soldiers. Throughout the early history of the colony the clergy were overworked and underpaid and seem to have been unappreciative of the real tragedy of the transportation system.

Two of the worst abuses of English clerical life were reproduced early in the history of the new settlement. Before 1800 two clergymen, Johnson and Marsden, had been made justices of the peace and in later years other parson-magistrates were appointed. It also became the practice for the clergy to farm their own land, and Marsden especially was known more as a pioneer of the wool-

growing industry than for his ecclesiastical duties. The magisterial appointments made the Church part of the governmental machine and prevented it from criticizing the penal system, though it did its best under difficult circumstances for individual convicts. Marsden in particular was noted for the severity of his sentences, and his position was summed up succinctly by the convicts, who said that though he prayed for mercy on their souls on Sundays, he had little mercy on their bodies on weekdays.

It is an astonishing fact that, after the departure of Johnson, the Clergy of the Church of England never protested against the system as a whole and only occasionally complained of specific abuses. It was left to the representatives of other religious bodies, Elizabeth Fry and the Quakers, Lang the Presbyterian, Whately of the Church of Ireland, and Ullathorne, the Catholic Vicar-General, to rouse British public opinion against the transportation system.

"In England at this time", said Leslie Stephen, "the Church, considered as a whole, could hardly be called an organism at all, or, if an organism, it was an organism with its central organ in a permanent state of paralysis."[52] Its perpetual subservience to the ruling classes and to their contempt for all religious enthusiasm as "lack of breeding" brought about the Wesleyan and Evangelical movements, with their insistence on the need for a vigorous Christianity and humanitarian reforms. The Wesleyans, as Lecky has justly observed, planted a fervid religious sentiment among the most brutal and abandoned sections of the population, and "taught criminals in Newgate to mount the gallows in an ecstasy of rapturous devotion", but they entirely missed the real significance of the coincidence of poverty and crime.[53]*

Raikes, Howard, Hanway, Wilberforce, Granville Sharp and Hannah More were all reformers produced by the Evangelical revival and revulsion from the lackadaisical attitude of the Established Church. They founded Sunday schools, taught the poor to read, visited gaols, rescued pauper children and sought to remove the canker of the slave trade from British commerce; but their reaction was instinctive and they had no sense of the necessity for that clear-cut and radical reform which characterized Beccaria and Bentham and even William Eden. The Humanitarians were among the noblest men and women that have ever honoured the

---

* It was typical of religious enthusiasm at the time that only one minister was sent to attend to 1000 people on the First Fleet, and that he remained alone until 1794, attempting to cope with the needs of increasing numbers of convicts in a parish that extended to Norfolk Island. The well-meant contribution of the S.P.C.K. to the first chaplain was also typical of the mentality of the Evangelicals: with Bibles and Prayer Books they included several other publications, including 200 *Exercises Against Lying*, twenty-five *Plain Exhortations to Prisoners*, fifty *Woodward's Cautions to Swearers*, 100 *Exhortations to Chastity*, six *Worthington on Self-Resignation*. It would be easy, and probably unjust, to become facetious when reviewing this list; but considering that most of the wretched prisoners were illiterate, the Church could have made a better contribution by sending additional clergymen, whom they could easily have spared from hundreds of idle, absentee benefice holders.

name of England, but they were essentially short-sighted and confined their efforts to reforming the morals of the poor, without attempting to tackle the political controls which brought about social conditions and crime. In fact, it may be said that the Evangelical revival resisted every attempt to interfere with existing institutions and thereby unconsciously helped to perpetuate the overlordship of the capitalist and the submergence of the poor.

THE CRIMINAL LAWS AND PUNISHMENTS

In the preceding chapter the prevalence of crime in England was noted, and an attempt was made to show how far social conditions might have been responsible for it. That criminality did exist to an astounding degree cannot be denied; it explains the panic of the legislators. In a debate in the House of Commons on the London and Westminster Police Bill in 1785, the Solicitor General remarked that "nobody could feel himself unapprehensive of danger to his person or property if he walked in the street after dark, nor could any man promise himself security in his bed". Robbery and villainy had become so daring that they were no longer accompanied by cunning and caution, but were perpetrated openly, and with undisguised violence in the most populous places and frequently before it was near dark. He adverted to the crowds of felons with whose weight "the gallows groaned", and yet the example was found ineffectual, for the evil was increasing. Young children were initiated by the elder rogues, and at length terminated their existence on the gallows at seventeen or eighteen, though old and accomplished in the mysteries of their profession; for it was a certain truth that of the whole number hanged in the metropolis, eighteen out of every twenty were under twenty-one.[1]

Sir Walter Besant, the historian of eighteenth century London, described the increasing criminality of the London mobs as "absolutely intolerable". A race of vagabonds, thieves and rogues grew up in terrifying numbers, so that it became customary for respectable citizens to carry cudgels for self-protection.[2] We have already referred to Colquhoun's description of the existing crime, in which he ascribed its causes, not only indirectly to the abuses of the poor-relief system, but immediately to the low-class taverns which were no more than dens of prostitution and receiving-houses for stolen goods. London was a comparatively small city, three miles long, with a population, in 1801, of about 641,000 people, 20,000 of whom led absolutely useless lives. There were 5000 public houses, and 50,000 women supported in some way by prostitution. River thieves, highway robbers, organized gangs of professional criminals, in league with hackney coachmen and dockyard officials, terrorized the community. Several thousand

persons were engaged in "coining", and the number of houses for receiving stolen goods had increased from 300 to 3000. The detection of criminals was impossible under existing circumstances, where ex-convicts at the rate of nearly 600 a year were released upon society from the prisons and hulks and where order had to be preserved by 189 paid officers, by 1000 perfunctory, un-remunerated parish constables, and by 2000 watchmen, who were paid at from 8½d. to 2s. a night and were often chosen from the ranks of the most indigent and feeble in order to keep them out of the workhouse. The revenue raised by crime, according to Colquhoun, amounted to £2,000,000, and the sums lost in gambling-houses approximated £7,000,000 annually.[3] Colquhoun suggested that the remedy lay in the creation of an efficient police force, in the amendment of the criminal laws to ensure a greater certainty of punishment, and in a systematic attempt to set men to work rather than encourage crime by subsidized idleness. None of his suggestions were listened to until much later, in the nineteenth century when Peel's police force attempted to cope with the problem. The parliamentary solution was, however, to multiply statutes against crime and to affix the capital penalty to them.

The accumulated penal enactments, which we shall call loosely the Penal Code, must be viewed from various angles. Theoretically it was sanguinary; in practice it was severe, but not so severe as it might have been. It was definitely taken for granted that it would not be universally applied. The code was a chaos of impossible statutes, leaving gaps to be filled up by the judges and the Common Law. Hence, despite its inflictions, it neither protected property nor checked crime.

In the speech which "marked the beginning of the long duel with France", Pitt had declared that "it was the boast of the law of England that it afforded equal security and protection to the high and the low, the rich and the poor". In 1826, however, when moving the consolidation of the Criminal Laws, Sir Robert Peel made a memorable survey of penal legislation in the past century. In that time new capital offences had been multiplied at the rate of more than two a year, until there were two hundred specified crimes punishable by death. "It is clear," said Peel, "that criminal legislation has been heretofore left to the desultory and unconcerted speculations of every man who had a fancy to legislate. If an offence were committed in some corner of the land, a law sprang up to prevent the repetition, not of the species of crime to which it belonged, but of the single and specific act of which there had been reason to complain. The new enactment too was frequently stuck into the middle of a statute passed probably at the latter end of a session, to the compounding of which every

man who saw or imagined a defect in the pre-existing law was allowed to contribute." As an instance of such chaotic legislation, Peel quoted an Act, the official title of which was: "An Act to continue several laws therein mentioned for granting liberty to carry sugars . . . of His Majesty's sugar colonies in America . . . in ships built in Great Britain; for the preventing of frauds committed by bankrupts; for . . . further encouragement for the importation of naval stores from . . . America . . . *and for preventing the stealing or destroying of madder roots.*" He remarked that there were no less than twenty statutes to protect trees and timber from theft or injury, but the incorporation of many of these statutes within others that were essentially dissimilar in purpose was frequent and ludicrous. He hesitated to define the statutes lest his listeners might think he was fabricating titles for the purpose of his argument. Sixty years previously, he said, it was realized that the numerous statutes referring to trees had not specifically mentioned hollies and thorns. Therefore, instead of amending the existing law, new Acts to cover the deficiencies were passed, so that to an Act "for the better securing the duties of customs upon certain goods" in outlying ports, for regulating customs fees in the province in Senegambia, and for providing for certain public offices in Scotland, was appended a new provision *"for the better preservation of hollies, thorns and quicksets in forests, chases and private grounds"*. Peel, at this late stage in the history of English criminal law remarked that in consolidating some of the criminal laws he did not propose to lessen the security given by the law to the owner of the madder roots or to throw open the holly or thorn to depredation, but only "to transplant them to a soil more congenial than the province of Senegambia".[4] Peel proved that much of the legislation had been "hasty and slovenly". Frequently new statutes made no reference whatever to the host of antecedent statutes, and in the same session, as in 6 Geo. III, a later statute might be found to impose a fine of twenty pounds for an offence which a few months previously had been declared a capital felony. Had the latter statute been passed in a succeeding session, it would have amounted to a virtual repeal of the former. There were in 1826 no less than twelve statutes relating to the offence of stealing goods, founded not on a general principle, but referring to separate articles of property. Nevertheless, despite the minuteness of definition one of the main defects of the criminal law was the facility with which criminals could escape from it, by appealing to the fact that some particular crime was not technically and completely such as that defined by statute. We shall refer to this when discussing procedure.

The legislation was, therefore, the desultory product of a

propertied class who were inexpert in legal matters and ignorant of the psychology of crime. To protect themselves they threatened people with the gallows for every offence "about which there was a temporary panic". Before considering the code in its practical application we shall describe it as it existed theoretically—the product of past and contemporary legislation. Broadly speaking, the subjects of criminal jurisdiction were distinguished as treasons, felonies and misdemeanours, and the punishments varied from death to brief imprisonment or the pillory. For the purposes of the general reader, and for the convenience of a non-legal writer, it will be sufficient to show the broad significance of certain terms that were most frequently used, particularly the divisions of clergyable and non-clergyable offences, and the distinctions between grand and petty larceny. Both misdemeanours and felonies were crimes, but the trials of both differed in procedure and no misdemeanour was a capital offence. Some misdemeanours, however, were punished more severely than certain felonies. In earlier centuries the number of felonies at Common Law was small—homicide (in its two forms of murder and manslaughter), rape, burglary, arson, larceny, robbery and mayhem. All of these, except petty larceny and mayhem, were punishable by death but were originally subject to the privilege of clergy.[5] Larceny was ordinary theft but did not comprehend real or immovable property, a fact which explains many of the absurd statutes against the cutting down of trees. Growing trees, crops and minerals were not subjects of larceny at Common Law, not being regarded as personal property until severance. They were part of the realty. Special statutes were therefore multiplied to cover these objects.

Grand larceny was the stealing of goods above twelve pence in value and was usually a capital offence. Petty larceny occurred when the goods stolen were of a less value, and was punishable by whipping and imprisonment. But, in the statutory provisions made during this period the two great classifications were those of *simple* and *compound* larcenies. Simple larceny—unaccompanied by aggravating circumstances—was punishable as a clergyable felony with imprisonment not exceeding two years, transportation not exceeding seven years, burning in the hand or whipping. Even simple larceny was non-clergyable for the second offence. There were many stated exceptions, for which the death penalty was applicable even on the first offence, such as the stealing of horses or cattle. Compound larceny, however, denoted an aggravation according to time, place or manner. In nearly all instances the offence became capital if goods were taken from the person, at night, on the highway or from a dwelling-house (housebreaking by day and burglary at night). Moreover, violence was always an

aggravation which lifted the offence from the simpler category, and in every case of compound larceny the theft was capital if the goods taken were above the value of one shilling.[6] At one time great numbers of people suffered the capital penalty, but the *privilege of clergy*, originally meant to free the clergy from the jurisdiction of secular courts, was gradually extended through varying classes, allowing educated persons and others to plead this benefit and to submit to a purgation by burning on the hand. The purgation provision was abolished in 1576, when it was enacted that persons claiming the privilege of exemption from the death penalty should be discharged or imprisoned for a short term. The education qualification for the privilege was further extended to include women, and then abolished altogether, allowing it to be invoked by all persons in certain defined circumstances, when other punishments might be inflicted. Accordingly, in the eighteenth century, when benefit of clergy had been thus extended, the punishment for all the offences in Common Law diminished; if a man was not hanged he was discharged, or at most imprisoned for a year without hard labour. Yet hangings were numerous. Certain felonies had been defined by statutes as non-clergyable, but these were few. Any person charged with a clergyable felony was entitled to benefit of clergy for the first offence. He was pardoned from the death sentence; but if his offence was larceny he might be transported for seven years.[7] The death penalty and forfeiture of land and goods were applicable, however, to all felonies except petty larceny and mayhem until 1828, though many of these felonies were subject to benefit of clergy. The work of the eighteenth century legislators fell into the two categories of withdrawing from the privilege of clergy numerous capital felonies and multiplying by successive statutes new offences which they expressly declared non-clergyable. This was the process which the jurist, Blackstone, saw in two different lights. As a very typical man of his century he was convinced that the English legislature "in the course of a long and laborious process extracted by noble alchemy rich medicines out of poisonous ingredients"; but, as an observer of the ineffectiveness of parliamentary procedure in multiplying statutes he had to remark that "among the variety of actions which men are daily liable to commit no less than 160 have been declared by Act of Parliament to be felonies without benefit of clergy". Hence, even so great a reactionary as he could "occasionally find room to remark some particulars that seem to want revision and amendment".[8]

Blackstone's list of 160 capital offences was not complete. It has been said that in Walpole's time there were 253;[9] throughout the period the number might be regarded as about 200, and, perhaps,

before the inauguration of reform the total reached 222.[10]* In 1795 Colquhoun made a selection from the crimes for which sentences of death were imposed. The list, which is given in Appendix A, covered a variety of offences ranging from murder, arson and rape, to "privately stealing or picking pockets above one shilling", cutting down trees and "breaking down the head of a fish-pond". Since these were non-clergyable offences the judge had to impose the death penalty, but it was left to his discretion to order transportation in certain cases, and this was equivalent to a conditional pardon. The obligation to pronounce the death sentence in cases where it was obvious that it would not be carried out was withdrawn in 1823 (4 Geo. IV, c. 48), when judges were empowered in all felonies except murder merely to record the death sentence and to impose transportation directly. Prior to 1768 pardons had been made by the King through one of the Secretaries of State; after that date the Judges of Assize were allowed to order that persons convicted of non-clergyable offences should be transported for whatever term they thought proper, or for fourteen years "if no term was specially mentioned".[11]

Apart from the recognized procedure of commuting death sentences in the majority of cases into other punishments, it has to be observed that the failure to consolidate crimes and the multiplication of specific statutes proved to some extent a measure of protection to the people of this period. Sir J. F. Stephen has remarked that a few general enactments would have been much more severe than a great number of special ones; if a general Act had excluded all forms of larceny or of forgery from benefit of clergy, the effect would have been greater than that of fifty acts specifying fifty different objects and circumstances. In the notorious Black Act (9 Geo. I, c. 27; 1722) fifty-four capital offences were defined, but in such a way that three different classes of people were forbidden to do any one of eighteen acts. Nevertheless, this eminent criminal lawyer particularly emphasized that the existing law "was severe to the highest degree and destitute of any sort of principle or system".[12]

Even as late as 1839, the crimes excluded from the death penalty were classified in thirty-eight classes of felonies and ninety-six classes of misdemeanours.[13] The list of crimes for which transportation might be the sentence can be seen in Appendix A. The principal one among these is larceny above the value of one shilling, except in cases where statutes distinguished otherwise. The

* Of the 160 capital offences referred to by Blackstone four-fifths were made during the reigns of the first three Georges. In practice, owing to the clemency of juries, there were only about twenty-five offences for which anyone actually suffered death. In 1823 five statutes, exempting from the death penalty about a hundred felonies, were passed into law. In 1832 forgery ceased to be a capital offence. Between 1820 and 1860 over 190 capital offences were abolished. (Cf. J. Laurence: *A History of Capital Punishment*, pp. 12-15.)

list contemplates serious crimes as well as petty offences, even, in certain specified instances, petty larcenies below one shilling in value. The particular point to emphasize in this list of transportable offences is "the wide though capriciously restricted discretion left to the judge". Whenever an enactment provided for transportation it generally made provisions for a maximum, an intermediate and a minimum term of transportation. As alternatives, left to the discretion of the judge in all but two instances, it provided for a maximum term of imprisonment with or without hard labour, a minimum term of imprisonment, and power to inflict whipping, publicly or privately and more than once, also solitary confinement during a part of the imprisonment.[14] These provisions for the transportation punishment were variable in many ways. In seventeen cases the sentence might be for life. In two cases the punishment was to be absolute, without alternative. In two cases minimum terms of ten and fifteen years were specified; in fifteen cases the maximum was fifteen years; and the instances in which the punishment for seven years might be inflicted presented twenty-three varieties.[15] Within this confusing ambit the judges sought to introduce an element of proportion between the crime and the punishment among transportable felons. But the intricacies of a cumbrous system left a very wide discretion to the judges, who, moreover, were empowered and expected to commute most of the capital sentences into transportation. In 1823 Mackintosh's proposal to define the procedure in inflicting punishments was negatived; but in 1826 Peel was at last able to state that "the laws relating to the punishment of transportation have been revised and collected into one statute".[16] Transportation, therefore, was a sentence passed in two circumstances. It was a condition of pardon allowed in many crimes excluded from the benefit of clergy, and prior to 1823 was pronounced after it was determined that the capital sentence should not be executed. It was also a substantive punishment for a great variety of crimes specified by statutes in the eighteenth and the nineteenth centuries, and as such could be directly imposed or altered according to the provisions described above.

The list of misdemeanours, punishable by fine, imprisonment, whipping and the pillory can be seen in Appendix A. To this long list Colquhoun appended a note which is worth repeating. "There are," he wrote, "a great many other trivial offences denominated misdemeanours, subject to pecuniary fines, which it is not easy to enumerate. Since almost every statute, whether public or private, which passes in a session of Parliament, creates new offences—the shades vary as society advances, and their number is scarcely within reach of calculation."[17]

C

While the severity of the code had been deliberately intended by the legislators, it is equally clear that acquiescence in its non-application was manifested throughout many years. The laws were more of a solace to enraged individuals than a warning to others or a means whereby the injured party might receive compensation. The official mind was often clearly manifested in this direction, particularly when opposing reforming legislation, but occasionally, as Romilly remarked, the temper of Government was exerted in an opposite direction to enforce the application of the laws to at least a degree proportionate to their intentions. Even the non-official mind acquiesced in this cumbrous system. Paley admitted that a critic of English law would look in vain for order and proportion, but the system suited "the accommodation of the inhabitant".[18] Goldsmith, a man less in sympathy with officialdom than Paley, also saw virtue in a system where the severe code acted as a parent, brandishing a rod but applying it only when insubordination "rose into enormity".* To some extent his argument might apply to any rational executive system, but the weakness of the eighteenth century system was that the law could not be applied in a variety of cases that called for punishment, and when applied to other cases was usually too extreme to be justifiable. The following paragraphs give a short description of the procedure of trial, and incidentally show the deficiencies in the system and the ways by which it could be circumvented.

Non-indictable offences were tried before, and summarily dealt with by, the Justices of the Peace. Indictable offences, treasons, felonies and misdemeanours, were tried under the Common Law system in its criminal jurisdiction. A man guilty of an indictable offence ordinarily came before the magistrate, and if the evidence warranted he was commited for trial at Assizes or Quarter Sessions, according to the gravity of the offence. Apart from cases committed by a magistrate certain cases might be preferred by bill before a Grand Jury at Quarter Sessions or Assizes. The Grand Jury consisted of from twelve to twenty-four country gentlemen selected by the sheriff. If they were satisfied that there was in the evidence a *prima facie* case, they found a "True Bill"—and the accused was then obliged to stand his trial. In the interval between commitment and trial, which could amount to six months, the

---

* From Goldsmith's *Citizen of the World* (1760): "There is scarcely an Englishman who does not, almost every day of his life, offend with impunity against some express Law, and for which, in a certain conjuncture of circumstances, he would not receive punishment. Gaming-houses, preaching at prohibited places, assembled crowds, nocturnal amusements, public shows, and a hundred other instances, are forbid—and frequented. These prohibitions are useful; though it be prudent in their Magistrates, and happy for their people, that they are not enforced, and none but the venal or mercenary attempt to enforce them. The Law in this case, like an indulgent parent, still keeps the rod, though the child is seldom corrected. Were those pardoned offences to rise into enormity, were they likely to obstruct the happiness of society, or endanger the State, it is then that justice would resume her terrors, and punish those faults she had so often overlooked with indulgence. It is to this ductility of the laws that an Englishman owes the freedom he enjoys superior to others in a more popular Government."

accused probably lay in an insanitary gaol, which was filled with other persons awaiting trial. In their courts of summary jurisdiction the magistrates naturally acted in the interests of the property régime. The Hammonds devote a special chapter to show the fallacy of the prevailing belief that the magistrates, being squires of their people, were as a class disposed to treat them with mercy.[19] In a class that regarded the defence of the rights of property as the main business of society the spirit and the working of English institutions all tended to protect the one class that was officially recognized by the State. Hence, in summary jurisdiction and particularly in enforcing the Combination and the Sedition Laws, the country magistrates became "a most effective part of the system of repression". The magisterial abuse of power under the Vagrancy Laws robbed the populace of the most fundamental rights of liberty. A parson magistrate seized two men who were found distributing Cobbett's pamphlets in 1817, and had them both flogged at the whipping-post under the Vagrancy Laws. With a multitude of supporting facts the Hammonds establish the fact that the county magistrates became a political force for maintaining the rigorous code, using even the questionable means of *agents provocateurs* and bribery. Within their summary powers floggings and imprisonments were imposed, and, as we have seen, men were committed for trial in thousands by them, only to be liberated again in thousands, perhaps after six months' gaol, by judges and London jurymen. From another point of view, however, a defensive case may be made for the county magistrates, and the Hammonds impartially state it in *The Village Labourer*. Other reputable historians have differentiated between magistrates and credited many of them with a rough sense of justice.[20] The French historian, Halévy, spoke of them as generally a class of rough, well-meaning men, popular with the people, and administering the law with a rude justice and careless mercy.* Much may be said for many of them, and it has been said in the chapter that discussed the philanthrophic work in which some of them were interested. But their functions covered all control of county life, exercising justice in Quarter or Petty Sessions or in the house of a single magistrate, managing prisons which they hired out to contractors, and administering the poor laws. When the Industrial Revolution set classes one against the other it was found that

---

* Mais, une fois cela dit pour expliquer les attaques dirigées vers 1815 par les démocrates anglais contre les institutions établies, il ne convient pas de considérer le régime comme un régime d'oppression, ni de méconnaître les éléments de liberté vraie qu'il renferme . . . il y a plus d'un tyranneau, prêt à abuser des pouvoirs que la loi lui confère pour terroriser le bas peuple. . . . D'autres . . . rappellent le Squire Western du roman de Fielding, grand buveur, grand chasseur . . . Leur justice apparaît, somme toute, comme nonchalante et débonnaire; leur administration des lois d'assistance publique est relâchée jusqu'au gaspillage. Faut-il louer tant de mansuétude et de générosité. A vrai dire, ce n'est pas seulement la volonté qui leur manque pour gouverner en despotes: les moyens nécessaires leur font défaut." (E. Halévy: *Histoire du Peuple Anglais au XIXe siècle*, Vol. I, p. 39.)

justice, administration and influence were concentrated within the hands of this personally interested group, so that their wide executive power combined with their domination in the legislature made them a feudal oligarchy.[21] The traditions of a professional magistracy were started by Henry Fielding and his brother, Sir John, at Bow Street, but the professional aspect of such an important position was not recognized by Act of Parliament until 1792. Outside London and Middlesex the magistrates were unpaid. "The use of the term 'despotism' for the rule of the squires is no exaggeration," wrote J. Holland Rose. Against their verdict in summary jurisdiction appeal was impossibly expensive; they pronounced judgment without expert advice; the Draconian code of the game laws was absolutely in their hands, made for them and administered by them.[22] The severity of their justice in summary convictions does not particularly concern this study of more serious offences; but the contribution made by the county magnates to the transportation system is to be estimated by the multitudes of men whom they committed for trial. However, it has to be observed that owing to the definitions in the laws the magistrates were compelled to commit large numbers of these men for trial, and the only protection for the people against the prevailing despotism lay in the common sense of judges and juries, by whom half of those committed were liberated. Nevertheless, even in the jury process the power of the landed gentry was noticeable, for ownership of land was a necessary qualification, the jurors being selected from a list compiled by the local magistrates. However, in London and Middlesex the property qualifications were considerably relaxed, and, consequently, acquittals were more numerous there than in the provinces.

Prior to 1772 the prisoner might refuse to plead, choosing the alternative of being pressed to death, by which he lost his own life but saved his family from beggary. After 1772 no such advantages were to be gained from a refusal to plead. His rights of challenge of a jury were liberal. Though in theory the prosecutor represented the outraged State, in practice the trial was more of a private litigation, in which the injured party had to pay the costs of prosecution in the first instance, which, after a successful issue in the trial, were occasionally refunded to him from county rates. In some cases the accused was not allowed counsel, though on matters of law counsel were available for both sides. The prisoner was allowed to cross-examine witnesses, but the law did not provide for him the same coercive measures for the attendance of witnesses as it allowed to the plaintiff. Though hearsay evidence was excluded the great deficiency in the trial was the refusal to allow the prisoner to give evidence in his own behalf. The prisoner

was not allowed before the trial to see a copy of the indictment, and his knowledge of it depended on what he could glean from the reading of it in the court. His defence was necessarily restricted. The judge gave his summing up and the jury retired, excluded from fire and food until they brought in their verdict. If the verdict was favourable to the prisoner, he was released; if unfavourable, the judge used the wide power of discretion which we have described.

During and after this simple but defective process the opportunities available to the judge and jury to exercise clemency were many and varied. In the trial the popular revolt of jurymen against the unjust system, which applied death to the murderer or to the boy who stole apples from an orchard, was shown by the artifices of exaggerating flaws in the indictment or deliberately reducing the value of the alleged damage committed. The law itself, despite its minuteness in hundreds of specific statutes, left many loop-holes of escape. For example, until 1803, no special punishment was provided for wounding with intent to murder or for doing grievous bodily harm, and until that date such acts were technically misdemeanours punishable by fine and imprisonment.[23] In 1826, when moving the consolidation of the Criminal Laws, Peel stated that such consolidation was necessary, not to protect the criminal against severity, but to supply "those omissions in the law which ensure the impunity of guilt".[24] According to the letter of the law it was not an offence to rob a furnished house though it was a serious crime to rob a furnished lodging. In such a circumstance acquittals had been recorded though there was no doubt of the guilt of the defendant. To steal fish from streams was an offence only if the stream passed *through* an estate, and not, as was usually the case, between two estates. As Peel put it, the law provided that a man who stole a pocket handkerchief could be transported, but there was no way of punishing the culprit who stole title-deeds or a will upon which the disposal of a vast property depended. Procedure required that in cases of embezzlement the indictment must define not only the gross value of the fraud, but the particular coin or note that had passed in the transaction. In each case the proof had to be confined to a single act of embezzlement, and as one of many incidents in a career of embezzlement might have been trivial, though technically a felony, the jury leaned towards mercy and acquitted the offender. If the indictment stated that the accused "killed" rather than "murdered" the deceased, or if any Christian or surname was omitted or wrongly stated, or if the facts proved in the process differed in the slightest detail from the charges defined, if it was proved that a blow was given by the left hand rather than the right designated

in the indictment, the "variances" invalidated the whole prosecution, whether the objection was raised before or after the verdict.[25] About the time of Blackstone this strictness was being somewhat relaxed, and, much later, in 1826 (7 Geo. IV, c. 64) the proving of immaterial facts became less important. In the literature of the period dozens of such instances are recorded. Colquhoun describes how intimidation of witnesses was practised by gangs of criminals so that evidence at the trial differed materially from that given before the magistrate; and in numerous instances the injured party, realizing that a trivial damage became in law a capital felony, refused to prosecute, or altered the assessed damage so as to make the offence a misdemeanour. This procedure was not due to carelessness; it was a popular revolt against the severity of the law by those who, as functioning jurymen, had the power of refusing to apply it. Sir J. F. Stephen, while sympathetic with the popular indignation against the penal code, remarks that the capricious methods turned the law into a "solemn farce", by which a small proportion of prisoners might be said to have "been allowed to toss up for their liberty".[26] Two results followed from the severity of the law and from the refusal to apply it in many instances. The acquittals were numerous: in 1794 of 1060 prisoners tried at the Old Bailey 567 were released, and in 1795 of 1894 prisoners tried at the same Court and at the different Assizes 845 were acquitted or discharged;[27] between 1809 and 1816 of 47,522 committed for criminal offences only 29,361 were convicted; from 1818 to 1825 out of 93,718 committed, a much higher proportion, 63,418, were convicted.[28] All sections of the community saw the necessity for reform. The law had proved ineffective. Legislators periodically demanded that the law should be enforced, but only rarely insisted upon its enforcement. The Reformers, too, emphasized the fact that notorious criminals were allowed to commit crime with impunity, relying on the idiosyncrasies of the executive. Over and above the loopholes provided in the trial itself, the procedure after trial was, as we have seen, inconsistent and careless. The majority of those convicted were sentenced to short terms of imprisonment, during which the petty criminals became confirmed villains by reason of their associations with greater criminals, and were than released to renew a life of crime. The pardons and commutations were so frequent as to belie the fact that the sentences had ever been seriously intended. Between 1809 and 1816 of 4126 persons sentenced to death 536 were executed, and between 1818 and 1825 the proportion was 579 out of 7770.[29] The commutations in transportation sentences were such as we have already described.

Generally, it might be said, the major sentences were rarely

executed as they had been originally defined. A state of general confusion existed, in which the law might be described as defeating its own purposes in a legal manner. The legislature refused to recognize the anomalies. It was left to practical reformers, like Colquhoun, to suggest that the phenomenon of increasing crime could best be tackled by an efficient police force. But the theorist reformers went to the root of the matter, finding the penal system so severe as to be impossible of application. When resentful jury-men refused to submit a petty offender to a capital sentence, they could not sentence him to a lighter penalty, which he probably richly deserved. They had necessarily to acquit. In numerous instances, however, the severest penalties of death and transpor-tation were imposed in most unjustifiable circumstances. Pope's often quoted allusion to wretches hanging that jurymen may dine must be regarded as unjust to a large proportion of those ordinary men who rebelled against the severe code which threatened life and liberty in England. "But for sleeping Dogberries and reluctant jurymen," wrote Prof. J. Holland Rose in his estimate of justice during the Pitt régime, "a tenth part of the population might have lodged in filthy gaols which formed the fruitful seed-bed of crime."[30] Nevertheless, because the system was inconsistent and dependent on the whims and prejudices of diverse types of judges and juries, the reformers of the period realized that a large proportion of those who were convicted were unjustly treated, particularly because they were subjected to extreme punishments, absolutely disproportioned to the nature of their offences. The system may be fairly judged by the number of its victims, by the nature of the punishments recognized by law, and by the attitude of the ruling classes towards the aggravating circumstances which attempted to make extreme penalties even more extreme. It would be worth observing, in this connexion, that the secondary punishments inflicted on convicts in Australia from 1788 to 1821, in their worst excesses were modelled on the régime that existed in England, and generally speaking, were far less severe and more cognizant of human rights than those sanctioned and approved by certain Englishmen whom history and *belles-lettres* would incline us to regard in a far different light. On the Continent the imposition of torture was far more frequent, though the English gaols in Howard's and Romilly's time were worse than those of Europe. Nevertheless, Sir J. F. Stephen came to the conclusion that "the English people have been singularly reckless (till very lately) about taking life, but they have usually been averse to the infliction of death by torture".[31]

Much has been written on the subject of criminal executions in England, but the subject need not be discussed in detail in this

book which is primarily concerned with transportation. Horace Walpole described the country of his day as little better than a shambles; men were shipped to the Plantations because on the weekly hanging-day at Tyburn there was not room for them on the gallows, where others, after "a triumphal procession" were hung up in tens and twenties to the huge entertainment of the mob.[32] This public procession pleased Dr Johnson, who in 1783 regarded its abolition as an infringement of the people's right to gratification. The spectacles at Tyburn are well known. The last execution there was on November 7, 1783, and later executions usually took place at Newgate. On the day before death a special sermon was preached to the unfortunate wretches, which was made realistic by an empty coffin set in a pew in the midst of the condemned. Aggravations of the sentence, such as burning alive and disembowelling alive had either been abolished or fallen into disuse at the end of the century. Instances of posthumous mutilation and drawing of criminals on hurdles can be found, but generally speaking, the most barbarous incidents of execution had disappeared or were disappearing. Dissection of a murderer's body was made optional in 1832, and abolished in 1860. The most remarkable and revolting features of the executions were the publicity of the act and the morbid satisfaction of onlookers who comprised people of all ranks in life. Hanging in all its frightfulness was carried out in public until 1868, when it was at last realized that the spectacle tended to brutalize the onlookers. Hanging in chains was abolished in 1834. But throughout the period of reform it would seem that the youth or sex of offenders mattered little in this punishment. In 1818 two women were hanged for forgery. In the days of George II the hanging of children was frequent and on one occasion ten of them were hanged as a warning; in 1808 a brother and sister, aged seven and eleven, were hanged at Lynn for felony; in 1833 the death sentence was passed on a boy aged nine, for housebreaking, but after a public protest by the people of Maidstone the sentence was not executed, and in 1831 a boy of nine was publicly hanged at Chelmsford for having set fire to a house.[33]

Other punishments adopted in the period were the pillory, abolished for all crimes except perjury in 1816; the stocks, "superseded" by the treadmill in 1820; forfeiture of property and fines. Whipping was an outrageous form of punishment, carried to extremes in England and Australia. In the army and navy the practice became an abuse, courts martial sentencing men to 1500 lashes. In 1807 the limit was reduced to 1000 lashes, but all through the Napoleonic campaign discipline was maintained to a great extent by whipping.[34] Naturally, the English system was

introduced in Australia by naval and military governors, and though the infliction of it depended upon a magisterial sentence the cases in which it occurred were not few and, in certain instances, the number of lashes was excessive.

Imprisonment was the most common punishment of all. Prior to the American War, as Hanway stated, death and transportation were the most common punishments,[35] but after the abolition of American transportation imprisonment became much more usual. Because its deficiencies were responsible for the decision to found the settlement in Botany Bay, we shall examine it in detail in a later chapter. Here, we need only call attention to the prevalence of placing men and women in irons to prevent their escape. The practice, regarded by Blackstone as illegal, was described by Elizabeth Fry as being used on female prisoners as late as 1823— iron-hooped round their legs and arms and waists.[36] In the chapter on social conditions we have already referred to the findings of the Select Committee of 1792, concerning the misery of men liable to be imprisoned for life at the discretion of creditors in gaols "almost in a state of putrefaction".[37] It was not until 1813 that insolvent debtors were allowed to obtain their discharge from gaol.

The punishment of transportation will be described elsewhere in this book. One form of it, seldom put into operation, was exile or "abjuration of the realm"; but this was never pronounced as a formal sentence, and was sometimes permitted as an alternative to capital punishment. The procedure in determining those to be transported was, as we have seen, capricious. Those capitally convicted, if not hanged, were generally transported for terms of life or fourteen years. Others sentenced to transportation were not necessarily transported; in many instances the deportation depended on their subsequent conduct in overcrowded hulks. As a punishment it was regarded as the next in severity to death, although prisoners at various periods welcomed it as a departure from the frightful conditions of English prisons. At various times in the course of the transportation system the chief complaint against it will be that it did not sufficiently terrify English criminals. The complaint will be particularly noticeable round about the periods of 1817 and 1833. In 1789 at the September sessions of the Old Bailey, it was recorded how "a vast number of prisoners who had on former occasions received sentence of death, but whose executions had been delayed during the late Royal indisposition", were asked whether they would accept the Royal mercy on condition of being transported. Most of those who preferred transportation to death did so "with great hesitation"; eight, however "peremptorily preferred their previo us sentence of death". A rather amusin

situation ensued. "It is shocking," wrote Grenville, "that men can be so lost to every sentiment of gratitude not to feel mercy shewn them in sparing their lives ... though on the terms of transportation." While the King's pardon existed it was doubtful whether they could be executed. Five of the prisoners obligingly solved the problem by allowing themselves to be persuaded into accepting the mercy, but three, one of whom had been guilty of robbery with the violence of a stick carved to resemble a pistol, persisted in refusing the pardon. Correspondence followed with the King, Lord Thurlow and various others, and a temporary respite was granted in order to allow a decision to be made. Grenville suggested that one of the three should be executed as an example which might induce the others to claim their pardon; but, in the end both Grenville and George III were relieved by the prisoners' accepting the mercy and "being ready to make such submission for their obstinacy as may . . . be thought necessary".[38]

In the Old Bailey sessions for 1790 forty-eight men capitally convicted accepted pardon on condition of transportation, but one woman refused. In the summer session of the same year all did the same, except two, "who preferred hanging and were immediately gratified with the object of their choice".[39] However, the procedure of trial, sentence, execution and pardon on condition of being transported continued absolutely unreformed until after 1821, "although it had been long condemned by the opinions of almost all reasonable men".

Opinion adversely critical of the excessive severity and the futility of the penal system had been unanimous throughout the whole period, apart from the legislators and some French philosophers who emphasized the more liberal process of an English criminal trial compared with their own summary procedure. Even when it functioned properly its ineffectiveness in checking crime and reforming criminals was well known. Goldsmith in his *Vicar of Wakefield* expressed doubt as to whether the licentiousness of the people or the stupid severity of the law had been responsible for the fact that English convicts doubled those of Continental countries. The Select Committee of 1785 declared that "the late increase in the number of public executions had had no effect in reducing crime".[40] In 1798 a Parliamentary Committee observed that though a general revision of the Statute law had been recommended by a committee as far back as 1666, Parliament had never undertaken to make this necessary consolidation and revision; hence reform had been "suffered to sleep for a century", and the delay of it had annually augmented its necessity. In 1810 Romilly tried in vain to have the death penalty removed from the offence of stealing from a shop to the value of five shillings and stealing

from a dwelling to the value of forty shillings. When the reform was thrown out in the Lords, Lord Ellenborough expressed the hope "that the laws which a century had proved to be beneficient would not be changed for the illusory opinions of specialists". The struggle for reform continued with scarcely any success until 1826, when Peel expressed his determination to rationalize the law. Even then reforms were slow in coming, but an attempt was made to consolidate the cumbrous system.

"It is impossible," wrote Sir J. F. Stephen, reviewing the whole penal system, "to defend its principal characteristic, its lavish and cruel employment of the punishment of death; but it is right to say that the law was not, and was not intended to be, strictly enforced. This certainly modified its cruelty, but it did so at the expense of making its administration arbitrary and capricious to the last degree."[41] Getting rid of an increasing criminal population by death and transportation had proved eminently satisfactory to English legislators of that time, and the distance of Australia from the homeland was regarded as its chief advantage. But, as Bernard Shaw has remarked in a refreshing introduction to the study on English prisons written by Sidney and Beatrice Webb, "all the social problems of all the countries can be got rid of by extirpating the inhabitants. But to get rid of a problem is not to solve it". "It may be argued", he wrote with particular applicability to the eighteenth century at least, "that if society were to forgo its power of slaying and also its practice of punishment, it would have a strong incentive to find out how to correct the apparently incorrigible."[42]

THE CRIMINAL LAW REFORMERS

THE barbaric penal methods and laws described in the previous chapter prevailed all over Europe at the beginning of the eighteenth century. By the outbreak of the French Revolution, however, the reign of the benevolent despots had inaugurated a series of enlightened reforms in which many of the worst tortures and punishments were abolished and the abuses of the old system were slowly whittled away. If men such as Leopold of Tuscany, Pombal, Struensee and Joseph II were responsible for actually carrying out these reforms, to Voltaire and Beccaria belongs the honour of having created the public opinion which enabled them to do so. The influence of Locke in stimulating the "Age of Reason" in Europe reacted on his native land in the works of Blackstone, Eden, Paley, Bentham and Romilly, after being refined by the scintillating minds of the *philosophes*.

Locke's immediate disciple was Montesquieu, the young scion of the *noblesse de robe*, the audacious irony of whose *Lettres Persanes* (1721) took the *salons* of Paris by storm. Montesquieu was the spiritual parent of the whole school of Encyclopaedists, and also of Beccaria, who, though no Frenchman, was intellectually an outstanding member of the great band of philosophers that France produced in the eighteenth century. There is little actually about criminal law and penal practice in the *Lettres Persanes*, but several ideas that appear later more fully in Beccaria are to be found there in embryo. Montesquieu sees clearly the danger that harsh penalties will defeat their own purpose by inducing brutality in criminals: "Dans un Etat les peines plus ou moins cruelles ne font pas que l'on obéisse plus aux lois. Dans les pays où les châtimens sont modérés, on les craint comme dans ceux où ils sont tyranniques et affreux."[1] In the later *Esprit des Lois* (1748) his thoughts on the maladjustments of the contemporary penal system are expanded further. He demands that penalties should be proportionate to the heinousness of the offence and free from judicial caprice, and reiterates his opinion as to the folly of harsh punishments. The twelfth book of *Esprit des Lois* is the germ of Beccaria's *Dei Delitti e delle pene*.

To the placid rationalism of the later Montesquieu succeeded the pungent manifestos of the Encyclopaedists and the devastating

assaults of Voltaire. Next to *Esprit des Lois*, Helvétius' *De l'Esprit* (1758) seems to have been the principal source of Beccaria's inspiration. Though not paying any special attention to penal problems, the attitude of Helvétius, as of the Encyclopaedists in general, was subversive of the *status quo*. The first great philosopher next to Hume to make utility the keystone of his thought, Helvétius held that laws must always seek the public good and promote the maximum happiness, to which end a suitable system of rewards and penalties was necessary. Diderot, d'Alembert, d'Holbach, Raynal and Morellet were all imbued with the same spirit, but apart from the article on crime in the *Encyclopédie*, they made no special study of penal problems. In general, they agree that utility and legitimacy are the two main desiderata in a penalty, and go to the root of the problem in insisting that prevention is better than punishment.

Voltaire, on the other hand, was the paladin of the *philosophes*, ceaselessly crusading against the inconsistency, the harshness, the uncertainty and the arbitrariness of the laws of France. He strove his utmost to avenge individual injustices and to curb the powers of the obscurantist magistracy, whom he called "barbares en robe". On every side he assailed cruelty and corruption, denouncing the inhumanity of torture, exposing the irrational law of evidence and proofs, thundering against the futility of harsh sentences, and reiterating that prevention is better than cure: Il vaut mieux prévenir les malheurs que de se borner à les punit."[2] Capital punishment he also condemned, preferring hard labour or transportation, which gave criminals a chance to become respectable citizens again: "On remarque la même chose dans les colonies anglaises; ce changement heureux nous étonne; les occasions du vice leur manquent; ils se marient, ils peuplent".[3] While this was true of the system of transportation to America, which prevailed when Voltaire wrote, it was by no means borne out by Australian experience of twenty years later.

Beccaria, the great apostle of criminal law reform, received his first inspiration from the *Lettres Persanes* and was later powerfully influenced in his general philosophical outlook by the writings of the Encyclopaedists. In 1764 he published his great work, *Dei Delitti e delle pene*, a brilliant indictment of the iniquity and irrationality and cruelty of the laws of Italy, and a monument of calm and utilitarian reasoning on the principles which should govern changes in them. After Beccaria, little or nothing remained to be said about criminal law reform that had not already been said in *Dei Delitti*. Nearly all the arguments used by Voltaire, the Encyclopaedists, Blackstone, Eden, Bentham and Romilly on this subject are taken straight from Beccaria, with or without acknowledgments, or are at least amplified and amended versions

of his reasoning. For that reason it seems worth while considering Beccaria's philosophy of punishment rather more closely than would at first sight seem necessary in a history of Australian transportation. The penal settlement in New South Wales was founded twenty-four years after Beccaria wrote, after a valiant effort had been made to inaugurate a more humane penitentiary system at home, and the unhappy experiences of its early years bore out to the full his warnings as to the folly of harsh and uncertain punishments.

The foundation-stone of Beccaria's philosophy[4] and his touchstone for good laws is the utility principle, "la massima felicità divisa nel maggior numero", which he derives straight from Helvétius. Laws must not only conduce to the greatest happiness of the greatest number, but must be certain in execution, invariable in interpretation, and quite independent of the caprice or temper of the judge. Crimes should be measured not by the intention of the criminal, but by the amount of damage sustained by society, hence punishments should be proportioned to social injury. The object of punishment, he insisted, is neither revenge nor compensation, but purely to deter others from committing a like crime. Rigorous penalties, therefore, defeat their own end, for the criminal classes come to think they may as well be hanged for a sheep as for a lamb.

Promptness and certainty of punishment are more important than the nature of the penalty, as a criminal will fear a mild sentence that he knows will be executed at once more than a severe one that may never be executed at all. For this reason clemency and pardons become unnecessary and even dangerous if penalties are humane, and asylums and sanctuaries of all kinds are indefensible. The rule of law must prevail indiscriminately throughout the country, and no social classes can be allowed privileged treatment.

Beccaria classifies three kinds of crimes, acts subversive of society or of its sovereign, acts injurious to the life, property or honour of individuals, and acts contrary to the positive or negative obligations which bind every individual to the public weal. Each type of crime should be appropriately punished, injuries to a man's person by whipping and damage to his honour by disgrace. Theft, on this principle, ought to be punished by a fine, but as it is usually a symptom of extreme indigence, which would only be aggravated by a pecuniary penalty, resort must be had to the compensatory principle, and the criminal set to work for society with hard labour. To imprison an innocent debtor or bankrupt, however, is simply barbarous. For crimes involving a disturbance of the public peace, an efficient police force is the best preventive.

Turning from species of crime to modes of punishment, we come

to that part of Beccaria's work for which he is most widely and most justly famous. In considering capital punishment, he did not hesitate to ask boldly by what right men made a practice of judicially assassinating their fellows. This placed him at one bound well in front of Montesquieu and the Encyclopaedists whom he regarded as his masters. The irreparable nature of a death sentence and its ineffectiveness in preventing crimes committed in hot blood particularly impressed Beccaria.

Ostracism, he thought, would often be more effective than positive sanctions, but should be sparingly used. Indiscriminate and absolute confiscation of property he thought indefensible. Ordinary banishment or exile might legitimately be used in cases of doubt when an atrocious crime had been committed, to give the accused a chance to establish his innocence. Transportation he considered "a distant and therefore almost useless servitude" because the punishment of lesser crimes, which are likely to be committed on the spur of the moment, should be in public in order to drive home the deterrent lesson to the full, the same argument applying to long terms of ordinary imprisonment.[5] In discussing the archaic methods of procedure still current in the courts of law throughout Europe, Beccaria condemned unreservedly *lettres de cachet*, secret accusations and torture.

Summing up, he propounded the thesis that it is better to prevent crimes than to punish them, and therefore the police should be improved, virtue rewarded, the laws made clear and simple, and above all, education encouraged. "In order that every punishment may not be an act of violence committed by one man or by many against a single individual, it ought to be above all things, public, speedy, necessary, the least possible in the given circumstances, proportioned to its crime, dictated by the laws."[6]

The rise of the criminal law reform movement in England was bound up with the growth and spread of the Utilitarian philosophy. At the beginning of the Hanoverian epoch, only a few isolated thinkers, such as Gay and Hutcheson and Hume, had discovered the greatest happiness principle. In the middle of the century, however, the doctrine crossed the Channel and, passing through Helvétius and Beccaria, came back to inspire Paley, Bentham and Priestley, who prepared public opinion for the wholesale adoption of Utilitarianism which ensued in the next hundred years. The influence of Beccaria can be seen in the works of the conservative thinkers, no less than in the radicals. Blackstone, Burke, Paley and Eden were his disciples, no less than Bentham and Romilly. This is what makes *Dei Delitti* one of the world's great books; its publication was a definite step forward in the realm of criminal law, and could not be gone back on.

To the maligned Blackstone fell the honour of being the first Englishman to honour the name of Beccaria. The Vinerian Professor of English Law has been so often derided as a reactionary—Dicey has made "Blackstonian optimism" almost a term of abuse—that we are apt to forget that only a year after the publication of *Dei Delitti* he wrote appreciatively of the Italian author and paid him the compliment of subscribing to several of his suggestions for the reform of the criminal law. It cannot be denied that Blackstone looked at the British Constitution through rose-tinted glasses, but even in the midst of his most eulogistic adulations he was willing to admit that it had some defects: "Though we may glory in the wisdom of the English law, we shall find it more difficult to justify the frequency of capital punishment to be found therein."[7] He also adopted Beccaria's idea that certainty is a more important attribute of punishments than severity, and condemned the application of the same penalty for crimes of differing degrees of guilt. Like Paley, however, he still found it reasonable that severity of punishment should vary according to the difficulty of committing the crime. In the next chapter we shall see how Blackstone attempted to carry his reforming theories into practice in the ill-starred penitentiary scheme.

Thus, if only because he was the first eminent professional lawyer to doubt the wisdom of a universal application of the death penalty, Blackstone deserves to be honoured as a pioneer in criminal law reform, along with the two other judges who were disciples of Beccaria, Lord Kames in Scotland and Lord Mansfield in England. Kames attacked capital punishment by the roundabout method of praising the ancient Egyptians who almost eliminated it, and found himself in agreement with Goldsmith and Johnson as well as with Beccaria.[8] Mansfield is said never to have mentioned Beccaria's name without respect.

The first concrete result of *Dei Delitti* in England seems to have been the committee of inquiry into the state of the criminal laws, set up by the House of Commons, in 1770 on the motion of Sir William Meredith. Two years later the Lower House plucked up courage to rescind the death penalty for the crime of belonging to the "people who call themselves Egyptions" and for desertion from the army, and to make it no longer high treason to attempt the life of a privy councillor. The Upper House, however, took a firm stand against this backsliding, and rejected the measure out of hand, declaring that it was "an innovation and subversion of the law".[9]

Among the other conservative and utilitarian philosophers of England, two deserve special mention, as representing a misinterpretation of Beccaria's doctrines which was to have a disastrous

effect on the progress of criminal law reform. Martin Madan and Archdeacon William Paley were both clerics, and were much more uncompromising in their attitude than Blackstone. Madan, who had already become notorious as a "lawyer turned divine" and an advocate of polygamy, published in 1784 his *Thoughts on Executive Justice, with respect to our Criminal Laws*, which Romilly described as "a strong and vehement censure upon the judges and the ministers for their mode of administering the law, and for the frequency of the pardons which they granted".[10] Taking Beccaria's principle that certainty of punishment is more effectual than severity, he transformed it into a statement that the only "complete and adequate redress" of criminality is a strict application of the full rigours of the law, the rigour being equally important with the strictness of execution, because it produces fear, which is the best preventive of crime. Madan was specially indignant at the practice of magistrates and judges in making frequent use of their power to remit the death penalty, and of juries in refusing to convict where penalties were disproportionately harsh, a phenomenon on which Blackstone and Paley also remarked. The author of *Executive Justice* feared that commutation of the death sentence to a mere term of transportation or imprisonment on the hulks was insufficiently deterrent and only led to an increase of crime. Though it was much read at the time and led to a brief outburst of judicial severity, his book had no intrinsic importance in the history of penal thought. Nevertheless, it provoked Romilly to start on his great career as a criminal law reformer.

Paley was a man of very different calibre from Madan. A more thoroughgoing utilitarian, he brought the theological and conservative aspects of that philosophy to high water mark. With Blackstone he contrasts curiously. The judge eulogized the British Constitution, but ventured to point out some defects in the criminal law. The clergyman, however, deliberately sacrificed his chances of preferment by satirizing the organization of society in the passage which earned him the nickname of "Pigeon Paley",[11] and yet in a chapter of the same book supplied Ellenborough with all the arguments which enabled him to keep the criminal law intact until the third decade of the nineteenth century. More than any other thinker, Paley held back the rising tide of opinion in favour of criminal law reform. Like Madan, he emphasized Beccaria's principle of the efficacy of certainty of punishment, but suppressed the accompanying strictures on the folly of severity, and with Blackstone, he thought crimes should be punished not according to the degree of guilt, "but in proportion to the difficulty and necessity of preventing them".[12] "It was", he thought, "the peculiar merit of the English law that it swept into the net every crime which under any possible

circumstances might merit death, whilst it only singled out a few cases in each class of crime for actual punishment; so that whilst few really suffered death, the dread and danger of it hung over the crimes of many. The law was not cruel, for it was never meant to be indiscriminately executed, but left a large margin for the exercise of mercy."[13]

Transportation fell under the ban of Paleyan disapproval. It was, he thought, a very imperfect deterrent, because it was really only a slight punishment to those with neither property, friends, reputation nor employment at home, and whatever miseries the transportee endured would be too distant to influence the potential criminal in Great Britain. Although he dismissed public torture as likely to excite too much sympathy for the victim, Paley was greatly concerned how to find a worse punishment than death for the graver crimes, and even went so far as to suggest the plan of "casting murderers into a den of wild beasts, where they would perish in a manner dreadful to the imagination, yet concealed from the view".[14] Such was the mentality of the man whose thought dominated the governing classes of Great Britain throughout the first three decades of the Australian experiment.

No survey of any aspect of eighteenth century philosophy in England would be complete without some reference to Edmund Burke, though the Irishman made no special study of the philosophy of punishment. He was, however, a conservative utilitarian and performed the function of Voltaire to Eden's Beccaria, attacking abuses as and when they arose. Imprisonment for debt and the proposed West African transportation scheme were the two principal objects of his reforming fervour. Anything in the nature of a wholesale reform he would have reprobated as severely as Paley himself.

There has been no more neglected man in the history of English penal thought than William Eden, later to be created Lord Auckland for his services in connexion with the famous commercial treaty with France in 1786. Eden's *Principles of Penal Law* (1771) revealed its author as an ardent follower of Beccaria and put him midway between the cautious reformism of Blackstone and the thoroughgoing revision of the law advocated by Bentham. What marked him off from the conservatives was his conclusion that a reform of the criminal code had become "an important and necessary work", though he fully realized the nature of the opposition he was up against, and when in 1772 an under-secretaryship of state was offered him, he allowed himself to be muzzled. In spite of this capitulation to what Bentham later called "Judge & Co.", he pursued his reformist ideals in company with Blackstone in the more limited sphere of prisons and did yeoman work on the penitentiary scheme described in the next chapter.

It is difficult to give the substance of Eden's *Principles* without repeating much of what has already been said in the summary of *Dei Delitti*. In sharp contrast to Paley and Madan he condemned the severity of the English penal code because "the excess of the penalty flatters the imagination with the hope of impunity", and deprecated the continuance on the statute-book of hoary old laws imposing heavy punishments for trivial offences, which had fallen into desuetude, serving only to bring the existing law into contempt. The haphazard accumulation of disparate laws which made up the English criminal code came in for a searching criticism. Eden emphasized especially the folly of punishing similar crimes with diverse penalties, and of using the same penalty for crimes as different as parricide and picking pockets. He reminded the legislators that they must bear indirect responsiblity for every individual punishment, and that they were "mediately" the executioners of every man executed under a penal statute. Capital punishment he considered to be not a punishment, but "a last melancholy resource" to exterminate those whose continued existence was a menace to public safety. "Nothing but the evident result of absolute necessity can authorize the destruction of mankind by the hand of man."[15]

Transportation he condemned on utilitarian grounds as being too often beneficial to the criminal—this was in the days of transportation to America—and as costing the kingdom a subject while in no way acting as a deterrent. As an alternative he suggested that criminals should be kept at hard labour in the dockyards or mines, or even sent to Tunis and Algiers in exchange for the Christian slaves of the corsairs. The latter suggestion shows Eden to be still fundamentally an eighteenth century aristocrat, whose reformist fervour could not always overcome the prejudices of his class. Ordinary imprisonment he disapproved of because "it sinks useful subjects into burthens on the community" and had a most disintegrating effect on their morals. Debtors and unconvicted persons he thought should receive special attention and better accommodation in the gaols. The later developments in Eden's penal philosophy are studied in the next chapter in connexion with the hulks and penitentiary schemes.[16]

The part played by the Evangelicals, especially John Howard and Jonas Hanway, in the movement for the reform of the criminal law in the eighteenth century was mainly in the sphere of prison reform, and is therefore also considered in the next chapter.

The influence of Beccaria is seen again in the work and writings of Sir Samuel Romilly, perhaps the greatest practical criminal law reformer in English history. In his later career, Romilly was

undoubtedly deeply influenced by Bentham, but, as his writings before he met the sage of Queen's Square Place in 1788 showed, he was by no means a slavish imitator of the older man. Indeed, his more intimate knowledge of the world led him to take up a much less intransigent attitude than that which Bentham was able to cultivate in the calm of his study, and this led later to a breach in the friendly relations between the two. Romilly himself frequently acknowledged Beccaria and Blackstone as his masters, and it is therefore strange that Halévy should attribute his belief in the superior efficacy of certainty over severity of punishment to the influence of Bentham, when the emphasis of this very point was one of Beccaria's chief claims to fame.[17]

Romilly's first essay in the field of criminal law reform was written in reply to Madan's *Thoughts on Executive Justice*, whose "folly and inhumanity" had "so much shocked" him that "instead of enforcing the same arguments" as Lord Lansdowne had recommended him to, he "sat down to refute them".[18] The pamphlet which resulted was his *Observations on a late publication intituled Thoughts on Executive Justice*, which was published anonymously in 1785 and seems, like Hume's first book, to have fallen still-born from the press. Three years later, in 1788, Romilly went to France in the Long Vacation, and "was much shocked and disgusted" with what he saw on a visit to the hospital and prison of Bicêtre. On the advice of the younger Mirabeau, whom he had known for four years, he wrote down his impressions of it, which Mirabeau translated into French and published as *Observations d'un Voyageur Anglais sur la Maison de Force appellée Bicêtre*, with some general remarks on criminal law which, as Romilly says, "were very nearly a translation" of the *Observations on a late Publication*. Later Romilly published the *Observations sur Bicêtre* in English, but for some reason let it be understood that it was the work of Mirabeau.[19]

In his reply to Madan Romilly showed himself a worthy disciple of Beccaria.* "Je soutiens que ce code, si toutefois on peut appeler de ce nom un assemblage informe de lois incohérentes, qui montre de la sévérité quand il faudrait de la douceur . . . [lois], qui pour la plupart, loin d'être l'ouvrage de la réflexion, ne sont que le fruit du besoin du moment et du caprice du législateur, je soutiens que ce code est, dans une foule d'occasions, absurdement inhumain."[20] He specially condemned the lack of proportion between punishments and crimes in so many instances, the injustice of expecting the unlettered populace to know what acts were crimes and what were not in a code of which many lawyers even

* As the *Observations on a late publication* only sold a hundred copies, it is now almost unobtainable (there is no copy in the British Museum), and we are forced to quote from Mirabeau's *Observations sur Bicêtre* for the substance of the former pamphlet, of which as has been said, Mirabeau's work is virtually a translation.

were ignorant,* and Madan's theory that certainty of execution was necessary to make the existing law adequate. He agreed that laws, if they were to be respected, must be strictly executed, but suggested that "a far more indispensable requisite to that end is that those laws be wise and just".[21] Like Eden he concluded that an absolute and entire reform of the criminal law was necessary.

Enough has been said of Romilly's early penal thought to show that the foundations of his brilliant later career had already been laid before he met Bentham in 1788. Sir James Mackintosh, his collaborator and successor in the great fight against Eldon, was more concerned with political than penal problems before the turn of the century,† and the repercussions of the French Revolution also attracted the attention of the other great thinkers of the age, such as Godwin and Paine, to the neglect of the problems raised by the continuing high level of crime.

With the advent of Jeremy Bentham, the rather half-hearted air that hangs over all eighteenth century attempts at reform began to disappear. Where Eden had called for a revision of the whole criminal code, but on realizing the strength of the reactionary forces confined his efforts to co-operation with Blackstone in the penitentiary scheme, and where Romilly, with a similar realism, set himself a lifelong task of propaganda and piecemeal reform, Bentham boldly applied the principle of utility to the problems of human conduct and drew up a series of codes for its regulation. Where Eden and Romilly were concerned merely to show how greatly the existing law was inconsistent with the tenets of Beccaria, Bentham went on to erect upon those principles a new science, the science of legislation which, as its author claimed, was universal and could supply laws for Hindustan as easily as for Great Britain.

As early as 1772 Bentham had begun work on the great legal code that was to occupy the rest of his days. The *Fragment on Government* (1776) and the *View of the Hard Labour Bill* (1778) were excerpts from his main work dealing with constitutional and penal law, and published with the specific objects of attacking Blackstone's *Commentaries* and praising the Blackstone-Eden penitentiary plan. By 1780 he had written and printed his *Introduction to the Principles of Morals and Legislation*, which outlines the main tenets of his philosophy, but this was not published until his friends, fearful that he would be accused of plagiarizing Paley, persuaded him to do so in 1789. The full exposition of the penal code was not published until 1802, and then in French by Dumont at Paris in the *Traités de Législation*. An English translation did not come until 1812.

---

* "Même le plus grand criminel n'en est pas moins un homme, et comme tel il a des droits à l'équité." Mirabeau: *Observations sur Bicêtre* (Œuvres, tome III, éd. 1835, p. 251).

† *Vindiciae Gallicae* was published in 1791.

Like Blackstone and Eden, Bentham was roused by the indefatigable labours of Howard to make a special study of prisons, and like them he attempted to put his theories into practice in a specially-designed penitentiary. This was the famous Panopticon, the place of which in Australian history as a rival to the New South Wales settlement is discussed in the last chapter of this book.

In Bentham the utilitarian philosophy reached its highest pitch. Like all the other utilitarians his thought is based on the greatest happiness principle, but where he advanced from the position taken up by Paley was in recognizing that "a science of morality pre-supposes certain principles which belong to the sciences of psychology and sociology".[22] He saw that if the *a priori* method of assessing moral principles was to be abandoned, some concrete method of measuring happiness must be adopted if moral philosophy was not to relapse into a "chaos of empirical doctrines".[22] This was where the pleasure-pain psychology and the celebrated "felicific calculus" came in. All laws must seek the greatest happiness of the greatest number. This happiness could best be attained by remembering that love of pleasure and fear of pain are the dominant motives of human conduct. For this reason the philosophy of punishment stands at the very centre of Bentham's system. He saw quite clearly that it was an evil, a necessary evil no doubt, but no less to be avoided wherever possible. As Halévy says, "from the point of view of utility all punishment is an evil, since it consists in the infliction of a pain, and pain is an evil",[23] and the idea that penalties are a kind of counter-crime is the fundamental principle of Bentham's penal code. "According to the principle of utility, legal penalties are evils inflicted under legal forms on individuals proved guilty of some harmful act which is forbidden by law, and inflicted with a view to preventing the occurrence of similar acts."[24] The evil of the punishment, he thought, should exceed the profit of the offence, or in other words the pain of the penalty should outweigh the pleasure of committing the crime.

Bentham's teachings, even in the limited field of penal thought, are so discursive and insusceptible to compression, that the following summary of them must perforce be restricted to those points which are most germane to our subject. Bentham's penal code* is a great advance on Beccaria's rather vague classification of crimes as treasonable, private or public. He defined a crime as any act detrimental to the whole or any part of the community and proceeded to discover four main categories of such delinquencies; *private*, which affect one or more persons other than the criminal; *semi-public*, which affect a number of unassignable persons other

* The following summary of Bentham's penal code owes much to these three authoritative and indispensable works: Coleman Phillipson's *Three Criminal Law Reformers*, 1923; Leslie Stephen's *English Utilitarians*, 1900; and Elie Halévy's *Growth of Philosophical Radicalism*, 1928.

than the criminal; *reflexive*, which affect the criminal himself; and *public*, which affect the whole community. Then, employing his "dichotomic procedure", Bentham proceeded to subdivide these into crimes against the person, against property, against reputation, crimes of malice, and seven other classes. Further dichotomization led to crimes against the person, for example, being resolved into simple corporal injuries, irreparable corporal injuries, and so on.

Crimes are social diseases and call for remedies, which Bentham carefully classified into preventive, suppressive, satisfactory and penal. Penal remedies, as has been said, he defined as evils deliberately imposed by society on persons who have committed crimes with the object of preventing the commission of similar crimes. Some of the canons of punishment laid down by Bentham had already been enunciated by previous reformers: the certainty and severity of a punishment should vary in inverse proportion; equal punishments should not be given for unequal offences; to punish a small offence with a heavy penalty is like using a three-man beetle to crush a cob-nut; the same punishment for the same crime should not be inflicted on all offenders regardless of their sensibility. The essential qualities of a punishment Bentham considered at great length and under twelve headings, for which he invented descriptions; some of these by themselves are meaningless (e.g. commensurability, characteristicalness), but equability, variability, exemplarity, frugality, remissibility, subserviency to reformation and compensation, and simplicity of description convey the drift of his intention.

Turning to individual punishments, the encyclopaedic mind of Bentham is found again classifying and categorizing everything within reach. Transportation he regarded with especial disfavour as possessing all the defects and none of the advantages of a good utilitarian punishment. Under the American system it was too easy for a convict to buy his freedom from the contractor, and thus leave only the poor in bondage, and too many returned before the expiry of their sentences. Under the Australian system the exemplary and reformatory qualities were absent and it was too difficult for convicts who had served their time to return. "The punishment of transportation, which . . . is designed as a comparatively lenient punishment . . . is, in point of fact, frequently converted into capital punishment. . . . This monstrous aggravation falls almost exclusively upon the least robust and least noxious class of offenders. . . . Justice . . . becomes, under the system in question, a sort of lottery, the pains of which fall into the hands of those that are least deserving of them."[25] Ordinary imprisonment, especially in the noisome gaols of contemporary England, Bentham thoroughly disapproved of, but imprisonment with hard labour, especially if imposed through

the medium of his own plan, the Panopticon, appeared to him to combine all the desirable qualities of a punishment.

Bentham's disciples were legion, but most of them did not come under his influence until after 1800. One early follower who deserves special mention is Patrick Colquhoun, the public-spirited metropolitan police magistrate, whose *Treatise on the Police of the Metropolis* (1795) warmly praised the Panopticon and showed many other signs of Bentham's influence. His great humanitarian work has been discussed in previous chapters.

It is interesting to observe how the phases of the early history of the New South Wales settlement can be paralleled in the history of the attempts to reform the prisons and the criminal law in England. Up to 1784, when the Act authorizing the Privy Council to select a site for a new penal settlement was passed, the Blackstone-Eden penitentiary plan* (first-fruits in England of the labours of Beccaria in the realm of thought and of Howard in the realm of action) held the field as a serious rival to the idea of transportation in the field of reformist philosophy. This philosophy revived for about twenty years after 1790, or corresponding to the history of the settlement up to the 1812 Report, and during that period Bentham's Panopticon became a potential substitute for the settlement if it was found to be too expensive. In 1800 the Government had thought of abandoning the Settlement for that reason. The next phase up to the arrival of Governor Darling, in 1825, corresponds roughly to the criminal law reform campaign of Romilly and Mackintosh; and the final and successful attempt to abolish transportation in New South Wales, 1830-1838, was organized by Bentham's heirs, the Philosophical Radicals led by Molesworth.

---

* America had ceased to co-operate in the transportation system, and the English gaols were overcrowded with criminals, many of them sentenced to transportation. It was important, therefore, that the temporary inability to continue transportation should not make it necessary to abandon that statutory sentence of transportation. Hence, transportable prisoners were frequently confined in Hulks, anchored in the Thames and elsewhere, and were then deemed technically to be in a condition of transportation. Meanwhile, search for a penal station was being made, to which these prisoners could eventually be sent.

THE PRISON REFORMS

(a) John Howard and the State of the Prisons

Two quite distinct kinds of prison existed in England in the middle of the eighteenth century, the common gaol and the bridewell or house of correction. The common gaol was maintained by the sheriffs in the counties and by the municipal authorities in the towns. Originally it was purely a place of detention, where accused persons lay awaiting their trial, and not at all a place of punishment, convicted offenders being either hanged, whipped, pilloried, fined or put in the stocks. The bridewell, on the other hand, originated as part of the system of poor-relief, and its inmates were mostly vagrants and sturdy beggars. Whereas the common gaol was run by the chief gaoler for his own profit, the bridewell was more closely supervised by the justices, though by the eighteenth century this distinction was becoming blurred, and the gaolers of the bridewells, too, waxed fat on the fees of their prisoners.[1]

A system whereby the gaoler made his living out of the prisoners committed to his charge not unnaturally led to grave abuses. When the prison needed structural repair, he found it cheaper to chain the prisoners up or to put them in airless dungeons, than to fill up the holes in the walls.* Food was stinted almost as a matter of course,† sanitary measures were unheard of, and not the slightest effort was made to stop the contamination of young first offenders by seasoned rogues, or the prostitution of female prisoners by everybody from the head gaoler downwards. "The felons in this country", complained the Gentleman's Magazine in July 1767, "lie worse than dogs or swine. . . . The stench and nastiness are so nauseous . . . that no person enters there without the risk of his health and life." Mr and Mrs Webb, to whose indefatigable labours students of this, as of every other branch of social history, will always be indebted, quote a medical eye-witness's experience as one of many samples: "Vagrants and disorderly women of the very lowest and most wretched class of human beings, almost naked, with only a few

---

* In the bridewell at Clare, Suffolk, in 1779, Howard found three female prisoners heavily chained, and two men with chains and logs. No justices had visited the prison, which was ruinous for many years. (John Howard: State of the Prisons, 4th ed., 1792, p. 305). See also the Ely case, quoted by the Webbs in English Prisons under Local Government, p. 3, n. 2.

† Convicted felons had an allowance from the county, meagre in most cases, but enough to keep them from absolute starvation; debtors and persons awaiting trial had to beg, borrow or steal what they could.

filthy rags almost alive and in motion with vermin, their bodies rotting with the bad distemper, and covered with itch, scorbutic and venereal ulcers; and being unable to treat the constable even with a pot of beer to let them escape, are drove in shoals to gaols, particularly to the two Clerkenwells and Tothill Fields; there thirty, and sometimes near forty of these unhappy wretches are crowded or crammed together in one ward where, in the dark, they bruise and beat each other in a most shocking fashion. In the morning . . . the different wards . . . are more like the Black Hole in Calcutta than places of confinement in a Christian country."[2]

The prisons of England, in fact, were sinks of every conceivable iniquity and vice and permeated by all the foulest diseases of an insanitary age; and so far were they from being isolation wards for these ghastly conditions, that every contemporary who investigated the problem lamented that the gaols of the country were even worse hotbeds and nurseries of crime, immorality and noisomeness in general than the rookeries of St Giles-in-the-Fields and St George's-in-the-East. The pleasant custom of giving the judges at the Old Bailey little nosegays of herbs dates from the time when they were needed as deodorants against the vile stench of the occupants of the dock. The fearful ravages of gaol fever are well illustrated by three examples quoted by Howard. At the Black Assize at Oxford in 1577, all who were present died within forty hours, the lord chief baron, the sheriff and about three hundred others. The Taunton Lent Assizes in 1730 were almost as bad, and the Black Sessions at the Old Bailey in October 1750 led to the death of the lord mayor, an alderman, two judges, an under-sheriff, and two or three counsel. This last disaster goaded one of the surviving sheriffs into the unprecedented step of ordering Newgate to be cleansed, and the prisoners to be washed before being brought into court.[3]

Into these unspeakably revolting dens were thrust not only hardened criminals, drunkards and prostitutes, but any person who had the bad luck to be unjustly suspected of a crime or was unable to pay his creditors, and there he would stay until the next gaol delivery, which might be anything up to three years,[*] or until his creditors saw fit to let him be released. Even when he was acquitted or his creditors satisfied, he could not go free until he had paid the gaoler's fees, which resulted in many poor wretches lingering on for weeks in prison, their food allowances withdrawn and subsisting on what scraps of food they could earn by appealing to their fellows' charity or pandering to their lust. It was these two worst abuses of gaolers' fees and debtors that first attracted the attention of the reformers.

* At Hull; Lecky: *History of England in the Eighteenth Century*, 1892 ed., Vol. VII, p. 330.

The prison reform movement began in England as early as the end of the seventeenth century, when a Member of Parliament named Pocklington exposed the iniquitous state of affairs in the Fleet Prison before the House of Commons in 1696. A Select Committee was appointed, but nothing was done except to abolish the ancient privilege of sanctuary at Whitefriars and the Savoy, the House of Lords rejecting, in 1701, a Bill to lessen the overcrowding in the Fleet and King's Bench prisons, on the ground that this would diminish the gaolers' profits.[4] When the Society for the Promotion of Christian Knowledge was founded in 1699, Compton, the zealous Bishop of London, induced the Society to appoint a committee which investigated the condition of Newgate and the Marshalsea and issued a very able report in 1702.[*] No legislative action resulted, although the S.P.C.K. continued to interest itself in the subject, and the early Methodists in the days of the "Holy Club" included prison visitation in their works of mercy.[5][†]

The next step was taken by General Oglethorpe, the founder of Georgia, in 1729, when a committee of the House of Commons under his chairmanship again exposed the horrors of the Fleet and the Marshalsea.[6] Once more, however, the legislators shrank from cleansing the Augean stables. The House of Lords, on the other hand, having appointed a committee in the same year on the condition of imprisoned debtors, went so far as to promote an Act (2 Geo. II, c. 22) which was intended to alleviate some of the worst hardships, but never became operative. In 1740 Bishop Butler, in his Spital Sermon, urged cogently the need for some separation of sheep and goats in the gaols; in 1751 an Act (24 Geo. II, c. 40) forbade the grant of a licence for the sale of spirits in a gaol; and in 1754 the indefatigable Oglethorpe obtained yet another committee, this time on the King's Bench Prison, the report of which showed no whit of abatement in any of the excesses or abuses. Four years later Parliament plucked up the courage to pass an Act (32 Geo. II, c. 28) requiring creditors who put their debtors in prison to allow them fourpence a day for maintenance,[‡] forbidding officers to take prisoners to taverns without their consent, or to charge them for things they had not freely and particularly asked for, and ordering the Justices at Quarter Sessions to draw up rules for the better government of the gaols under their jurisdiction, and a scale of fees to be charged to debtors.

Debtors were perennially before the consideration of Parliament.

---

[*] Printed for the first time in W. H. Dixon's *John Howard and the Prison World*, 1849.

[†] A prayer for the visitation of prisoners was inserted in the Irish Book of Common Prayer at a synod held in Dublin in 1711 (Howard: op. cit. 29).

[‡] Howard, however, found that few debtors ever managed to secure their "Lords' Groats", on account of the tortuous mechanism of the law (op. cit. 5).

As long ago as 1671 an Act (23 Car. II, c. 20) had ineffectively ordained their separation from other criminals, and right through the eighteenth century, especially after 1770, repeated efforts were made to alleviate their lot, which were invariably scotched by the House of Lords, the vigilant guardian of the sacred rights of property.

In spite of this somewhat half-hearted legislation, the state of the gaols and bridewells remained as if it had never been passed. Magistrates were apathetic or ignorant and the general public, never having seen the inside of a prison, did not heed the wails of those who thought they were never going to see the outside of it. Only a few obscure humanitarians* and public-spirited magistrates ever gave a second thought to the living cesspools maintained by Quarter Sessions in every county in England or to the great quags of iniquity known as Newgate, the Fleet and the Marshalsea.

In Ireland conditions were just about as bad as in England. Two Acts of 1763 (3 Geo. III, cc. 5, 28) brought in some of the reforms that had been enacted in England in the previous reign, such as the prohibition of the sale of liquor by gaolers and of the keeping of pigs and cattle in gaols, but, as Howard remarked, though the Irish prison code contained "many articles highly laudable and worthy of imitation . . . the policy of this country in these matters is as defective in point of execution as it is commendable in theory". On the Continent prison reformers, spurred on by the great work of Beccaria, had been more successful, and the crimelessness of the Dutch towns was one of the seven wonders of the Grand Tour. Leopold of Tuscany and his Imperial brother Joseph II vied with each other in their humanitarian reforms. Portugal abolished imprisonment for debt in 1774 and even in backward Russia the criminal code distinguished between different classes of prisoners.[7]

Such were the conditions in the gaols of England when a certain country gentleman of Bedfordshire, a Nonconformist, John Howard by name, was picked sheriff for that county on February 8, 1773. He had already experienced the rigours of imprisonment on the Continent, having been captured by a French privateer and kept prisoner at Brest and Morlaix, when on a voyage to Lisbon in 1756. Like most of his countrymen, however, he had no notion of what went on inside English prisons until a chance pin-hole set him on a road which was to lead him to lasting fame. He was of a simple and somewhat naïve disposition, and took the duties of his shrievalty rather more literally than was the wont of

---

* e.g. Robert Raikes, the founder of Sunday Schools, who made a graphic appeal on behalf of the prisoners in Gloucester Castle in 1768, and carried on a campaign on their behalf in his paper the *Gloucester Journal.*

eighteenth century country gentlemen. Not content with a mere ceremonial parade, he noted how some prisoners, even when acquitted, were dragged back into the county gaol until they paid the gaolers' fees, and applied to the justices for the gaoler to be salaried instead of dependent on his fees. The bench, confronted with so simple a remedy for an abuse that had been going on under their eyes for longer than any of them could remember, could hardly do other than assent, but their instinctive conservatism asserted itself so far as to demand a precedent for charging the county with the expense. The High Sheriff accordingly rode into several neighbouring counties and discovered the same disgraceful conditions wherever he went. This was the beginning of a pilgrimage round the prisons of Europe, which occupied Howard for the rest of his life and took him nearly 50,000 miles over the by no means smooth roads of those days, pursuing his tireless investigations and, in his own words, wiping the tear from many an eye.[8]

The concrete manifestation of this ceaseless peregrination, which continued right up to the weary traveller's death in Russia in 1790, was his monumental *The State of the Prisons in England and Wales*, first published at Warrington in 1777, with its companion volume, *An Account of the Principal Lazarettos in Europe*, which appeared twelve years later. The state of affairs revealed by Howard's enquiries appalled even the tough social conscience of the English aristocracy. He resorted to no rhetoric or hyperbole to embellish his shocking story. He had no need to; the plain, ungarnished facts were more eloquent than the silver tongue of Edmund Burke. Under the heading of "General View of Distress in Prisons" he marshalled his grim array. Bridewells where the prisoners were given no food and not allowed to work, while the magistrates callously said: "Let them work or starve"; debtors starving and uncared-for while highwaymen were fed and attended by a doctor; water allowances limited to three pints a day for all purposes; air so foul that the leaves of his notebook had to be spread two hours in front of a fire before he could use it; dungeon floors under two inches of turbid water; the straw bedding worn to dust; striplings listening eagerly to the tales of hardened rogues; idiots herded in with all the other prisoners. His investigations led him to the conclusion that more people died of gaol fever "than were put to death by all the public executions in the kingdom", which vividly illustrates an expression which has passed into the idiom of the language—"rotting in gaol". He confirmed Sir John Fielding's observations about the gaols being nurseries of crime and said: "Half the robberies committed in and about London are planned in the prisons by that dreadful assemblage

of criminals and the number of idle people who visit them."[9]

Nor was this all. The second section of the *State of the Prisons*, entitled "Bad Customs in Prisons", is equally damning to the system—if so chaotic a collection of archaic survivals can be called a system. The custom of garnish stripped new-comers to the gaols of most of their clothing if they could not pay for drinks all round; gaming of all sorts, from faro to fives, was endemic; prisoners in the more ruinous gaols were loaded with heavy chains; wives and children often accompanied debtors in prison; and many gaols were adjuncts to already fat rent-rolls, that at Windsor going to swell the King's.[10] There follow a number of common-sense suggestions for remedying these abuses.[11]

Meanwhile, ten days after the commencement of Bedfordshire's most memorable shrievalty, Popham, the Member for Taunton, had quite independently introduced a Bill into the House of Commons to authorize the defrayal out of county funds of the gaol fees of prisoners who were acquitted or otherwise discharged.[12] Lack of interest and active hostility led this Bill to the usual doom of first attempts at social reform.[13]* Popham, however, was not daunted, and returned to the attack in the following spring with the support of Samuel Whitbread,† the elder, and an enlarged measure, both to pay the prisoners' fees and to preserve their health. By this time "rumours of the eccentric conduct of the High Sheriff of Bedfordshire had got abroad" and Howard was called as a witness before the House of Commons Committee which was considering the Bill, probably at the instance of Whitbread. His evidence so startled a House unaccustomed to such businesslike exposures of social evils that they not only passed the Bill, after splitting it into two, but thanked him at the Bar of the House for his public-spirited labours.[14] After laying before the Committee a detailed statement of the abuses of the prisons, he went on to propose some strikingly modern suggestions for their reform, including the provision of adequate prison buildings, the conversion of the gaoler from a fee-taker to a salaried public servant, the disciplining of all prisoners by diet, work and religious services and instruction, and a scheme of inspection of the prisons by some outside governmental authority, either central or local.[15]

The two measures thus passed, "An Act for the relief of prisoners who shall be acquitted or discharged" (14 Geo. III, c. 20) and "An Act for preserving the health of prisoners in gaol and preventing the gaol distemper" (14 Geo. III, c. 59), together with

---

* A Bill requiring the appointment of prison chaplains did, however, reach the Statute book this session. Jonas Hanway, some years later, found that it was little complied with (*Distributive Justice and Mercy*, 1781, p. 83).

† The Whitbreads were neighbours of Howard in the village of Cardington, a few miles out of Bedford town.

the Act of the previous session providing for the appointment of
chaplains in gaols (13 Geo. III, c. 58) represented a notable
advance in prison reform.* Not only were discharged prisoners
to be set free in open court and the gaolers to be compensated
by the county treasurer, but the prisons were to be periodically
cleansed, the prisoners to be washed, separate sick-rooms and a
prison doctor to be provided, and a quarterly report made to the
magistrates on the general health of the prisoners. The advance,
however, was mostly on paper, in spite of Howard's generous
action in having copies of the Acts printed at his own expense
and sent to the keeper of every county gaol in England to be hung
up in the prison as Parliament had directed.[16] Sir George Paul,
writing in 1784, found that Clerks of Assize and Clerks of the
Peace were still claiming fees from acquitted or discharged
prisoners.[17]

(b) History of Transportation to 1776

The system which later became known as Transportation
derived from two ideas of primitive justice, the idea of exile or
banishment and the idea that criminals could be called upon to
do any dangerous or difficult task for the common good. The
Greek custom of ostracism, the unhappy fate of Shakespeare's
Romeo, and the exile of Bolingbroke by Richard II in 1398, and
of Clarendon by the Cavalier Parliament in 1679, are good
examples of the idea of simple banishment, which was usually
reserved for political offenders. The second idea is seen at its
worst in the grim fate of the galley-slaves. When Sir Martin
Frobisher sailed on his second attempt to discover the North-
West Passage he took certain "prisoners and condemned men"
with him,[18] and it was not infrequent for condemned felons to be
pardoned on condition of enlistment in the armed forces of the
Crown or of the East India Company. Spain, Portugal, France
and Sweden all made use of malefactors as colonizers, the first
Spanish edict being issued only five years after Columbus's
discovery of the New World.[19]

In England, however, according to Blackstone, "Transportation
is a punishment unknown to the common law. It is only inflicted
by choice of the prisoner himself, to escape a death sentence, or
by express authority of a modern Act of Parliament."[20] The proviso

* In Ireland the Act 3 Geo. III, c. 5, provided for the discharge of acquitted prisoners without
fees, but it was hedged about with so many restrictions that it was disregarded as often as it was
enforced. It was not until an Irish Act of 21 and 22 Geo. III that food allowances were given to
acquitted persons who could not pay their fees, and even then the provision was accidentally
omitted from the gaol code. The preservation of the health of prisoners was provided for by the
Irish Act 17 and 18 Geo. III, c. 28, which Howard found to be generally neglected (Howard:
op. cit., 203, 205).

whereby a person convicted of one of the capital crimes with which English criminal law abounded could be reprieved and transported instead was responsible for a very large proportion of those actually transported, and Jonas Hanway found that death and transportation were the only common punishments imposed by English courts in 1775.[21] William Eden, in his *Principles of Penal Law*[22] traced the origin of transportation back to the ancient custom of sanctuary, which was abolished under James I. Wrongdoers who succeeded in reaching the sanctuary were allowed to abjure the realm and were given a certain time in which to flee the country.

The first of the modern statutes mentioned by Blackstone was a Vagrancy Act passed in 1597 as part of the Elizabethan poor law code. Entitled "An Acte for Punyshment of Rogues, Vagabonds and Sturdy Beggars" (39 Eliz., c. 4); it laid down that "such Rogues as shall be thought fitt not to be delivered shall be banyshed out of this Realme and all the domynions thereof and shall be conveied to such partes beyond the seas as shalbe at any tyme hereafter for that purpose assigned by the Privie Counsell".* There is no evidence of any immediate action being taken by justices in Quarter Sessions under this Act, but from the foundation of Virginia in 1606, irregular batches of "dissolute persons" seem to have been transported there, especially after 1618.[23] Of the 1608 expedition to Virginia, of nine ships with five hundred settlers, one historian remarks that they "were for the most part the very scum of the earth—men sent out to the New World because they were unfit to live in the Old".[24] It was possibly this expedition which incurred the wrath of Bacon in his much-quoted words: "It is a shameful and unblessed thing to take the scum of people, and wicked condemned men, to be the people with whom you plant."[25] The newly-founded East India Company, however, heeded his words no more than the Virginia Company, for we find three Orders in Council of January 1614-15, July 1615, and March 1617-18, directing certain reprieved criminals to be delivered over to the Governor of the Company to be transported to the East Indies.[26]

In 1617 an Order in Council was issued to the effect that:

Whereas it hath pleased his Majestie out of his singular Clemencie and mercy to take into his princely Consideration the wretched estate of divers of his Subjects who by the Lawes of the Realme are adjudged to dye for sondry offences though heynous in themselves, yet not of the highest nature, soe as his Majestie both out of his gracious Clemencye, as also for divers

---

* The rogues were to be branded "R" on the left shoulder, and were guilty of felony within benefit of clergy if they returned without licence.

weighty Considerations Could wishe they might be rather corrected than destroyed, and that in theire punishmentes some of them might live, and yealde a profitable service to the Commonwealth in partes abroad, where it shall bee founde fitt to employ them, for which purpose his Majestie having directed his Commission under the great Seale of England, to vs and the rest of his privy Counsell, gyving full power warrant and Authoritye to us or Sixe or more of vs whereof the Lord Chancellor and Lord Keeper of the Greate Seale to be two, to Reprieve and stay from execution suche persons as now stand Convicted of any Robbery or felony (Willful murther, Rape, witchcraft or Burglary onely excepted) who for strength of bodye or other abilityes shall be thought fitt to be imployed in forreine discoveryes or other Services beyond the seas.[27]

It was probably in pursuance of this order that James I in 1619 directed the Virginian Government to receive "a hundred dissolute persons".[28] Thereafter, there was a steady stream of reprieved felons transported to the American colonies, including enough Scottish soldiers* taken prisoner at the Battle of Worcester in 1651 to enable an American writer to claim that the majority of persons transported to New England were prisoners of war.[29] The total number of persons thus dealt with in the seventeenth century will probably never be known, but it has been estimated that 10,000 servants were exported to Virginia, Maryland and the West Indies from Bristol alone between 1654 and 1679.[30] In Virginia so many convicts infested the colony that there was great fear of an insurrection in 1663, and in 1670 the settlers persuaded the English Government to prohibit the importation of convicts in several of the colonies for a few years.[31] The Monmouth Rebellion resulted in the transportation of many deluded yokels, 841 rebels being sent to the West Indies from the Bloody Assize at a profit, it was rumoured, of £1000 to the Queen.[32]

The Restoration Parliament resorted to transportation as a punishment in five Acts, viz. 13 and 14 Car. II, c. 1 (the Conventicle Act, 1664) which prescribed it for the third offence of a Quaker denying any oath to be lawful or assembling under the pretence of joining in religious worship; 18 Car. II, c. 3, empowering the judges to exile for life the notorious "moss-troopers", or border brigands, of Northumberland and Cumberland to any of the American colonies (this Act expired in 1673); 22 Car. II, c. 5, which gave justices the power to transport certain petty thieves, and was invoked as late as 1763; and 22 and 23 Car. II, c. 7, which gave fire-raisers the choice between transportation and

---

* According to Clarendon, 1500 were granted to the Guinea merchants and sent to work in the gold mines of West Africa (*History*, Book XIII).

death. Transportation was also allowed by the Habeas Corpus Act (31 Car. II, c. 2, sec. 14).[33]

The beginning of the regular transportation system, however, came in 1718 and 1720, when Acts of 4 Geo. I, c. 11 and 6 Geo. I, c. 23 condemned any person convicted of any larceny or felonious stealing to be transported to America at the discretion of the court.* Fifteen other Acts between then and 1765 prescribed transportation as a punishment for offences ranging from perjury and poaching to the second offence of Episcopalian ministers in Scotland not praying for the King and the Royal Family by name.[34] The preamble of the Act of 1718 reveals that the motive of its passing was both the ineffectiveness of the practice of allowing felons to transport themselves to the West Indies and the lack of cheap labour in the American colonies. The actual transporting was farmed out to contractors, who were given a property in the service of the convicts, which they sold to the planters on their arrival in America.† Duncan Campbell, one of the principal contractors, giving evidence before the House of Commons Committee of 1779, said that until about 1772 he had received a Government bounty of £5 per convict,‡ but had since agreed to make all his profit out of disposing of their labour. Many convicts were able to buy off their servitude with their own money, thus converting their punishment into mere banishment. He traded only in Maryland and Virginia and sold common male labourers at £10 apiece, females at £8 or £9 and artificers at from £15 to £25. The old and infirm he gave to those humane people who would take them and sometimes even had to offer a premium to anybody willing to relieve him of them.[35] Several of Defoe's novels, notably *Moll Flanders* and *Colonel Jack*, contain vivid, if rather journalistic, descriptions of the operation of the transportation system on both sides of the Atlantic, including the practice of kidnapping people in the streets and shipping them off to America to be sold as indented servants.[36]

No official records of the numbers transported were kept, even after 1718, and we have to rely on unofficial sources in making any estimate. A footnote in Phillip's *Voyage to Botany Bay*[37] states that the mercantile returns of the old system amounted to £40,000 per annum, about 2000 convicts being sold for £20 each. Most

---

* The 1718 Act had a curious effect, which was commented on by Commissioner Bigge on p. 138 of his first report. Persons transported under it were deemed to be pardoned after they had served their sentences, whereas persons transported under later Acts were liable to the legal disabilities consequent on a conviction for felony, even after completing their sentences.

† The Act 8 Geo. III, c. 15, for the more speedy and effectual transportation of criminals, reinforced these provisions, and extended them to capital offenders who were respited on condition of transportation.

‡ The Government paid the bounty in London and the Home Circuit; elsewhere it came out of county funds (Webb, op. cit., p. 44n).

historians have adopted this estimate without further ado* and have computed the whole number transported at 50,000, a nice round figure, though there is some difference of opinion as to whether it applies to the whole period, or only to the sixty years after 1718. Several other contemporary estimates exist, mostly for the septennium, 1769-1775. Duncan Campbell, in a letter to Under-Secretary Nepean, dated January 29, 1787[38] refers to a calculation he made for the information of the House of Commons "some years since" that in the period 1769-1775 he transported on an average 547 convicts per annum from London and six of the Home Counties, 117 of whom were females,† and adds that he always "looked upon the number from the other parts of the kingdom to be equal to what was transported by me". If the calculation in question was the one he gave to the Select Committee on the Returns of Felons in 1779, it appears in the report of the Committee[39] as 473. Sir George Yonge, speaking in a House of Commons debate in 1776, suggested that 1500 convicts were transported every year from Great Britain;[40] the Select Committee on the working of the Hulks Act, reporting in 1778, said that the yearly average of felons sentenced to transportation in 1769-1776 was 960, of whom 240 were women,[41] and Eden, in his *Draught of a Bill* in 1778 gave the annual average of transportees in the same period as 963 (or 936 if fractions are allowed for), adding that it was less than in former periods, as judges had already seen strong objections to transportation and had discouraged the use of it as far as was compatible with public convenience and safety.[42] If a balance is struck between these varying figures, we get a total of about 1000 convicts per annum being transported to America in the closing years of the system, but this does not justify us in making any assertions about the earlier period. Other estimates range from Barton's maximum of 120,000[43] for the period 1650-1775, obtained by averaging 1000 per annum throughout and allowing for the extra numbers after the rebellions of 1685, 1715 and 1745‡ and those who were allowed to transport themselves, to Jefferson's fantastic figure of

---

* Dr Lang, in his *Transportation and Colonization*, 1837, p. 35, attributed these figures to William Eden.

† They were carried from one to two hundred on each ship, with a two months' voyage, and about one in seven died either in gaol or at sea of gaol-fever or smallpox, the mortality among the females being only half that of the males (D. Campbell's evidence in 1779: *C.J.*, XXXVII, 306). In another place he says that on a voyage to America, a loss of 10 per cent can be reckoned on (*C.J.*, XXXVI, 926). The conditions during this white "middle passage" are further illuminated by Howard's remark that "many of those who survive their long confinement are by it rendered incapable of working, some of them by scorbutic distemper, others by their toes mortified or quite rotted from their feet, many instances of which I have seen," and the letter he quotes from a firm of Bristol contractors to the gaoler at Salisbury, dated September 13, 1774, saying that "sore feet prove fatal. The mortality we met with in our last ship, if repeated in this, will so surfeit us that we shall never take another" (op. cit., p. 20).

‡ For the numbers "barbadosed" after these three rebellions, see *Notes and Queries*, 10 Ser., Vol. VIII (1907), pp. 68, 135, 176, 235, 317; 12 Ser., Vol. LX (1921), pp. 33, 75, Vol. X, p. 361.

2000[44] for the total numbers transported to Virginia, about which the most charitable thought would be that he accidentally omitted a cipher. According to J. D. Butler, at least 10,000 convicts were sent to America from the Old Bailey alone between 1717 and 1775.* Margaret Wilson contents herself with a cautious three to four hundred per annum at the end of the system, and H. E. Barnes estimates that the largest number of convicts sent to any one colony was 20,000 to Maryland.[45]

Such was the thriving trade of transportation when the rising temper of the American colonists led to an open break with the Royal Government in 1775. Not unnaturally, one of their first actions was to refuse any longer to be a dumping-ground for English rogues. Trading was already restricted to the southern colonies; Campbell only exported to Maryland and Virginia, and when he found he could not dispose of any more convicts there, he refused to contract again. In reply to questions, he said that Georgia and the Floridas might take about 100 convicts per annum, hardly a ship-load and not a paying proposition, that none could be disposed of in Canada, and that it was illegal to import felons into the West Indies because of the necessity of preserving the balance of colour.[46]

The Select Committee of 1785 bewailed the loss of the American outlet: "The old system of transportation to America answered every good purpose that could be expected of it; it tended directly to reclaim the convicts and make them good citizens; the climate was good and the means of gaining a livelihood easy, so that country magistrates could safely be entrusted with the power of inflicting it; it applied to the whole country and not only to London; it was cheap, the men being taken out in Jamaica or tobacco ships; the colonies seem to have appreciated the benefits of the practice; the convicts were usually removed to the backwoods, away from the temptations of the cities, and the public order does not seem to have suffered."[47]

(c) The Temporary Solution—Hulks

The year 1759 was designated by eighteenth century Englishmen "Annus mirabilis", on account of the succession of victories won by their armies in all the theatres of the Seven Years' War, but could they have taken the longer view that we are able to take today, it is more probable that they would have fixed on 1776

---

* According to figures quoted by Howard (op. cit., p. 479), in 1749-71 5600 persons were sentenced to transportation at the Old Bailey, including 401 capital respites; 1179 were transported from Newgate in 1773-75, including 112 respites; and in 1750-72 1397, including 523 respites, were sentenced to transportation on the Norfolk Circuit and 1057 were transported on the Midland Circuit.

instead. In that one year, the Declaration of American Independence was signed, three great books were published—Adam
Smith's *Wealth of Nations*, the first volume of Gibbon's *Decline
and Fall*, and Bentham's first work, the famous attack on Blackstone in the *Fragment on Government*—Major Cartwright drew up
the democratic programme which was to become the banner of
the Chartists and Radicals, and a system of keeping convicts in
hulks was begun which lasted deep into the prosperous nineteenth
century, fully eighty-two years, a long time for a temporary
expedient, even in England.

The reason for this new departure is not far to seek. By 1775
at least a thousand convicts were being shipped off to America
each year, so that when the revolt of the colonies stopped this
steady flow, they were diverted to the insanitary and dilapidated
gaols of England. These gaols, to the nauseating and inhuman
conditions prevailing in which we have already had occasion to
refer, were quite incapable of accommodating an extra thousand
prisoners per annum, notwithstanding that they were by no means
full. By the spring of 1776, when many felons who would otherwise
have been on their way to America had already been cast into
them, Howard found only 4084 prisoners in all the prisons of
England and Wales, of whom 2437 were debtors, 653 petty
offenders (i.e. not liable to transportation) and only 994 felons;
and in 1779 as many as 130 prisons contained fewer than ten
prisoners each.[48]

At any rate, within a year of the opening shots of the American
War, the state of affairs compelled the Government to act, and
on April 1, 1776, the Prime Minister, Lord North, rose in the
House of Commons to ask leave to bring in a Bill "to authorise,
for a limited time, the punishment by hard labour, of offenders
who, for certain crimes, are or shall become liable to be transported
to any of His Majesty's colonies and plantations". The opposition,
in the person of Governor Johnstone, took the opportunity to
make a factious attack on the "pusillanimous administration, who
had betrayed the honour and character of this country to every
petty, shabby state in Europe, and reserved all their spirit for the
purpose of oppressing and massacring their fellow-subjects in
America". He "saw no reason why felons might not be sent to
the West India Islands or to the Falkland Islands" except that
the Government "probably in the prevailing rage of ministerial
cringing and subsidising had given up that island, which cost the
nation some millions, by private agreement to Spain".[49]

The Bill was introduced a few days later by Lord North,
supported by Sir Charles Bunbury, William Eden and Edmund
Burke, and in the debate on the Committee stage on May 9 came

under heavy fire from the Opposition.[50] The general opinion seemed to be that this was another of Lord North's clever tricks for aggrandizing the power of the Crown, and infringing the time-honoured liberties of Englishmen. The Rt. Hon. Thomas Townshend, later destined, as Lord Sydney, to make the final decision for the foundation of New South Wales, strongly opposed the King's being given power to mitigate punishments, and Governor Johnstone, Lord Irnham, Sir Philip Jennings Clerk and Mr Popham agreed with him. Sir Joseph Mawbey would rather have seen felons sent to the Floridas or the East or West Indies, and Mr Powis opposed the Bill on the ground that it made no distinction between different degrees of guilt. On behalf of the Government, the Solicitor-General urged that the Bill was only an experiment, an emergency measure for two years, at the end of which it could be amended or repealed if the pacification of America permitted of the resumption of transportation. Eden, then Under-Secretary of State for Home Affairs, said "he had had a hand in bringing in the Bill". He had consulted some of the judges and king's counsel who were unanimously in favour of it. Persons convicted of several species of felony might be punished according to the nature of their crimes; some being sent to garrisons in unhealthy climates and others employed in dredging rivers, or confined in houses of correction and made to work; and the term of punishment might be varied.* Sir Richard Sutton approved of the Bill because "it put a stop to sanguinary punishments which were a disgrace to the Government", and Mr Wenman was for it because he "thought hard labour worse than death for three-quarters of those annually hanged at Tyburn".

The debate on the report stage took place on May 13, when there was much ado about the proposal to vest the power of appointing the overseers of the hulks in the Middlesex Justices who, said Burke, had become a "standing reproach" and were "the most unfit persons on earth" to be trusted with such a power. Sir George Yonge† thought that the clause in question "looked like a designed insult on the Corporation of London" and added that Trinity House did not want any convict labour. Sir William Meredith, speaking for the Bill, said that all the gaols were full, and gaol fever must break out if they were not emptied, and Eden reiterated the experimental nature of the Bill.[51]

The Hulks Bill finally received the Royal Assent on May 23, 1776, as 16 Geo. III, c. 43. In its preamble it recites how "the

---

* This is probably the speech referred to in the *D.N.B.* as "his famous speech in the House of Commons, in which he proposed the substitution of hard labour for the transportation to America."

† Sir George Yonge was Secretary-at-War in the Shelburne and Pitt Ministries. He is not to be confused with Sir George Young, Admiral of the White, and author of a plan for the colonization of New South Wales in 1785.

transportation of convicts to America is found to be attended with various inconveniences, particularly by depriving this kingdom of many subjects whose labour might be useful to the community, and who, by proper care and correction, might be reclaimed from their evil courses"; it goes on to prescribe that able-bodied males who are sentenced to transportation, or reprieved from death on condition of being transported, may be kept at hard labour for the public benefit in raising sand, soil and gravel from, and cleansing, the River Thames, for any term between three and ten years, and females and the more infirm males may be kept at hard labour within the county of their conviction. Overseers were to be appointed by the Justices of Middlesex, a bounty of £2 to £5 was to be given to each convict on his release, and the King might pardon for good conduct.*

Accordingly, on July 12 the much-abused Justices of Middlesex appointed Duncan Campbell, the former contractor for transportation to America, as overseer of the convicts working on the Thames. To house the convicts, Campbell provided the *Justitia*, an old East Indiaman of 260 tons at Woolwich, to hold 120 men, and in August the first batch of eighty-five convicts arrived. In October, the indefatigable Howard, fresh from his Continental perambulations, paid the new-fangled prison a visit and was horrified at what he saw, many of the men being half-naked, the sick untended, the rations mouldy, no bedding, and a most disagreeable smell—this from one who must by this time have been well seasoned to insanitary conditions in prisons. The officers, he added, were evasive and told several palpable lies. He paid a second visit in January 1778, and found conditions much improved. A second hulk, the *Censor*, a French frigate of 800 tons, had been provided in April 1777, and many convicts said "that they were much better used than when he saw them last, which was very evident by their looks". Howard attributed such unhealthiness as there still was to the fact that the ship was only scraped, not washed.[52]

The Act of 1776 was only passed for two years, and early in 1778 the problem again came up for consideration. In his budget speech on March 6, 1778, North, referring to the £7846 which had been voted for the maintenance of the hulks, "took notice of the experiment he had made of criminal labour on the Thames, which had answered beyond all expectation, and hinted at a farther extension of the plan over the whole kingdom".[53] On March 23, he returned to the subject with a motion for leave to bring in a Bill to continue the existing system. Burke led the

---

* There appears to have been an Irish Act of 17 and 18 Geo. III, which was never put into operation (Howard, op. cit., 205).

attack by prognosticating the time "when we should put prisoners and felons to death on the principle of economy" and suggested that they should be transported to Canada, Nova Scotia and the Floridas. Sir W. Meredith disapproved of the hulks as being much severer than transportation and "totally repugnant to the general frame of our laws", and Sir Charles Bunbury, taking the same view, also advocated transportation to America. Townshend and Sir Richard Sutton agreed that the Act had not had the slightest effect on the number of robberies. Mr Gascoyne had visited the hulks and thought the punishment far from severe, the men not doing as much work in a day as might be done for hire for nine-pence. They were too well fed and "thousands" of people visited them and gave them money. Some, who escaped, at once returned to their predatory habits. The worst of their punishment was a want of room and air, which made them liable to illness and distemper. Mr Whitworth had also been on board the *Justitia* and was told by the overseer that the prisoners were very sickly except where the pitch and tar acted as a preventive. On the motion of Sir R. Sutton, a select committee was appointed to enquire into the working of the Act.[54]

The committee appointed Sir Charles Bunbury as its chairman and examined seven witnesses before reporting on April 15.[55] Duncan Campbell, much of whose evidence has already been quoted, was called first, and gave particulars of the rations,* sleeping accommodation, and type of work provided for the men. From August 1776 to March 1778, 632 convicts had been received on the two vessels, of whom 176 had died, twenty-four escaped and sixty had been pardoned. At first they had refused to work, but now he found they preferred to do so, and were less trouble to keep at work than to keep clean. He himself derived no advantage from the men's labour.† There was a staff of forty guards, but on the whole the convicts' behaviour was good, and he found that the prospect of being pardoned had an excellent effect on them. What sickness there was had been brought on board from the gaols. There were six or eight boys who were too small to work on shore, one totally blind man and one one-legged man on board. Steward Erskine, Campbell's principal deputy since September 1776, confirmed his chief's evidence. Howard followed with an account of his two visits in October 1776 and January 1778, and Dr Solander, F.R.S., the friend and fellow-traveller of Sir Joseph Banks, related how he had visited the hulks

---

* Bentham, in his *View of the Hard Labour Bill*, says that Campbell devoted some of his ground to growing vegetables for the convicts (*Works*, IV, 10n.).

† Later, the Clerk of the Works to the Board of Ordnance gave evidence that they had been working under his orders since January 1777.

three times in 1777, and found that all possible care was taken of the convicts, and that many of them worked but little. Two army doctors, the Surgeon-General to the Artillery and his assistant, told the committee how they had attended the convicts since October 1776, and were quite satisfied that they were being properly cared for, and that it was impossible for the convicts to have more air than they had.

Summing up, the committee found that there had been a progressive improvement in the condition of the hulks, which were "now convenient, airy and healthy" and recommended that the system should be continued. There were contracts for only 380 felons per annum, whereas an average of 720 were liable to be sentenced to hard labour on the hulks each year. The upshot of this report was the introduction on May 5, by Sir Charles Bunbury, of a Bill to continue the 1776 Act until June 1, 1779, which received the Royal Assent on May 28 as 18 Geo. III, c. 62.[56]

About this time the second draft of the Penitentiary Bill* was published, and in the explanatory memorandum attached to it, Eden made several references to the rival hulks scheme. It was, he said, a temporary measure, for dangerous males only, and was supported in both Houses of Parliament by "many most respectable characters who have not usually been unanimous in measures of a public nature", the opposition being founded chiefly on the fear that the plan constituted a threat to English traditions of freedom. The overseers, he continued, had "exerted the utmost humanity and attention in the discharge of a very unpleasant duty", and there was no motive to any undue severity in the treatment of the prisoners, as all the expenses lay on the public. It was not the cheapest method, but was thought the best in a new departure of this kind. Although 35,000 tons of sand and gravel had already been raised, it was not to be expected that any system of forced labour would ever become self-supporting. It had to be admitted, too, that hard labour on the hulks was too severe for any but the most atrocious offenders, and the more deserving felons were soon pardoned. The last report from the overseer had revealed only six sick out of 360.[57]

The next move was made on December 16, 1778, when the House of Commons ordered returns of felons and others who were imprisoned in the Home Counties to be laid before it.[58] After these returns had been made, Bunbury complained in the House on February 5, 1779, that the Hulks Act was a failure as many of the gaols were crowded with prisoners who had been sentenced to the hulks, but for whom there was no room on board. He moved for a Select Committee to consider various alternatives, such as the

* Dealt with fully in the next section of this chapter.

revival of the "old salutary law of transportation" or the enlisting of convicts and soldiers with the East India Company, and to enquire into the management of the hulks. Mr Luttrell and Sir George Yonge supported the motion, saying that they never liked the Act, even as a temporary expedient. It was like all North's plausible plans and had failed like the rest.[59]

The Select Committee was duly appointed with Bunbury again in the chair, and reported on April 1, 1779.[60] The enquiry dealt with three different aspects of the problem of disposing of convicts, the hulk system actually in operation, the proposed new penitentiary system, and the possibility of a resumption of transportation. Seventeen witnesses were examined. Richard Akerman, the Keeper of Newgate, was the first to be called, and deposed that many convicts who had been sentenced to the hulks remained in gaol because there was no room for them on board. If the young and robust convicts had not been removed to the hulks, he would not have been able to keep them in order; as it was, they often stole from strangers who came to see them. Duncan Campbell and Steward Erskine gave an account of the state of the hulks establishment. By the terms of the contract, 240 tons of shipping had to be provided to 130 men; 260 were on the *Justitia* and 250 on the *Censor*, of whom eight were boys under fifteen, eight more under sixteen, eleven more under seventeen, twenty more under eighteen, and two men over sixty. Thirty-one men were infirm and unfit for labour, including several deprived of the use of a limb. Since March 23, 1778, 132 convicts had died of disease (ninety of nervous, putrid fevers which they brought from the gaols), six had met an accidental death, and twenty-nine had been discharged. Altogether, a hundred convicts had been pardoned since 1776, of whom only six were known to have gone back to their criminal ways. Thirty or forty offenders under eighteen had recently been recommended for pardon. The men had been behaving very well for some time,* probably because they entertained a hope of being transported as a consequence of the present enquiry. Two of the three doctors who were paid by Campbell to attend the men also gave evidence.†️ Surgeon Dodo Ecken of the Royal Artillery said the hulks were much airier and roomier than last year, and were kept remarkably clean, but would be far healthier if there were fewer men on board.

* On June 7, 1778, the *Gentleman's Magazine* (Vol. XLVIII, p. 284) records that thirty-six of the convicts on the hulks "rose on their keepers, when a terrible engagement took place", in which a score of them escaped, and were only recaptured after committing several fresh robberies. On September 29 of the same year another affray is reported (ibid., p. 494) in which 150 convicts attacked the commander and tried to escape, but were routed with the loss of two ringleaders killed and seven wounded.

† Bentham (op. cit., p. 28) said that a surgeon of a battalion attended the convicts daily, and the surgeon-general of the artillery once a week. Spiritually, they were ministered to by a clergyman provided by the Countess of Huntingdon, who distributed Bibles among them and "endeavoured to direct their attention to the sacred writings, by giving them rewards for performing little exercises proposed to them as tests of their proficiency".

He advised the provision of a hospital ship or a quarantine hut on shore for convicts arriving from gaols with putrid fever, and told the committee how eight or ten men had died simply of "lowness of spirits". Dr William Smith thought there had been a great improvement since the system began, and opined that with some alterations in diet, and a little more space, the men would be very healthy. Sir Herbert Mackworth, M.P., described his impressions after paying a visit to Woolwich. The food was good and the work "of real public service", but the lame and decrepit convicts were "very improper objects and hurtful to the establishment". The committee observed in its report that whereas the Act of 1776 was a temporary measure, intended only for "the most dangerous and daring offenders", it had uwisely been extended to less suitable persons. The execution of the Act, however, had been continually improved since its inception and the labour done appeared "to be of solid advantage to the public", and its value was as much as one-third of the annual expense of the establishment. The committee made several recommendations, including a shortening of the term of imprisonment from seven years to a period of from one to five years, to be inflicted only by judges of gaol delivery;* a separate hospital and quarantine ship; the appointment of a magistrate as Inspector of the Hulks; and the extension of the system to other rivers and ports. They remarked on the general neglect of the clause directing justices to prepare their houses of correction for the reception of offenders, and went on to recommend the erection of two penitentiary houses.

As a consequence of this report, Bunbury and Eden were given leave on May 21 to bring in a Bill to continue 16 Geo. III, c. 43 until July 1, 1779, which received the Royal Assent on May 31 as 19 Geo. III, c. 54; and their Penitentiary Act (19 Geo. III, c. 74) which received the Royal Assent a month later, continued the system, with various minor amendments, until June 1, 1784.[61]†

Howard visited the hulks again on November 16, 1779, and found things much improved as a result of the parliamentary enquiries. A quarantine ship, the *Reception*, had been provided, where the convicts were examined by a surgeon on arrival and isolated for three days. The *Justitia* had been converted into a hospital ship and had twenty patients on board, and there were 526 convicts in the establishment, of whom 150 were at work in the warren. He paid two further visits, on December 27, 1782, when there were 204 convicts, and on October 19, 1783, when there were 194.

---

* It was the magistrates at Quarter Sessions who had sent the unsuitable offenders to the hulks.

† The philanthropist, Jonas Hanway, in a series of letters written about this time to Sir Charles Bunbury, complained of the failure of the hulk system. His specifics were solitary imprisonmen separation of the more from the less enormous offenders, and regular inspection.[62]

In 1782, the *Censor* and *Reception* were laid up, and twenty-four convicts were in the hospital ship; 116 convicts were employed in removing ballast and planking on shore and thirty-six were heaving ballast in the lighters.* In 1783, only twenty-two were in hospital, and few had died during the year, but Howard bewailed the association of so many criminals as "utterly destructive to morals". On the *Censor*, in addition, there were 137 convicts "for our settlements", many of whom were sickly.[63]

The next move in Parliament did not occur until 1784, when the Act of 1779 was due to expire, and a change of front is observable in the Government spokesmen in that, whereas in 1776 a sentence to the hulks was in lieu of transportation, in 1784 it was regarded as part of the sentence of transportation, a change due to the growing conviction that transportation in some form or other would have to be resumed. On March 1, leave was given to the Law Officers of the Crown to bring in a Bill to provide places for the temporary reception of convicts reprieved from death or sentenced to transportation; on the following day the Bill was ordered to be extended to include sick prisoners.[64] A debate took place on the report stage of the measure,[65] when Capt. John Luttrell opposed the Bill in principle on the grounds that moving persons from the gaols would only spread the gaol fever and that an *ex post facto* procedure such as "subjecting persons to hard labour who were sentenced to transportation was a severity that nothing could justify". Fox agreed with him that it was dangerous to alter sentences already imposed, though he was loath to see convicts idle. Even the capital respites had been offered a choice between death and transportation and had chosen the latter, and were therefore entitled to expect their choice to be respected. Pepper Arden, the Solicitor-General, replying for the Government, said that the Bill had been brought in at the suggestion of the judges, who reported that the gaols would soon be full to over-crowding, because it was still quite impossible to carry out the sentence of transportation. Duncan Campbell had contracted to carry 260 felons to America, though it was well understood that his contract could not be executed and was made solely to clear the gaols, as there were still 200 persons sentenced to transportation in Newgate alone. Legally, convicts on the hulks were supposed to be on their way to America, and he thought it only proper that as they cost the nation half a crown a week they should work for their living. In any case it was more merciful to let them work than to keep them idle, as none had died on the hulk where work was done, and sixty out of two or three hundred had died on the hulk where they were idle. In answer to criticisms, he agreed to delete

---

* Howard gives a diet table in full.

the word "hard" from hard labour. The Act eventually received the Royal Assent on March 24, as 24 Geo. III, c. 12,* but only for a year's duration. Its preamble referred to the "want of convenient and sufficient room" in many of the gaols, and the text prescribed the removal of prospective transportees to hulks, where they were to be allowed half their earnings, but not forced to work; their time on the hulks was to count as part of their transportation sentence; any court might order offenders to be transported to any place they thought proper, and might agree with contractors therefor. Later in the year, the Act 24 Geo. III, c. 56, which marked the resumption of the transportation system, repealed 24 Geo. III, c. 12, but continued the hulks as the first stage of transportation.

Early in 1785 rumours got about of the Government's plan for sending convicts to Africa and Burke and Lord Beauchamp raised the matter in the House of Commons on March 16 and April 11 respectively.[66] Burke drew attention to "the melancholy situation under which those unfortunate people laboured who were sentenced to transportation", of whom he alleged there were at least 100,000,† and complained of the lack of distinction between heinous and trivial crimes. He called for a reform in the prisons. Alderman Newnham said that convicts released from the hulks had been renewing their depredations on the public, and would be much better removed to the utmost distance. Lord Beauchamp called for a committee to investigate the working of 24 Geo. III, c. 56, which was duly appointed‡ and, having elected his lordship to the chair, took evidence from thirteen witnesses, and issued two reports on May 9 and July 28.[67]

The principal evidence relating to hulks was given by Evan Nepean, Under-Secretary of State for Home Affairs, in whose honour the Nepean River was subsequently named. He said that the Government had hired the *Censor* hulk from Duncan Campbell for 250 convicts, some of whom had originally been sentenced to America, and had provided H.M.S. *Dunkirk* at Plymouth for convicts from western gaols, of whom a hundred were at present on board, including fifty who had returned from transportation, and ten capital respites. Recently the *Ceres*, an old East Indiaman, had been hired by Campbell to hold 250 men, there being now 150

---

* There were two sessions in the regnal year 24 Geo. III. This Act was in the first session; 24 Geo. III, c. 56 was in the second.

† This is a typical piece of Burkian hyperbole, but has been taken seriously by many historians Actually, in 1782 Howard found only 4439 prisoners in all the gaols, bridewells and hulks in England and Wales, of whom 2197, or nearly half, were debtors. By 1787-88 the numbers had increased to 7482, of whom 2011 were debtors and 1412 petty offenders not liable to transportation. In Ireland there were 1574 prisoners in 1787-88, of whom 550 were debtors (Howard: *State of the Prisons*, 4th ed., 492; *Account of Lazarettos etc.*, 2nd ed., 242, 245).

‡ Burke, Eden, Fox, Hussey, Luttrell and Sheridan were among the members.

on board who were destined for Africa. The convicts on the hulks were of five classes: (1) those sentenced originally to America; (2) those reprieved on condition of transportation to America; (3) those sentenced to transportation at large; (4) those sentenced to transportation to Africa; and (5) those reprieved on condition of transportation to Africa. The Chairman of the Lancashire Quarter Sessions said that the gaols in his county were very full, but the justices had not considered themselves entitled to provide places of temporary reception without an order under the Sign Manual.*

In the second report, Lord Sydney told the committee that the hulks, however necessary as a temporary expedient, had materially contributed to the spreading of the contagion of criminality, and felons, on being released therefrom, almost invariably resumed their nefarious activities.

On March 7, 1786, when the choice of the destination of the convicts to be transported was still undecided, a Member of Parliament named Bastard called for information about the persons incarcerated in the hulks and the cost of their maintenance. The Government spokesman replied that the order could not be complied with as the books had been burnt in 1780.† Two or three returns, however, are recorded in the *Journals* of the House, and an estimate of £31,300 for the cost of the hulks establishment at Plymouth, Portsmouth and Woolwich for one year was presented on May 18.⁶⁸

On June 11, 1788, more than a year after the sailing of the First Fleet, the Act 28 Geo. III, c. 24, received the Royal Assent, which laid down that offenders conveyed to temporary places of confinement under 24 Geo. III, c. 56 should be treated as if they had been sentenced to hard labour under 19 Geo. III, c. 74. This signified that the hulks system, the "purely temporary expedient" of 1776, had become a permanent and integral part of the English penal system. Starting as a safety-valve to relieve the abnormal congestion in the prisons which followed the outbreak of the American War, and as the experimental beginning of a home penitentiary system, they gradually came to be regarded as the first stage of a sentence of transportation, and when that system actually became operative again, it was found that they still could not be dispensed with.

---

* During the course of the session, an Act was passed extending the provisions of 24 Geo. III, c. 56 to "that part of Great Britain called Scotland". It received the Royal Assent on July 24 as 25 Geo. III c. 46.

† According to Colquhoun, 2024 convicts were put on board the Thames hulks from July 1776 to January 1788 [*Police of the Metropolis*, 2nd ed. (1796), 328; in the 6th ed. (1800), 1788 is misprinted as 1778].

(d) *The Attempt at a Permanent Solution—Penitentiaries*

We must now turn to two further aspects of the prison reform movement, which at first sight may appear to be only remotely connected with the history of Australia, but which in fact led to a determined attempt to dispense with the punishment of transportation altogether. If it had succeeded, Australian history would certainly not have begun in 1788, and in all probability the first colonizers of the country would have been the French. The first section of this chapter described the atrocious state of the English prisons in the eighteenth century, and the third section showed how an emergency led to the establishment of floating prisons whose inmates were put to hard labour. The two strands of the prison reform movement now to be examined are the attempt to remedy the structural defects of the prisons, as distinct from the bad customs prevailing inside them, and the development of the idea that prisoners should be set to work instead of sitting around in idleness all day, drinking, gambling and indulging in lecherous practices.

In medieval times fortresses were used as prisons, but from 1340 onwards statutes were passed from time to time empowering or ordering the sheriffs or justices to build or repair gaols.[69] On the last year of the seventeenth century the Act 11 and 12 William III, c. 19, authorized justices to repair or rebuild at the cost of the county any gaols presented by the grand jury as "insufficient or inconvenient", and the Act 10 Anne, c. 14, eleven years later, empowered the magistrates to levy a rate for the repair and building of county gaols. Neither Act was effective, and an attempt to reinforce them in 1723 failed to reach the statute-book.[70] Such new gaols as did get built were constructed by the authority of special Acts,* and the only remedy that legislators could think of to stop prisoners escaping was to make aiding and abetting such an act a capital offence,† though some gaolers, as we have already seen, adopted the more practical measure of chaining their captives. No other steps towards the building and repair of gaols were taken until the arrival of Howard, Eden and Blackstone upon the scene, except the injunction of Parliament to the City Corporation in 1767 to rebuild Newgate, which was so slowly obeyed that although the first stone was laid in 1770 it was still unfinished when the Gordon rioters burnt the old prison to the ground in 1780.

The idea of hard labour came originally from the Poor Law. The first bridewell was set up in London in the reign of Mary Tudor, and an Act of 1576 resulted in the setting up all over England of

---

* e.g. Kent (*C.J.*, XXII, 16 and 24.ii.1736) and Devon (*C.J.*, XXVI, 23.ii and 5.iii.1753).
† By 16 Geo. II, c. 5 (1743).

houses of correction, where vagrants and sturdy beggars might be
set to work. An Act of 1608 (7 Jac. I, c. 4) directed that no expense
should fall on the county on account of their upkeep, but sixty
years later, 19 Car. II, c. 4 empowered justices to levy not more than
sixpence a week on each parish to provide a stock of materials on
which to set poor prisoners to work, the profits being devoted to
their relief, a provision repeated in 1739 by 12 Geo. II, c. 29.
An attempt was made, in a Vagrancy Act of 1744 (17 Geo. II,
c. 5) to make the justices inspect the houses of correction, but
otherwise their fabrics were equally neglected with those of the
gaols throughout most of the eighteenth century.*

The unceasing flow of pamphlets from the pen of Jonas Hanway
included several on the topic of prison reform, in which he advocated
his sovereign specifics of more religion and solitary confinement
coupled with hard labour, and at least once is found avowing that
religion and the gallows† are the only real remedies for crime.[71]
This was in 1775, when the event occurred on the other side of the
Atlantic which had so many far-reaching consequences, among
them that of taking the question of prison reform out of the hands
of isolated humanitarians and placing it in the forefront of practical
politics. A group of practical reformers, of whom Mr Justice Blackstone and William Eden were the leading spirits, were ready with
a plan, of which the essence was the substitution of imprisonment
with hard labour for transportation, in itself by no means a revolutionary proposal, for the principle had long been known in the
houses of correction and bridewells. As usual in English political
practice, however, the new scheme could not be launched straight
away, and resort had to be had to the temporary expedient of the
hulks until public opinion could be educated up to it. Sir George
Yonge, in 1779, referred to the hulks scheme as one of Lord North's
plausible plans, but from Eden's *Draught of the Hard Labour Bill*
of 1778, and from his speeches in Parliament, it would appear
that it was really part of the programme of the Blackstone-Eden
group.[72]

Accordingly, the Hulks Bill was brought in in April 1776, and
on May 23, the day on which it received the Royal Assent, North,
Eden and Burke introduced the first draft of the ill-fated Penitentiary Bill.[73] In the debate on the committee stage of the Hulks
Bill, Townshend referred to a Bill concerning houses of correction,
which, he understood, was to be brought in, printed, and sent into

* An attempt to substitute hard labour at the docks for death as the penalty for certain felonies
was defeated in the House of Lords in 1752 (Farrer: *Crimes and Punishments*, 51-2). The second
report of the Committee on the Poor Laws in 1776 recommended the amendment and stricter
enforcement of the Act of 1744, and that houses of correction should be separated from poorhouses
and properly regulated (*P.P.*, 1731-1800, Reps., Vol. IV, No. 32).

† The chief drawback to the gallows was, for Hanway, that there were too many criminals for
them all to be hanged.

the country, and suggested the same fate for the Bill under discussion. The Hulks Bill itself, it will be remembered, embodied the principle of hard labour, although it went no further than to suggest that females, infirm persons, and those for whom there was no room on the hulks should be "kept at hard labour within the county of their conviction". Justices were enjoined "to prepare their houses of correction for the reception of such offenders, and to give directions for their government and keeping them to hard labour". On the committee stage of the Bill, Sir George Yonge complained that this provision would involve a huge expense for the erection of houses of correction and the payment of managers, but he seems to have confused the limited provisions of the Hulks Bill with the extensive scheme of the Penitentiary Bill; nobody else seems to have paid any attention to this part of the Bill.[74]

Colquhoun, writing almost as a contemporary, curiously confuses the legislation of this period. Rightly attributing the provisions just mentioned to 16 Geo. III, c. 43, he then says that the hulks were instituted by a different Act of the same session (not specified), and "an enormous expence has been incurred in building Penitentiary Houses in various Counties, and many philanthropic individuals have exerted their best endeavours to carry this Act (i.e. 16 Geo. III, c. 43) into execution".[75] The plain facts are that the Act embodied both the hulks scheme and the plan for putting felons to work in the county houses of correction, and so far from enormous expenses being incurred, the chief complaint was that this part of the Act was completely ignored.*

In a pamphlet published in 1776† Jonas Hanway, "the benevolent Hanway", as Colquhoun called him, stated that the hulks would have to be much improved before they would effectively reform criminals, and that if they failed to do so, bigger prisons would become necessary. The biographer of that worthy magistrate, Sir John Fielding, quotes a letter written by him to Eden, in which he said he had "perused with attention his able and elaborate Bill to establish a system of penal labour", but suggested that the last Lighter (i.e. Hulks) Bill should be modified and tried for two more years before any great change is made. The date given is March 14, 1776, but the reference to the Hulks Act shows that to be an error; 1778 or 1779 is probably the correct date.[76]

In 1777 Howard came forward with his own suggestions for

---

* e.g. Howard, giving evidence before the Hulks Committee in 1778, said that the provisions of 16 Geo. III, c. 43 with respect to houses of correction had not been carried out, and few, if any, were fit to contain convicts. Felons were kept in the gaols because the hulks and bridewells were full up, but the term of their sentence did not begin until they were transferred thither, which might not be for three or four years.

† *Solitude in Imprisonment, with proper profitable labour and a spare diet, the most humane and effectual means of bringing malefactors who have forfeited their lives, or are subject to Transportation, to a right sens of their condition; with proposals for salutary prevention.* London, 1776

prison reform. He adhered to the traditional division into gaols and bridewells, and sketched out a plan for a gaol in which men should be separated from women, young offenders from hardened criminals, and debtors from common felons, with meticulous attention paid to sanitation and orderliness. In the bridewells adequate work-rooms and plenty of work should be provided, the motto being "Not one should be idle that is not sick". All his ideas are surprisingly modern and not a few of his suggestions are canons of present-day penal practice. In the 1792 edition of the *State of the Prisons*, he approved the proposed penitentiary houses.[77]

In 1778, Eden and Blackstone returned to the attack, having held their hand in 1777 in order to give the Hulks Act a full trial. It was now due to expire, and their Penitentiary Scheme had been before the public for two years, so another Bill was drafted, with some modifications on the 1776 Bill, and an explanatory memorandum, by Eden, was attached.[78] In consequence of the interest now aroused, the Hulks Act was renewed only for one year. One of the objects of Howard's Continental tour which began in April 1778, immediately after he had been a witness before the Hulks Committee, was to collect information on the *Rasphuizen* and *Spinhuizen*, the model prisons of Holland, to help Blackstone and Eden in their task.

The preamble of the 1778 draft of the Hard Labour Bill was the same as that of the 1776 draft, and recited how transportation had been found "insufficient both for the reformation of offenders and the example of others" and proposed to erect "houses of hard labour" to confine those persons who had hitherto been transported, with the object not only of deterrence but of reformation. The "work of long and continued labour and enquiry" and the revision of the Bill "by many very able hands" had reduced the ambitious scheme of 1776, for "a house of hard labour" in every place with a court of criminal jurisdiction, to two such houses in each of nineteen groups of English and Welsh counties, a change explained by Eden as due to the expense of the earlier scheme and the superfluity of prisons containing unequal numbers of convicts, which it would have entailed. The latter part of the Bill was designed to extend and perpetuate the hulks system, an indication that its temporary and experimental stage was already at an end, and the courts were to be empowered to order hard labour instead of transportation. It also set out to provide a new régime of health for the convicts, to enable them to be employed on different navigable rivers, to prevent very distant removals, to shorten the terms of imprisonment, and to restrict the power of sentence to judges of gaol delivery. Eden defined its main aims as solitary confinement, sobriety, instruction and well-regulated labour, the

profits from which would in some measure repay the community for its broken peace.

Attached to the 1778 Bill were nine pages of *Observations* by Eden, its chief promoter. This, together with the Bill, was privately circulated by the promoters and is usually referred to as Eden's *Draught of a Bill*. Among the advantages which would accrue from the enactment of the measure he cited the additional security of the public from the shutting-up of dangerous persons, the reformation of the criminal by reflecting on his sad fate while in solitary confinement, the deterrence of would-be law-breakers by force of example, the proportioning of the punishment to the crime, lack of which was tending to increase capital offenders because the poor thought they might as well be hanged for a sheep as for a lamb,* and a mitigation of the many statutes creating felonies without benefit of clergy which the waning terror of exile had induced Parliament to pass. It was to be hoped that the new scheme might supplant many bloody and inefficient laws, the strict execution of which would "exhibit a scene, rather of massacre and carnage than of justice and due restraint".

Among those into whose hands a copy of the Bill fell was Jeremy Bentham, then a young barrister of Lincoln's Inn in his thirtieth year. Although engaged on his *Rationale of Punishment†* at the time, Bentham was unaware of what had been done in 1776, and was agreeably surprised to find that many of his own ideas, particularly solitary confinement combined with hard labour, had been incorporated by Eden in the new Bill. He at once wrote a pamphlet entitled *A View of the Hard Labour Bill*, in general support of it, with various observations and suggestions for amendment, the preface being dated March 28, 1778.[79]‡ He spoke of his debt to Howard's great book and of his pleasure in seeing the new scheme sponsored from such exalted quarters;§ Eden he specially commended for his lucid preface. He also stated that "the plan is not yet looked upon as absolutely completed". The pamphlet proceeded to examine the Bill in great detail, descending even to the relative merits of shaving off one eyebrow or daubing the cheeks with a solution of gold in *aqua regia* as a method of marking the convicts. ‖ Bentham specially commended hard labour as against transportation because it admitted of a better discrimination between the different

---

* This is another colloquialism that comes down to us from the vernacular of a less humane age.

† Not published until 1811.

‡ Bentham sent a copy of his pamphlet to the two promoters of the Bill, and related in the Historical Preface to the second edition of the *Fragment on Government* (*Works*, i, 255) that he received a cold reply from Eden and a frigidly cautious letter from Blackstone.

§ The judges on circuit had been advertising it and discussing it with the county benches.

‖ He also suggested that a device in the form of a bas-relief of a wolf, a fox and a monkey (representing rapine, knavery and mischief) yoked together to a heavy cart and being whipped by the driver, should be fixed over the entrance doorway (*Works*, iv, 32).

degrees of guilt; and in general showed a modernity of thought far in advance of an age which still allowed the penalties of disembowelling men and burning women to remain on the statute-book.

The plan having been well ventilated, the final campaign for its enactment began in December 1778 with the motion calling for returns of felons in the prisons in the Home Counties. These were presented on February 5 and led to the appointment of the second Select Committee under the chairmanship of Sir Charles Bunbury. There was no reference to the Hard Labour Houses in the debate which preceded the setting up of the committee.[80] While the committee was sitting, its chairman, together with Sir Herbert Mackworth, sponsored a Bill for the better regulation of prisons and houses of correction in England and Wales,* but it never passed third reading.[81]

The Committee on the Returns of Felons issued its report on April 1.[82] Howard, in his evidence, related how he had found few convicts in the West of England with any work to do, and a discussion ensued as to how they might most profitably be employed, the manufacture of canvas bags, hop-bags, coarse cloth, and hempen rope for the navy, and stone-sawing, all finding advocates. In the course of the report the committee observed that there were unjustifiable variations in the prisoners' allowances in different prisons; that the sentences were "often longer than can be useful either for reformation or example"; that the work done was usually unprofitable to the public; and that the whole prison system was "ill-suited either to the economy of the state or to the morality of the people". They remarked on the neglect of the sections of the Hulks Act which ordered justices to prepare their houses of correction for the reception of surplus offenders and, considering that "solitary confinement, corporal punishment duly limited and privately inflicted, sobriety, well-regulated labour and instruction" were the best remedy, recommended the experimental erection of two penitentiaries, one for each sex, in the Home Circuit on the plan of the Hard Labour Bill of 1778. In these the punishment should be adjusted to the crime and the convicts properly classified and set to work of public utility. Justices should be given wider powers to improve the bridewells, institute lazarettos, and pardon boys on condition of enlistment and men who had definite jobs to go to.

Accordingly, a third draft of the Hard Labour Bill, whittled down now to two penitentiaries only, was brought in on April 19 by Eden, Bunbury and the Law Officers,[83] and received the Royal Assent as 19 Geo. III, c. 74, with a duration of five years.† As it finally

---

* On March 4, 1779.

† Blackstone inserted an account of it in the 9th, 10th and 11th editions of the *Commentaries*.

reached the statute-book, the Blackstone-Eden Penitentiary Scheme provided for the appointment of three supervisors, who were to build two "substantial edifices", one for 600 males, the other for 300 females, to which limited numbers of persons sentenced to transportation at the various sessions might be sent to be confined separately and kept, if hale, "to labour of the hardest and most servile kind", or if not, to less laborious work, the profits of which, it was hoped, would defray the salaries of the governors and warders.*

The three original Penitentiary Supervisors were Howard, who, though personally reluctant, yielded to Blackstone's request to take the office, his friend Dr John Fothergill, and George Whately. They reported to the Lord Chancellor and the other persons appointed by the Act as to suitable sites, but their suggestions were rejected. There followed disputes between the supervisors over fresh sites, and when Fothergill died in December 1780, Howard resigned shortly afterwards and set out on another Continental tour.† On March 2, 1781, three new supervisors, Sir Charles Bunbury, Sir Gilbert Elliot and Dr Thomas Bowdler were appointed, who proceeded to fix on Wandsworth Field for the male and Battersea Rise for the female house. The Lord Chancellor and his colleagues, however, approved the eighty-two acre Battersea site for both houses, a small canal to be cut from the Thames by the convicts for water supply. A public competition for the plans of the two penitentiaries was held, and out of sixty-three entries, the supervisors, in March 1782, awarded first place for the male house to William Blackburn and first place for the female house to Thomas Hardwick. These plans were officially approved on June 18, and five days later the Treasury issued the supervisors £1000 on account. In September a special jury assessed the land at £6600, but the Treasury now refused to pay the amount, on the ground that "new measures were about to be taken with respect to felons which made the hastening the penitentiary houses less necessary". Further applications produced only the evasive reply that the Act contained no section authorizing the Treasury to issue the money. The next setback occurred in February 1783, when the supervisors laid estimates of £149,982 for the erection of the male house, and

---

* In this connexion, another of Jonas Hanway's works is relevant. Beginning in March 1779, he wrote a series of thirty-three letters to Sir Charles Bunbury, which were published serially in the *Public Advertiser*, and later, in 1781, in book form as *Distributive Justice and Mercy: shewing that a temporary real solitary imprisonment of convicts, supported by religious instruction and well-regulated labour, is essential to their well-being and the safety, honour and reputation of the people.* He mentioned a series of conferences he had had with Bunbury and Sir Charles Whitworth, and called for a proper prison for convicts in the Home Counties, complaining that the third draft of the Bill had been "mangled and distorted from its first comely form". In a later pamphlet he criticized the Act on the ground of expense, but approved it in general.[84]

† On his return he began, in January 1782, his third general inspection of gaols in the British Isles in the course of which he gave evidence before a committee of the Irish House of Commons which was enquiring into the state of the Irish gaols.

£60,370 for the female house, before the Lord Chancellor, who considered that it could not be the intention of the Act to delegate to him the power of incurring so large a public expense. Lower estimates of £30,165 and £14,900 were accordingly prepared.[85]

By this time the Penitentiary Act was nearly due to expire, and on December 19, 1783, Bunbury obtained leave to bring in a Bill to amend and continue it. This Bill was not proceeded with, and on March 9, 1784, Bunbury secured the appointment of a select committee of enquiry, with himself in the chair,*which reported on March 22;[86] the report stated that on the revised estimates, the whole work would occupy five years at an annual cost of £40,000. Beginning in May 1784, it was hoped that in the spring of 1785 100 convicts could be housed in sheds, who would help with the construction, and that by September of that year progress would be sufficient to allow 200 convicts to be accommodated. The congestion in the gaols, however, was growing so great as to bring about the resumption of transportation within three years of this report, and although the Act 24 Geo. III, c. 56, which was the first step towards this goal, extended the Penitentiary Act for three years, the buildings were never erected, as the Government had lost interest in them.

The committee of 1779, it will be remembered, had also recommended wider powers for justices to improve the houses of correction, a sphere of their duties which they consistently neglected; thereby they helped in no small measure to bring about the resumption of transportation. The Act of 1779 which followed it provided that the existing local prisons should be deemed penitentiaries *pro tempore*, which led to hundreds more convicts being sentenced to rot in those already crowded and ruinous structures.† The situation grew so serious that, pending a decision on when and where to resume transportation, a course of action that was rapidly becoming inevitable, Parliament passed three more Acts to enable (not, unfortunately, to compel) the justices to build and repair gaols and houses of correction.‡ Little more notice was taken of these enactments than of previous ones, although the justices in many counties, led by that great reformer Sir George Onesiphorus Paul

---

* Eden, Hussey, Luttrell, Wilkes, Gen. Burgoyne and the Law Officers were among the other members of the committee.

† The Chairman of the Lancashire Quarter Sessions told the Committee of 1785 that owing to the uncertainty of the punishment of transportation, they had been sentencing felons to imprisonment, which had led to a great increase in the number of prisoners, for whom there was no proper accommodation and no facilities for labour. The Keeper of Newgate told the same Committee that he would soon have 600 prisoners in his custody, double the normal of 1780. Convicts under sentence of death could not be kept in separate cells, as there were only twenty-two such cells (*C.J.* xl, 954). The second report of the Committee referred to "the extraordinary fullness of the gaols", which rendered any separation of offenders impracticable and led to a promiscuous spreading of the "contagion of criminality". Later it recommended the resumption of transportation if only to relieve the pressure on the gaols and added that "the future public benefit is closely connected with the problem of the relief of the gaols" (*C.J.*, xl, 1161).

‡ 22 Geo. III, c. 64 (1782); 24 Geo. III, cc. 54 and 55 (1784).

of Gloucestershire and by the Duke of Richmond, the eccentric Lord Lieutenant of Sussex, secured special Acts for the building of local prisons. As early as 1775 a new prison was begun at Horsham, in Sussex, and after Paul had secured the Gloucester Act in 1785, largely based on the principles of Howard, Eden and Blackstone, the movement gathered ground so much that by 1789 Howard was able to record as many as forty-two new prisons under construction in the country.[87]* By that time, however, it was too late and the infant colony on "the Eastern coast of New South Wales" had already celebrated its first birthday.

* Two years later the first general Prisons Act, 31 Geo. III, c. 46, ineffective because it was permissive and not compulsory, brought to an end this chapter of English prison history.

PART II

THE BEGINNING OF TRANSPORTATION TO AUSTRALIA

THE RESUMPTION OF TRANSPORTATION

WHEN the outbreak of the American War of Independence, which now stands out as the real beginning of Australian history, brought the traffic in convicts across the Atlantic to a standstill, several lines of thought combined to prevent any immediate proposals for its resumption. There were first the humanitarians, both evangelicals such as Howard and Hanway, and the more rationalistic school of Eden, Blackstone and Bentham, who believed in the possibility of reforming criminals in the prisons at home. Second, we find a considerable body of evidence that transportation was not thought a severe enough punishment; and third there was a paradoxical fear of a declining population at a time when the nation was beginning to multiply itself at a phenomenal rate.

The first trend has already been fully dealt with in the sections describing the hulks and penitentiary experiments. Examples of the second line of argument occur fairly frequently in the literature and official documents of the period. In 1773, for example, we find the Lord Justice Clerk of Scotland complaining to the Home Office that "in this part of the kingdom transportation to America begins to lose every characteristic of punishment".[1] Jonas Hanway, in 1775, related that some criminals "actually wish for transportation as favourable to their fortunes",[2]* and Eden in his *Draught of a Bill* in 1778 referred to inadequate laws "which leave punishment uncertain and a bare probability of temporary removal to a continent peopled with the same race and a progressive society". It is an argument which it is interesting to find expressed so early, because allegations of a similar kind bulked large in the reasons which led to the appointment of Bigge as Commissioner of Enquiry in 1818.

Depopulationism was a widespread delusion in the eighteenth century. "It came to be believed, with a fervency that bordered on the fanatical, that a nation's strength depended entirely on the number of its inhabitants,"[3] in much the same way as the bullionists linked national welfare with gold and silver and the new industrialists thought factories and blast-furnaces the only possible gauges. In 1735 we find Bishop Berkeley suggesting that felons might more

---

* In 1776 he said it "seems to be even an encouragement to evil doers": cf. *Solitude in Imprisonment*, p. 6. Cf. also the *History of New Holland* in 1787, which says of the First Fleet that "there have not been wanting voluntary candidates for banishment to that remote shore" (2nd ed., Preface, p. xvii).

usefully be employed in public works at home than in being transported to America,[4] and in 1766, Callender, plagiarizing the Frenchman, De Brosses, set forth the pure milk of the depopulationist doctrine in doubting if any British citizens but criminals could be spared for colonization.[5]* After the rioting among the Glasgow weavers in 1773, when they threatened to emigrate to America in a body, the Lord Justice Clerk, in the correspondence quoted above, wrote "I pray God for the sake of this country that such ideas of migration to America may not become epidemical amongst the most useful of our people." The preamble of the Hulks Act of 1776, probably drafted by Eden, referred to the inconvenience of "depriving this kingdom of many subjects whose labour might be useful to the community, and who, by proper care and correction might be reclaimed from their evil courses", and Hanway talked in 1776 of "the drain of men in the prime of life by transportation". In 1780 he wrote: "Indiscriminate banishment is extremely absurd; we lose a fellow-subject who with proper treatment would have been profitable and useful to the community at home."[6] Arguments of this sort were a powerful influence in favour of the penitentiary experiment, but the plethora of felons in the gaols eventually overbore them, even before depopulationism received its *coup de grâce* from Malthus in 1798. The revelation of the 1801 Census, that the population was increasing rapidly, set up a clamour about overpopulation that has not died out even today. Matra, and the other authors of plans for colonizing New South Wales, however, were at some pains to combat depopulationist arguments, and might have quoted Adam Smith in their favour, the founder of economic science having pronounced that there was not "the least ground for any such opinion or conjecture".

Sir John Fielding, writing to Lord Suffolk in 1773, complained of the leniency shown towards felons sentenced to transportation, who were often released, or allowed to return before the expiry of their term to resume their life of crime. He considered transportation the most effective form of punishment because it rid the country of criminals and gave them a chance to start life afresh, thus fulfilling the ends of punishment, example, humanity and reformation, but if those who returned prematurely were not punished it detracted from these merits. He proposed that retransportation for life or fourteen years should be the penalty for the first offence of returning from transportation, and death for the second offence.[7]

It should not be thought, however, that there was any lack of vague proposals for transportation to other parts of the globe after

---

* In his collection of South Pacific voyages, published in 1770, Dalrymple made a similar reference to colonies drawing off the life-blood of the mother-country.

the outbreak of war. The East Indies, the West Indies, the Falklands and the remainder of British North America were all mentioned in parliamentary debates as possible repositories for convicts.[8] Eden suggested that some might be sent to garrisons in unhealthy climates,[9] Burke was in favour of Canada, Nova Scotia, or the Floridas,* and Bunbury also favoured a place in British North America.[10] Duncan Campbell, however, gave a quietus to these ideas, by telling the committee of 1778 that the Floridas could not take up even one load of convicts and that the importation of white felons was illegal in the West Indies.[11]

The North Government did not heed any of these proposals, and persisted in its hulks experiment, fervently hoping that a speedy end of the American Rebellion would enable them to resume the time-honoured system. But by February 1779, when the hulks had been in existence for two and a half years and the war for nearly four, and the gaols were still so crowded as to occasion "such scenes of cruel neglect and misery as were shocking to humanity and repugnant to sound policy", it was evident that some less happy-go-lucky policy would have to be adopted. On the 5th of that month, Sir Charles Bunbury moved in the House of Commons for a select committee to consider whether the East India Company could take any convicts as soldiers or whether the "old salutary law" of transportation could not be revived, the convicts being sent to the West Indies or part of the African coast.[12] It was before this committee, which reported on April 1, [13] that Sir Joseph Banks gave the evidence which has brought him the title of Father of Australia, and which is, indeed, the first recorded mention of Australia as a possible penal settlement. Asked where would be the most suitable spot for a penal colony in a distant part of the globe, whence escape would be hard, and where the convicts, from the fertility of the soil, might maintain themselves, after the first year, with little or no aid from the mother-country, Sir Joseph suggested Botany Bay in New Holland, which was remote, fertile† and inhabited by few and inoffensive natives. A colony there would certainly need a full year's supply of provisions, and afterwards, with reasonable industry, it might undoubtedly maintain itself without any aid from England. He recommended that at least two or three hundred felons should be sent. If they formed a civil government, they would necessarily increase and need many

---

* The Floridas, acquired at the Peace of Paris in 1763, were not restored to Spain until the Peace of Versailles in 1783.

† Cf., however, Banks's earlier account of the country. "In the whole length of the coast [i.e. New South Wales] which we sailed along, there was a very unusual sameness to be observed in the face of the country. Barren it may justly be called, and in a very high degree, so far at least as we saw. . . . A soil so barren, and at the same time entirely devoid of the help derived from cultivation, could not be supposed to yield much to the support of man." (*Journal of Cook's First Voyage*, 1768-71, ed. Sir J. D. Hooker, London 1896, pp. 297-8.)

European commodities, and England would certainly benefit thereby. Thus, it can be seen that the first penal colony envisaged on the Australian Continent was to be an autonomous settlement on the lines afterwards proposed in West Africa.

The Committee then turned to other parts of the world. Duncan Campbell told them again that the American colonies which remained faithful to the Crown would not serve as convict-markets. Georgia and Florida might, he thought, take a hundred felons a year, but Canada would not have any, and in any case the cost of transport would be too great. The Rt. Hon. Sir John Irwin, M.P., said that if they slept in hulks and were segregated from the troops and kept from escaping to Spain, convicts could be used at Gibraltar to repair the fortifications. The African project, however, was clearly regarded by everybody as the most practicable. Transportation to Africa was no new thing. Between 1755 and 1776, 746 convicts had been sent to man the garrison at Cape Coast Castle, probably as a condition of being respited from death, and of these 334 had died, 271 had either deserted or been discharged, and of many of the others there was no account. The climate made the mortality so great, that the African Committee had in 1774-76 only sent out seven officers and manned their garrisons with natives and mulattoes. The new scheme was sponsored by John Roberts, an ex-Governor of Cape Coast Castle and supported by various other persons who had lived in the country. The site of the colony was to be Yanimarew, 400 miles up the River Gambia, though some witnesses, with their own axes to grind, suggested Podore,* seventy miles up the River Senegal. 150 men and sixty women were to be sent out at a cost of £3000, and £6000 for two years' maintenance, after which it was hoped they would be self-supporting. It was contemplated that not more than one-tenth to one-sixth would die of fever. Summing up, the committee said:

> It is not in the power of the Government now to dispose of convicts in North America, and every other plan of transportation hitherto suggested appears to be fraught with difficulties. Sending atrocious criminals to unhealthy places where their labour may be used, and their lives hazarded in the place of better citizens, may in some cases be advisable, and in the case of capital respites is indisputably just.

> The plan of establishing a colony or colonies of young convicts in some distant part of the globe, and in new-discovered countries, where the climate is healthy and the means of support attainable, is equally agreeable to the dictates of humanity and sound policy, and might prove in the result advantageous both to navigation and commerce.

* This fort had had to be abandoned on account of native turbulence.

It might be of public utility if the laws which now direct and authorise the transportation of certain convicts to His Majesty's colonies and plantations in North America were made to authorise transportation to any other part of the globe that may be found expedient.

No action was taken at this time to form another penal colony, either free or disciplined. Instead, the hulks were continued, and an endeavour was made to give a practical demonstration of the penitentiary scheme. The Penitentiary Act, however, did authorize the courts to order persons liable to transportation to America to be sent either there or elsewhere. It seems, too, that commutation of capital sentences to service in the fever-ridden garrison of Cape Coast Castle had not wholly ceased.* One witness before the 1785 Committee, Mr Sturt, M.P., related how he had visited Africa in 1782 with three men-o'-war and the *Mackerel* transport with 350 convicts enlisted as soldiers for Cape Coast Castle, of whom a score or more died at sea, many deserted to the Dutch and manned their forts, some stole a Portuguese vessel and escaped, and nearly all the rest either died or decamped. Evan Nepean, however, told the committee that the African Company had refused to take any more convicts into their forts and settlement.

By 1783 it was evident that the hulks were only making matters worse, acting as reservoirs and hotbeds of criminals, and the penitentiaries were not likely to be erected till the Greek kalends.† Accordingly, the war having limped to its ignominious close, the new Coalition Government tried to carry out the promises of 1776 and resume transportation to America. A London merchant, named George Moore, was found who undertook to carry thither on the *Swift* transport, 150 convicts "whose original sentence had been to America at large". On August 12, a warrant was issued to Duncan Campbell, ordering him to deliver up the bodies of fifty-six convicts to be "effectually transported to North America", and on August 24, Lord North wrote to him asking him to take 200 convicts on board the hulks pending their transportation to the same destination.‡ Some prisoners were taken straight from Newgate on August 14. From the first the venture was disastrous. The men mutinied and ran the vessel ashore near Rye in Sussex, many

* Cf. Colquhoun, who refers to the many persons who have, from motives of humanity, obtained "free pardons for convicts, or pardons on condition of going into the Army or Navy" (*Police of the Metropolis*, ed. 1800, 450). Also two letters from Earl Temple to W. W. Grenville in *Dropmore Papers*, I, 182, 184 (January 1783), referring to thirty or forty military deserters sentenced to serve in garrisons in Africa and the East Indies.

† It was in the autumn of 1783 that the Treasury refused to purchase land for the penitentiaries on the pretext that other steps were pending.

‡ Note, however, the Solicitor General's statement on March 11, 1784, that though Campbell had contracted to carry 260 felons to America, "it was well understood that his contract could not be executed and was made solely to clear the gaols". (*P. H.*, xxiv, 755.)

escaping,* the rest eventually being disposed of in the United States. Next year Moore tried again, but was refused admittance to American ports, being chevied down the coast to Honduras, where the convicts got into quarrels with the log-wood cutters. In 1784 he received the sum of £1512 17s. 6d. for his pains.[14] This seems to have been the end of transportation from Great Britain to North America, though, as will be described later, the Irish Government tried to resurrect the practice in 1789.[15]†

About the time that George Moore was sending off his ill-fated vessel, James Mario Matra, who had sailed with Cook and Banks when New South Wales was discovered and was later to become British Consul-General at Tangier,‡ came forward with the first definite scheme for the colonization of New Holland. On August 23, 1783, he addressed his "Proposal for Establishing a Settlement in New South Wales" to the Fox-North Coalition, hoping that it might "in time atone for the loss of our American colonies".[16] The project, however, had nothing whatever to do with convicts. Once again the American War of Independence intrudes itself into the beginnings of Australian history. Even in 1782, England, and London in particular, was swarming with American Loyalists, driven from their homes, and subsisting mostly on public and private charity. Many, of course, had crossed the border into Canada, but the others were a constant anxiety to the British Government, who cast round for a plan to rid them of this hungry, homeless, and most embarrassing host of patriots. In July 1783, Matra wrote to his old shipmate Banks, "I have heard a rumour of two plans for a settlement in the South Seas; one of them for New South Wales to be immediately under your direction, and in which Sir George Young, Lord Sandwich, Lord Mulgrave, Mr Colman and several others are concerned. . . . I have frequently revolved such plans in my mind, and would prefer embarking in such to anything that I am likely to get in this hemisphere."[17] Matra seems to have become the voice of a kind of casual committee, consisting of Banks and the others mentioned in his letter, and the proposal may not be entirely his own work.[18]

---

* Five of these were subsequently engaged in a fierce fight with the police in Saffron Hill, London, three being captured. At the Old Bailey on September 19, twenty-nine of the convicts were sentenced to death for being at large after being sentenced to transportation; six were hanged at Tyburn three days later, the rest being sentenced to retransportation for life, except one for seven years. (*Gentleman's Magazine*, 1783, pp. 800-02.)

† Nepean told the 1785 Committee that he knew of no plan to send convicts to British North America, and that the Nova Scotians, not surprisingly, were "strongly against it". Grenville, in December 1789, explicitly stated that "No convicts have been transported from this country to any of the British colonies in America since the last peace, and all the colonies have uniformly expressed a decided resolution not to receive them." George Moore later became British Consul at Salonika, and in 1787 made over to William Richards, Jun., his rights in the fifty-one convicts whom he had transported and who had escaped, but were then supposed to be on their way to Botany Bay. (*C.J.*, xl, 954; *Dropmore Papers*, I, 548; *C.O.*, 201/2.)

His eventful career is sketched by Nepean in the "Chatham Papers", 163.

In the plan, Matra contemplated colonization both by American Loyalists and by native-born Englishmen, the author considering it better that the latter should emigrate under the Flag than to the United States, and pooh-poohing the fears of the depopulationists. The chief advantages held out were commercial and Matra had an eye on the trade with China, Japan and the Spice Islands.* New South Wales would also make an excellent naval station from which we might "very powerfully annoy" either Holland or Spain if we were at war with them. The Government was advised to send out an expedition of two vessels, with two companies of marines and about twenty artificers, who would take on supplies of livestock at the Cape and prepare the settlement for the arrival of the Loyalists. One vessel would then return home and the other go off and collect "a few families" and enough mistresses for the marines and artificers from Tahiti and New Caledonia or even from China. The whole expense was not to exceed £3000. Banks was constantly cited throughout the document and was obviously closely connected with its formulation.

The plan was quite well received, and Matra, to use his own word, was "pestered" with letters on it, largely from persons seeking jobs. The Coalition Government does not seem to have taken it up, but early in 1784 Lord Sydney gave him an interview and having inherited a legacy of overflowing gaols from his predecessor, at once "observed that New South Wales would be a very proper region for the reception of criminals condemned to transportation". On this encouragement Matra amended his plan to allow for criminals to be given a few acres of ground in absolute property as soon as they arrived in the colony, very sensibly realizing that this would be a more effective way of reforming them than any system of forced labour.[19] Sydney turned the plan over to the Admiralty, but Lord Howe, at that time First Lord, rather threw cold water on it.[20]

In 1784 the Penitentiary Act was due to expire, so on March 1, a temporary Bill was brought in "to authorise the removal of prisoners in certain cases and to amend the laws respecting the transportation of offenders", pending the result of an investigation into the progress, or lack of progress, of the penitentiary houses.[21] The preamble of the Bill recited the customary excuses about the difficulties which prevented transportation and were unlikely to be obviated of some time, and also the fullness of the gaols. The usual remedy of the hulks was thereupon prescribed, time spent on which was to count as part of the sentence of transportation. The Bill, which eventually received the Royal Assent on March 24 as 24 Geo.

---

* Cf. a rumour in the *Dublin Chronicle* of May 31, 1791, that the Government were "about to establish a spice plantation on the N.W. side of New South Wales". (*H.R.N.S.W.*, ii, 781.)

E

III, c. 12, then went on to empower the courts to agree with contractors for the transportation of offenders, and to order them to be sent to any place they might think proper. This was an optional power which, as might be expected, caused great confusion whenever it was exercised. In the debate on the report stage, a Member of Parliament named Hussey said he was convinced that transportation was the only solution of the problem, and advised the Government to give every man a woman and establish them on some island such as New Zealand. The Government spokesman pleaded that "no place had yet been found" to which convicts could be sent.[22]

Later in the year was passed the Act which authorized the fateful Order in Council, fixing upon "the eastern coast of New South Wales" as the site of the new penal settlement. Government had now made up its mind that transportation must start again, the only question which remained was to fix on a site. The Act 24 Geo. III, c. 56, "an Act for the effectual transportation of felons and other offenders", re-established the ancient system of transportation and remained its legal basis for thirty-one years.* By it, the King in Council was authorized to appoint to what place overseas "as well out of His Majesty's dominions as within the same" felons should be transported; the contractors were to have property in the service of the offenders, as in the old American system; and the ridiculous provision of 24 Geo. III, c. 12 (which was now repealed), that the courts might order transportation to any place they thought proper, was repeated. The contingency that the Privy Council and the judges might have different ideas on the proper destination of the convicts does not seem to have been thought of.

Towards the end of the year Admiral Sir George Young, who had been named by Matra as one of the persons interested in the project for colonizing New South Wales, put his own ideas down on paper.† He then approached Lord Mansfield, who turned him over to the Attorney-General, Pepper Arden, who had already interested himself in the Matra Plan.[23] Arden seemed quite impressed with the scheme and wrote to Sydney on 13 January 1785, commending it to him and enclosing a copy.[24] Actually Young's plan differed very little from Matra's after its amendment to allow for convict colonization. The commercial advantages of a settlement so near the centres of Far Eastern trade were underlined and the utility of a naval station so near South America remarked upon. The New Zealand flax, it seemed, could be grown abundantly all over the country, as well as cotton, indigo, coffee, tobacco, sugar, tea, silk and madder, and metals of every kind were sure

---

* It was repealed by 55 Geo. III, c. 156, in 1815.

† Young's plan was published in London as a pamphlet of four foolscap pages on April 21, 1785.

to be found there. This Canaan, however, was not to be opened to the working citizens of the mother-country.* Far from it; to appease the fears of the depopulationists, only felons, American Loyalists and settlers "to be collected from the Friendly Islands and China" were to inhabit this fertile earthly paradise. Two economies would be achieved. The Government would be relieved of the expense of maintaining the Loyalists in England, and the heavy cost of the upkeep of the convicts in the hulks would be considerably diminished, and the risks of their returning to their ways of crime entirely removed. The cost of establishing the settlement would not be more than £3000, and after that the felons could be taken out by outward-bound China ships of the East India Company,† about twice a year, not more than seventy in each ship. A long list of "necessary implements" followed, ranging from mattocks and iron crows to fishing tackle and "hatts and caps".‡

No immediate action was taken by the Government on Young's plan, as the African plan, first mooted in 1779, was once more on the *tapis*. On 5 March, the Attorney-General was asked to draft an Order in Council under the Act of 1784, appointing Africa as the place to which convicts should be transported, and to advise whether such an order could change the destination of those already sentenced to America by the courts.[25] On 11 March, two Orders were promulgated by the King in Council directing that thirty-four convicts, including three women, be transported to Africa, and that twenty-five convicts, including four women and some capital respites, who had been sentenced to America or other parts beyond the seas, should be sent to Africa instead. This seems to have been kept secret, for it was not officially announced in the House of Commons until 12 April.[26] Nevertheless, rumours of it got abroad and led to Burke's rising on 16 March in his best fighting

---

* "At a time when men are alarmed at every idea of emigration I wish not to add to their fears by any attempt to depopulate the parent state."

† It is worth noting here that early in 1785 a group of speculators sought the Company's leave to establish a settlement on Norfolk Island, where cordage could be made for the Indian marine from New Zealand flax, and which would act as a centre for the Alaska fur and China trades and form an outpost against Spain in the Pacific. Dalrymple, the Company's hydrographer, scotched the idea, declaring it would lead to extensive smuggling, and later, when the Botany Bay project came up, condemned this, too. (Cf. *Australian Encyclopaedia*, art. "Norfolk Island"; and *C.H.B.E.*, Vol. VII, 60.)

‡ A third, and anonymous, plan for colonizing New Holland, which must have been written about this time, is to be found in the Home Office papers, and is reprinted in *H.R.N.S.W.*, II, 359. Its author who had "been employed abroad many years", had proposed to Lord North in 1779 that an expedition should be sent to the South Seas to foment insurrection in Chile and Peru. He now advocated a settlement in New Holland, New Zealand, New Caledonia or some other South Sea Island, in order that England might benefit from the South American revolt which he shrewdly saw must soon follow the successful revolution in the North. This would counterbalance to some extent the loss of the exclusive North American trade. The depopulationist argument is set out and dismissed as "specious", as it is better that emigrants should stay under the Flag than go to the United States. The American Loyalists are again urged to betake themselves off to the Antipodes, and the possibility of Chinese and Malayan colonists hinted at. After a denunciation of the existing system as one which nurtured and disseminated vice instead of curing it, the anonymous author praised the transportation system and the practice of the navy, the army and the East India Company in taking convicts into their service abroad. He proposed a free convict colony in New South Wales or New Zealand, but was not very clear as to the connexion between this and the other proposed colony.

trim to draw the attention of the House to "the melancholy situation under which those unfortunate people laboured who were sentenced to transportation". To what part of the world, he asked, did the Government intend to send them? Not, he hoped, to Gambia which, though represented as a wholesome place, was "the capital seat of plague, pestilence and famine". "The gates of Hell were there open night and day to receive the victims of the law." The House should remember that death was not meant to result from transportation, yet in Gambia it might truly be said that there "all life dies and all death lives". He hoped no contract had yet been entered into for sending convicts to the African coast, and was assured from the Treasury Bench, perhaps not without equivocation, that no engagement had been made.[27] The Whigs, however, were not to be put off, and returned to the attack a month later. Lord Beauchamp, on 11 April, moved for information as to the Government's intentions, and referred to a rumour that they were contemplating forming a convict colony on the African coast not on British territory.[28] Pitt, in reply, regretted that the pressure of public business had caused the neglect of so important a subject. Burke then intervened to say that he thought the African plan a very serious matter. "He could not reconcile it with justice that persons respited from death should, after a mock display of mercy, be compelled to undergo it, by being sent to a country where they could not live, and where the manner of their death might be singularly horrid, so that the apparent mercy might with justice be called cruelty, as the merciful gallows of England would rid them of their lives in a far less dreadful manner than the climate or the savages of Africa." The situation of the seventy-five felons now on board ship awaiting a favourable wind called for immediate attention. Pitt, to save the Government's face, interrupted here to say that Burke was assuming these things purely from hearsay, and should wait until he had official information.

The upshot of this incident was first, the appointment on April 20 of a committee of enquiry into the working of 24 Geo. III, c. 56, with Beauchamp in the chair, and second, an order in council on 27 April directing four male convicts to be transported to America.[29] The committee issued its first report on May 9, which consisted entirely of evidence.[30] The first witness was the Recorder of London, who deposed that when 24 Geo. III, c. 56, was passed the Old Bailey judges left it to the King in Council to declare where the transportable felons should be sent, but in a few cases specifically designated Africa.* The Government then ordered 100 convicts from Newgate to be sent to Africa, and about that number of men

* At the previous Sessions, five felons had been sentenced to Africa. and the rest to transportation at large.

and women were chosen, though after the necessary orders in council and of court had been made, it was found inconvenient to move the women and a few of the men died, so that only seventy-eight* were actually removed. The number was now being made up to 100 out of the most desperate and dangerous felons. Most of those now destined for Africa were originally sentenced to be transported to America, and none were respited capital offenders. The Chairman of the Lancashire Quarter Sessions said that after the Act of 1784 the Bench appointed two of their number to contract for the transportation of offenders, but that no ship's captain would undertake it.† A complaint to the Home Office about the overcrowded gaols had gone unanswered.

Evan Nepean told the committee that of the many schemes suggested to the Government, the one for a convict colony on the Island of Lemane, 400 miles up the River Gambia, was the most likely to be adopted. 150 convicts on board the hulk *Ceres* and some more who were still on shore, consisting of felons respited on condition of being transported to America or Africa, and felons originally sentenced to Africa, were destined to go, and would already have departed if the season had not been so far advanced. The plan was for 200 men and some women to be sent to Lemane in transports chartered from Mr Anthony Calvert, and left to found their own colony. Food and tools would be provided, but only a few firearms, as the natives were quite inoffensive, and the convicts would elect their own leader to distribute the provisions. A guard-ship was to be stationed in the Gambia to prevent escapes, protect trade, and visit the colony from time to time to find out its wants. Great Britain had as yet no territorial right to Lemane, but an annual tribute would be paid to the natives for the island. Calvert was to receive £10 a head for his services, and the cost for the first year would be no more than if they were kept at home in hulks, and would be greatly reduced later even if all the convicts lived. It was intended to have annual transportations to Africa.‡

Nepean was followed by Mr John Barnes, an African merchant, who claimed to be the originator of the Lemane plan, and to have elaborated it in conversation with Lord Sydney. He described the fertility of the soil there, the harmlessness of the natives, the relative healthiness of the climate, and the difficulty of escaping from it.

* These were obviously those to whom Burke referred on April 11.

† The form of appointing two justices to contract for the transportation of offenders seems to have continued even after the Government took over the responsibility under the Australian system (cf. MS. Minutes of Wilts Quarter Sessions, Hilary 1803). It is improbable, however, that any justices privately chartered vessels to take convicts to New South Wales or to anywhere else after 1787, as S. and B. Webb thought might be the case. (*English Prisons under Local Government*, 44n.)

‡ In *C.J.*, xlii, 700 (April 30, 1787) there is a record of the payment of £457 10s. 6d. to Thomas Cotton "for the purchase of the Island of Le Main, in the River Gambia, for a settlement for convicts"; and in Appendix L. 1 of the Twenty-Eighth Report of the Select Committee on Finance in 1798 are two items of £158 6s. 6d. in 1785 and £128 7s. 6d. in 1786 paid to Anthony Calvert "for the transportation of convicts".

He thought it would maintain three or four thousand Europeans. The eight next witnesses unanimously condemned the project. The climate, they said, was fatal to white men; an army surgeon deposed that two-thirds of the military died every year, and soldiers were useless for eleven months out of the twelve. An ordinary field labourer would not live a month without medical aid. Sir George Young estimated that a man-o'-war stationed off the coast would bury nine-tenths of her crew in a year, and the whole of it if stationed up river. Other witnesses spoke of the turbulence and thieving propensities of the natives, the poor prospects of trade, and the unlikelihood of a local chief willingly ceding any territory. These lurid revelations effectively damned the project, which may almost be said to have expired on the spot.

Nevertheless, two more orders in council were made on May 13, appointing Africa as the destination of eight male transportees and changing America to Africa in the case of nine more.[31]

On July 28 was issued the committee's second report, containing its recommendations.[32] Lord Sydney, apparently, had been asked for copies of all plans for the transportation of convicts which had been submitted to the Government, but replied that all the suggestions had either been made in conversation or appeared unworthy of the committee's attention; a curious statement, considering that both the Young and Matra plans had been submitted to him officially. Having bewailed the loss of the old American system, "which answered every good purpose that could be expected of it", and lamented the closing of United States ports against convicts "with severe penalties for any infringement", the committee went on to hope that "some arrangement may be come to in the future as to felons acquainted with husbandry or manufactures". The possibility of a European power taking convict labour was excluded as being outside the province of the enquiry.* The desiderata of a convict settlement were then considered. The climate and site should be healthy, as the fact that a man has been respited from death implies that his sentence should not expose him to imminent danger of his life. The end of transportation would be defeated unless the colony was far enough away to prevent its inmates returning, but otherwise a coastal site was better than one inland, because it would be easier to protect them from the natives and furnish them with supplies there. The committee condemned unhesitatingly the idea of a colony composed only of convicts and without external control, but recommended the resumption of transportation, with convicts

---

* See, in this connexion, A. Brésillion, *De la Transportation*, p. 11, who quotes an offer to the Russian Government to send transports to the Crimea, and also the probably jocular remark of George Wilson to Jeremy Bentham, who was then in Russia, in a letter dated September 24, 1786: "Will you have a few convicts for the Crimea?" (*Bentham's Works*, Vol. X, p. 164.)

as the basis of a new Trading Settlement, if only to relieve the pressure on the gaols. Criminals were being sentenced to be transported to Africa every session, and it lessened the respect shown to the administration of criminal justice if sentences were imposed which could not be carried out.

Having considered Africa, British America and other parts of the world as possible sites of a penal colony, the committee ruled the two latter out, as well as the schemes for transportation to Gambia and Guinea. The final recommendation was for a colony at Das Voltas Bay, between Angola and the Cape, which was said to be healthy and to have friendly inhabitants, and would make an excellent port of call on the way to India. Four slavers of 200 tons each would carry 500 convicts at a total cost of not more than £12,500. The officer commanding the African station should be the commander of the settlement, as it would be necessary to give him absolute powers over it, and the selection of a suitable man was most important. November would be the best month in which to found the colony, as the convicts would then have all the summer before them. Artificers, mechanics and husbandmen should be selected as settlers, and it was to be hoped that the American Loyalists would emigrate there and help to keep the convicts in order. If they did, they were to have convicts assigned to them. The committee used Matra's argument that it was desirable to divert the flow of emigration from the United States to territories still under the British Crown. In conclusion, they remarked that if the system of transportation to Africa was to be persisted in, the Das Voltas scheme was the only practicable one. Only if the colony flourished, could the English gaols be emptied annually, as was desirable, and in any case it would require help from the mother country for many years, so that it should only be adopted so far as the commercial and political benefits of a settlement in South-West Africa warranted the expense.

In pursuance of these recommendations, the commander of the African station was instructed to detach one of his ships to explore the "River or Bay Des Voltas (28° 29′ S.)", which appears to be the mouth of the Orange River, with a view to establishing a convict settlement there.[33] This was in August 1785, just after the luckless La Pérouse had set out from Brest on his ill-fated voyage. H.M. Sloop *Nautilus* was accordingly sent to explore the coast between the latitudes 15° 50′ and 33° S., but on her return her officers reported that the land was "sandy and barren and from other causes unfit for a settlement of that description". Thus ended the many and strenuous attempts to establish a convict colony on the African coast.*

* Many writers have stated that English convicts were sent to Africa (including Colquhoun,

Although Africa had been ruled out as a possible destination, the crime problem still remained pressing. The *Edinburgh Magazine* for March 1786 printed a petition of the City of London to the King, bewailing the unprecedented increase in crime, and praying for "a speedy and due execution of the law, both as to capital punishment and transportation".[34] Thus urged on all sides, the Pitt Government, or more probably its Home Secretary, came to its momentous decision some time in the summer of 1786.* On August 18, 1786, Lord Sydney wrote to the Lords Commissioners of His Majesty's Treasury saying that the King had "thought it advisable to fix upon Botany Bay" as the site of the proposed convict settlement, and requesting them to make provision for the conveyance of 750 convicts thither.[35] On 31 August, a similar letter was sent to the Lords of the Admiralty.[36] The reason given by Sydney for the necessity of making such a settlement was the familiar one of gaols so crowded as to give rise to the danger of wholesale escapes or an epidemic of fever. The general arrangements for the expedition, as outlined in these letters and in the "Heads of a Plan" which was attached to them, were much the same as were eventually carried out, and will therefore be discussed in the next chapter. One or two points, however, deserve special notice. In particular, the danger of the twin scourges of prostitution and unnatural vice was foreseen, and provided for, although the precautions were neglected in the actual outcome. One transport was to be properly fitted up for the accommodation of women "to prevent their intercourse with the men", and a proposal was made, but never adopted, to fetch a number of women from the Friendly Islands or New Caledonia, "from whence any number may be procured without difficulty, and without a sufficient proportion of that sex it is well known that it would be impossible to preserve the settlement from gross irregularities and disorders". The "Heads of a Plan" bears many evidences of the influence of its three fore-runners, especially in its references to the cultivation of New Zealand flax and other tropical products, and to the superior timber of New Zealand; but commercial advantages are clearly secondary to the necessity of emptying the gaols. Altogether this fourth scheme was far the most concrete that was put forward. Various estimates

op. cit., p. 461, *Phillip's Voyage to Botany Bay*, p. 6, and the Twenty-Eighth Report of the Select Committee on Finance, 1798, p. 352), but perhaps they refer to the men sent to the garrison at Cape Coast Castle. We have been unable to trace any records of any transportations other than these military cases. Various proposals for colonizing Gambia are to be found in the "Chatham Papers", 311. As late as January 12, 1787, there was a rumour that although the female convicts in the London gaols were going to Botany Bay, the men would be sent to Africa. (*H.R.N.S.W.*, II, 739.) The Orders in Council for the Second Fleet show that a few felons, mostly in London and Middlesex, were still being sentenced to Africa as late as September 1787.

* In March, Pitt is still found saying that "several new modes of disposing of the convicts had been pointed out, every one of which was attended with such difficulty and expense that Government was not a little embarrassed what method to take consistently with the public safety". (*P.H.*, xix, 329.) The prison population nearly doubled between 1782 and 1787-88 (see *ante*, p. 141n.).

were attached, including £1497 10s. for the salaries of the staff per annum, £2 19s. 6d. for clothing a convict for one year, and £1268 10s. for tools and utensils.

The decision at last having been made, preparations for the expedition were soon well under way. Phillip's first commission was issued on 12 October, and by the end of the month most of the other officers, the surgeon and the chaplain had been appointed. At a meeting of the Privy Council held at the Court of St James's on 6 December, two orders were made for the transportation of convicts to "the eastern coast of New South Wales". The first order related to 328 men and sixteen women, originally condemned to be transported to "parts beyond the seas", of whom 307 men and fifteen women were for seven years, eleven men for fourteen years, ten men for life, and one woman for five years; eleven of these were being retransported, having returned before the expiry of their first sentence. The second order was for 286 men and nine women originally sentenced to America, of whom 246 men and six women were for seven years, eleven men and three women for fourteen years, fifteen men for life, and fourteen men no sentence stated; and for 101 men originally sentenced to Africa, of whom eighty-seven were for seven years, thirteen for fourteen years and one for life. Among the Africans, seven had originally been tried in 1782, nine in 1783, fifty-five in 1784, twenty-eight in 1785 and two in 1786. Ten convicts in the second order were being retransported. Two more orders were made on 22 December, relating to 100 women, of whom in the first category seventy-seven were for seven years and four for fourteen years; in the second category two each for seven and fourteen years, and in the third eleven for seven years and two each for life and fourteen years.[37]

These orders were presented to the House of Commons on 29 January 1787, a week after the King's Speech, in which it had been announced that a plan had been formed "in order to remove the inconvenience which arose from the crowded state of the gaols in the different parts of the kingdom".[38] The Government's decision was approved in the Addresses of both Houses, Lord Compton in the Commons remarking that "it was a measure of absolute necessity", and "the only remedy for an evil which required immediate redress", none of the promised penitentiaries having yet been built. Charles James Fox also implicitly blessed the scheme.

On 12 February two more orders in council were made, consigning five men and thirty-two women convicts to Botany Bay, all with seven years sentences, except one woman for five years. Two of the women and one man had originally been sentenced to America, and one man to Africa. On 20 April the last two orders in council

for the First Fleet were made, when three men and twenty-seven women were designated as future inhabitants of Australia, all with seven years sentences, except one woman each for five years, fourteen years and life. One man had his sentence altered from America, and one man and one woman from Africa. Seven of the women had been tried as lately as the Lent Assizes, 1787. The total number of convicts specified in the eight orders in council was 883, of whom 184 were women, 279 men and fifteen women had originally been sentenced to America, and 103 men and sixteen women to Africa. 793 convicts were sentenced for seven years, forty-four for fourteen years, twenty-nine for life, three for five years, and in fourteen cases no sentence was stated.[39]

The motives of the Pitt Government in making this fateful decision have been the subject of controversy ever since. Whig historians maintain that there was no other motive than that of getting rid of the convicts; Imperialists, with a nice disregard for cold facts and an unfortunate tendency to be misled by contemporary pamphleteers, have declared that their intention was to found a second, and less rebellious America in the South Seas, which was to be the chief jewel in the new Imperial diadem. Careful study of contemporary sayings and doings compels one to the conclusion that this time those "horrid Whigs" were right. In spite of the three plans in the Home Office papers for a commercial colony in New South Wales, there is no shred of evidence that if the gaols of England had not been unwontedly full, the colony would ever have been founded when it was. Admittedly, once it was decided that the gaols and hulks should be emptied, not into a West African swamp or into the peaceful homes of the Nova Scotians, but on to the barren, though supposedly fertile, shores of Botany Bay, various plans began to be drawn up for using this settlement to the best advantage, and by the time the First Fleet sailed, nine months after the original decision, the idea of a commercial settlement was very definitely in the air. This must be the justification of the Imperialists, and such writers as Sir T. A. Coghlan, who says "they [the authorities] did not consider they were founding a mere gaol but an industrial colony, from which would arise in due season a new home for the British people".[40] It is incontestable, however, that the disposal of the convicts was the paramount motive which led the British Government to embark on the hazardous and costly experiment of founding a colony in the Antipodes. This opinion is borne out by Professor Melbourne in his erudite work on the early constitutional history of New South Wales. Referring to the decision to found the colony, he says that it "was occupied deliberately, in order to relieve the overcrowding of the gaols", and later, when discussing Phillip's Instructions, adds that the Government probably

had some of the prevalent reformatory ideas in mind, and to that extent "was seeking to found a colony rather than create a gaol".[41]

The doctrine of collective responsibility made all the members of the cabinet responsible for the decision; but in fact it is probable that Lord Sydney* and, still more, Home Office officials such as Evan Nepean, were the real initiators of the scheme, and should, therefore, get any praise or blame that is to be apportioned. Pitt, on whom eager biographers have often showered the highest praise for his "far-seeing" action, seems to have been entirely unconscious that he was authorizing the birth of a new nation, and to have paid no more attention to the project than any Prime Minister does to an irritating and persistent departmental problem. As Dr Holland Rose says, "the painful truth must be faced that in this matter Pitt lacked the Imperial imagination. Despite vague assertions to the contrary by professed panegyrists, I cannot find a word in his speeches or letters which evinced any interest in the Botany Bay experiment". It must not be forgotten, too, that over four hundred American Loyalists were living in penury in London at this time, whose claims might have been advantageously disposed of by some such scheme as Matra's, and who in fact were compensated at considerable expense in 1788.[42]

Indeed, only poets such as Erasmus Darwin, and other lesser and anonymous fry, seem to have had any conception of the possibilities of the occasion.[43] The *Annual Register* did not mention the project until the First Fleet reached the Cape, and the memoirs of contemporary statesmen are singularly lacking in any reference to it. Several political pamphlets and *livres de circonstance* need to be noticed, however. Chief among them is the anonymous *History of New Holland*, written probably between October 1786 and January 1787, and published before the New South Wales Judicature Bill was presented to Parliament.† The attempts to plumb the anonymity of its authorship have led to the most incompatible results. Until recently, the British Museum and many other library catalogues have attributed it to George Barrington, the notorious pickpocket, who at this time was earning a dubious living on the turf, and who seems to be the last resort of bibliographers seeking the authorship of anonymous Australian works. In the 1935 edition of the British Museum catalogue the description has been altered to anonymous. Many historians, however, go to the other extreme, and by misreading the title, attribute the book to Eden

---

* He was said to have "too hastily" rejected "a much better plan": William Pulteney to Pitt, September 14, 1786, quoted Holland Rose, op cit., p. 438.

† Its full title is: *The History of New Holland, from its first Discovery in 1616, to the present time, with a particular account of its produce and inhabitants; and a description of Botany Bay: also, a List of the Naval Marine, Military and Civil Establishment. To which is prefixed an Introductory Discourse on Banishment by the Right Honourable William Eden* (Stockdale), London, 1787.

himself.* The fact is, that far from writing the whole book, Eden did not even, as has often been supposed, write the introductory *Discourse on Banishment* specially to commend the scheme sponsored by the Government of his friend Pitt. The celebrated *Discourse* is, in fact, nothing but the fourth chapter of the *Principles of Penal Law*, first published fifteen years previously, and was republished possibly with the author's permission, with the object of adding the lustre of a famous statesman's name to an anonymous publication. It certainly does not indicate that Eden gave any spontaneous support to the Botany Bay idea, and cannot be quoted to show that the author of the Penitentiary Scheme had abandoned it in favour of a penal colony, or that an intimate friend of Pitt had prophetic visions of the great destiny of the settlement.†

The body of the work consists entirely, as its unknown author acknowledges, of a digest from the works of previous writers of all that was known of the "island or continent of New Holland" up to Cook and Banks. The preface, however, contains some interesting incidental remarks on the merits of the expedition, although the editor considers himself precluded "from attempting to add to the multiplicity of opinions already advanced", which indicates that the work was a journalistic venture, rather than a political pamphlet. A favourable opinion of the project is nevertheless expressed, and criminals are warned that "when their lives or liberties are forfeited to justice", they "have always been judged a fair subject of hazardous experiments, to which it would be unjust to expose the more valuable members of a state", and they must not imagine that they are going to sit for the rest of their lives "on a bed of roses"—an argument which paraphrases the words of the 1779 Committee. The chapter from Eden's *Principles* is put in to bolster up this argument. Some comments about the "unhappy influence" of "a King [James I] who affected to be a legislator" suggest that the editor was inclined to Whiggism. He then suggests that the Dutch colony at the Cape should be the model for Botany Bay, and supposes that the latter can never have any commerce of its own so long as the East India Company's charter exists. In the preface to the second edition, published later in 1787, but before the fleet sailed, the colonial idea becomes more prominent still, and the editor dilates on the advantages of such a settlement in a war against the Dutch,‡ and on the possibility of tobacco, indigo,

---

* Among those who have so described the work are Eden's biographer in the *D.N.B.*, Prof. Ernest Scott in *C.H.B.E.*, vii, p. 58, n. 2, and Prof. A. C. V. Melbourne in *Early Constitutional Development in Australia: New South Wales, 1788-1856*, p. 4.

† Another less well known pamphlet, *Copious Remarks on the Discovery of New South Wales, etc.*, London, 1787, also contains "Prefatory Observations on Transportation" by the Rt. Hon. William Eden, which is the same chapter from his *Principles*.

‡ For Dutch opposition to the New South Wales settlement, see *H.R.N.S.W.*, ii, p. 737.

silk and wines being produced there, and goes to considerable lengths to refute the depopulationists.

Another pamphlet which favoured the Government's scheme was *An Historical Narrative of the Discovery of New Holland, etc.*, published anonymously in London in 1786. The author considered that the new settlement would be useful as a base for trade with Japan, China and the west coast of America, and for attacking the Spanish colonies in case of a war with that country. The whole appears to be merely a journalistic rehash of previous authors.

Against the proposed expedition was the unknown author of *A Short Review of the Political State of Great Britain at the commencement of the Year* 1787, which was published by J. Debrett in London, and ran into seven editions within a year. He made a trenchant onslaught upon the Pitt Government in general, and smote the Botany Bay scheme hip and thigh, comparing it to Thule and Lilliput and suggesting a lumber-camp in Newfoundland or a colony on the Gold Coast instead. He gloomily prognosticated the time when the convicts would fill the Indian and Chinese seas with slaughter and depredation, and concluded that anyhow, England would reap no advantage from it.

Dalrymple's opposition has already been referred to. The pamphlet associated with him is *A Serious Admonition to the Public on the intended Thief-Colony at Botany Bay*, published by Sewel in 1786, and consisting of a letter from him to the East India Company prefixed to remarks by an anonymous commentator. He marshalled a formidable, if somewhat rancorous, array of arguments against the foundation of the colony, ranging from the great expense to the undesirability of infringing the East India Company's charter, and his editor recommended that the felons should be dumped on Tristan da Cunha.*

Considerable controversy also ensued in the public press, and comment, both editorial and in letters from correspondents, was acrimonious in the manner of an age which had given birth to Junius; but on the whole, opposition came only from parties who thought their interests would be likely to be infringed, or who fancied that the South Sea Islanders were about to be debauched by the dregs of the English gaols. In general the ayes had it, especially as commercial advantages were expected to accrue. Strangely enough, hardly a thought was spared for the convicts themselves, except by stern moralists, who bade them prepare to suffer the punishment they had so justly incurred.†

---

* There were also *Proposals for Employing Convicts within this Kingdom instead of sending them to Botany Bay*, by G. R., London, 1787, and an anonymous plan, also dated 1787, for sending convicts to the coal mines, which is in the "Chatham Papers", 311.

˙ A full study of public opinion on the foundation of the penal settlement is beyond the scope of this book, although much of it has in fact been considered. Those who wish to pursue the subject further should consult the files of contemporary newspapers and periodicals in the British Museum; and also Ferguson's Bibliography of Australia (Vol. i.)

The decision of the British Government, however, did not affect Ireland, nominally independent since 1782. In that year a Select Committee of the Irish House of Commons had enquired into the state of the gaols of the kingdom and heard the evidence of Howard, but this seems to have had little effect, for in December 1785 the *Hibernian Journal* is found bewailing that "notwithstanding the enormous numbers of transports lately sent from our prisons", the gaols were still overcrowded with felons, and murder and rapine were rampant throughout the country.[44]

In 1786 an Act (26 Geo. III, c. 24) was passed by the Irish Parliament authorizing the Lord Lieutenant to sent "convicts to any of His Majesty's plantations in America, or to such other place out of Europe as shall be expressed in such sentence, rule or order". Under the old system, which had prevailed since the reign of Anne, transportation from Ireland had only been permissible to the British colonies and plantations in America, and the sheriffs of the different counties contracted directly with the masters of vessels trading with North America, but by the Act of 1786 all convicts had to be sent to Dublin and transported from there by warrant of the Lord Lieutenant.[45] Although we have not been able to find any direct evidence, it seems very probable, from allusions in the journals and correspondence of the day, that the traffic in Irish convicts to America continued, at least sporadically, even after 1776.

On 8 December 1788, the *Annual Register* records that "the season is over for sending [convicts] to Quebec and Nova Scotia; but assurances have been given that two ships, properly fitted up, shall be ready by the latter end of March next, to carry convicts to America".[46] In the following year a transport, which was probably one of those referred to in the *Annual Register*, sailed for Newfoundland with eighty Irish convicts under warrant from the Lord Lieutenant of Ireland, thereby stirring up such a hornet's nest as to produce one of the few really Gilbertian situations in the long and sordid history of Transportation. The unfortunate Irishmen arrived at St John's in July 1789, and were so unwelcome to the inhabitants that they were promptly cast into gaol by the Governor, Admiral Milbanke. There they stayed until October, when Milbanke, finding that as they had committed no offence against the laws of Newfoundland he had no legal right to keep them in prison, released them and sent them back to England. In November the eighty arrived at Portsmouth, where they found that the English Government did not want them any more than Dublin Castle or Admiral

at Hendon, e.g. *The Times*, the *Morning Post*, the *Public Advertiser*, the *Morning Herald* and the *Gentleman's Magazine*. Extracts from some of these papers are to be found in J. Bonwick: *Australia's First Preacher*, ch. iv; Barton, op. cit., 466; *H.R.N.S.W.*,II, 737; see also a letter from George Wilson to Jeremy Bentham on 24.ix.1786 in Bentham's *Works*, X, 164.

Milbanke. After a brilliant suggestion that they should be tried for having returned from transportation before the expiry of their sentences had been rejected, on the ground that the jury might acquit them and release them upon English society to resume their interrupted depredations, it was finally decided, on the advice of the Lord Chancellor and the judges of the King's Bench, to ship them back to Ireland. The Irish Government, however, was grimly resolved that its eighty black sheep should not return to their fatherland. They took the extraordinary step of sending out a revenue cruiser with an agent on board who was instructed to bribe the captain of the transport not to put into an Irish port. At length, however, after a heated correspondence, Grenville prevailed upon the Irish Government to take them back and to forget the insult implied in an Irish Act of Parliament being overridden by the Governor of Newfoundland. The eighty unhappy subjects of this interlude arrived back in Dublin on January 21, 1790, and forthwith disappeared from history.[47]

When the unwanted Irish convicts, six of whom were said to be boys under fourteen and some even under twelve,[48] were still waiting on their transport in Spithead, Grenville, having procured a warrant for their conveyance to Dublin, wrote sharply to Chief Secretary Hobart:

The awkwardness, inconvenience, and expense of this whole business is so very great, that I must earnestly request of you to consider again with the Lord Chancellor as to the means of preventing any repetition of it. The landing convicts in the territories of the United States (even if the masters of the ships perform their contracts for so doing) is an act highly offensive to a country now foreign and independent; and as such, very improper for the Government to authorize. And it is besides an act of extreme cruelty to the convicts, who, being turned on shore without any of the necessities of life, are either left to starve, or (as has sometimes been the case) are massacred by the inhabitants. And as to transporting to the King's American colonies, you may depend upon it that, after the example set them by Admiral Milbanke, none of our Governors will suffer any of these people to be landed in their governments; and that, if landed by stealth, they will send them back at a heavy expense which must fall upon the Irish government.[49]

After much wrangling among the lawyers it was decided that although the Irish Act of 1786 was valid, it only authorized transportation to the colonies and plantations; Newfoundland was legally neither a colony nor a plantation, but a fishing-station;

and in any case the Irish Parliament, unlike the English, had no jurisdiction outside Ireland.

Another transport, possibly the second ship mentioned in the *Annual Register*, appears to have reached the British island of Barbuda in the Leeward Islands, and there to have landed "a fresh set of miscreants". Grenville anticipated more trouble from this, as there was no doubt that Barbuda was a colony, but the inhabitants must have been in need of cheap labour, as no more was heard of the matter.[50]

In 1789, however, the Irish authorities were already contemplating sending their surplus felons to New South Wales. On 9 July, Secretary Grenville wrote to his brother, Lord Buckingham, Lord Lieutenant of Ireland, that he had "enquired about the convicts" and found that "the expense of transporting them this year will be about £14 per head". Buckingham, who was taking the waters at Bath, replied two days later: "I have writ to Ireland about the convicts whom I am anxious to send to New South Wales."[51] Later in the year, when Grenville wrote to Hobart about the Milbanke episode, he added:

> I had some little conversation with you before you left this country on the subject of the expense to be incurred by Ireland by transporting to New South Wales. The convicts whom we now send out are contracted for at £17 per head, besides which they are victualled for the passage, and for one year after their arrival. This is the whole expense which Ireland would pay on account of the convicts themselves, and this might be lessened to the Government by charging a proportion of it on the counties who formerly bore the expense of transporting to America.
>
> Besides this, if the King authorized the receiving these men into the settlement in New South Wales, we should naturally expect that Ireland should contribute to the increased body of troops which an increased number of convicts would require. This might easily be done by raising an additional company in Ireland to be added to the New South Wales Corps, and to be borne on the Irish Establishment, in the same manner as the troops which Ireland now furnishes for the protection of the West India colonies. This mode would avoid the introduction of any new principle of contribution.[52]

The result of Buckingham's enquiries was seen on February 15, 1790, when the Irish Chancellor of the Exchequer, Sir John Parnell, who about this time became interested in Bentham's Panopticon, drew the attention of the Irish House of Commons to "a matter of very considerable importance", "the subject of those wretched

people who were sentenced in this country for transportation". He proposed the erection of penitentiaries for the lesser offenders, as being less expensive than transportation to Botany Bay, which should be reserved as a life punishment for the greater criminals. He quoted the example of several British prisons where the produce of the convicts' labour had "more than compensated the whole expence of the establishment and the rent of the building", and said that he proposed to introduce a Bill on the subject within a few days.[53] It was not until the following year that any convicts were actually sent from Ireland to New South Wales, 155 convicts sailing on the transport *Queen* in April 1791.[54] They were the first of many transported for political and criminal offences.

PREPARATIONS, AND DEPARTURE OF THE FIRST FLEET

(a) Governor Phillip's Instructions

THE reason why Arthur Phillip was chosen to be Governor of the settlement in New South Wales is not clear. He was then forty-eight years old, the son of a German father, and had retired from the Navy, in which he held the rank of captain. On 3 September 1786, Lord Howe wrote doubtfully of the choice that had already been made by Lord Sydney. The little knowledge he had of Phillip would scarcely have led him to choose such a man "for a service of this complicated nature", but as Sydney had already determined that Phillip's abilities were equal to the task, and the settlement of the convicts was a matter for the Home Department rather than the Admiralty, Howe was willing to concur and to facilitate transport arrangements through his own department.[1] The compiler of *The Voyage of Governor Phillip*, published in 1789, stated that Phillip had been chosen because of his fitness "to conduct an enterprise which required professional knowledge and habitual prudence."[2] It has been suggested that his living at Lyndhurst, near the residence of Sir George Rose, the Treasurer of the Navy, may have brought him under that gentleman's notice.[3] At all events, Phillip soon after the establishment of Sydney gave the name of Rose Hill to one of the new settlements. The choice of Arthur Phillip was a happy one. Endowed with common sense, kindliness, breadth of vision, firmness and sincerity, he was an ideal founder for any new colony. But for the tradition which Phillip began, the system of government control in the colony would have proved chaotic in the extreme. It degenerated as soon as he left it.

After the decision to send convicts to Botany Bay the general administrative plans for the projected settlement were quickly formulated. On November 12, 1786, Arthur Phillip received his first commission as Governor "of the territory called New South Wales". The Territory, so little known, was defined as all that lying between Cape York in the north and South Cape in the south, westwards as far as the 135th degree of longitude, and eastward indefinitely, so as to include all islands in the Pacific Ocean within the latitude of 10° 37′ South and 43° 39′ South.[4]

The second commission, dated April 2 of the following year, defined his position and powers more fully, and more clearly showed that Phillip was directed to act as a colonial governor as well as a gaoler.[5]

The title by which possession of New South Wales was taken was that of "occupation" of desert and unoccupied lands, but the exceptional circumstances of the settlement, differing considerably from those that had existed in American colonies where convicts were simply transferred to plantation owners, necessitated a peculiar form of government. In New South Wales the Government had to "assume a responsibility" for the convicts, which in America it had been able to evade, and was obliged to become the employer itself.[6] Convicts in England were accordingly handed over to contractors, who on arrival had to relinquish all control and rights to the Governor of the territory without further compensation than the rates allowed for transport. In the Act of Parliament authorizing the resumption of transportation (24 Geo. III, c. 56, 1784) the convicts subject to transportation were defined in three classes. First, those convicted of any offence for which they were liable to be transported; second, those convicted of "non-clergyable" offences who had been pardoned on condition of transportation, by the courts and with the subsequent approval of one of His Majesty's Principal Secretaries of State; and third, those who were allowed to transport themselves voluntarily. Except in the case of the voluntary exiles, the courts were empowered "to order such offenders to be transferred to the use of any person" . . . "who shall contract for the due performance of such transportation" for the term of years specified in the condition of transportation.[7]

The contractors, in return for a stipulated sum of money according to the tonnage of the vessels employed by them, were held responsible for the safe custody of the convicts until their arrival in New South Wales. Upon arrival they had to hand over their interests in the convicts absolutely to the governor in command. In Governor Phillip's Instructions, issued on April 25, 1787, he was told that before discharging the transport-ships he should take care to have an assignment made by the masters of vessels to himself, or the governor-in-chief for the time being, "of the servitude of the several convicts for the remainder of the times or terms specified in their several sentences of transportation."[8]

The colonial idea in arranging for the formation of the first settlement was undoubtedly present in the minds of ministers, developing considerably in the long interval that elapsed between the date of Lord Sydney's letter, August 18, 1786, and the

departure of the First Fleet in the following May. Lord Sydney said that it had been determined that the "convicts should form a settlement." Phillip's first commission was vague on this point, and the commissions issued to the civil staff were stated as being subject "to the rules and discipline of war". A military government was contemplated, and 28 years later Bathurst notified the Deputy Judge Advocate that even then he was not prepared to alter the military restraint which had characterized the colony since its commencement.[9] The first omission of the martial law restrictions was made in the commission given to Deputy Judge Advocate Bent in 1809.[10] In Phillip's second commission, April 2, 1787, the colonial idea was exemplified in the regulations made for the new styled "Captain-General and Governor-in-Chief" to observe the laws relating to trade and the plantations. In the Act (27 Geo. III, c. 2) establishing a court of criminal judicature, the imperial policy was again mentioned. For some unaccountable reason this Act has been described as "The Act of Parliament establishing the Colony", [11] but its sole purpose was to establish a court of justice. (See Appendix F). The Act cites 24 Geo. III, c. 56, the two Orders of Council of December 1786, and the decisions of the two Exchequer Barons who had already set the system in motion on December 30, 1786, by determining certain convicts as its subjects. By it a criminal court "with power to proceed in a more summary way than is used within this realm", was established; but the preamble of the accompanying "warrant for the Charter of Justice", April 2, 1787, stated that "whereas we find it necessary that a colony and civil government should be established in the place to which such convicts shall be transported", legal provisions would be made in civil and criminal jurisdictions in the settlement.[12] Immediately before the First Fleet sailed the colonial prospects of the settlement were more clearly envisaged. In Phillip's Instructions, issued on April 25, 1787, the governor was notified that further batches of convicts would be sent in the near future and that convict labour was expected to exploit the natural resources of the country and make it self-supporting to an appreciable extent. Norfolk Island was to be occupied and settled in view of possible advantages. Land was to be given to emancipated convicts "with all convenient speed", on condition of their residing on it and farming it; and in order to facilitate colonization the Governor was instructed to introduce native women from the Pacific Islands "whenever the *Sirius* or the tender shall touch at any of the islands in those seas". To the convicts who should marry, land grants would be increased and additional acreage provided according to the number of their children. But over and above such questionable colonization schemes as these, the Govern-

ment expressly mentioned the possibility of free settlement by some of the military who might desire to remain in the colony, and by "others who may resort thither upon their private occupations". On April 20, 1787, Lord Sydney stated that the Admiralty would authorize petty officers and men of the *Sirius*, to a number not exceeding forty, to remain as settlers in the penal colony. Phillip was accordingly instructed to report on the state of the land and to propose how it might be apportioned among all settlers, in order that proper instructions could later be issued to him for the purpose of colonization.[13] Two years later, August 20, 1789, the policy of encouraging free settlers was more clearly defined.[14] But at the commencement, in 1787, while it is evident that colonization was contemplated with the unpromising ingredients of convicts and island women, problematical military settlers and others who might later be tempted to try their luck in this distant place, it is clear that the transportation of criminals was the dominant intention. Had there been no criminal problem, there would not have been a settlement.

The provisions made by Government for the management of this peculiar colony, established at so great a distance and in an unexplored land, show that the problems of settlement were not understood. Whatever theoretical excellence was in them was later diminished by the carelessness which characterized the practical preparation and caused much disquietude to Governor Phillip. Haste was evident in the earlier provisions, as it was hoped that the fleet, for which a large number of convicts were in readiness as early as December 1786, might be able to leave early in the new year. Its delay until May 1787 was in some measure due to Phillip's insistence on more adequate equipment. Before the end of the year commissions had been issued to Phillip, to Major Ross as Lieutenant-Governor, to David Collins as Deputy Judge Advocate, to John White and William Balmain as surgeons, and to Richard Johnson as chaplain.

Phillip's Commissions and the Instructions which were issued to define his powers gave him autocratic control in the new settlement—an autocracy which continued without change in the commissions of four succeeding governors. In administration he was to be assisted by a civil staff, "an extraordinary" judicial system was devised to enforce and interpret the law, and a military force to maintain general order within the settlement. The various officers and systems of control were made subject to his immediate supervision, under the rules and discipline of war. The judicial system was peculiar. Although a court of civil jurisdiction was authorized by a warrant under the Privy Seal on April 2, 1787, it was not mentioned in the Act of 1787; consequently its legality

was questioned in later years. (For an outline of the defects of Civil Jurisdiction see Appendix F.). This court was placed under the control of a deputy judge advocate and "two fit and proper persons to be appointed by the governor", who though inexperienced in law, might give judgments from which an appeal lay to the governor, with a further appeal to the King in Council when the sum involved exceeded £300 in value.[15] The criminal court, consisting of a deputy judge advocate, together with six officers of the sea or land forces, nominated by the governor for this office, was empowered to hear and determine all criminal cases and to punish them according to English law "as nearly as may be, considering and allowing for the circumstances of the . . . Settlement and the inhabitants there". The decision of the bench was to depend on a majority vote. It is interesting to note that when Pitt submitted the draft of the Bill for establishing summary jurisdiction in New South Wales to the Lord Chief Justice, Earl Camden described it as "a novelty in our constitution". "In the present state of that embryo (for I can't call it either settlement or colony)" trial by jury was impossible, he wrote. He recommended that an annual report of all capital convictions made by this inexperienced body should be sent to England for supervision, and that when the number of inhabitants increased in New South Wales trial by jury should be introduced "as soon as it can be done with propriety".[16] Trial by jury had to wait for a considerable time before entering on the slow development that lasted from 1823 to 1839, but the Lord Chief Justice's recommendations were followed in the Letters Patent to the extent that no death sentence might be carried out without the governor's consent, and when the capital charge was upheld by less than five members of the bench, the sentence was to be suspended until confirmed by the Crown. Only two punishments might be imposed by the criminal courts; in certain cases death might be pronounced, otherwise corporal punishment had to be the sentence.[17]

Not only in the functioning of justice, but in every detail of administration the governor's power was unfettered; he was to nominate the bench, to decide when the sessions should be held, to act as a court of appeal, and to have the right of pardoning all offences committed in the colony except wilful murder and treason, but even in these he had the power to reprieve. Without a legislative or an executive council to advise him, his mere command would be authoritative for executing acts and his daily orders would be the only mediums for legislation.[18] His Commission foresaw a great number of eventualities in which he was empowered to act—to levy forces for defence, to proclaim martial law, to erect fortifications, to control naval discipline by specially constituted legal machinery

to meet all circumstances, to regulate ports and shipping and markets and to provide for his successor in the event of his absence or death.[19] The Instructions issued to Phillip were more explicit about his immediate task.[20] Whereas "about 600 male and 180 female convicts" had been ordered to be put on board the transports already engaged for their reception, Phillip was to take them and the people who comprised the civil establishment to Botany Bay. At various places, particularly at the Cape of Good Hope, he was to take on provisions, seed grain, hogs, black cattle and sheep. Arrived at Botany Bay which, from information received, appeared to be "the most eligible situation on the said coast", he was to discharge the vessels speedily, to have the convicts assigned to him, and to set them to work on the land. It was presumed that the convicts were fitted for cultivation and that the supply of implements was adequate. In the provisions made for the commissariat the lack of official comprehension of the problems that faced such an expedition is extraordinary. They had forgotten Banks's first description of New Holland as "the most barren country I have seen", and only remembered his unjustifiable evidence, recorded nine years later, that Botany Bay was a place where two or three hundred convicts might be settled with one year's allowance for food, clothing, seeds and animals, after which they could "undoubtedly maintain themselves without any assistance from England".[21] On such dreams the pamphleteers had fed the populace, and the Government, convinced or unconvinced, was prepared to experiment at so great a distance with a thousand souls and even to economize in supplies. The result was, as will be seen, that the convict settlement was threatened with starvation even at Sydney, a much more fertile district than the swamps of Botany Bay.

The remaining clauses of the Instructions covered a wide field. Explorations were to be made; Norfolk Island, "as a spot that may hereafter become useful" and in order to prevent its occupation by any other power, was to be settled; the aborigines of the country were to be conciliated and protected. Phillip was also instructed to "enforce a due observance of religion". It has been suggested that the Government failed to appoint a chaplain to the fleet until constrained to do so by Sir Joseph Banks, when the ships were on the point of sailing. From the official letters of the period, however, it is certain that a chaplaincy was spoken of as early as August 1786 and that the Commission given to the Rev. Richard Johnson by Royal Warrant was dated 24 October 1786, only twelve days after Phillip's Commission as Governor.[22] Unfortunately, the Catholics were not so successful. An offer made by two priests to act as chaplains without any salary apparently remained unanswered.[23]

The practical arrangements made by the Government, apart from those already mentioned, provided for transport, victualling, and supervision during the voyage. The Commissioners of the Admiralty advertised for vessels to convey about 750 convicts to the settlement; and in the beginning there was no question of economy, because it was hoped that the new transportation scheme would be a solution for the problem of crime, which having increased "to an alarming degree", had proved insoluble by all former expedients.[24] Economy was introduced later. Two King's ships were provided, one under Phillip's flag being of 520 tons and classed as "sixth rate", and the other an armed tender of 170 tons. The five transport ships originally provided had a total tonnage of just over 1800 tons, and after complaints of inadequacy of accommodation for so large a complement, another transport, of 350 tons, was added.[25] There were also three small storeships. The tonnage of the whole fleet amounted to 3892 tons, and these vessels were expected to convey over 1400 persons to New South Wales by way of Rio de Janeiro and the Cape of Good Hope. The transports were hired at the rate of ten shillings per ton per month, over a period covering the outward and return journeys, except in the case of certain ships belonging to the East India Company whose contract ceased on arrival.[26] Further contracts were let for victualling the fleet and for supplying provisions sufficient to feed the settlement for two years after arrival. In this estimate provision was made for 200 additional women, who were to be procured from the islands and fed on half rations, but it was also contemplated that during the voyage the deaths would approximate forty-five.[27] The two years' provisions were expected to last three, because in the second year the populace would be placed on half rations, and at the end of the third year it was expected that local industry "would be fully sufficient".[28] Extra provisions were to be purchased at the Cape of Good Hope. The provisioning contracts which were let out variously, but chiefly to Messrs Richards and Thorn,[29] specified supplies for each prisoner at the rate of two-thirds of the weekly allowance given to seamen in the navy, which was: seven pounds of biscuit, four pounds of beef, two pounds of pork, "two pints of pease", three pints of oatmeal, six ounces of butter, three-quarters of a pound of cheese, and half a pint of vinegar. On shore the rations of meat were to be increased, flour or bread allowed,[30] and clothing, valued at £2 19s. 6d. for each convict annually, provided.[31]

A military garrison, for the defence of the settlement and for enforcing "due subordination", was appointed and 160 private marines were detailed for the purpose, and were divided among the transports to assist the crews in maintaining order. It was ordered that the owners and masters should be responsible for

the safe custody of the convicts and the ships were fitted up for this purpose, having "thick bulkheads filled with nails run across from side to side 'tween decks", with loopholes for muskets in case of disturbances. Hatches were strongly secured, and structural arrangements were made for sentry controls in order to prevent intercourse between convicts and seamen.[32] The responsibility thrown upon the contractors was not relished by them, particularly when Phillip took a hand in demanding that the essential arrangements should be carried out. When Sir Charles Middleton was requested to forward official complaints to the contractors that the female convicts were to be placed on a ship by themselves and that the owners of the chartered vessels were bound by law to sign contracts for the safe custody of the convicts, he felt compelled to speak in defence of the contractors. In the existing transportation system of negro slaves from Africa to the West Indies, he said, both sexes were confined in separate compartments on the same vessels, hence he saw no reason why the same practice should not apply to the convicts. Moreover, the new system held out only small inducements to the contractors, who now had no pecuniary interest in their freights other than the mere transport and victualling charges, whereas formerly they had enjoyed a profit by sale of their cargoes.[33] Nevertheless, the contractors were held to their responsibilities for the security of the convicts.

Arrangements for assembling and victualling the fleet were quickly put in hand. On October 24, 1786, twelve days after receiving his commission, Governor Phillip hoisted his flag on the *Sirius* at Deptford. On December 6, the Order in Council proclaiming New South Wales as the site of the new penal settlement was made. On the first day of the new year, Evan Nepean stated that convicts, already selected, should be removed from the hulks to the transport *Alexander*, and on January 3, Duncan Campbell, the Superintendent of the Hulks at Woolwich, received a warrant to allow transportation to begin by handing over the selected convicts, under bond to the contractor and the master of the ship to which they had been allotted.[34] Eight days later Phillip had to warn Nepean that fatal consequences would follow if the convicts, already crowded into one of the transports, were to be kept under such conditions for months pending the departure of the ship.[35]

In his *Journal*, White, the Surgeon-General, described the early embarkations in the *Charlotte* and *Friendship* transports at Plymouth. On March 9 the marines were embarked on these ships, and on March 11 the convicts were removed from the prison-ship to the transports, "all secured in irons, except the women". The transports sailed for Spithead, where they arrived on March 17,

joining "the rest of the transports and victuallers intended for the same expedition".[36] The other convicts had been embarked at Portsmouth and Woolwich, and the whole fleet lay at the Mother Bank off the Isle of Wight until the date of sailing, May 13.[37]

Looking at the arrangements made for the establishment of this new settlement one may find instances of ingenuity and carefulness. The machinery provided for government, though crude, attempted to be comprehensive. A variety of eventualities possible in an unprecedented settlement were provided for; others were left in abeyance, and perhaps, wisely so, until the Governor might be able to report on conditions in a country of which everyone was completely ignorant. As it was intended to be primarily a penal settlement, it might be expected that the Government would have been explicit and comprehensive concerning convict management, but in all the provisions made for the control of the territory the penal aspect figures least. The definition of Phillip's power and responsibilities in this respect occupy only a few lines in many pages. He was to receive from the contractors ownership in the services of the convicts on their arrival in the colony; after a legal process the convicts and others might be punished for offences committed in the colony; the convicts were to be set to public works; he might emancipate and discharge from servitude any convicts whose good conduct would make them deserving of favour. To these he was instructed to make free grants of land, and assist them by family endowments of provisions, tools, seed and stock for twelve months. In general terms he was empowered to appoint justices, constables "and other necessary officers . . . for putting the law into execution". These were the sum total of all penal provisions made up to the date of departure, and some of them, particularly the power of emancipation, were the results of Phillip's own suggestions.[38] The problem of convict management was left absolutely to the Governor, and although in the course of time customs, approved or disapproved in England, tended to regulate the disposal and discipline of convicts, no comprehensive set of instructions was issued by the Home Government for standardizing convict control until 1842, when Lord Stanley compiled a system for the direction of convicts in Van Diemen's Land. In these circumstances it was fortunate that the first Governor was a man whose appreciation of the responsibilities and the difficulties connected with the experiment was greater than that entertained by the Government that employed him.

(b) Equipping the Fleet

From October 1786 to May 1787 Phillip was prevented from joining his fleet and was occupied in arranging the details necessary

for the equipment of the fleet, the welfare of the garrison to accompany it, and the government of the new settlement. The most interesting document in all the mass of papers connected with the foundation of the colony is the one in which Phillip expressed his own views on the subject and specified the problems he would have to meet. He would have preferred to land at the settlement three months before his fleet, so that huts might be built to accommodate the sick, and vegetables be available to counteract the scurvy which would be sure to break out on so long a voyage. He suggested that the transports should travel directly, without stopping at ports for supplies, so that the convicts might be set on land as quickly as possible in view of diseases. Moreover, lists of convicts, specifying ages, crimes, characters and trades, should be sent, so as to allow a proper separation of the less evil from the villainous criminals. (In this suggestion he struck on the basic principle of reform, but governments failed to appreciate this obvious provision throughout the whole régime.) The women on board the transports should be classified in this way and kept from interference by the crews. Realizing that fevers would most certainly occur in crowded conditions among people deprived of exercise, he asked that hospitals should be provided. He determined to see that no venereal cases were embarked, to inspect the ships personally while at sea to see that cleanliness was observed and that the rations were fairly distributed, and to inform the convicts that he would reward their good conduct. He also attempted to formulate a plan for the guidance of his conduct at the settlement. He would keep the worse women apart from the rest of the convicts, but allow the better ones to associate with the men in view of marriage, which he would encourage by concessions. The provision for introducing women from the Islands might be adopted, he thought; but to his credit it must be said that he did not allow that provision to be executed. He would protect the aborigines and punish with the utmost rigour any convict who abused a native woman. Rewarding and punishing the convicts would be in the governor's control, but death would never be necessary, for he thought that the fear of death never yet prevented a man of no principle from committing a crime. Over a wide range of topics he foresaw difficulties and determined to submit them for government decision. How would he clothe the convicts when the need arose? he asked himself—a question which a few years later Governor Hunter had to repeat when the convicts were forced to work naked in the fields. Two striking excerpts from Phillip's list of suggestions and resolutions may be quoted in full. They show that he wanted to found a colony rather than a gaol, and that, if a gaol had to be, it was not to entail assignment of convict labour such as had existed

in America. "As I would not wish convicts to lay the foundations of an empire," he wrote, "I think they should ever remain separated from the garrison and other settlers that may come from Europe, and not be allowed to mix with them, even after the 7 or 14 years for which they are transported may be expired." The laws of England would be introduced into the new settlement, but "there is one that I would wish to take the place from the moment his Majesty's forces take possession of the country: That there can be no slavery in a free land, and consequently no slaves."[39]

For months he pursued the authorities with complaints and demands. On January 4 he foresaw the difficulty that would most perplex him and his successors in the settlement. Where would he obtain and how would he pay people to superintend the convicts in their various labours? They could not be taken from the garrison and no provision had been made for these necessary officials.[40] The matter was not decided despite its urgency, and the unsatisfactory system of setting convict overseers to control their fellows had to be resorted to. On January 11 he had to report that the 184 men already on board the *Alexander* more than crowded a ship intended for 210 convicts; in such insanitary conditions sickness must arise, particularly as there were several men on board who were "unable to help themselves". He had to ask that surgeons' instruments should be supplied for every ship,[41] that the convicts confined in the transports should be allowed fresh meat and vegetables prior to their departure,[42] and had to insist again when the contractors failed to comply.[43] He asked that the allotment of 16 lbs. of bread for each convict over a period of six weeks should be increased,[44] and that the marines, upon whose health the success of the expedition depended, should be made an allowance of flour in place of a portion of the salt meat provisions, so as to prevent illness on so unprecedented a journey; but as the request necessitated the alteration of an age-old naval custom it was opposed. Phillip was indignant and sent a protest to Lord Sydney "to prevent my character as an officer from being called in question", should the consequences which he feared be realized. The contracts for victualling the convicts and the garrison had been made before he had been appointed, he wrote, and though he had no power to interfere he had not ceased from exposing the dangers to which men, crowded together in such numbers on small ships, were subjected. The economies exacted and particularly the refusal to place anti-scorbutics on board, must lead to fatal consequences. He charged the Home Office with equipping this fleet, destined for "the extremity of the globe", as if it were destined for a six weeks' passage to America. He foresaw the loss of half his garrison, but

though he was prepared to meet all difficulties, he shrank from the inevitable public criticism that might later charge him with having assumed control of an expedition, knowing full well that he would lose half his full complement of garrison and convicts because of crowded and insanitary conditions. The public, being ignorant of the fact that he had never been consulted in the equipment, and that he had disapproved of the arrangements, would blame him. Hence, he wrote to clear himself of responsibility and begged Sydney to produce his letter should this defence later become necessary.[45]

In a series of letters written during this period of preparation Phillip stated that among the convicts embarked on the *Alexander* transport during the past two months one man in every six had to be sent to hospital. [46] A few weeks later he urged the Navy Board to send lighters to Spithead to take off the convicts temporarily so that the transports might be fumigated. Once again he repeated his request for anti-scorbutic supplies, and stated that if the convicts' welfare had to be put out of the question, the predicament of the marines, at least, called for care. They were being sent "in a worse state than ever troops were sent out of the Kingdom". He proposed that the *Friendship* transport might be used as a hospital ship. He had taken it upon himself to order clothing for the convicts embarked at Plymouth, but as other convicts were due to be sent on board he asked that they should be clothed and washed so as not to contaminate those he had already provided for. "The situation in which the magistrates sent the women" convicts on board the *Lady Penrhyn* "stamps them with infamy", Phillip boldly declared. Almost naked, and filthy, fever came upon them before clothing could be got to prevent their perishing, and veneral diseases were also prevalent. He foresaw the spreading of these illnesses despite his precautions, particularly as several of the women were pregnant. If the one surgeon on it died, a hundred women would be left without aid. "Let me repeat my desire", he wrote, "that orders may be given to increase the convicts' allowances of bread". His complaints, he said, were not to be regarded as unexpected; he had foreseen them from the beginning and pointed them out to the department, when they could easily have been remedied at little expense. Even now they might be redressed "and the intentions of the Government by this expedition answered". If Government persisted in its neglect it might expect to hear that the marines would desert the infected ships or the ships might be refused entry into a foreign port.[47] The official reply was addressed by Evan Nepean to Sir Charles Middleton on April 18, stating that Phillip's complaints about deficient clothing were to be remedied and that the wives and children of the marines were to have better food

allowances. Nepean apologized for having to worry Middleton about this business which had caused them all much perplexity, but he hoped he would not have to write again as "Phillip will probably get away on Saturday".[48] Middleton's reply to Sydney claimed that the convicts' allowances were ample, particularly suitable for people who were prevented from taking exercise, and much preferable to the prison allowance of bread and water. It was then too late to alter the contracts, and delay would not only necessitate expense but also incur further risks to the health of the prisoners. However, even at this late date, fresh food was sent to the convicts and Phillip was empowered to supply flour to those on board his fleet.[49]

It is possible that Phillip, realizing the great responsibility of so many lives on so perilous a voyage, exaggerated the sickness of the convicts on board the transports. The two contemporary journals written by Tench and White might at first sight indicate that Phillip's anxieties were not founded in fact. In a brief reference to the period of waiting, March to May, Tench wrote that but for a slight contagion in one of the transports the convicts were "universally healthy" and uncomplaining. "I should feel myself wanting in justice to those unfortunate men, were I not to bear this public testimony of the sobriety and decency of their conduct". The soldiers and convicts "were indiscriminately supplied with fresh beef", he wrote. Tench, however, was only indirectly concerned with the health of convicts and his narrative at this point is very cursory.[50] John White, as the principal surgeon, must be regarded as more authoritative. In his *Journal* he noted with some acerbity how a medical gentleman had demanded the landing of convicts suffering from "malignant" diseases at the end of March on board the *Alexander*.* The assistant-surgeon, Balmain, ridiculed the malignancy of the diseases, and on inspection White upheld his view. However, he found the convicts depressed, weak from long imprisonment and wretchedly clothed in bitterly cold weather. For four months they had lived on salt beef and had been imprisoned below decks. He immediately arranged for them to have access to purer air, and wrote to Phillip urging him to have fresh meat supplied to all, and a little wine to the sick, in order to prevent their commencing so long a journey "with a scorbutic taint", which would possibly prove fatal to many on the journey. By return post he received the necessary authority to do this, and learned that long before his application a similar permission had been given but had not been acted upon. He also took precautions for disinfecting the ships, and within a fortnight an improvement in health was

* Sixteen men died on the *Alexander* between embarkation in January and the sailing of the fleet in May. (See Appendix B.)

noticeable. White's *Journal* merely emphasizes the personal care taken by Phillip in the preparation of the fleet and shows that the failure to provide fittingly for the health of the convicts was due, not so much to the Government, as to the delay and economies of officials and contractors to whom those tasks had been assigned. White remarked on the public apprehension of disease among the convicts: "the newspapers were daily filled with alarming accounts of the fatality that prevailed among us". But, because of the precautions demanded by Phillip and White the health of the convicts was considerably improved by the time the fleet was due to sail.[51]

In the course of his letters Phillip had suggested among other things that he should be allowed to establish the settlement in whatever part would best suit its purpose.[52] He had doubts about Banks's favourable description of Botany Bay.[53] In Lord Sydney's reply he was given permission to make the settlement at any place convenient to Botany Bay, but he was not to delay on arrival there "under the pretence of searching after a more eligible place". He was empowered to suspend and appoint officers; the victualling contracts, it was stated, had been already made and any further necessary supplies for the voyage would be obtained by the contractor. If disease were to break out the infected should be quarantined, but if the epidemic became widespread Phillip might convert a transport into a hospital ship. For founding the new colony he would be paid £1000 a year.[54]

Phillip's departure had been long delayed, due to his own exactions and to other causes, one of which, it was suggested, was the impending second trial of Lord George Gordon, some of whose followers had been sentenced to transportation.[55] He was prevented from sailing when he expected because the ships were short of water and provisions; on 11 May he grudgingly approved of the quality of bread supplied but was obliged to begin the first stage of his journey without an adequate supply of women's clothing.[56]

It is difficult to determine the number of convicts on board the First Fleet, as contemporary sources give different totals. According to calculations made in Appendices B and C in this book, it seems that 778 were embarked in England in 1787. Of these 586 were men and 192 were women. Among them were fifty-two people who were incapacitated through old age or infirmity. Thirteen children of convicts sailed. The number of free people is usually estimated at 695, comprising 252 officials, marines and officers with their wives and children, 210 seamen of the Navy and 233 merchant seamen.[57]

(c) The Voyage

On May 13, 1787, the fleet passed the Needles. The experiment had begun—for good or evil. Some saw in it a veritable colonizing enterprise. Officialdom felt satisfaction that the gaols would be relieved by this and future transportations which Phillip had been warned to expect. A contemporary caricature expressed another side of public opinion: instead of convicts the Prince of Wales, Burke, North, Fox, Sheridan, the Duke of Portland, and others, were depicted as leaving for Botany Bay, while Mrs Fitzherbert and two Jewish money-lenders remained disconsolately on the shore.*

The voyage has been described by several who took part in it. Generally speaking, it was uneventful; conscientious care and supervision by those in charge ensured discipline and checked the illnesses and epidemics natural to such crowded conditions. On board it was found that, without any evident signs of implements experienced prisoners were able to make counterfeit coins from buttons and other materials; the fatalities were few, accidental and inevitable; at least six births occurred on the voyage. Morality was enforced under strict supervision, one private of the marines being punished by 100 lashes for immoral intercourse with a convict woman, and another member of the marines being sentenced more severely for conniving at such conduct. First the fleet went to Teneriffe, arriving there on June 3, in order to get supplies of fresh vegetables and meat, which were liberally distributed to all classes on board. Phillip then reported that the convicts had improved considerably in health, although eighty-one were still sick, but among these there were ten venereal cases, thirty suffering from debility and two from dropsy. Here at Santa Cruz Phillip had his first chance of inspecting the convicts over whom he had been placed in control. A conspiracy to seize the ships had been easily checked and two of the leaders punished, but in general, he reported, they had behaved well, and were "quiet and contented, though there are among them some compleat villains".[58] The journey to Rio de Janeiro was unavoidably uncomfortable in tropic heats, the women suffering most because they had to be locked up at night. On August 4 they reached Rio and Phillip was able to report that he had increased the food rations allowed to convicts and that all were liberally supplied with meat and vegetables. But the clothing given to the women, being of defective quality, had fallen to pieces in a few weeks; as an expedient Phillip proposed using sacking to provide clothing for the convicts, "many of whom are nearly naked". The total deaths since leaving England now numbered fifteen; there were eighty-one sick, among whom was

* Cf. Frontispiece to this Volume.

one case of cholera.[59] From Rio the fleet sailed to the Cape of Good Hope—an extraordinary route, but adopted in order to avoid the calms on the African coast.[60] Leaving Rio on 4 September the fleet reached Table Bay on 13 October, and remained there for a month. Phillip experienced difficulty in obtaining provisions, but was able to give fresh bread and 1½ lbs. of fresh meat to each convict daily. The number of sick on arrival was twenty marines and ninety-three convicts. In his *Journal* Surgeon Bowes recorded that on the day after arrival a convict woman aged eighty died.[61] Plants, seeds, provisions, horses, cattle and sheep were taken on board, and after Phillip had transferred himself to a faster vessel which he hoped would bring him to New Holland in time to make necessary preparations, the fleet set sail on 13 November on the last stage of its journey. On 18 January 1788, the forward party arrived and on the 20th the entire fleet was anchored in Botany Bay.

This remarkable feat of seamanship, in which 15,063 miles were covered, occupied eight months and one week and was accomplished on a fleet of miserable vessels the total tonnage of which was less than 4000 tons. In every journal connected with the fleet the most evident satisfaction was expressed on the happy conclusion of the venture. The voyage had been such as the mind dared hardly contemplate, wrote David Collins: on a journey over "an imperfectly explored sea", conveying a large body of convicts crowded together, many of whom were sick on leaving, the total deaths among more than 1400 people had been only thirty-two, two of which had occurred by accident. Collins remarked that the small number of deaths in such circumstances was all the more surprising as it had been feared, before leaving England, that sickness would have necessitated the conversion of one ship into a hospital. He attributed this pleasing result to the liberal supplies of fresh food that had been obtained at the ports of call, and to the quality of the provisions which had eventually been supplied in England.[62] Captain Tench, however, was more critical of the provisions made by the Government for this hazardous journey. "I wish I could answer to the liberal manner in which Government supplied the expedition", he wrote; but "some of the necessary articles allowed to ships on a common voyage to the West Indies were withheld from us", and the only anti-scorbutic supplied had been "an inadequate quantity of essence of malt". The risks taken had been enormous, for the people sent in these ships were not a healthy race, but "the major part a miserable set of convicts emaciated from confinement" and lacking clothing. Nevertheless, he, too, stated that the provisions which were served on board had been "of a much superior quality than those usually supplied by contract".[63] Sir Joseph Banks

F

attributed the success of the voyage to Phillip's supervision. When Banks later wrote in praise of Phillip he had before him the frightful statistics of mortality and disease that occurred on the Second Fleet and remarked that although the Government was always willing to bear the necessary expense, it was not always able to find proper people to command its convict transports.[64]

It did not take Phillip long to prove the inaccuracy of the English opinions expressed about Botany Bay; the ground was low and unfertile, "there was a small run of water there, but it appeared to be only a drain from a marsh". On January 22 he set off to examine Port Jackson, which had been named by Captain Cook in 1770 without entering it, and having found a site suitable for his purpose, called it Sydney Cove. On January 24 he returned to Botany Bay. Leaving behind him the two French vessels which, under the command of La Pérouse, had just arrived at Botany Bay, Phillip returned again to Sydney on January 25. On January 26 the transports followed him into Port Jackson, and on that day a party was landed and the British flag unfurled.

THE FOUNDATION OF THE PENAL SETTLEMENT

(a) General Survey

PHILLIP had fortunately selected a site which was advantageously situated for maritime communications and commerce. Port Jackson, he wrote, was "the finest harbour in the world, in which a thousand sail of the line may ride in the most perfect security",[1] but the barren mountains thirty miles west of the sea hemmed in the colony to a narrow strip of unsatisfactory farming land which, while making an effective gaol wall, lessened the opportunities for cultivation. This barrier was not crossed until a quarter of a century later. The country was totally unexplored, covered with great trees, to remove which was a labour as formidable as it was necessary, devoid of animals fit for food, domestication or transport, and sparsely inhabited by tribes of aborigines, treacherous, primitive and absolutely unacquainted with any form of agriculture or housing construction. Phillip's resources on arrival were meagre and his responsibilities overwhelming. "The settlement will be amply supplied with vegetable production and most likely with fish", he had been told in England. He had been ordered to commence agriculture immediately. It was expected that he could maintain the convicts and the military on a portion of the crops and animal progeny to be raised in the settlement, and he was warned to conserve the remainder of the stores "as a provision for further numbers of convicts who will shortly follow". He had what were supposed to be provisions sufficient for two years,* but the numbers of the surviving breeding stock were small, much of the seed had been ruined in transit, and the agricultural tools, which, incidentally, did not include a plough, were "the worst that ever were seen". Such were the material resources with which Phillip had to commence and continue to support 1030[2] persons, including 736 convicts. Many of these were "helpless and a deadweight on the settlement", most of them were idle and unwilling to work, scarcely

---

* The stores brought out comprised among other items: clothing valued at £4939; "victualling and providing for convicts and marines for two years, £16,205" (approximately £8 per head per annum); wine, essence of malt, etc., £381; tools, etc., £3056; medicines and surgical equipment, £1429; seed grain, £286; "old canvas supplied from Portsmouth dockyard for tents for convicts until huts can be erected, £69". The total value of stores brought out for use in the colony was stated to be £29,548. (Cf. *P.P.*: 1731-1800, Accounts & Papers, XXXIV (1790-91), No. 740, 8.iv.1791.)

any of them were experienced in farming or shepherding, and few of them had been trained as carpenters, brickmakers or smiths. The useful convicts had been retained in England. The bulk of the official population was equally unsatisfactory, contributing little to the development of the settlement, but depending on it for subsistence and refusing to co-operate in solving the most pressing problems faced by the Governor. The original plan had envisaged a community dependent on a central commissariat store for a brief period. When the crops failed and provisions did not arrive from England, the helplessness of the people intensified the attitude of dependence on government support to which the criminal classes and the military guards were naturally prone. On the general principle that neither criminals nor warders can make a positive contribution to the economy of production and exchange, Professor Shann has remarked that this policy of government support, necessary though it was, "confirmed in economic childishness that first company of marines and convicts".[3] These two classes constituted the population of Phillip's settlement.

In addition Phillip had a small civil staff to assist in administration. Without advisers, and being in most instances the court of appeal, the Governor was burdened with personal responsibilities. His Commissions and Instructions defined and limited his jurisdiction only in general terms, leaving much to his own discretion. He regulated rations, labour, grants of land, hours and conditions of employment, mustered the population, transferred the convict part of it to other settlements, convoked the courts and modified judicial sentences. Adopting the method of governing by the frequent promulgation of public orders Phillip acted as both legislature and executive. This procedure was continued for several years without challenge, during which there accumulated a series of regulations which were not collected and printed until 1801. Commenting on the fact that disobedience to the governors' regulations in the later years had in some instances been punishable by fine of £100 or by 500 lashes, the Select Parliamentary Committee of 1812 observed that this concentration of power within the hands of an individual was open to abuse and that it would naturally be resented by men who had been unused to such methods in England.[4] The subsequent history of this autocratic procedure, which in the beginning Phillip was compelled to adopt because oi the deficiencies in the machinery of government, necessitated in 1819 a validating Act of Parliament.[5]

The authorities in England never appreciated the peculiar circumstances of the settlement which they had called into being. It would have been quite possible for a colony of free men to develop its own institutions and gather its own equipment by a

gradual process extending over years. This had happened in America. To accommodate and control hundreds of prisoners, however, a specially prepared and planned organization was necessary. In Australia there was no system except such as Phillip devised and altered to meet changing conditions. Looking back over the many years through which this lackadaisical attitude prevailed, Earl Grey said that the failure of the transportation system was due to the mistakes made in the earliest years. "Too much economy" and insufficient preparations for so sudden and large a foundation necessitated subsequently a lavish and unavailing expenditure.[6]

(b) The First Years, 1788-1790

After having approved the Port Jackson site Phillip returned from Botany Bay on 25 January 1788, and on the following day cleared sufficient land for the first camp at a deep-water cove into which a freshwater stream flowed. He named the place Sydney as a compliment to the Home Secretary. In the evening the convoy arrived, and on the following day the disembarkation of the male convicts commenced. During the next few days the convicts were employed in the preliminary works of such a settlement, closely guarded by the soldiers within defined limits of territory, which a Provost-Marshal, appointed by Phillip, patrolled. Despite the precautions a few convicts escaped with the intention of being received by the French on board their fleet at Botany Bay; but La Pérouse refused to take them. On February 6 the female convicts were landed, "many of them well dressed", and that night there followed "a scene of debauchery and riot" that "may be better conceived than expressed".[7] On board ship the sexes had been rigorously kept apart, but on land it was found impossible to restrain not only the criminal population, but also the merchant-seamen of the vessels.

On February 7 the whole population was assembled to hear the reading of the Governor's Commissions and to witness the formal ceremony of taking possession of the country, which had been privately anticipated on January 26. The Governor addressed the convicts in firm but hopeful language. From what he had seen of them he was convinced that a great number of them were incorrigible and deserving of the utmost severity. On shore they had proved an idle lot, not more than 200 out of 600 occupying themselves at work, and several of them wandering around the country. He made it clear that the food problem of this settlement differed from that of England. The lives of more than a thousand people depended on the conservation of food and the co-operation

of all in industry. Even in England to steal a fowl was punishable by death; in this colony, where seed and stock were needed for breeding purposes, there was special justification for regarding theft as a crime against the community. Immorality would be punished with the utmost rigour, and anyone attempting to enter a female convict's tent at night was liable to be shot by the sentry. Phillip realized the severity of the intended discipline, and made it clear that he would execute the law without favour to anyone. They would be expected to work, but not so hard as the average English farmer had to work to support a wife and family. Everyone would be asked to contribute his share to the common welfare, and those who refused to work need not expect to be fed. As soon as the stores and military quarters were built they would be allowed to erect houses for themselves.[8] He further emphasized that co-operation and good conduct would be recognized and marriage encouraged.[9] Phillip's disposition to regard marriage as a means of public control was marked particularly in his instructions to the women convicts whom he sent to Norfolk Island at that time, recommending them to choose their partners among the convicts destined for that place, to whom they could be married immediately.[10]

Exclusive of thirteen men who were later drafted from the crews of the fleet into the service of the settlement, the total population was 1030. There were 736 convicts—548 men and 188 women—and seventeen children of convicts. In addition there were 211 marines and officers, with twenty-seven of their wives and nineteen children, Phillip and his staff of nine, the chaplain and his wife, five members of the medical staff and two servants.[11]

To comply with his Instructions and to begin a settlement which might relieve the pressure on Sydney, Phillip issued to Philip Gidley King, on February 12, a Commission as Commandant of Norfolk Island. King was instructed to settle that island, to study its natural resources and to commence the cultivation of flax, cotton and corn. In command of a party of twenty-three persons, including nine male and six female convicts, King sailed for the island on February 14.[12] He took with him provisions for six months.

Phillip was now faced with the task of forming a settlement. Of the 736 convicts landed at Sydney, he had 721 to accommodate and render profitable. But scurvy appeared among them and the ships' crews soon after landing, and in May was raging "in a most extraordinary manner". The sick were accommodated in tents, and to obtain anti-scorbutics seeds were sown, which withered soon after germination. The numbers of sick so increased that a spot for a hospital was chosen and the building of it was commenced as soon as possible.[13] Meanwhile efforts were concentrated on clear-

ing land for government farming and building storehouses to accommodate the stores on board the ships, two of which were freed in March. It was a higgledy-piggledy town of tents and frame huts, slowly taking on the rough semblance of order, from which storehouses, quarters for the civil staff, and barracks for the marines were the first to emerge. In the work of building and farming Phillip was handicapped by the lack of craftsmen. There were only twelve carpenters among more than 500 male convicts, and only sixteen craftsmen were temporarily available from the ships.[14] Moreover, death, sickness and physical unfitness were proving serious burdens on the settlement. Six months after landing it was reported that twenty-eight convicts and eight of their children had died in the settlement, and the total of convicts under medical treatment was sixty-six. In another category were fifty-two, whom White described as "unfit for labour from old age and infirmities"[15] and Phillip regarded as a "burthen" on the community. It was natural, therefore, that Phillip should express the hope that further batches of convicts should be delayed, and if sent, that they should include "carpenters, masons, bricklayers or farmers, who can support themselves and assist in supporting others".[16] By July order was fairly well established. The hospital, two storehouses and an observatory were complete, but the marines and convicts were still encamped. Most of the male convicts had been employed on public work, but others had been handed over to the officers to assist in clearing the ground for private enterprise. Phillip regarded the assignment of convict labour to private individuals as essential for the expansion of the colony, and on the departure of the first ships sailing for England, asked for directions concerning this practice, which was destined to become an essential part of the penal régime.[17] From the women convicts servants had been drawn for the civil and military staffs, but generally speaking, the women "lived in a state of total idleness, except a few who are kept at work in making pegs for tiles and picking up shells for burning into lime".[18]

The convicts, although under severe discipline, were well treated. Working under supervision, road-making, farming or building, they were indulged by being exempted from labour every Saturday afternoon and Sunday. On Sundays they were mustered for divine service, which was performed in one of the storehouses or under a tree.[19] The weekly rations for each consisted of 7 lbs. of bread, or 7 lbs. of flour, 7 lbs. of beef, or 4 lbs. of pork, "three pints of pease", 6 ozs. of butter, and ½ lb. of rice.[20] Women received two-thirds of this ration. Commenting on the mortality that had taken place in the first half-year of the settlement, Tench emphatically denied that scarcity of food or excessive toil could be regarded as a

cause. The convicts received the same food allowances as every soldier and officer in the garrison.[21]

The chief difficulty experienced by Phillip was the supervision of the convicts. He had hoped that the military garrison, three companies of Royal Marine Light Infantry commanded by Major Robert Ross, would co-operate in this work, and had foreseen the dangers of insufficient policing, but the matter had been left in abeyance in England. Although it had been arranged that the military garrisons would be relieved in three years, when the non-commissioned officers and privates would be discharged in England or be allowed to settle permanently in Australia, the military felt aggrieved with their situation in the settlement. Major Ross resented the way in which the Governor concentrated power within his own hands and felt that his Lieutenant-Governorship was a sinecure; but the most general grievance lay in the fact that, while Phillip's Instructions provided for the granting of land to emancipated convicts, land-grants were not contemplated for the soldiers. From the commencement the military insisted on confining their activities to garrison work, leaving Phillip in the awkward position of policing the convicts and settlement with convict overseers and watchmen. Phillip frequently represented the unsatisfactoriness of this situation to his superiors in England. The officers, he said, were few in number, but most of them declined any interference with the convicts "except when they are employed for their own particular service". All he had asked them to do was to encourage the worthy prisoners and to take notice of the idle, but even this they refused to do, saying that "they were not sent out to do more than the duty of soldiers". The consequences of this action, Phillip observed, were obvious. The convict overseers, fearing to exert their authority, were unable to compel the convicts to work satisfactorily "in a country which required the greatest exertions". Collins and Tench both regarded this situation as undermining discipline and reform. It was much to be regretted, wrote Collins, that the necessity arose to use convicts to fill the position of overseers and watchmen. In too many instances the trust placed in them was abused, though the choice was confined only to those with the best testimonials and those best fitted to instruct the convicts in their various occupations. In some instances, however, the new responsibility inclined them to honest industry.[23] Tench declared that within the first six months the imperfect plan had shown signs of defeating the purpose for which the prisoners had been sent out.[24] Phillip asked that men should be specially appointed for the position of overseers, and a few men, experienced in trades and farming, were sent out, but the anomalous system of setting convicts to maintain discipline among their peers continued indefinitely.

The conflict with the military was early evidenced in the execution and administration of justice also. They regarded themselves free from any but military discipline,[25] and refused to be interested in the administration of justice. It had been provided that the criminal courts should be presided over by the judge-advocate and six officers chosen by rote from the garrison. Pleading ignorance of this provision before leaving England, several officers were strongly disinclined to act on the criminal bench, regarding the office as a hardship and outside the duty for which they were paid. Disgruntled officers described the Governor's compelling them to act in this capacity as oppressive. Phillip, however, in reporting the occurrence, suggested that all future appointees should be warned that "a young colony requires something more from officers than garrison duty", and presuming that an additional force would be sent to the colony, suggested that grants of land should be made to the military in order to satisfy their grievances.[26] In answer to these complaints Grenville wrote in 1791, deprecating "arbitrary behaviour which was ill-calculated to promote the good understanding so essentially necessary for securing the prosperity of the colony". Instructions were issued that where conduct was not defined "all persons in the settlement should accommodate themselves to the circumstances and situation" and "that they must carefully avoid any nice distinctions in point of duty which might tend to occasion embarrassment in the execution of the public service".[27] The order, as so frequently happened in these years, lacked precision and a social sense was never developed among the military, who took undue advantage of their precedence in the colony and the distance from their English superiors, to further their own rather than the community's welfare. As an attempt at a solution of the military problem in the settlement, it was decided to replace the discontented marines by a body of troops raised specially to act as a garrison. This was the New South Wales Corps, which arrived in Sydney in 1790 and 1792. A miscellaneous collection of officers, flotsam and jetsam from many regiments, and of privates whose past history in several cases would not bear too close an examination, the corps merely accentuated for twenty years the unfortunate precedent which the earlier garrison had established in the beginning of the settlement.

The judicial system was defective in many respects, and was not amended until 1814. Presided over by a judge advocate quite inexperienced in legal matters, and associated with six equally inexperienced officers, the court could hear evidence and sentence a prisoner in only two ways, death or corporal punishment, though sentences of confinement were in fact imposed.[28] The death sentence, however, could not be executed without the governor's consent,

and when the verdict rested on a majority of one, the capital sentence had to be confirmed in England. "No convict during the time of his servitude could sue or be sued in these courts, or suffer imprisonment for any debt incurred by him";[29] a convict, however, could apply for redress of his own grievances to a magistrate. Such makeshift gaols as were erected were for the temporary accommodation of prisoners arrested for crimes committed within the colony, whose sentences were quickly executed. Petty offences were tried before a magistrates' bench; Collins tells how Captain Hunter had been sworn in as a magistrate soon after the arrival of the fleet, and with the Judge-Advocate and the Surveyor-General determined minor cases once a week.

Punishments during Phillip's term of office were severe, but, in view of the necessity for enforcing order in such a community, and particularly because individual thefts of provisions jeopardized the lives of a thousand people who were dependent on rationing, no other course lay open to the Governor. It should be noticed also that the severity of which Phillip was accused was exercised towards soldiers and convicts impartially. Within a few days of landing, on February 11, Phillip was compelled to assemble the criminal court. Three prisoners were found guilty—for assault one received 150 lashes; another for stealing a convict's rations was ordered to be confined for a week on a small rocky island in the harbour, which subsequently became known as "Pinchgut"; and the third, sentenced to fifty lashes for stealing a plank, was pardoned. In Collins's view the leniency of these punishments had a bad effect upon the convicts, for within a month and despite the fact that the prisoners had been granted the same rations as the free men, attempts were made to rob the common stores. One of these offenders was put to death as an example against a crime "big with evil to our little community", others were pardoned on condition of being banished from the settlement, and the pardon of James Freeman was made conditional on his accepting the office of public executioner. In May a youth of seventeen suffered death for theft of goods valued at five shillings. Severity appeared to have little effect upon the prisoners, and kindness was equally unsuccessful. On the King's birthday the convicts were indulged and those confined in chains on the harbour-island were liberated: on that night, however, further depredations occurred. "Exemplary punishments seemed to be growing daily more necessary" among men "so inured to habits of vice and so callous to remonstrance that they were only restrained until a favourable opportunity presented itself". Collins explained that the prevailing disorder arose often among men who consumed their week's rations within a few days and had to steal

for the rest of the week. Much of the irregularity was due to the companionship of seamen who, in spite of Phillip's regulations to the contrary, brought intoxicating liquor to the settlement from the ships; but the chief cause was the absence of proper overseers and the abandonment of the convicts to the discipline of men selected from themselves. Nevertheless, Collins stated that in general the prisoners conducted themselves better than had been expected "from people of their description".[30]

After the first six months Phillip was better able to estimate the prospects of the settlement. In a series of letters written before the sailing of the transports in July, Phillip described the course of events and made suggestions for the future. As no indent papers had been sent with the fleet, he was at a loss to know the dates when the sentences of the convicts were due to expire, and would consequently have to detain many claimants for liberation until further particulars were received. In a later letter he adverted to the inconvenience of sending out men with only short terms to run, and recommended that the fourteen years category would be more suitable. Whatever might be decided about the sending out of convicts he was emphatic that artificers should be included among them and that overseers should be specially appointed for regulating convict labour. He was opposed to the government proposal to bring women from the islands, who would "pine away in misery", but he strongly recommended the sending out of more convict women as an "absolute necessity". However, when a shipload of females arrived later, when the settlement was starving, he and many others deprecated so useless a cargo. He had used the convict labour for the public profit, as he had been directed; but he had found the necessity to give some of this labour to the officials who had undertaken agriculture; and he strongly urged the sanctioning of this procedure in the future. Grants of land to freed convicts had been permitted in his Instructions, but he was convinced that such men would need to be supported by Government for two years, or more, at the commencement of their career as farmers. If the colony was to become self-supporting, he said, industry must be carried on by free men. In this respect fifty farmers would do more than a thousand convicts. Hence, he strongly recommended that free farmer-settlers should be encouraged to go to the colony, that they should be supported by Government for the first two or three years, and that during these years they should be afforded convict labourers who, also, would be dependent on the Government stores. After two or three years the farmers ought to be able to relieve the public funds of all expense.[31]

The ships that sailed from the settlement in July 1788 carried

letters, private and official, which must have bewildered their recipients in England. The verdict of the military was almost universally condemnatory. Major Ross, the Lieutenant-Governor, declared ther ˙ was not an officer who did not wish to return from the settlement, which could never be expected to become self-supporting and was destitute of the most usual natural resources. Phillip's autocratic control was particularly displeasing to the military, and, rather than continue to finance the penal settlement at Sydney, it would be cheaper for the Government to lodge prisoners at London taverns and to feed them on venison and turtle.[32] During the following two years letters in a similar strain were sent to England.[33] Phillip, however, took a more moderate view of the disadvantages and an optimistic view of the future. Success would depend on regulation in England and organization in Australia. Looking to the future he had made a regular plan of the settlement, in which sites were provided for various public buildings and the size of building allotments was specified along streets two hundred feet wide. Difficulties were numerous, and he presented them boldly to the Government. No country offered less assistance to its first settlers, he said, and no colony has ever been so dependent on the mother country as the penal settlement was and must continue to be for a few years. Nevertheless, he had no doubt that this "country will hereafter prove a most valuable acquisition to Great Britain", though to bring this about would require a degree of patience and perseverance which he, for his part, was prepared to give.[34] Captain Tench, also, took a reasonably optimistic view of the situation in the *Narrative* which he sent on this occasion for publication in England. He referred to the fact that at the departure of the fleet from England public opinion had been divided as to the wisdom of the venture. If his book did not help them to decide this question, he hoped it would induce adverse opinion to give a fair trial to "an experiment, no less new in its design than difficult in its solution". As a penal settlement the country was well adapted, he said, but Englishmen should convince themselves that the notions of the colony's being able to support itself were chimerical; therefore, he warned the Government that if supplies were not sent regularly "the most fatal consequences would ensue". The following months proved that his fears were not unfounded.

Until the end of the year the settlement was busily occupied. Reports had come from Norfolk Island that the land was suitable for cultivation, though heavily timbered. The chief drawback, however, was the absence of any kind of harbour; ships had to anchor on either side of the island according to the wind and to land passengers and freight in small boats over a dangerous sea.

In New South Wales it was decided to concentrate agriculture in a more fertile district, fifteen miles or so from the settlement. To this settlement Phillip gave the name of Rose Hill. A convict base was made there and the commanding officer was made a magistrate and vested with power to inflict corporal punishment on the disorderly and idle. Collins records how the convicts had to be driven to work, showing no interest in their labour, determined to subsist on the public stores, and quite oblivious of the fact that they were part of a community on whose united efforts in agriculture starvation or affluence depended. Convict behaviour in general was perfunctory, though violent disorder was not common. One convict, Daley, who had ingeniously hoaxed the community into believing that he had discovered gold in the settlement, was subsequently hanged for burglary, and an unfortunate wretch was sentenced to 500 lashes for stealing soap valued at eightpence from another prisoner.[35] To stop the prevalent practice of selling their clothes, orders were issued proclaiming that the receivers of these goods must return them and forfeit the money paid in the transaction. Another order proclaimed that stragglers at night would be fired upon by the guard. But, as Collins remarked, the population, having never been trained to an observance of written laws, disregarded any but oral injunctions, pleaded ignorance of the regulations or believed that orders had only a momentary significance.

Soon the spectre of famine began to appear in the settlement. Crops had failed, the last of the transports had left for England and the colony realized that only the limited stores and the promise of future supplies from England stood between them and starvation. The writings of the period now became tinged with a note of expectancy and men were described scanning the seas for a sail and trying to conceal well-grounded fear. In October Phillip took the precaution of sending the *Sirius* to the Cape of Good Hope, stripping her of guns in order to provide more space for flour and provisions, and one pound of flour was deducted from the weekly ration of the males and eleven ounces from that of the females. This special rationing system, based on a central commissariat-store, commenced at the end of 1788 and destined to continue with increasing severity until June 1790, has been aptly described as the economic last ditch, communism, but it sufficed to hold off wholesale death by famine.[36] By the end of the year sixty-two adults, including men and women convicts, were already at Norfolk Island;[37] the returns of Surgeon White state that seventy-seven convicts and twenty-seven others were then under medical treatment, and fifty-one were unable to work because of old age and disease.[38] On December 31, Collins enumerated sixty-

five deaths in the first year of the settlement, six belonging to the garrison, twenty-eight convict men, thirteen convict women and nine of their children; four had been killed by the natives, five had been executed, and fourteen had absconded or were missing.[39]

Early in the following year twenty-seven more convicts were sent to Norfolk Island, where it was learned that an insurrection among the fifty-one male and twenty-three female convicts to seize the island had been narrowly averted, and a stricter discipline was enforced under the control of the commandant, King. At the main settlement the conduct of the military occasioned much concern. Immoral practices between them and the convict women were frequent, and in their capacity as custodians of the public stores they not only showed no higher sense of the common need than the convicts themselves, but also betrayed their trust by robbery. For neglect of duty as a sentinel one soldier received 700 lashes, inflicted in two instalments within three weeks, and later six soldiers were executed for robbery of the stores. In times of such distress robbery was the worst possible crime, and convict and freeman suffered alike. In May, after an absence of seven months, the *Sirius* arrived back from the Cape with a cargo of flour, sufficient for about four months' supply and, as Tench remarked, serving merely to procrastinate the day of famine. Further explorations were made in which arable but comparatively distant land was discovered along the Hawkesbury, near Richmond, and later on, in the neighbourhood of the Nepean River.[40] Under the control of Henry Dodd, who had arrived as the Governor's servant and was described by Phillip as the only person who had any knowledge of agriculture, the settlement at Rose Hill became more orderly, allowing for the reduction of the military guard placed there, and at the end of the year produced a modest harvest of wheat, barley, oats and corn. At Port Jackson employment was concentrated on building and brick-making, and among the diversions of the populace was a play presented by the convicts on King's birthday night, in which a prologue and an epilogue facetiously depicted the social position of men who had been deported for their country's good. Nevertheless, constant supervision and severity were essential to check the criminality of soldier and convict alike. One soldier, for raping an infant, was deported to Norfolk Island. In mentioning the fact Collins unconsciously revealed the mentality of the settlement, which was exercised more in conserving food than in preserving morality. The crime, he stated, did not call for "immediate example", as it was not likely to be followed by others, for "the chastity of the female part of the settlement had never been so rigid as to drive men to so desperate an act".[41] "From the peculiarity of our

situation", wrote Collins, "there was a sort of sacredness about our store, and its preservation pure and undefiled was deemed as necessary as the chastity of Caesar's wife." Consequently, when the convicts unjustly accused the assistant-commissary of embezzlement, instead of being reprimanded they were commended for manifesting a public spirit.

The frequency of the depredations, particularly by convicts living in isolated huts at night, impelled Phillip to institute in August a night-watch composed of convicts. He issued a series of orders by which the settlement was divided into four districts, in each of which three patrols were empowered to enter huts and to arrest all suspicious persons who were found prowling after "the taptoo had beat".[42] Collins remarked on the unfortunate situation in which the Governor was placed in having to institute a police force from convict members, but as there was no section of the population between the military and the convicts from whom such a force could be drawn, there was no alternative. The military naturally resented supervision by such a body, and when on one occasion a soldier was detained for a breach of the regulations, the commanding officer, although at the time Lieutenant-Governor of the settlement, indignantly repudiated the right of convicts to interfere with the military. Such interference, he stated, was to be regarded as an insult and would not be tolerated by the military "while they had bayonets in their hands". Phillip was consequently obliged to issue an amending order excluding the military from supervision,[43] and to content himself with reporting to Lord Sydney a condition of affairs in which "every obstacle is thrown in the way of civil government" by those whose duty it was to co-operate in government.[44] Three months after its institution Collins expressed the opinion that the work of the patrol had proved beneficial in bringing to trial men who otherwise would not have been detected. Many streets in London, he said, were not so well guarded as those in the settlement. But the members of the patrol were detested as much as they were feared by the convicts, from whose ranks they had risen to a position of authority. He further observed that the decrease of the weekly rations, which were consumed within three days of being issued, had a large influence on crime conditions. This fact was appreciated, and though a further reduction in the amount issued had to be made, the rations were in future given out twice in the week. Moreover, discontent was occasioned by the fact that several of the convicts were claiming that their sentences had expired in the first two years of the settlement, and demanded their rights as freemen. Having no indent papers by which to decide their cases, the Governor compromised by ordering the Judge-Advocate to take

affidavits of these claimants, and directed them to continue working for the public until he received information from England. Though all were convinced that many among these men were suffering an injustice, the Governor must have felt that he had no other alternative pending the establishment of their claims, for when one vehement protester insultingly demanded his rights he was brought before the criminal court on a charge of insubordination and sentenced to 600 lashes and to wear irons for six months.

At the end of 1789, two years after landing, seventy-three deaths had occurred, some of which, as in the case of a woman who was insane when she arrived, were unavoidable. During 1789 only two had been executed, and twenty-five births were recorded.[45]

The year 1790 was one of the utmost despondency. Every chronicler was obsessed with fear of abandonment, preferring to believe that shipwrecks had delayed further communications from England, rather than that the Government should have risked the lives of a thousand people by forgetting their existence during the greater part of three years which had elapsed since their departure. From sunrise to sunset telescopes swept the horizon. "To say that we were disappointed and shocked", wrote Tench, "would very inadequately describe our sensations. The misery and horror of such a situation cannot be imparted, even by those who have suffered under it."[46] Phillip, who had sent urgent demands to England in seven separate despatches fifteen months previously, hoped against hope, endeavouring by repeated reductions in rations, which he attempted to compensate by greater indulgences to the convicts, to postpone the day of famine as long as possible. To Batavia, as the nearest source of supply, he decided to send the *Sirius* for food, but in order to reduce the numbers at the chief settlement, he determined first to send that ship to Norfolk Island where harvests were more hopeful and conditions less crowded. In March the small stock of the settlement was divided, part of it being put on board the *Sirius* and the *Supply*, which carried 116 males and eighty-six female convicts and one child to Norfolk Island.[47] The people on that island now numbered ninety officials and military, 191 male and 100 female convicts, and thirty-seven children. At Sydney there were 141 of the civil and military classes together with sixty of their women and children. The convict section comprised 297 male convicts, seventy female convicts and twenty-three children.[48] Immediately the rations, which had been reduced by a third in November, were reduced to one-half. Phillip remarked that on such rations he could not expect work from emaciated convicts. The weekly ration was now but four pounds of flour, two and a half pounds of pork, and one and a half pounds of rice. It was issued in one-seventh parts daily, and served to all

alike, whether free or convict. Working-hours were reduced, lasting only from sunrise to one o'clock, with an interval for breakfast, and Phillip urged the convicts to devote their afternoons to raising vegetables for themselves.

But further disaster was at hand, for the *Sirius*, after disembarking its batch of convicts on Norfolk Island, was wrecked before the provisions were landed. The population, now beyond the capacity of the island, was placed on reduced ration and martial law was proclaimed to enforce contentment under starvation. In April the *Supply* arrived back alone "with an account that was of itself almost sufficient to have deranged the strongest intellect among us", wrote Collins. Immediately, Phillip took counsel with his officers to decide on future procedure on which life more than ever depended. Martial law was proclaimed, all private stock was to be commandeered for the public benefit, and justice was to be administered by a court martial of seven officers, the concurrence of five of whom could pass sentence of death. The whole population was assembled and the new regulations proclaimed to them. The ration was further reduced to two and a half pounds of flour, two pounds of pork, one pint of pease and one pound of rice for each person during seven days. Children under eighteen months only were excepted, and to these was allowed one pound of the salt-beef which had been brought from England three years previously. The only craft that remained, the *Supply*, was fitted and sent to Batavia for supplies. On April 12, it was estimated that on the starvation ration the meat supply would last four months, rice and peas for five months and flour for eight months.[49]

Phillip set an example, surrendering flour from his own private stock and contenting himself with the ration of the populace—a fact which his contemporaries justly recorded with much gratification. Phillip's attitude was masterly. He had to hide the fact of distress from the aborigines lest they take advantage of the weakness of the people. In view of the uncertainty of oversea supplies special attention had to be paid to future agriculture, for which land was cleared and prepared. The physical condition of all was impaired and at least two deaths were recorded as direct results of the famine. Crime naturally increased in such circumstances, Phillip and the contemporary historians ascribing it equally to hunger and natural inclination. Punishment became severer in order to protect the food rights of the weaker convicts against the stronger. However, Phillip was not oblivious of good conduct, commending attempts to grow vegetables, in one case issuing a public order to remit the remainder of the sentence of John Irving, a convict who had been "bred to surgery" and appointing him as assistant to the surgeon at Norfolk Island,[50]

and in another case, presenting an ex-convict with land on which he might support himself. On April 15, 1790, he requested leave of absence in order to see his wife, who had been in a dying state when he left England three years previously. Nevertheless, he was quite willing to return to the settlement and felt confident, even in such circumstances, that disaster would be averted from the colony, even though seven-eighths of the inhabitants richly deserved to starve.[51]

On June 3 the long-awaited sail from England appeared. The chroniclers described the intense relief of the people, but in more graphic terms they recorded the deep mortification that was felt on all sides when it was found that the ship, the Lady Juliana, was a transport whose only cargo was the "unnecessary and unprofitable" one of 221 female convicts.[52] The transport had left Plymouth on July 29, 1789, with 226 women, five of whom died on the passage. It was learned that the Guardian, a faster ship which had left England in September 1789 carrying provisions, had been wrecked near the Cape after striking an iceberg. The Lady Juliana carried supplies sufficient for the women on board over a period of two years, and a third of the stock of provisions which had been transferred from the wrecked Guardian. It also brought the unwelcome news that 1000 convicts were on their way to the settlement.

It is difficult to understand why so long a delay was occasioned in England before further supplies were sent to the settlement. Provisions, estimated to be sufficient for two years after arrival, had been put on board the First Fleet. The estimate was too exact for so precarious a venture, and did not allow for the risks that were necessarily to be associated with a long sea voyage and a country whose resources were unknown. Phillip's urgent demands for supplies, sent from the settlement in May, July and November 1788, had reached England in March 1789. Sir Joseph Banks recorded the receipt of "the first news from Botany Bay, March 25, 1789". Moreover, Captain Tench's Narrative of an Expedition, in which the needs of the colony were emphasized, had appeared in April 1789 and was so widely read that it ran through three editions in that year; on May 1 The Voyage of Governor Phillip to Botany Bay was published, and excerpts from Phillip's despatches had meanwhile been printed in the newspapers.[53]

Officialdom appears to have been less concerned with the food problem in the settlement than with the riddance of more felons, for arrangements were already in hand for transporting additional convicts on the Lady Juliana. On April 29, however, the Home Office requested the Treasury, in view of Phillip's statements that provisions were being rapidly expended, to prepare a ship on

which to send out new supplies and to increase those on the transport also.[54] This was Sydney's last official act, as he retired from the Home Office on June 5. A fortnight later Grenville evidently determined to exercise economy. On June 19 he informed Phillip that the supplies forwarded to the colony corresponded to the Governor's demands except in the matter of provisions, in the use of which he recommended caution as they had cost a considerable sum. Despite the disquieting news from the settlement he continued to empty the gaols and adhered to the old illusion that the colony was soon likely to be largely self-supporting. In this strain he wrote to Buckingham on July 9, optimistically estimating the future costs of transport at only £14 per head, and stating that although "they must be victualled for some time longer . . . this expense may probably cease in a year or two at furthest."[55] However, H.M.S. *Guardian*, a fast sailing ship, was equipped and left England in September 1789—nearly two and a half years after the departure of the First Fleet.[56] As Phillip observed, the delay had retarded the colony's progress and necessitated support over a longer period than if it had been allowed to develop normally from the beginning.[57] The arrival of the *Lady Juliana* and of the *Justinian* storeship, which followed her within a fortnight, did prevent the wholesale destruction of the settlement, but even had the *Guardian* not been wrecked it would be difficult to acquit the Government of a charge of gross delay and negligence in a duty that concerned a thousand of its subjects. To leave them on the high seas or at the other end of the world, without enquiry or assistance from May 1787 to January 1790—the earliest possible date at which supplies could have arrived by the *Guardian*—was nothing less than an act of criminal negligence and quite in keeping with the moral outlook of ministers who had proposed previously to send convicts to a probably worse fate on the west coast of Africa. Various happenings in the subsequent history of the transportation system were condemned by parliamentary committees and zealous reformers, but in most of the cases it is possible to find some palliation of official policy. The perfunctoriness with which the system was commenced, however, can neither be explained nor excused, not so much because of what resulted from it, but rather because of what might have resulted.

(c) The Convicts in Transport

With renewed provisions it was possible to reorganize the settlement, and with suddenly increased numbers of convicts reorganization became a necessity. On June 20 the *Justinian* storeship arrived with stores for the whole settlement, having been

only five months on the voyage, and on the following day full rations were restored, served out weekly as hitherto, and the afternoon remission from labour was cancelled. In the following month supplies were sent to Norfolk Island to relieve the famine there, rescuing the population only a few days before absolute starvation would have occurred. Had the island not provided a plentiful supply of sea-birds their condition, wrote Collins, would have been "too distressing to be contemplated". Creditable reports of the convicts' conduct on the island throughout the famine period were recorded.[58]

On June 20 the *Surprize*, one of three transports that had sailed from England on January 19, arrived, and a few days later the *Neptune* and the *Scarborough* followed, bringing convicts and a detachment of the new military corps.

In his early despatches from the colony Phillip had recommended that the transportation of convicts might be curtailed until the colony was better able to stand on its feet, though he was anxious that skilled prisoners, farmers and artificers, and also females, should be sent. His request for skilled men was heeded only to the extent of sending out twenty-five artificers on the *Guardian*, and his suggestion for limiting the numbers was absolutely ignored, the Government resolving to equip a great fleet on which all convicts sentenced to transportation or respited were to be sent away "in order that his Majesty's gaols in this Kingdom may be at once cleared".[59] His demand for female convicts was acceded to with embarrassing prodigality. An attempt was made to induce the convicts to take their wives with them, "or even women that cohabited with them"; but despite tempting inducements very few of these women, wrote Grenville in 1789, accepted the proposal.[60] Nevertheless, 226 female convicts were sent immediately by the *Lady Juliana* to promote matrimony among the bachelors of the settlement. This transport arrived at Sydney on June 3, 1790, and only five had died in a long voyage of ten months. Before the month was out the Second Fleet, consisting of the *Neptune*, the *Surprize* and the *Scarborough* followed her. On these three ships 939 men and seventy-eight women had been embarked, of whom eleven had died and eleven had been disembarked before they sailed; also twenty convicts from the wrecked *Guardian* had been taken on board at the Cape. In this terrible voyage, 267 out of 1017 died: on the *Neptune* 147 out of 424 males and eleven out of seventy-eight females perished, and on the two other vessels 109 out of 615 males were lost.

The case of the Second Fleet was the worst in the history of transportation. Twenty-six per cent had died, and 488 were landed sick from scurvy, dysentery and infectious fever, so that

the total of deaths increased by fifty within a few weeks of arrival. The outraged feelings of the colonists were expressed in indignant descriptions written by Phillip, Collins, Tench and others. In his capacity as surgeon of the settlement John White visited the vessels, where he saw "a great number of them lying, some half and others nearly quite naked, without either bed or bedding, unable to turn or help themselves. The smell was so offensive that I could scarcely bear it. Some of these unhappy people died after the ship came into the harbour, before they could be taken on shore. Part of these had been thrown into the harbour and their dead bodies cast upon the shore, and were seen lying naked on the rocks. The misery I saw among them is inexpressible." The description given by the Rev. Richard Johnson was even more expressive. Coming into contact with the fresh air men fainted and died when being taken on shore to the inadequate hospital, or to beds of grass on which demented wretches lay, covered with vermin and madly stripping blankets and clothing from their neighbours as they died. Those who were not sick were "lean and emaciated". Within six weeks of the arrival of the fleet Johnson buried eighty-six people.

In the First Fleet the Government did not relinquish responsibility in the details of transport. Vessels were taken up by the Navy Office for the outward journey, and the distribution of food and clothing was supervised by officers specially detailed for that duty. Consequently, the mortality on that fleet had been small. Subsequently, under a contract system responsibility was handed over to private contractors. It is difficult to determine on what basis the contracts were made. In the case of the first transport sent after the First Fleet, the *Lady Juliana*, the contractor, Richards, was compensated at the rate of 9s. 6d. per ton, as well as at the rate of 6d. for each convict daily during the voyage. The sum of £2 was also allowed for clothing for each convict.[61] For the Second Fleet, contracts were made with G. Whitlock as agent for the owners to supply ships, equip them for their special purpose, and victual and transport convicts at the rate of £17 7s. 6d. per head. A separate contract was made between the contractors and the masters of the vessels to carry out the engagements already entered into.[62] On the Government's side it cannot be said that the provisions were defective. Rations were defined with minuteness, each batch of six convicts being entitled to receive, over a period of seven days, sixteen pounds of bread, twelve pounds of flour, fourteen pounds of beef, eight pounds of pork, twelve pints of pease, one and a half pounds of butter and two pounds of rice. For women the ration was increased, and special provision was made for the supply of fresh meat and vegetables at ports of call. Clothing also, which was described in the contract, was to be

provided. Surgeons were placed on board and a commissioned officer of the navy was appointed to act as agent and to supervise sanitation and the distribution of rations.[63] The contractors were paid £15 per head before departure, and the remainder was to be paid after the Governor had certified that the merchandise sent in the vessels had been delivered. But the chief defect in these arrangements was that there was only one Government agent on the fleet, and consequently, when he died the masters of the vessels, in whose jurisdiction the distribution of rations and the general arrangements of sanitation lay, were uncontrolled. As Collins remarked, it was to the advantage of the contractors to overcrowd their ships and of the masters to curtail rations. Dead convicts were more profitable than living ones.[64] There was no condition for the safe landing of the convicts, though two contracts required the safe landing of the merchandise.

On the Second Fleet the conditions of contract were not observed. An attempted insurrection on the *Scarborough* had been followed by stern disciplinary measures and close confinement. Men were huddled together almost naked, without bedding, and in a state of indescribable filth. Many of them were in irons, chained together for days on end, some even dying in their fetters; others were "standing up to their middle in water"; men and women were denied access to fresh air, and the stench of a corpse, concealed by convicts anxious to take advantage of rations supplied heedless of numbers, sometimes called the attention of the surgeon or officer to the necessity for its removal.[65] Writing to Grenville, Phillip emphasized the evils arising from the long confinement of prisoners in the holds without access to air and the assertions of the master that the convicts had been ill when sent to the transports from the hulks.[66] He keenly resented the lack of co-operation between England and the settlement. He had asked that transportation should be curtailed for a few years, but now, faced with the problem of caring for 450 sick prisoners, a hundred of whom were a "permanent dead weight", and having been told to prepare for a thousand more after the English and Irish Spring Assizes, Phillip charged the Government with retaining the healthy and useful in England and transporting only the refuse to Australia. "The sending out of the disordered and helpless", he wrote, "clears the gaols and may ease the parishes from which they are sent; but, Sir, it is obvious that this settlement, instead of being a colony which is to support itself, will, if the practice is continued, remain for years a burthen to the mother country."[67]

Meanwhile, the Third Fleet arrived. With it word came that Grenville had decided to adopt a systematic transportation of criminals and the sending of supplies twice yearly; but this advan-

tageous proposal was not put into execution until many years later. Although the Third Fleet had left England before news was received of the mortality on the preceding vessels, conditions of transport were much improved. During 1791 eleven transports, excluding the *Pitt*, which arrived in February 1792, came to the colony with a freight of 1864 prisoners, 1696 of them males and only 168 females. One of these was an Irish transport, the first sent by the Irish Government, with 126 male and twenty-one female convicts of desperate character.[68] Out of the total who were sent on this fleet only 198 died, and the chief charges laid against the contractors were that the prisoners had been too closely confined and, in certain instances, deprived of rations by masters who were more concerned with what they could make by private trading than with the care of the convicts. Phillip exposed the actions of masters who utilized valuable space for the transport of copper and lead, and was subsequently ordered by Dundas to confiscate such illegal cargoes.[69] Though deaths were fewer, Phillip observed that "the greatest part of them are so emaciated, so worn away by long confinement or want of food, that it will be long before they recover their strength, and which many of them will never recover". At the end of that year, 626 prisoners were under medical treatment, and 576 of these had arrived in 1791.[70]

Phillip's reports on the mortality in the Second Fleet considerably awakened English public opinion to the horrors of the system. Dundas declared that the Government was determined to punish those who had been responsible for the "shocking calamity",[71] and after an investigation the Commissioners of the Navy in 1792 reported that the mortality and sickness had been chiefly due to the withholding of provisions,[72] whereupon the master of the *Neptune* promptly absconded in order to escape punishment. The incident inspired a new and temporary zeal, and in view of the public concern all documents concerning the transporting of convicts in these years were officially published.[73] As a result only three transports sailed that year, and one of them was delayed twelve months in preparation.[74] A proposal made by the East India Company, that such convicts as were ready to leave should be sent at a cost of £20 per head on the ships chartered by that company and at their usual times of departure, was favourably reported on by the Commissioners of the Navy. By this arrangement it was ensured that the prisoners would receive adequate clothing and the same rations as were given to the ship's company; moreover, it was hoped that a saving would be effected by the elimination of the agent and the members of the guard, who would no longer be necessary. For the return journeys these ships were fully under the control of the East India Company, but for

the outward journeys contracts continued to be made with private individuals, dependent on or independent of the company, and the private contractors were alone responsible for observing the conditions of transport.[75]

The unfavourable disclosures about transportation brought about some response to Phillip's demands. In July 1791, Dundas informed him that the 356 male and fifty-six female convicts, about to be transported on the *Pitt*, had been carefully selected with a view to their usefulness in the colony.[76] An anonymous critic, who alleged that the crowded conditions on that ship would speedily exterminate two-thirds of the prisoners, of whom several were "old men about sixty", led Dundas to call for an investigation. As this charge was found to be true, 34 "sick and diseased" prisoners had to be disembarked. In the prison-room a space six feet square was occupied by eight men, so that with a full complement "every berth or space of eighteen inches would be occupied" by men, sick or well, in unavoidable physical contact with one another. There were three women's apartments: two of these, 6 ft. 7 ins. by 7ft. 10 ins. were designed to hold ten women in each, and another 13 ft. 7 ins. by 8 ft. 4 ins. accommodated twenty-seven women.[77] This was a typical transport ship. In estimating a ship's capacity it was also reckoned that for every two tons one convict might be carried. The *Pitt* sailed on August 17, 1791, carrying 340 males and fifty-eight females, as well as a detachment of the New South Wales Corps and their commanding officer, Major Grose. Despite the precautions, and probably because a case of smallpox had appeared on the ship just prior to sailing, the *Pitt* "buried thirteen soldiers, seven seamen, twenty male and nine female convicts and landed 120 sick prisoners". Phillip, in recording this fact, however, also noted that the men received from that ship were less emaciated and better fitted for labour than any of those hitherto arrived.[78] The *Royal Admiral* which arrived in October 1792, carried 348 convicts, of whom twelve died and eighty-eight were landed sick. Four children were born on the voyage. Hence, while Phillip looked forward to improved conditions under the new system of transportation by ships employed in the service of the East India Company, he had to advise Dundas that ships were still being overcrowded.[79] The *Kitty* transport, which had sailed in March 1792, carried only ten men and thirty women. The male convicts had been specially selected as artificers, but, as the ship had been forced to return to port soon after leaving, eight of the ten men escaped. The women included fourteen convicts from Dublin, half of whom were under twenty years of age. No particulars of their sentences were given, as was usual with Irish prisoners, and of all the others originally embarked only

three had sentences above seven years.[80] This ship, with its thirty-two convicts and attended by a special naval agent and a surgeon, lost three females on the voyage.

As the system of transportation was not considerably modified in the eighteenth century, a paragraph may suffice to describe its outstanding characteristics. During the investigations of 1791 it had been twice suggested that the contractors should be paid, not according to the numbers embarked, but according to the numbers whom they landed in satisfactory health. The suggestion was not heeded. Before the Committee of 1812 Governor Hunter described the system as it had existed in his time and Alexander McLeay, the Secretary of the Transport Office, gave evidence over the whole period. The hiring of vessels at *per capita* charges was abandoned in favour of contracts for transport on the basis of payments according to the tonnage of the vessel. In this way, large ships could be chartered, upon which private individuals and provisions could be sent as well as prisoners. The Victualling Board entered into a separate contract for feeding and clothing the convicts on board the ship, and for nine months after arrival. Before departure the convicts were provided with a new outfit of clothing and inspected by medical officers, the contractors being theoretically bound to place a surgeon on each ship. However, as Governor Macquarie observed many years later, the surgeon was often but an incompetent apprentice, although in the evidence of 1812 it was asserted that only approved surgeons were sent. No person, other than an agent of the contractor, was appointed to supervise the distribution of food. This matter was left absolutely to the master of the vessel. Although the contracts were meticulous in laying down the conditions for rationing and for allowing the prisoners access to fresh air, the regulations were frequently abused. The medical officer was expected to submit a report on the conditions obtaining during the voyage. In some instances the masters were rewarded by a gratuity of £50 for careful supervision and surgeons received a gratuity of ten shillings for every convict landed in good health. On board the transports a military guard of thirty men was usually placed, frequently composed of detachments going to the settlement for service.[81] It had often been suggested that the Navy Board should transport prisoners in its own vessels, under naval supervision. The practice was adopted in two instances in 1803—H.M.S. *Glatton* and H.M.S. *Calcutta*—but was abandoned owing to the necessities of war. The practice of transporting convicts twice annually, approved twelve years previously, was then commenced and with advantageous results.

On arrival in the settlement the convicts were mustered on board ship and an attempt made to classify them. As no information

was sent from England about the past history and qualifications of the prisoners, the task was difficult; only in a few instances, as in the case of the convicts on the *Kitty*, were the trades of prisoners specified, and, in point of fact, the procedure of classifying convicts before leaving England was not adopted until after 1834. Moreover, the failure to send out records of the terms of sentences and the date of their expiry made classification even more difficult. The preliminary muster, which signified the transfer of the prisoners from the master of the vessel to the Governor, was conducted by the Governor's secretary and the superintendent of convicts in the presence of the captain, the surgeon and the ship's company. Convicts supplied information concerning their identity, age, time of trial and term of sentence, and occupation, but in most instances it was found that the information they gave could not be relied upon. After a medical examination, details of health and physical characteristics were noted, and the prisoners were invited to make their complaints concerning their treatment on the voyage. A report of these complaints was sent to England.

(d) Conditions in the Settlement, 1790-1792

In July 1790 the population of the settlements had increased to 2239. In New South Wales there were 1715 people, all victualled from the public store. The convicts comprised 908 males, 358 females and forty-seven prisoners whom Phillip described as children. The wives of convicts numbered six and their children five. At Norfolk Island the total population was 524, including 191 male, 100 female and thirty-six child convicts.[82] The problem of administration, therefore, comprised not only the controlling of the convicts and forcing them to work, but also feeding them.

A promise had been made to send supplies twice yearly to the settlement, but it was not observed; and until the end of Phillip's tenure of office the food problem was acute. When ships arrived with convicts they only carried supplies sufficient for their complement for nine months; a paltry supply which in one case Collins described as sufficient to provide for the settlement during forty days. The food transports came irregularly, and as the supplies were based on the assumption that the settlement was becoming more and more self-supporting by its own agriculture, they proved inadequate. At Norfolk Island, just released from real famine conditions, the promising harvest was ruined by caterpillars; in New South Wales agriculture was still in its beginnings. These eventualities had not been contemplated in England when purchases were made, although the amount expended on provisions and accessories, and in transporting them, was colossal. The food supplies

of 1790 were being quickly exhausted, and in 1791 when drought conditions prevailed in the settlement and more than 1800 additional convicts had arrived, it was found necessary to reduce rations considerably. The military, too, were compelled to share in the general discomfort, being told to bring their own bread with them when invited to the Governor's table; but they resented this equality of treatment and demanded special favours, which being refused, they chartered a vessel privately to bring their own provisions from the Cape. Among the convicts, however, the situation was becoming intolerable. Rations were being constantly reduced and crime naturally increased as men grew weaker under starvation conditions. In May 1791 Collins described how the convicts showed every indication of the baneful effects of the reduced rations, particularly as they had scarcely recovered from the famine of the previous year and large numbers of them had been the victims of the dreadful conditions obtaining in the Second Fleet. Phillip recognized the influence of such conditions in promoting crime. "The throes of hunger will ever prove too powerful for integrity to withstand", he wrote. At Parramatta in November 1791, 400 prisoners were prostrated by sickness; to this number more than 100 others might be added "who were so weak that they could not be put to any kind of labour, not even to pulling grass for thatching the huts. Forty-two convicts died in November, and in these people nature seemed fairly to be worn out; many of them were so thoroughly exhausted that they expired without a groan, and apparently without any kind of pain."[83] In 1791, 155 male and eight women convicts died. The total deaths in that year were 171 persons and 626 people were under medical treatment and incapable of labour. The total population at the end of 1791 was 4059, of whom 3178 were convicts. Phillip complained bitterly that the colony had been generally on a reduced ration since 1789. It was just four years, he said, since he had landed in the settlement, and in that period he had repeatedly requested that competent farmers should be sent to direct agriculture and that healthy, useful convicts should be selected. During all these years, however, "all the publick live stock which has been received is not more than would be necessary for one good farm; nor has that been received till within these three months". Therefore, England must recognize "how far distant that period must be" when the settlement will be able to give its population a local supply of meat.[84]

The *Pitt* transport arrived in February 1792, with 368 convicts and a supply of food sufficient at the much reduced ration for forty days for the whole settlement. Supplies were then estimated at flour for fifty-two days and salt meat for twenty-one weeks at the rations then in force, which was five pounds of flour and four

pounds of pork for each man over a period of seven days. Narrating the history of this period Collins referred to the increased mortality and the distress of observing "poor wretches daily dropping into the grave" and other emaciated prisoners who were soon to follow. Every endeavour was made to alleviate their lot and the weakest of the convicts were excused from any kind of hard labour; "but it was not hard labour that destroyed them; it was an entire want of strength in the constitution to receive nourishment or to throw off the debility that pervaded their whole system". Out of 122 male convicts who had arrived from Ireland in September 1791 only fifty were alive in May 1792. Collins records the fact that most of the robberies committed were "confined to this class of the convicts", but the men who were apprehended for those offences "were in general too weak to receive a punishment adequate to their crimes". "Their universal plea", he wrote, "was hunger."[85] When supplies eventually arrived in June but thirteen days' rations of flour remained; and much of the food now received was unsatisfactory in quality.[86] Within the settlement the wheat harvest had been small and it was deemed advisable to conserve a great part of it as seed for the following sowing. At the end of June the ship which Phillip himself had sent to Calcutta for supplies arrived, bringing grain, an inferior flour, and some breeding stock. As the meat supplies were insufficient Phillip diplomatically issued a public order by which, to palliate the reduction in the meat ration, he increased the grain supplies, and after detailing the ration which the law prescribed assured the prisoners that what had been deducted from their allowance would later be made up to them. They need have no fear that supplies would not be sent, he told them, because the Government had pledged itself to ship supplies twice yearly. However, he did not reveal the fact that this official proposal had been made by Grenville seventeen months previously. Clothing, too, was deficient, Phillip reporting in June that "not a month's wear was in store". In the course of the year, the rations were considerably increased as ships arrived. Clothing was distributed in October, some garments being of coarse and "unsubstantial" fabrics, "in which there were seldom found more than three weeks' wear". In December rations were restored to almost normal, and as a last act, before quitting the colony, Phillip ordered that an extra pound of flour should be added to the weekly rations of the prisoners, who throughout a difficult period had conducted themselves "in a better way than could have been expected of them."

Fortunately, it is not necessary for us to pass judgment on the procedure adopted in England to supply the colony with food. Before leaving the colony Phillip himself expressed an opinion,

which was fair and typical of this just man. He warned the Government that the contractors were filling their ships with private merchandise, which occupied a space three times as great as that which they spared for the official supplies. "It has been my fate to point out wants from year to year", he wrote; "it has been a duty the severest I have ever experienced. Did these wants only respect myself or a few individuals I should be silent; but here are numbers who bear them badly; nor has the colony suffered more from what we have not received than from the supplies we have received not arriving in time".[87]

THE DISPOSAL OF THE CONVICTS

(a) Conditions of Public Labour

IN the early years methods of procedure were adopted either by design or by necessity which became permanent features of the system. Among the most important of these were the communal system of labour, the assignment of convicts to private settlers, and the pardons issued under the forms of absolute or conditional emancipation. As the general principles of this procedure did not change they may be described here.

To devise a system of control for so varied a population was difficult. Besides the military and civil staffs, with their dependants, the convicts towards the close of Phillip's administration numbered 3099, of whom 737 were at Norfolk Island and 2362 at the settlement in New South Wales, which comprised Sydney and the districts of Rose Hill and Toongabbie in the region of Parramatta. In New South Wales the disparity between the sexes was 414 women to 1948 men, but at Norfolk Island the women were more than fifty per cent of the 488 males.[1] There were prisoners of all terms, the seven years category predominating, and of all ages, though in the earlier period of the system the convicts were generally of a more advanced age than in the later years, when one-fourth were under twenty-one.[2] Also, there were child convicts, some of those on the Second Fleet being under fourteen years of age. They were not a numerous body; the returns sent by Phillip in July 1790 appear to differentiate between child convicts (forty-seven at Sydney) and children of convicts (five at Sydney); this is evidently a mistake, for all other lists classify only according to sexes. Child prisoners continued to arrive throughout the following years, but no really scientific classification of them as a body was made until 1819, when separate barrack accommodation was provided for 150 boys.[3]* Children of convicts and ex-convicts, who at the end of 1792 numbered 127 on the mainland and 119 at Norfolk Island, had arrived with convict mothers in a few cases or had been born in the settlement, either from legitimate unions, or from

---

* In the *Journal* of George Thompson (Appendix to Dyer's *Slavery and Famine*, p. 22), he notes that on board the *Royal Admiral* (1792) there were four boy convicts, aged fifteen, sentenced to seven years; two girls, aged sixteen and eighteen, with life sentences; and one boy, Scott, aged thirteen, sentenced for life.

promiscuous unions made with convict men or the military. The popularity of marriage, arising from Phillip's promise to reward the parties who would enter into it, had waned when the Governor later made it clear that no convict who had made such an alliance could leave his wife and children behind him when he wanted to retire from the settlement after the expiry of his sentence. Nevertheless, by 1792, many of the convicts were married and 112 ex-convicts were settled on the land, the majority of these, as of the children, being at Norfolk Island. The attempt to induce wives of convicts to follow their husbands to the settlement was not successful, though the practice became so popular after inducements offered in 1812 that restrictions had to be made so as to guarantee the support of the migrant on arrival.

The fundamental means of control were the Public Orders, by which the regulations were promulgated, and the regular musters of convicts, by which personal contacts were made with this class as a body. Before religious service on Sundays the convicts were assembled in the different districts, when they were inspected and given an opportunity to lodge complaints to magistrates. At regular intervals a general muster for census purposes was ordered and attendance was compulsory on all classes.[4] Not many years passed before the Sunday musters came in for much criticism, as it was believed that the assembling of large numbers of prisoners at one place on their day of liberty offered opportunities for crime and drunkenness. Immediate control of convict labour was, as we have seen, entrusted to overseers drawn from their own ranks. In response to Phillip's frequent complaints Grenville, in 1789, attempted to remedy this deficiency by sending out free and salaried superintendents and skilled convicts to direct industry, but after the wreck of the *Guardian* only five superintendents and a score of artificers arrived. As their numbers were never adequately increased, being only sixteen in 1792, the system of drawing overseers from the convicts continued as a permanent arrangement. Phillip had to complain of the "useless" procedure of sending out superintendents who were not masters of some trade, and in 1796 Governor Hunter, weary of "the sad impositions" and drunkards who had been appointed to responsible positions, suggested that proficient convicts ought to be given the posts with compensation as an inducement to their industry.[5] The general direction of industry and of convict labour was entrusted to the superintendents, and the overseers took charge of small gangs of twenty or thirty convicts, exercising authority over these but being themselves responsible to the superintendents, who, as the years passed, were frequently emancipists. Legally, none of these might impose punishment, for the infliction of which the sentence of a magistrate was necessary.[6]

Nevertheless, the overseers and superintendents were unsatisfactory taskmasters, sometimes courting the favour of prisoners by a relaxation of discipline under which labour suffered and at other times becoming unduly repressive. Many years passed before barracks were provided for prisoner accommodation. Convicts generally lived in separate huts, within a prescribed area that was patrolled at night by convict-police. The bulk of the convict population, however, was concentrated at Parramatta, where supervision was more efficient and crime less frequent. Secondary offenders were usually liberated after punishment or placed under stern discipline in special gangs at harder work, which, in certain cases, they had to perform while chained.

Labour was necessarily of the more arduous kind, clearing forest land and building roads and bridges. Tench and other contemporaries described it as fit only for beasts of burden, but it should be remembered that these descriptions were much influenced by the abnormal famines and sickness of the early years. George Thompson's *Journal*, for instance, has a description of conditions that were particularly characteristic of the famine period. He arrived in 1792, when there remained but one week's meat supply in the stores. He described convicts as working till eleven, without breakfast, because they seldom had anything to eat; because of the lack of food "and the ill treatment they received from a set of merciless wretches (most of them of their own description) who are their superintendents, their lives are rendered truly miserable". At night they were placed in huts, accommodating from fourteen to eighteen men, without beds, blankets, bowls, spoons or knives. His description of superintendents was true in some cases, and the lack of ordinary comforts and conveniences was applicable to the whole period. However, an attempt was made to regulate the system, distinctions being made between classes, and the unfit were exempted. Thompson admitted that "the women have a more comfortable life than the men; those who are not fortunate enough to be selected for wives, which every officer, settler and soldier is entitled to", were made hut-keepers, set to work at sewing or at picking grass in the fields. Discipline over the female section remained a scandalous reproach for thirty years, and when an attempt was made many years later to set some of them to work in the factory at Parramatta disorder characterized their work by day, and professional prostitution engaged large numbers of them at night.[7] Educated convicts, whom we shall have occasion to notice in the next chapter, were given special privileges. Large numbers of the male prisoners were employed at agriculture, and others at building or brick-making. For all classes employed by Government the hours of labour were regulated, being from

sunrise to sunset, with two and a half hours off for meals and rest. Phillip readjusted these hours according to the intensity of the famine conditions and the strength of the convicts. In general the work done by convicts was regarded by them as part of their punishment and not as a contribution towards the common welfare. The hours of liberty—from 7 a.m. to 9 p.m. daily, and on Saturdays after 10 a.m.—came to be regarded by the prisoners as a period when they could hire themselves to private employers. Two systems of labour, therefore, grew up side by side, one being forced and unremunerative and the other free, at which large wages could be earned. When a system of task-work was introduced later on the public work suffered and Governor Hunter had to order that prisoners employed by Government should return to the full hours of work that had obtained in Phillip's time and that superintendents who used convict labour for private purposes would be dismissed.[8] These regulations were not observed and in June 1799 Hunter remarked that owing to the shortness of the winter days and the late hour at which the convicts assembled it was impossible to complete a fair day's work by 1 p.m.; he therefore ordered that the working gangs should continue their labour until 2 or 3 p.m.[9] This system of task work with a few minor adjustments, remained the general rule among government workers until 1811.

The freedom accorded to convicts to enable them to hire their labour had many advantages, and, as Hunter observed, the progress of agriculture was largely due to it. But in a community where prisoners were allowed this liberty, where others were assigned to private employers and where convicts in ever increasing proportions were obtaining their liberty after expiration of their sentences, the employment of labour could not be left to desultory self-adjustment. Consequently, in 1794 a Government regulation stabilized the rate of wages for free men at ten shillings for reaping an acre of crop, being the equivalent of half-a-crown daily. The natural reaction was that convicts in government employ, among whom the practice of completing the government task-work by 1 p.m. had arisen, claimed their liberty after that hour or that they should be remunerated by Government for working overtime. Hunter indignantly repudiated the claim, but was unable effectively to extend the hours of labour beyond 3 p.m., so that if extra work was required from the prisoners the Government was forced to pay wages at the same rates as those by which private employers were bound.[10] In 1797, when settlers had complained of the arbitrary demands of labourers, who were demanding four or five shillings a day and when 700 men had been liberated and were open to employment, Hunter drew up a scale of wages for all classes. Apart from the fixing of wages according to the amount of work

G

done the following regulations were made for general employment: yearly wages with board £10; weekly with specified provisions 6s.; daily, with board 1s., without board 2s. 6d. But a "government man", assigned to settlers and working for these permanent employers on any occasion outside his specified hours, was to be remunerated at the rate of 10d. daily.[11] Shortly after this date Hunter had to complain that the schedule of wages had not been observed by employers, and in 1800 Governor King disclosed the fact that wages were twice as high as those stipulated hitherto by Government. However, while employers then complained that industry was unable to pay the costs of labour, the labourer had the disadvantages of having to purchase his provisions at an excessive cost from private retailers.

The hardships of convict labour in government service, therefore, admitted of degrees and much depended on the overseer or super-intendent who was the immediate master. The real hardship arose from the frequently recurring reductions of food rations, due to the non-arrival of store ships from England, which continued at intervals until the end of the century, and after that date with less frequency in 1802, 1806 and 1807. But the stipulated ration was not insufficient and was provided whenever it was possible to do so. One other cause of hardship was the weakened physical condition of the prisoners, several of them being constitutionally incapable and very many rendered unfit by privations on the voyage. The chief cause, however, was the lack of proper accommodation and scientific discipline suitable for the punishment of some and the reformation of others.

(b) The Private Assignment System

Some convicts, while still in a state of servitude, were employed privately. In Phillip's original Instructions he had been authorized to make grants of land to emancipated convicts and was asked to report on the conditions under which similar grants could be made to the military who might choose to remain at the settlement. On arrival at the settlement Phillip realized the necessity for individual effort in farming and encouraged the military and civil population to cultivate the land. Acting on his own initiative he allowed the services of convicts to these temporary settlers at the expense of the Crown. In 1789, in answer to his strong recom-mendations, permission was accorded to him to make grants of land to settlers, non-commissioned officers and privates, and the assignment of convict labour to private employers was approved on condition that the labourers should be clothed and fed and housed without cost to the Government. By the end of 1791 the

Governor had made grants of land to eighty-seven persons, of whom fifty-seven were ex-convicts and the rest chiefly ex-marines. The policy then begun was enlarged under the succeeding governors.

Although Phillip saw the necessity for assisting farmers by a grant of labour, he did not take kindly to the proposal to hand over convicts indiscriminately to the military.[12] In England, however, the proposal was welcomed with enthusiasm, being regarded as a means of transferring the maintenance of convicts from Government to private individuals. In the colony the military argued that in the early years when all work was unproductive, it was essential that the assigned labour should be wholly supported by Government, although the employer would reap the advantage of free labour. In the precarious state of the settlement, where it was essential to begin agriculture, Phillip agreed with the argument. The Home Office, however, remained adamant against the project of supporting the assigned servants at Government expense, though it was insistent on the principle of assignment. Phillip's hesitant policy, by which he had assigned only thirty-eight convicts in 1790, led Dundas to compromise by proposing to support these labourers for one year. Phillip, however, pressed for a longer period of support, and on January 10, 1792, Dundas agreed to the proposals on the following basis: that civil and military officers might have two convict servants each, supported by Government for two years, and that all other settlers were to be allowed the same privilege over a period of eighteen months.[13] After eighteen months the servants were to be supported by the masters. This was the position when Phillip left the colony a few months later.

The assignment system, which became so important in the penal system, had a long and varied history and has been subjected to severe criticism. Under the Australian system of transportation the governor, who possessed a property in the services of the convict, transferred that right to a settler, under certain specified conditions. The distinction has been drawn that this transfer of rights did not comprise the right over the person of the convict, which is the essential of slavery. However, in practice the assignment system differed very little from slavery. Earl Grey believed that "the assigned servants were in fact slaves, and there is only too painful proof that in many instances the evils inseparable from slavery were experienced".[14] The Select Committee of 1838, relying on the condemnatory evidence of Governors Arthur and Bourke and Captain Maconochie, all of them highly qualified to speak on the subject, absolutely reprehended the system.[15] The practice had been a vast lottery, the Committee declared, under which men and women transported for similar offences and having a right to equal punishment were apportioned to Government or private

employers, and among the latter prospered or suffered according
to the disposition of the employer to whom fate had assigned them.
These verdicts, however, were made after the system had been in
operation for half a century and after moral and economic abuses
had come to be associated with it. Assignment was a compromise
between colonization and criminal punishment, welcomed both
in England and in the colony for economic reasons.
It suited a system by which the State paid the enormous expenses
incident in the foundation and equipment of a new colony, made
free grants of land to settlers and gave them free and forced labour
to make fortunes for themselves by the production of cereals and
meat, which they then sold to the patronizing Government.
This trade was profitable and remained stable over many years,
during which the demand always exceeded the supply.[16] Convicts
were assigned to various classes, the military, the free, the freed,
and in instances rare at the beginning, but more frequent in the
later years, to their own wives or husbands who followed them to
the country or became free before the indented partner had served
his sentence. Phillip's assignments had been few, but under the
military despotism that followed a policy of wholesale distribution
of land and convict labourers to civil and military settlers was
adopted. This will be described in the next chapter. The system was
placed on a better regulated basis in 1801, but after developing in
a scandalous fashion through the following years it was amended in
1827, restricted in 1837, and finally abolished in 1841, much to
the discomfiture of private employers.

(c) Remissions of Sentences

Before a prisoner in the settlement could look forward to being
released he had to continue to keep himself out of the hands of
the law. Punishment was summary and severe, and a second
sentence would not only prolong his original term but also rob him
of the chance of remissions for good conduct. Secondary offences
were punished usually by the lash, by a committal to the gaol-gang,
where men worked at more laborious tasks, "double ironed and
on a single ration",[17] or by re-transportation to Norfolk Island.

In the official documents of this early period more emphasis
is given to the restrictions placed on subordinate officials against
inflicting punishment than on the extent to which punishment was
inflicted by authority. This is natural as excessive corporal punishment was a recognized practice in that period. Apart from
executions, which decreased towards the close of Phillip's régime,
the extreme severity of the floggings belies the suggestion made
by Hunter that a magistrate's sentences were usually in the vicinity

of twenty-five strokes. Collins records sentences of 500 lashes, 400 of which, on one occasion, were remitted by Phillip because of a personal interest in the case; another of 600 lashes together with servitude in irons for six months was apparently executed; instances of 100 and more strokes were numerous, and it is recorded that one of the indulgences granted to celebrate the King's birthday took the form of issuing a pardon to all those men who for stealing corn had been sentenced to wear iron collars around their necks.[18] It is difficult to judge how far this severity was justifiable. Phillip was not a martinet and probably, considering the people with whom he had to deal, his discipline was no worse than that in the English Army and Navy. In nearly every instance where excessive corporal punishment is recorded, it is remarked that the punishment was meant to be exemplary to prevent rising waves of theft. The *Journal* of George Thompson describes penal discipline as it was in 1792. For a trifling offence a convict was put in the stocks until it was convenient to examine him. If guilty he was taken to a cartwheel to receive a "Botany Bay dozen", which was twenty-five lashes. Thompson, however, believed that the punishments at Sydney were greater than those in England, two or three hundred lashes being imposed there in cases where the equivalent would be a dozen in England. If the crime were serious, such as theft, he said, death or transportation to Norfolk Island followed. But, at the same time convicts as well as others had the benefit of the laws. "No person, unless those immediately concerned with them, is allowed to strike them or by any means ill use them. All complaints must be made to the Justice, who must be consulted on the most trifling occasions".[19] Whatever may be thought of the Phillip régime, it must be granted that his law was no worse than the penal code of England under which the Australian convicts had originally been transported.

The natural termination of the punishment by expiry of time was considerably hampered in the earlier years owing to the lack of official information concerning the duration of the sentences. An incomplete list of these was sent in 1790, but complete returns were not made available until 1797, and, as we have seen, the absence of particulars for the Irish prisoners remained for many years a disquieting problem for governors. Phillip in 1791 complained that large numbers were claiming the right of liberation and refusing to remain in the settlement; while believing it would be dangerous to compel them to remain he doubted if any ship would receive some of them who, being "aged and infirm" could not be expected to work in return for their passage. We have already referred to the opposition made by the English Government to the return of convicts who, having been refused assistance towards

repatriation were forced to remain or to seek employment in returning vessels. The attitude of Government caused considerable discontent, which manifested itself in a stubborn reluctance to work and in attempted abscondings. As a letter of 1791 put it: "any fate appeared better than that of perpetual slavery".

Abscondings from the settlement were a serious problem. In the earliest years men had escaped into the unexplored country and were killed by aborigines or starved in forests where game and food were scarce. However, with the arrival of Irish convicts in 1791 more daring and more frequent efforts at escape were made. These unfortunate people, resenting the forced labour to which the earlier convicts had submitted, were obsessed with the idea that Java and China were easily accessible either by land or by sea or that a settled colony existed north of Sydney. With scarcely any food and with a compass drawn on paper they set off in small stolen, open boats. On one occasion twenty men and one woman among these Irish convicts set off, and when later they were rescued by a fortuitous visit of an exploring party near Broken Bay, were found to be almost starving and naked. Phillip was more concerned in convincing them of their folly than in punishing them, for, as Collins observed, they were part of a mass of 402 prisoners who had been treated at the hospital on the day when Phillip had to disillusion them. Before Phillip's departure forty-four men and nine women had escaped.

The most striking of these escapes was that which occurred in March 1791. William Bryant, a convict who had been transported for seven years for "interrupting revenue officers in the execution of their duty", was the leader. On arriving with the First Fleet in the colony he immediately married Mary Broad, who was serving a seven years term as a commutation of her original death sentence for stealing a cloak on the public highway. As Bryant's sentence had recently expired he ingeniously set about preparing for flight, providing himself with a small fishing-boat, provisions, a compass and some trusted companions with a knowledge of navigation. On March 28 his party absconded. They included his two infant children, his wife, who still had two years to serve, and seven convicts who had arrived in the first two fleets and were not yet free of servitude. The crimes for which they had been transported included stealing handkerchiefs, stealing three pigs, a net and a watch, and stealing twenty pounds of "old lead and iron". They set sail for Timor, more than 3000 miles away, which after many hazardous adventures they reached in ten weeks. For a while they deceived the Governor there into believing that they were survivors from a shipwreck, but when a chance conversation revealed their true identity they were handed over to the captain

of the wrecked *Pandora* who had managed to reach Kupung. On the voyage back to England Bryant, his two children and three of the convicts died. The five survivors were tried at Bow Street in July 1792. They contended that they had escaped because of the starvation conditions existing at the settlement, and though "Governor Phillip had used them very well" they preferred "to throw themselves on the mercy of the sea rather than perish on this inhospitable shore"; they "would sooner suffer death than return to Botany Bay". All of them were committed to Newgate to await their execution in London. In May of the following year, however, Governor Phillip, who had just returned from the colony, related how an officer of high rank visited the extraordinary and long-suffering Mary Bryant at Newgate and after hearing her story returned the next day with the King's pardon in his pocket and took her off with him in his carriage. It would not be difficult to imagine that the kindly ex-Governor had been a sympathetic abettor of this act of humanity.[20]

The absconding habit, begun in the earliest years, was continued and China remained, particularly for the Irish prisoners, a perpetual land of dreams more enticing than the nightmare of the Australian settlement. In 1798, on hearing that sixty of the "Irish Defenders" were about to abscond, Governor Hunter arrested twenty of the leaders, but taking pity on their illusions, decided to provision and send the four strongest of them into the forest country to learn what dangers it held for the inexperienced. They returned "most completely sick of their journey". Nevertheless, another party of fourteen of them set off and abandoned half their number on a small island in Bass Strait, 500 miles from Sydney, where they were "miraculously" picked up by Bass in a state of starvation. Escapes, though not numerous considering the numbers of the convicts, produced some epics of navigation and not a few absconders became roamers or pirates of the South Seas.

The attitude of the Government in discouraging the return of ex-convicts, who by servitude had been restored to civil rights, did not pass unchallenged in England. In February 1791 Grenville acknowledged that no legal barrier stood in the way of their leaving the colony, but he made it clear that men of their criminal records would not be acceptable and that no facilities were to be offered for their return voyages. His declaration caused considerable relief in the colony, and it was remarked that had it been made earlier it would have prevented abscondings and discontent. Criticism of the official opposition to repatriation continued, one newspaper describing it as "a circumstance novel in the annals of transportation" and stating that the question was to be raised in Parliament.[21] In the colony, however, while ex-convicts were

generally allowed to leave if they could manage to do so, the antipathy of Government to their return was on one occasion misinterpreted as a prohibition, and in 1796 the Duke of Portland had to issue an emphatic protest against an opinion that had been current at Norfolk Island, declaring that no official had "discretionary power" to detain free men.[22]

Phillip endeavoured to persuade the expiree convicts to become settlers, presenting them with the alternatives of signing an agreement to work for the Government for eighteen months or to find a passage as best they could; but neither at the main settlement nor at Norfolk Island were they willing to remain any longer than would enable them to save sufficient to pay for their passage.[23] Those who did not return were employed by the private settlers or wandered about the country proving a menace to life and property. Some of them became settlers with varying success and helped to provide employment for others.

In the second Commission granted to Phillip in April 1787 the power to pardon and reprieve had been inserted at his own request. Though it appeared to be no more than the power usually granted to colonial governors to pardon crimes committed within their territories, the accompanying Instructions made reference to the emancipation and discharge from servitude of all convicts, who from their good conduct showed a disposition to industry and were worthy of being rewarded with land grants. However, as the prerogative of pardoning "any kyndes of felonnyes . . . comytted in any parties of this realme" was vested in the Crown alone, by 27 Henry VIII, c. 24, it could not be delegated without statutory authority. In 1790, therefore, a special enabling Act, 30 Geo. III, c. 47, was passed to enable the governors of oversea penal settlements to remit the sentences of transportees. The power was conveyed to Phillip personally by Letters Patent in November 1790, and it was distinctly provided that the pardons granted by the governor should be notified to England, where they would be inserted "in the next general pardon which shall pass under the Great Seal of Great Britain".[24] Two conditions were therefore necessary, a special delegation to each individual governor of this power and a ratification in England of all pardons granted in Australia. For twenty-eight years it was believed that the procedure of pardoning which had been followed in the colony was valid and restored ex-convicts to their full civil rights. It was subsequently discovered, however, that a special delegation had not been made to Governor Macquarie; moreover, by a judgment of the King's Bench in 1818 it was decided that a prisoner, whose pardon had been recorded only by a governor within the territory but had not been inserted in any general pardon under the Great Seal, was not restored to

the civil rights which he had previously lost by attainder for felony. Bigge, reviewing the past history of the colony in 1821, stated that "as this direction has never been literally complied with in New South Wales, no one of the many persons who have received absolute and conditional pardons from the respective Governors" was removed from the disabilities arising from his original attainder, and the only legal right which the colonial pardon gave him was to entitle him to claim the general pardon which would operate only from the date of its being granted.[25] Special Acts of Indemnity were subsequently passed to remedy the awkward position which had arisen from this misapprehension and by that date involved a considerable amount of real estate, which had been transferred during more than twenty years. In the early days of the settlement Phillip was careful to send particulars of emancipations to England, and at the 1812 Enquiry Hunter asserted that he had always done so. Nevertheless, omissions had occurred and though no serious consequences were experienced for many years, the legal disqualifications existed. As a matter of fact Phillip, misconstruing his earlier Instructions, had absolutely pardoned three convicts, one bred to surgery, one a bricklayer and another a man who had saved the wrecked *Sirius* from fire, before the special powers of 1790 reached him.

Pardons were absolute and conditional. The word "emancipist" was subsequently employed to describe all classes of ex-convicts, and a counter-term, "exclusives", to denote those who had never been under bondage, grew up in later years when the classes became sharply divided and antagonistic. But technically the word "emancipist" applied only to those who had been pardoned before expiry of sentence. By an unconditional pardon the term of the sentence was remitted, and, except in specially defined cases such as political "exiles" or among men transported for life terms, the ex-prisoner was entitled to leave the settlement immediately.*

An intermediate method of indulgence, which was introduced in later years, was the ticket-of-leave. This was a declaration, signed by the governor or his secretary, dispensing a convict from attendance at government work and enabling him, on condition of supporting himself, to seek approved employment within a stated district. The indulgence was dependent on good behaviour and the governor's pleasure, and was easily obtained, on the recommendation of a superintendent or on the likelihood of the convict's being able to support himself under these conditions. It was frequently granted to women and to educated convicts, often immediately at their arrival, at marriage, or at the arrival of a free wife or husband from England. Under a ticket-of-leave

* Copies of these certificates of pardon are in Appendix D.

a man was still subject to supervision in its more general aspects, but his liberty was such that he could sue and be sued in the courts, could carry on trade and even become a land-holder.[26] Whenever supervision had been exercised over this body of people, Bigge regarded the system as beneficial in stimulating industry, but it had the disadvantage of placing men too suddenly on a footing of equality with the free and the freed who had served sentences. Its greatest disadvantage, however, was the lack of any guiding principle for granting the concession, and it was not until 1811 that regulations were drawn up to determine after what period of service a convict was entitled to the remission. Even after that date the conditions were not always observed.

The conditional pardon contained a declaration by the governor, under his hand and seal, that the unexpired term of the convict's sentence was remitted on the condition of his continuing to reside within the territory of New South Wales during the term of his original sentence.

To such emancipated convicts as wished to become settlers grants of land and assistance were made: to every male thirty acres of land, twenty more if married, and ten more for each child in his family at the date of settling. He was to be furnished with a year's supply of provisions for himself and his family, and with seed and stock to commence his farm, on which he was supposed to reside. He was given an assigned servant, supported by Government over a period of eighteen months. He might, and did, employ other convict labourers, but at his own expense. There was no regulation specifying the number of years which had to be served from a sentence before a convict became eligible to apply for emancipation. A scale of this kind, differing according as the sentences were for life, fourteen or seven years, was drawn up after 1810, but though its originator was Governor Macquarie, his neglect of his own rules made emancipation a scandal and a menace in the colony. Emancipations were granted readily, for marriage, good conduct, meritorious or special service, to useful and educated men, and in the early years as a solace to men whose terms of sentence were believed to have expired, or to those who were willing to undertake military service. Phillip used this pardoning prerogative sparingly and with discretion, regarding emancipation as a reward for industry and good behaviour. The prospect of its being accessible only in such cases, he believed, was a strong incentive to reformation.

The verdict of contemporary Governors was unfavourable to the emancipists, who soon began to form a mixed population ranging from members of the lowest English criminal classes to others who had previously held comfortable positions in life. However, even

in the earliest years exceptions were to be noted among the ex-convicts. One case in point was that of the first emancipist farmer. In December 1789, when the opinion became prevalent that no ex-convict was fitted to take up a life of agriculture and when it was believed that the rations allowed by Government were insufficient to maintain a man at hard work, Phillip determined to make an experiment to discover whether the proposals made for convict colonization were feasible or not.[27] Among the convicts claiming that their sentence had expired at this date was James Ruse, who in 1782 had been sentenced at Bodmin Assizes to seven years' transportation, and was subsequently selected to be transported to Africa,[28] but, on the abandonment of that project, was kept in custody until he sailed with the First Fleet to Australia. In 1789 he was emancipated, pending the arrival of his papers, given land, seed and live stock, and was assisted in clearing his holding. By perseverance and industry, not, as he said, by merely scratching the land as was done at the government farms, he was able to declare himself self-supporting in a little over a year. When rumours spread that Ruse was starving, the Governor endeavoured to persuade him to use his right of sustenance from the public stores, but the settler refused. In the same year he married, allowed his wife to be supported for a few months and in December 1791 triumphantly undertook to support himself, his wife and child. He was the first settler to be given the stipulated grant of thirty acres, which was made to him on February 22, 1791. Two years later he sold his grant and removed to the more fertile Hawkesbury district where he continued his industry for many years. By this experiment the possibility of convicts becoming self-supporting pioneers of agriculture was proved; unfortunately, however, the Ruses among them were few, although they were not absolutely lacking.

About the time when Ruse was put to farming, Phillip placed twenty-seven other ex-convicts on the land. The returns of November 1791 show that twenty-two free settlers, mainly recruited from retired marines, had been given land in lots averaging sixty acres and fifty-two ex-convicts had been settled on farms usually of thirty acres. Twenty of these were married.[29] The returns of December 1791 increase this number and state that sixteen expirees had left the settlement.[30] Twelve months later, when Phillip left the settlement, sixty-five settlers had come from the ranks of free men and 113 from ex-convicts. At that date there were only fifteen with conditional pardons.[31]

One other convict emancipated and favoured before Phillip's departure may be mentioned, as his name became almost world famous. This was the notorious impostor, Waldron, better known

by his assumed name, George Barrington. Born at Maynooth in 1755 he was educated by a clergyman of the Church of Ireland until about the age of sixteen, when he joined a theatrical company and began his celebrated career as a pickpocket. He was always extraordinarily successful in convincing his victims, his judges, and later Phillip himself, of a deep and permanent repentance. His first victim failed to appear against him; in his second case he was sentenced to three years' hard labour and released for good conduct after twelve months; in a third case his eloquent appeal from the dock succeeded in having his five years sentence commuted to banishment; and so on, through a further history that comprised twelve months in Newgate, three further acquittals and outlawry; then after a career of stealing on racecourses he was sentenced in September 1790 to seven years' transportation. His histrionic experience at once asserted itself in grovelling correspondence meant for the official eye. His power of ingratiating himself was such that even on the transport ship he was given control of convicts and twice every Sunday conducted services and preached a sermon. On arrival at the settlement he impressed Phillip so well that he was almost immediately appointed a policeman and in 1792 was emancipated and given land as a settler. Phillip, Collins and Hunter wrote of him in the most complimentary fashion. Hunter made him chief constable and superintendent of convicts at Parramatta in 1796, a position which he held until 1800. He died a lunatic in 1804. There is no occasion to doubt his usefulness in the colony, but his case is interesting because of the ingenuity he displayed in identifying himself with officialdom in Australia. His literary reputation was largely not of his own making, but having compiled, or claiming to have compiled, a work entitled *A Voyage to New South Wales*, which was published in London in 1795, his name was wrongly linked with several works of the same kind which appeared about that time. His faculty of deception in life was equalled only by his posthumous literary celebrity, which endured until comparatively recent years.

(d) Estimate of the First Five Years

When Phillip departed in December 1792 the penal settlement had been in existence for five years. Opinion as to its success or failure depended on whether it was viewed from the English or the Australian point of view. English opinion was divided, one side accepting it as generally fulfilling its main purpose and the other side recommending its total abolition on the ground of its extravagance and ineffectiveness in reforming the criminals. Opinion in Australia varied also, but among officials of broader vision the

ideal of a free colony was not regarded as hopeless. However, even optimists were convinced that a reform of the existing system was essential, and hopes were chiefly centred in a plan for the introduction of free settlers, whose interested labour would increase production and set an example to ex-convicts engaged in the same work.

In a book written in the colony by Tench in 1791 and published in 1793, the fundamental defect in the penal system was exposed in a single sentence, which he urged all Englishmen to consider attentively. "Punishment," he declared, "when not directed to promote reformation is arbitrary and unauthorized."[32] This was at the root of the failure of the penal system from the Australian and from the convicts' points of view. It was not a system but a haphazard attempt to combine penal and colonial purposes. It is difficult to find evidence of any sincere intention to promote the reformation of the convicts; certainly, as Tench observed, the system had not been directed to that purpose. Although official despatches during these five years occasionally manifested a humanitarian interest in the welfare of the convicts, and it might be argued that the emancipation policy supports this view, the tenor of the correspondence revealed an eagerness to get rid of the prisoners, whatever the expenditure in money or human lives. In the main, the emancipation and assignment procedures were but parts of a debased colonial policy which sought to plant as many ex-convicts as possible and to give to settlers as many convict labourers as they could support. The shameful conditions of convict transport and the recurrent periods of starvation, or semi-starvation, in the colony are sufficient indication that the British Government, once it had paid the costs, did not much care what happened to the prisoners either in transit or at the settlement. Under the contracting system responsibility was conveniently transferred to others, and transportation consequently tended to become a matter of commerce. This shelving of responsibility was even more evident in the settlement. The task of founding a penal colony, involving momentous decisions and attention to detail, was left almost absolutely to a handful of officials in New South Wales.

The constitutional bases of government and the regulations of discipline and procedure which had been formulated before the departure of the First Fleet were inadequate, and were not modified to any appreciable extent for many years. Moreover, the men who were entrusted with this task were given insufficient material equipment for their work: prison discipline was to be maintained without proper warders or any of the essential paraphernalia of a gaol; an agricultural community was to be formed without farmers and

with the most primitive implements of labour. None of those on whom this great responsibility had been thrust were men of outstanding ability or experienced previously in colonial administration. Many of them were decidedly antagonistic to their duties. The planning and the execution devolved upon Phillip, Collins, White, Tench, Grimes, King, Hunter and Johnson chiefly. Phillip's absolute power could have been dangerous in another man; Collins was inexperienced, a soldier struggling to act as judge; King and Hunter were absent over long periods; Tench retired in 1791; Grimes arrived well after the settlement had begun; and White and Johnson worked well at their unwholesome but necessary tasks, the one as doctor and the other as clergyman. Others, too, contributed their share in the foundation. These few men were the organizers, or rather the creators, of a settlement built upon hopelessly inadequate material.

As a disciplinary institution the penal settlement was a failure; order could not be maintained among the convicts, except by arbitrary punishment, since reduced food allowances could nearly always be invoked as an explanation, and perhaps as a justification, of their maraudings, and many of them enjoyed a liberty and lack of restraint which, being criminals, they naturally abused. The condonation of promiscuous intercourse, tolerated because of its supposed necessity and the impossibility of preventing it, was an incentive to crime, a means of reducing the lesser criminal to the lowest levels, and a general preventive of possible reformation among the convicts. Reformative aspects in the system, whether material or spiritual, were lacking.

Nevertheless, there were experienced men in the settlement who looked with hope to the future and felt some satisfaction with what had already been achieved under adverse circumstances. The views expressed by Phillip when leaving the colony are significant, because of the conservative though optimistic attitude he had maintained throughout his term of office. The year 1792 had been particularly disastrous, the death roll in the community of four thousand totalling two civil officers, six soldiers, 418 male and eighteen female convicts, and twenty-nine children.[33] Moreover, it was only in the last few weeks of the year that he had been able to restore the full food ration to the community. Despite his frightful experience, when he received permission for leave of absence he expressed his misgivings about departing at a time when "the colony is approaching to that state in which I have so longed and anxiously wished to see it".[34]

In 1792 exploration had been extended as far as the Nepean and Broken Bay and beyond Botany Bay. The penal portion of the New South Wales settlement had been concentrated near

Parramatta, Sydney being, as Tench described it, no more than a headquarters for officials. Around the settlements at Parramatta 1700 acres were under cultivation and 100 acres of corn had been planted at Norfolk Island. The total population of the colony in October 1792 was 4222 at both settlements. The returns of December give the total of convicts as 3071, comprising 2387 men and 684 women. Children were 255. The earlier returns, differing slightly from the later one, show the distribution as 2372 at the main settlement and 737 at Norfolk Island. In these places the proportion of males to females was approximately five to one and two to one.

People settled on the land totalled 177, of whom 112 were of convict origin.[35] Following the inaccurate returns made by Governor Hunter on September 25, 1800, it is frequently stated that Phillip's land-grants were only 3889 acres; but Phillip's official returns of November 1791 and October 1792 specify individual grants totalling just on 6000 acres. (cf. *H.R.A.*, I i, 279, 401). The actual total was somewhat above that figure.

The costs of the penal system will be considered in the last chapter, but in order to compare the costs and the gains and to make it clear that the British Government had not been niggardly in expenditure a few general facts may be given. On May 30, 1793, a detailed analysis of expenditure on the settlement from the beginning was compiled by the Navy Office.[36] As this statement includes only about £10,000 belonging to the beginning of 1793, it will serve as a review of expenditure during Phillip's administration. Round figures are here used for convenience. The total cost of the First Fleet amounted to £84,000, of which half was expended on actual transport and fitting of vessels for service.

The subsequent cost of transport and provisions for new batches of convicts was £102,000; expenses of other vessels employed in the service of the colony, £116,000. The maintenance expenditure was thus classified: provisions £50,000; stores and clothing, etc., £83,000; bills drawn on the Treasury by the Governor for necessary supplies £28,000. Expenses of the military and civil establishments amounted to £67,000; two wrecked ships in the service were valued at £60,000. The total cost to within a few months of Phillip's departure was £473,044, and taking the period as having commenced in May 1787, the average annual cost had been £78,840. To the date at which these returns were compiled, June 1793, 5214 convicts had been sent from Great Britain and Ireland; therefore, the satisfaction felt by Government in being able to send its criminals overseas had necessitated an expenditure of at least £90 for each individual transported. It should be remembered that an average struck over the six years

was not conclusive, for maintenance costs in the later years increased as greater numbers were sent. The majority of these convicts still had long periods of sentence during which they had to be clothed and fed and guarded.

Commentators on this expenditure looked forward to a considerable reduction in the future. It was hoped that the expenditure for 1794 would be only £41,000, or £13 14s. for each convict in bondage. In that year, however, "owing to the high price of victualling, the demand for shipping, and the risque of capture", a contract for transporting criminals was accepted at the high rate of £80 per head.[37]

THE CHANGING ENGLISH BACKGROUND

THE history of the founding of the new penal system might properly be concluded with the departure of Governor Phillip from the colony, where, after the vicissitudes of the first five years the first hopeful signs of order and permanency had emerged. As the collapse of these hopes came with such suddenness and endured over so many years, it is advisable to show that while the system continued to serve the purpose of emptying English gaols it completely lost adaptability for reforming criminals and scientifically settling the new colony. Most of the general principles and practices of the system have already been described, and in some cases the development of these in subsequent years has been anticipated. To the general history of the colony, which then began to comprise new political issues naturally arising from an increased population of free and military settlers, only the briefest notice can be given in this chapter. However, the broader changes which took place in the execution of penal control in the colony, and the new element of divergent degrees of guilt which characterized many of the transportees in this period, will be indicated. For the latter it is essential that the reader should recall the altered social and political conditions in Great Britain and Ireland at this time.

"The Pitt Terror" in Great Britain and Ireland

The well-known and salient facts to be kept in mind, when the history of England from 1790 to 1800 is brought into indirect association with Australian conditions, are the increasing impoverishment of the labourers, and the influence of the French Revolution upon the proletariat in bringing them into the political field and upon the Government in inclining it to repress these democratic tendencies. The direct relationship between England and Australia, manifested in modulations of the penal and transportation policies, will be described in the following chapter.

After the French Revolution the Pitt Government commanded a power absolutely independent of the Crown and was strengthened by the support of Portland and Burke, who with their followers

had deserted the Whigs. From this time authority was irresistibly directed to the defence of property. The conditions of the poor were deplorable: the enclosure policy was being pursued with greater vigour; the inventions of Hargreaves, Arkwright and Crompton were now extensively in use and the Industrial Revolution, the effects of which upon the labour of men, women and children have already been noticed, had become a feature in national life.* Population was increasing at a rapid rate, being nearly nine millions at the beginning of the century, and in 1803 according to Pitt himself there were 1,234,000 people in England and Wales who were subsisting on parochial poor relief.[1]

The parliamentary reforms of which the earlier years of Pitt had given promise failed to eventuate, and such relief measures as he did propose were checkmated under a régime impregnated with Burke's teachings and fearful of Rousseau's. The attempts made by Price and Priestley in their writings to reform the constitution without destroying it had failed to convert the aristocracy and exerted little influence over the uneducated masses. Paine's work, however, was of a different character. The first part of his *Rights of Man*, published in 1791, did reach the multitude, teaching them that government was derived from the people, could be altered by them and should be exercised in their interests. The second part of that work, published in the following year, was revolutionary in its doctrines, advocating that hereditary offices should be abolished and less offensively, to our way of thinking, that government should be confined to the people's representatives. Here then, was French radicalism firmly implanted in England. The *Rights of Man* was suppressed and its author only evaded prosecution by flight; but his influence did not wane. Two hundred thousand copies of his book were sold in one year, despite the campaign waged against doctrinaires throughout the kingdom. Two political societies formed by the radical leaders attracted attention. Hardy's "London Corresponding Society" and Grey's "Friends of the People," though ostensibly confined to the education of the people in political affairs so that public opinion might be strengthened in the legitimate demands for universal suffrage and annual parliaments, gradually lost control over the multitude of branch organizations that sprang up in England and Scotland. The progress of the political movement cannot be described here, but one phase of it was destined to have a direct connexion with the Australian penal system. Before describing this it must be emphasized that although Jacobinism and revolution were not the avowed intentions of the leaders, the radical doctrines spread so quickly among the downtrodden and hungry masses that they

* Cf. Part I, Ch. I Section (d), p. 34.

easily took on the complexion of sedition; moreover, there was a real danger of perverting the armed forces at a time of national emergency. After the French massacres of 1793 panic seized the aristocracy and the Government, manifesting itself in ruthless prosecutions of newspaper editors, withdrawing the right of free speech outside Parliament, and billeting the military all over the country at an expense of nearly one and a half million pounds.

Scotland, however, hitherto resigned to its ridiculously small representation in Parliament, where Henry Dundas and his nephew ruled its destiny according to the best interests of the aristocracy, suddenly joined forces with, and speedily outdid, the English radical associations. The Scottish political organizations, whose vice-president was the capable young advocate of Huntershill, Thomas Muir, expanded rapidly. In December 1792 a Convention of Scottish Delegates assembled at Edinburgh, at which the most orderly and moderate proposals for reform were made. Muir, however, against advice presented an address from the United Irishmen in Dublin, in which concerted action was advocated and defiance was suggested. The incident provoked alarm at Dublin Castle, where the Committees of Secrecy were even more active than in England. At the instigation of the Lord Advocate, Robert Dundas, Muir was arrested at Belfast and brought to trial in Scotland before a packed jury and the biased and ignorant judge, Braxfield, on whom the mantle of Jeffreys had descended. The irregularities in the case were scandalous; it was questionable whether the indictment for sedition was sustainable under Scottish law, and evidence was rejected and accepted contrary to rule. He was found guilty and sentenced to fourteen years' transportation.

This was the beginning of the trials of the men known as the "Scottish Martyrs", who were transported to Australia. (Two of them were really Englishmen.) Around them and their cases a great mass of literature arose within a few years, which, however, can only be mentioned in this cursory survey of the political transportations.* The next victim came from Dundee, where radicalism had taken firm root among the starving weavers. *An Address to the People*, published in 1793 and containing very true but impolitic condemnations of the "wicked Ministry and complacent parliament", was found to have been transcribed by the Rev. Thomas Fysshe Palmer, a Unitarian minister educated at

* Cf. Trials of Muir, Palmer, Skirving, Margarot and Gerrald: Howell's *State Trials*, xviii; *passim. Parliamentary History* for Debates and Questions on the trials, as indicated in the Bibliography, and *Lords Journals*, xl, 15, 123-126; *Reports of Committees of Secrecy*, 1794 and 1799, Appendix XV; Dyer, G.: *Slavery and Famine* (1794); *A Narrative of the Sufferings of T. F. Palmer and W. Skirving, etc.*, by T. F. Palmer (1797); Muir, T.: *The Telegraph* (1796); Campbell's *Lives of the Lord Chancellors*, VIII, 143. Much of the documentary history and evidence, as well as the opinions of contemporary newspapers, has been collected in a special appendix to the *H.R.N.S.W.*, Vol. II, 820-886. For general reviews of the subject see J. Holland Rose's *William Pitt and the Great War*, ch. vii; Lecky's *History of England, etc.*, Vol. VII; and Holden Furber's *Henry Dundas* (1931), ch. iii, in which the argument for Dundas is presented fairly. Other works are indicated in the Bibliography.

Eton and Cambridge. Though manifestly not the author, Palmer was arrested and, to provide an example, was sentenced to five years' transportation. In this case, as in the other, the gross abuses in the procedure of the trial were glaringly apparent. These two cases were raised in the House of Commons on five occasions in 1794. On March 10, Whitbread, Fox, Sheridan and Grey presented a brilliant exposure of the injustices which had been committed during the trials, but after uncompromising replies from Dundas and Pitt the motion for a reconsideration of the cases was rejected by a majority of six to one.[2]

In November of the same year the Edinburgh Convention attracted delegates from forty-two kindred societies of Ireland and Scotland, and Joseph Gerrald and Maurice Margarot attended as representatives of the London Corresponding Society. Advanced doctrines were boldly stated and the close alliance with the Irish societies was indicated in boastful speeches. It is clear that in Great Britain and Ireland the radicals underestimated the extraordinarily expert espionage forces which were at the disposal of Government and kept authority in close touch with every movement. The result of this convention was that four of the leaders were placed on trial, at which the presiding judge established a novel precedent by declaring that those who created dissatisfaction such as tended to rebellion were to be held guilty of sedition to all intents and purposes, even though that intention was not in their minds at the time.[3] Braxfield further distinguished himself by a subsequent declaration that he had had no idea that his sentences of transportation involved servitude and hard labour.[4] All were sentenced to fourteen years' transportation, and Skirving, the cultured Gerrald and the irascible Margarot were sent to Australia.*

English public opinion was so aroused by this exploitation of justice that the London juries began to refuse to convict for sedition. In the two celebrated trials of Hardy, the founder of the London Corresponding Society, and Horne Tooke, an equally prominent leader of radical opinion, acquittals were recorded to the obvious delight of the populace and the discomfiture of the Government. The Prime Minister lost much of his prestige: "the hero of the year 1794", wrote Professor Holland Rose, "was not William Pitt but the British nation".

The further history of the severe repressions need not be described at any length, as these were the only transportations, so far as we

---

* When Robespierre was tottering to his fall and people were being executed on suspicion of being English spies, the following Bulletin was sent from Leghorn to Lord Grenville: "Mars 11, 13, 15, Paris; Le 13, le Ministre de la Marine écrivit au Comité qu'il lui proposoit de faire tout ce que dépendoit de lui pour procurer la liberté au nommé Margarot et ses collègues qu'on alloit déporter à Botani Bay, et de décréter, s'il parvenoit à arriver en France, que la Nation donneroit, en pur don à Margarot, toutes les possessions qu'avoit en France le Duc de Richemont sous le titre de Duché d'Aubigny." (Cf. *Dropmore Papers*, II, 544.)

know, directly resulting from sedition trials in England and Scotland at this time. It is of some interest to note, however, in the Returns of Convicts compiled in 1810 that nineteen prisoners were transported in 1794 after having been sentenced in Scotland. There had been no other transportation of Scottish prisoners since 1791 and the next transportation, in 1800, was of four prisoners, sentenced between 1796 and 1799. The political societies, far from being intimidated by these sentences, continued often in an inflammatory manner, which was justifiable according to their demands and the necessities of the people, but dangerous in a country that was already at war. The espionage system continued unabated and prosecutions were particularly directed against newspaper editors and publishers or sellers of seditious literature. Alarmed by plans for a General Convention of Radicals and excited by exaggerated reports from the Committees of Secrecy, the Government redoubled its efforts to stem this "enormous torrent of insurrection". The Habeas Corpus Act was suspended, it was made illegal to hold public meetings and every innocent attempt by the working population to form trade unions was checked. While the intensity of the anti-sedition campaign waned, the magistrates continued to sentence half-intoxicated unfortunates for "damning the King", and prisoners against whom no sufficient evidence was forthcoming languished in gaol until near the end of the century.[5]

After considerable agitation concessions were granted to Palmer, Skirving, Muir and Margarot, who were placed together on the *Surprize* transport; the unfortunate Gerrald, gentler in disposition and far less self-assertive than the others, lay in prison for fourteen months and was then brought manacled to the ship, *Sovereign*. However, the influence of friends gained him some privileges, and he was the only transportee on board that ship, which sailed in January 1795. The tuberculosis from which he suffered increased in virulence on the voyage, and he died not long after landing in the colony, on March 16, 1796. Palmer and Skirving paid their own passages and the former was accompanied by his servant. By special permission Margarot's wife sailed with her husband. During the passage an attempt was made to seize the vessel by convicts and soldiers who were impregnated by the new revolutionary ideas. Palmer and Skirving were accused of complicity and for a considerable time afterwards correspondence followed from these literary gentlemen, establishing their innocence and protesting against the confinement to which they were subjected as a result of the mutinous charges laid against them. On arrival at the settlement the accused were found not guilty of complicity. Before the prisoners left England it had been made clear that

their sentences were to be interpreted as banishment. Accordingly, the Lieutenant-Governor, Grose, was informed that as a property in their services had not been made over to the contractor, he would not be able to compel their services at government work. He was strictly enjoined, however, to keep a firm control over their insidious practices, and it was further ordered that they should receive no benefit whatsoever from the public stores, unless they worked for it.[6]

One other feature of the unrest during these years, which had an important relationship to Australian transportation, was the disaffection existing in the English Navy. The Navy, victorious though it was, was the more neglected of the services. Men were recruited to it in large numbers from the dregs of English society. Naval service was a recognized commutation of capital sentences, and when men were needed, county magistrates and corporations readily emptied their gaols into the King's ships, even paying a bounty for the privilege. In Ireland the practice was carried to extremes by magistrates, at first in open disregard of the law, and later legally, and it sometimes happened that as many as a hundred men were sent from one gaol to begin a naval career.[7] The severity of discipline in the ships became a scandal, and although reforms were made in the service extreme cases of corporal punishment continued, one man being flogged to death as late as 1805. Loyalty was expected from half-starved, half-naked and underpaid crews. The immediate cause of the naval unrest which occurred in these years was economic, and the mutinies were attempts to force the authorities to improve conditions.[8] At least one incident in these mutinies can be connected with Australia. In 1797 a young assistant-surgeon on H.M.S. *Standard*, William Redfern, aged about nineteen, took a minor part in the general mutinous risings at the Nore; his death sentence was commuted because of his age, and in 1801 he was transported to the Australian penal settlements, where, in the following year he began a career as a medical officer. He was pardoned absolutely in 1802 and continued his work until 1819, proving progressive in his scientific methods and being largely responsible for the equipment of the Sydney hospital. Throughout his long career he was practically ostracized by the "exclusive" section of the population, and in 1819, when it was suggested that he should be made principal medical officer the proposal was rejected by the British Government, chiefly because of his previous history. His case was one of the most interesting in the colony, illustrating the degrees of guilt among convicts and the reluctance of officialdom to rehabilitate men of at least average integrity.

It is difficult to determine how many naval and military

offenders were sent to Australia under sentences directly imposed by court martial. In the incomplete 1810 Returns there is no mention of these transportations until June 1801, but in that year thirty-six offenders were sent out, having been sentenced on various ships and at Gilbraltar between 1797 and 1800, and in 1802 four men, similarly sentenced, were sent to Australia.[9]

As the criminal and political situations in Ireland have already been briefly described, only a passing reference need be made here. An important point to emphasize is that the seditious tendencies and activities of this period were sufficiently real to make them national dangers from the point of view of England. This explains how men of the stamp of Pitt and Burke, who in the past had held more liberal views, became convinced that a national emergency had arisen in which repression was necessary.[10] The admission that widespread disaffection existed need not involve agreement with the violent policy that was pursued in Great Britain and Ireland, and in the Navy, to stamp it out. Neither does it imply a condonation of the shameful social conditions to relieve which the radicals strove, or, as in Ireland, the provocative attitude of Government in goading the people on to a state of real rebellion. The documentary evidence of this period reveals the far-reaching influence and efficient organization of the Society of United Irishmen, under the leadership of Wolfe Tone.* Within the radical societies of England and Scotland the power of this body was such as to divert moderate opinion along more extreme courses, as was seen in the cases of the Scottish Martyrs. In the Navy, where Irishmen in 1797 numbered about 15,500, the Jacobin activities of the Irish secret societies were far from negligible. Wolfe Tone's perfervid addresses to the Irish sailors— informing them that they were no longer subjects of the King, instructing them to convince others that mutiny would be to their own advantage, and demonstrating how a vessel might be seized by a mutinous crew—these direct communications from Tone reveal the great extent to which this highly disciplined body attempted to control the activities of men beyond Ireland.

The intimate sway held over the minds of the United Irishmen in Ireland and exercised by deputies of the supreme control stationed throughout the country, and the enthusiasm and loyalty felt by the members for their leaders, were phenomena far in advance of those that had characterized other rebellions. This devotion was more in evidence in the later period of the movement, when it became accentuated by the English practices of

* Cf. "Rebellion Papers" (State Paper Office, Dublin); Reports of the Committees of Secrecy (Irish), 1793, 1797, 1798 (August 21, 30); for transportation references see Appendices, pp. 45, 56, 74, *passim*. English P.P., 1731-1800, Accounts and Papers, XXXIV (1791), No. 740, p. 14. See also T. W. Tone: *Memoirs*, II, 326-28; C. Gill: *Naval Mutinies of 1797*, 330 *et seq.*

espionage and cruelty, and finally, after defeat, it persisted vividly in the minds of the victims, who refused to acknowledge that the cause for which they had suffered was irrevocably lost.

If this fact is kept in mind it will explain the conduct of the Irish prisoners in Australia. Conscious of their lack of real criminality, they more readily set themselves to organize revolt against a system which, by its nature, was repressive and degrading. Hitherto, prisoners generally had submitted doggedly to the penal system, unconscious of their power by united effort to overthrow the small and disgruntled guard that kept order in the colony through the years of starvation. The sudden introduction of great numbers of experienced insurrectionaries into the colony made itself immediately felt by the subversion of such law and order as existed there. Transportation from Ireland did not begin until 1791, when 155 persons were sent out in the *Queen*, but from then until 1802 2086 criminals and political prisoners were transported from Ireland. In that period, 1793 to 1802, when 1917 Irishmen were embarked and 1736 arrived, 41 per cent of all the transportees who reached the settlement had come from Ireland. In 1800 Governor King estimated that there were 450 "United Irishmen" in the colony and in the following year he increased this total to 600. From the "Rebellion Papers" it is evident that large numbers of disaffected Irish soldiers were sent to Australia, and complaints were made frequently by officers that these men were accumulating without facilities being provided for their transportation. Soldiers in Irish regiments which had shown signs of disloyalty, wrote Professor Scott, were clapped on board ship and transported by the simple order of a commanding officer, without even a list of their names being sent with them.[11] He estimated that the Irish political "exiles" numbered about 2000; but although all these prisoners were saturated with the revolutionary doctrines, it must be granted that many of them were transported for crimes that were not political, some being hardened criminals and others merely victims of the property laws.*

Therefore, while granting that the punishments inflicted upon the unfortunate and misguided ringleaders of the Irish in the settlement, particularly the atrocious floggings inflicted by Governor King in 1803 and 1804, were unjustifiable, it must be recognized that the influence of this large body in a small, incompetently controlled community of felons was disquieting to governors. It is now certain that the tactics that had been followed in Europe were attempted in Australia, and word was sent to the French

* *Bell's Weekly Messenger* (3.1.1802) referred to this distinction between the transportees. On the *Luz St. Ann* (arrived 16.ii.1801), besides political offenders, there were "miscreants of all descriptions, convicted of the worst of crimes, such as murder, etc." Bentham quoted this journal in *Panopticon versus N.S.W.* (*Works*, IV, 205).

that if an attack were made on the settlement the invader might rely on Irish assistance.

However, the most striking feature about the Irish prisoners and their procedure is that the revolutionary principles which they introduced into Australia vanished absolutely within a few years of the arrival of the last of the "Defenders". It may be argued that the stern repressive measures taken against them by the military and the deportation of their leaders to Norfolk Island produced this result. But it seems more likely that with their gradual restoration to civil rights and their separation from the troubles of their native country, they settled naturally, quickly and profitably in the land which but recently they had regarded as the symbol of oppression. Very few of the Irish returned to their homeland and twenty years later some of the former rebels were among the well-to-do citizens of Sydney. Apart from the repression immediately connected with the insurrection years, governors displayed a sympathetic understanding of the Irish prisoners' condition, granting them the usual concessions of land and convict servants, and frequently commending their conduct in terms complimentary to themselves and derogatory to the military settlers. The blame for withholding religious rights from them is more to be credited to the British Government and English policy prior to 1829, than to the governors in the settlement.

Among the better known of those deported directly as a result of the rebellion in Ireland were Joseph Holt, a land-holder of Wexford who had led a detachment of yeomanry during the rebellion; Michael Dwyer, another leader in the guerilla warfare; Henry Fulton, a Church of England clergyman; and three Catholic priests: James Harold, James Dixon and Peter O'Neil.*

* Holt was banished, not transported as a felon, and sailed, accompanied by his wife and daughter, in the *Minerva* on August 24, 1799. In 1800 he became manager of William Cox's farm at Sydney. He was arrested on suspicion of being concerned in the Irish insurrection of 1800, but was restored to liberty. He bought land, but was wrongly imprisoned in 1804 for alleged complicity in the succeeding rebellion and was exiled to Norfolk Island; after his release he was entrusted with important work at Hobart. He returned to Sydney in February 1806. In 1811 he was granted a free pardon and left the country in December 1812, and after many adventures returned to Dublin in April 1814, where he died in poverty in 1826, regretting he had ever left N.S.W. His *Memoirs* (edited by T. C. Croker) were published in two volumes in 1838.

Henry Fulton, an Irish Protestant clergyman, confessed "under pressure" to having been implicated in the rebellion, and being allowed to transport himself for life sailed with Holt. In 1800 he was given a conditional pardon, and for seven years worked at Norfolk Island as a chaplain. He was fully pardoned in 1805, resumed his duties in N.S.W. and was made a member of the civil court. He loyally supported Bligh on the deposition of that Governor and was favourably regarded by Macquarie, who made him a magistrate. He worked as a chaplain in the Penrith district until his death in 1840.

James Harold, transported for complicity in the rebellion, came with Holt. (Cf. Bentham's *Panopticon versus N.S.W.*, Works, IV, 176.) Dixon, on a life sentence for the same offence, arrived in 1800. O'Neil, in a similar position, arrived in 1801: his case had occasioned much publicity in Ireland, and after the intervention of friends on his behalf with Lord Cornwallis, he was pardoned, and returned home in 1803. (See *Correspondence between Lord Redesdale and the Earl of Fingall*, Dublin, 1803; *Observations on the Remonstrance of Rev. P. O'Neill*, Dublin, 1804.) Dixon was conditionally emancipated and temporarily sanctioned to act as chaplain in the districts of N.S.W. (April 19, 1803); he was made by the Pope, on receipt of this news in Europe, Prefect-Apostolic of New Holland. Meanwhile Harold had been implicated in the Irish insurrection, and being found guilty, was re-transported to Norfolk Island, where he remained without recognition, leaving the colony in 1810. Dixon returned to Ireland in 1808.

THE BREAKING OF THE SYSTEM

(a) The Military Oligarchy

For nearly three years after Phillip's departure control of the colony was exercised by the New South Wales Corps. Whatever good Phillip had done was undone, convict discipline was undermined, and by methods of unscrupulous exploitation a few men concentrated power so effectively within their hands that they were able to retain it for seventeen years, defying Governor Hunter and bringing about his recall, stultifying the well-intended efforts of Governor King, and, when faced finally with a martinet, deposing him by force from his governorship. The brevity of this interregnum period might lead one to underestimate its importance, which, from two points of view, was fundamental in shaping subsequent colonial history. From the land-grants then made originated the land problems which were partly solved by the abolition of the free grant system in 1831 and the introduction of sale by auction.

In the second place, the penal system which Phillip had tried to adapt for the reform of criminals was made to serve an opposite purpose, establishing precedents of laxity which produced men and women of unambitious outlook who profoundly influenced the minds and actions of those who came after them.

As a solution of the difficulty that had arisen from the refusal of the marines to co-operate with Phillip's government, this guard had been withdrawn and a corps specially raised for the colony was instituted. In accord with English procedure in colonial affairs, it was largely composed of rejects from other corps, sent to Australia whenever they could be collected and having among its members many young soldiers, adventurers, deserters and mutineers.

In 1794 among a party of twenty privates arriving, there were six deserters and a corporal who had been found guilty of mutiny at Quebec. As Collins indignantly observed, the personnel of this body was "disgusting" and such men exercising authority presented no "counterpoise" to the vices of the prisoners. It was even provided that a supplementary company should be raised within the colony from such marines as chose to stay, from

freed convicts, and, as happened frequently, from convicts themselves who were emancipated on condition of joining the corps
indefinitely or until their being discharged. The first detachment of
the corps reached Sydney in June 1790, but the former marine
guard did not leave until December 1791. The commander of the
new corps, Major Francis Grose, arrived in 1792 and by virtue of a
commission as lieutenant-governor succeeded Phillip on December
11, 1792.

Within a month of Phillip's departure the whole system of
government was altered, and it was made evident that the
Lieutenant-Governor was under the sway of a force which he
could not control. Hitherto the military, other than the Lieutenant-
Governor, had taken only a small part in the civil government
of the colony, their chief duty being to guard the stores and to
exercise a general control when called upon. Complaints against
convicts and all minor offences within the colony had come before
the civil magistrates, who were five in number and at regular
sessions imposed sentences which they reported to the Governor,
but Grose's first act was to define the absolute power of the military
captains at Parramatta and Sydney, whom he ordered to review all
existing sentences. Another order directed "that all inquiries by the
civil magistrate were in future to be dispensed with" pending a
new arrangement, and convicts were to be punished only by the
Lieutenant-Governor's particular order. With military and judicial
power concentrated in their hands it was easy for the corps to
go forward for their own benefit. The working-hours of convict
labour were reduced and the practice hitherto obtaining by which
the civil, military and convict populations shared equal rations in
prosperity or famine was altered, two scales being defined, one
of which considerably favoured the ruling class. This marked the
end of the national experiment in co-operative living.

From the beginning the military officers had resented the fact
that no legal provisions had been made for their being accommodated with land. Phillip had agreed that their contribution to
agriculture would be advantageous and, pending a decision,
allowed them to clear and farm land with the help of two assigned
servants supported by Government. The same concession was
later authorized for non-commissioned officers, and a month after
Phillip's departure another despatch was received by Grose
allowing grants of land to officers as a speculation, from which
they might benefit by selling it when they left, but conditionally
on its being allocated in such districts as might encourage settlement in an orderly fashion later on.[12] The privilege was acted
upon immediately.

The economic and social aspects, and consequences, of this

entry of the officers into agriculture will be specially considered in the following section. But, in order to maintain continuity in the historical narrative, the main facts about the distribution of land in this period are indicated in the following paragraph, although they must be repeated in the latter section.

Only two official returns of land-grants were made in this period. The first states that, between December 31, 1792 and April 1, 1793, only 1590 acres were distributed between 11 settlers of official origin, 5 free settlers, and 5 expirees. The distribution was in small lots between 20 and 120 acres. The next return indicates that, between June 1, 1793 and April 1, 1794, only 2663 acres, comprising 59 grants and 4 leases, were distributed among 28 officials and 35 members of the penal classes. Again the lots were small, from 30 to 120 acres. (Cf. *H.R.A.*, I, 1, pp. 438 and 472). Included among the grantees were such highly placed figures as Paterson, Macarthur and Foveaux.[13] The figures are incomplete and omit the period between April 1794 and September 1795. Moreover, it should be observed that the distribution of land was made in a haphazard way. As Governor Hunter remarked, the deed of grant was usually informal, merely indicating that someone had the Lieutenant-Governor's premission to settle on land, and any private soldier could get 25 acres of land wherever he wanted it. (Cf. *H.R.A.* I, 1, pp, 667, 670). Governor Hunter's estimate, made in 1800 was more accurate, defining a total of 10,674 acres granted by Grose and 4965 acres by Paterson, who succeeded Grose. The total for this administration was 15,639. (*H.R.A.* 1, II, p. 566). A distribution of even this extent could not be regarded as excessive; Governor Phillip's grants probably had approximated 6000 acres, and Governor Hunter's own distributions within a period of five years totalled 28,279. However, while appreciating the moderation of the grants made during the military regime, due regard must be given to purchases or seizures of land made by the official group from indigent settlers. The extent of such transactions cannot be computed satisfactorily.

The military have been blamed for thus robbing the emancipists, but it is clear that some worthless settlers only waited for Phillip's departure to get rid of the stock which he had carefully reared and nursed and apportioned to the settlers whom he placed on the land. Had this stock not been purchased when it was, it would certainly have been destroyed within a few weeks and sold as meat. According to Grose's opinion, the settlers were a good-for-nothing crew, lacking every other ambition than that of saving sufficient money from their land to enable them to purchase a return passage to England.[14] From the economic point of view the only sane policy was to give land to a class that was anxious to have

it, capable of using it and inspired by the chief motive under which economic prosperity is usually achieved—personal profit.

In many respects, this official attitude and opinion had much to justify it. To depend absolutely on settlement by convicts, considering their dispositions, natural and developed by force of circumstances, was folly; and to await sufficient free immigrants for colonizing was speculative in the extreme. The colony was in a precarious state for food, and as it had now become evident that regular supplies could not be expected from England, it had necessarily to become self-supporting as quickly and as far as possible. This distribution of land to military, free and ex-convict settlers had many disadvantages, but some such impetus had to be given to industry. The officers chartered ships, importing under the greatest difficulties stock from abroad, and the foundations of the great wool industry were then laid by John Macarthur, one of the foremost members of this oligarchy.

Much, therefore, must be conceded in justification of this policy, even though the methods by which agricultural progress was eventually made were questionable in the highest degree. Those aspects will be discussed later on in this book. Where the system failed was in the lack of control. In previous instructions to the governor the board principles of land distribution had been laid down by the British Government. Phillip had even gone so far as to plan his town with a view to the future. The foundation of a new colony, wrote R. C. Mills, offered an unexampled opportunity for laying down a fair and equitable system of land holding and settlement, elastic enough to adapt itself to the needs of a growing community, and it might be expected that the authorities would have adopted some system or, at least, acted cautiously in view of the possibility of failure and the difficulty of retracing steps wrongly taken at the beginning.[15] Under the system inaugurated by Grose, in disregard of definite instructions, a chain of farms was begun, connecting Sydney with Parramatta, but without regard for systematic sub-divisions. Phillip's plan of a future city was permanently marred when the military began to restore to Sydney the population which Phillip had confined to Parramatta. Land was granted in the most haphazard fashion, to ex-convicts liberally, to all degrees of the military from officers to drummers, who were allowed to settle where they pleased.

From the penal point of view the methods adopted in this change were disastrous. The officers justified themselves in their purchase of stock from the wasteful settlers, but the sheep were sometimes bought at two gallons of rum per head—which is quite another question and only one example of a nefarious practice which was then introduced. The wholesale bartering of stock and

farms for spirits was a breach of two regulations, one that had prohibited the sale of spirits to prisoners, and the other issued by Dundas in June 1793, according to which land could be granted to emancipists only on condition that they resided on it and cultivated it for five years, any intervening sale being voided and the land reverting to the Crown.[16] But the practice continued over many years, whereby unfortunate, drunken settlers sold their properties for little or nothing, anxious to be rid of the obligation to work and craving for liquor. In this way the original grants of land made to military and other settlers increased in size by accretions from the farms surrendered by helpless ex-convict settlers.

The liquor trade and the monopolist commerce of the official coterie must now be considered. At the commencement of his career Grose lamely excused his purchase of a large quantity of spirits, on the grounds that the military required the stimulants and that the ship's captain had refused to sell his other cargo except on this condition. When he asked for directions from London, Dundas's reply was definite: spirits must not be sold or conveyed to convicts, and commerce in this commodity was to be under the strictest supervision. This first cargo was sold to the officers at prime cost, but before the month was out a system of barter between settlers and military traders, in which spirits were sold at 600 per cent profit, had become so great a menace that Grose had to issue an Order making such sales punishable except by special licence. The Order was ignored, and in the following years the passion for liquor became a mania. Illicit stills were set up, and it was found more profitable to distil wheat than to sell it to the public store. From one bushel of wheat, wrote Collins, five quarts of spirit were distilled, which were sold in exchange for labour at five and six shillings a quart. By another estimate spirits which had cost 7s. 6d. were sold at £8 the gallon. However, the monopoly was not the main evil; the degradation of the population by this commerce had a far greater significance.[17]

Officers were allowed to engage in private trading. They chartered ships to bring foodstuffs from abroad and encouraged frequent trading by American merchant-ships, the cargoes of which they purchased absolutely, dividing them up according to the amount invested by each in these wholesale importations. In these years, when the community was literally in a state of semi-starvation, monopolies were formed among the officers over even the necessities of life, and in order to make their commerce more effective they entered into a "combination bond", by which each contracted not to overbuy or undersell the other. Consequently, fortunes were quickly made; Captain John Macarthur commenced

operations at this time £500 in debt, and in 1808 it was said that
he had amassed a fortune of £20,000. Prices of commodities were
exorbitant, and while labour was expensive in theory, it was in
practice cheap to one class of employers who paid wages in a
liquor equivalent. As the colony totally lacked a currency, grain
had been the recognized item of barter, being purchased by
Government and paid by bills on the Treasury. Rum now began
to take the place of grain.*

This system of national exploitation was ingenious. It was more
reminiscent of ancient commercial methods than of the contemporary English system, bad as this was.

Unrestricted in trade, indulged with land, and in some cases
with women to satisfy their lustful desires, this commonplace body
of men devised a system under which they were paid threefold by
Government. They had their military pay, they were given land
to become farmers, and had the free labour of the men whom they
were sent to guard. The assignment system was carried to an
extreme. Grose illegally granted ten convicts to every officer, and
invited the Government to send out as many convicts as could
be afforded, who, he candidly admitted, could readily be absorbed
in the colony. Dundas ruled that each civil and military officer
was entitled to only two convict servants, to be supported by
Government over a period of only two years, and if they employed
more they must support them. Grose re-submitted the question,
and temporarily allowed the assignment of ten to continue. When
the Duke of Portland wrote in 1795 to state that the original
instructions "did not admit of any discretionary construction on
the part of the Lieutenant-Governor", Grose had already left the
country and the system had become so firmly established that
despite his best efforts, Governor Hunter was unable to bring about
its complete reform.[18]

The altered conditions of assigned convicts may be viewed
from three angles.

In the first place, under the system of labour endowment the
military settlers grew rich doubly at the expense of Government.
The assigned servants were maintained, except in a few instances,
by Government and the products of their labours were sold back
to the government stores. Moreover, where assigned servants were
supported by the employers, these servants received rations from

---

* At the end of 1793, prices and values were as follows: Wheat, 10s. per bushel, cash; as
payment for labour, 14s. Maize, 7s. cash; 12s. 6d. for labour. Ewes, £6 to £8; wethers, £4 to £5.
Breeding sows, £3 to £6. Pork, per lb., 9d. Mutton, per lb., 2s. to 2s. 6d. Tea, 10s. to 16s. lb.
Labour: carpenter, 3s. per day; clearing and hoeing an acre of ground, £4. Collins regarded wages
as high; but commensurate with prices of commodities they do not appear to be so. (Collins,
Account, etc., 334.) In the Records of the Macarthurs of Camden (p. 51) Mrs John MacArthur stated
that beef cost 4s. or 5s. per lb., "a good horse", £140. No horse sold at less than £100. A cow in
calf fetched £80.

the stores, which, in their turn, were compensated by payments made with produce from farms.

In the second place the transference of such large numbers of these servants to private employ practically brought government production to a standstill, and much of the labour still available to Government was diverted from public agriculture and employed in building barracks for the soldiers. The colony had therefore degenerated into a state where its chances of ceasing to be a burden on the mother country were more remote than ever. It had stultified its original intention and was fast becoming similar to the previous American system, under which convicts were transported to become the slaves of private owners. The great difference, however, remained that in Australia Government still owned the prisoners and had to maintain them for the privilege of supplying them to individual farmers. That this was a studied policy among the military is clear from the aggressive attitude taken by Grose against King, the reliable Commandant at Norfolk Island. At this settlement prosperous seasons and interested labour had brought a fruitful harvest. Having more than his needs and in accordance with the previous regulations laid down by Phillip, King shipped his surplus to New South Wales, where, on behalf of his state farms and his industrious settlers, he expected it would be bought by the Government. Despite the fact that the colony at Sydney was generally in a famine state, necessitating huge purchases of supplies from India, which were authorized by Grose and paid by bills drawn on the Treasury, Grose refused emphatically to purchase the products of Norfolk Island, contending that by such an arrangement all private initiative would be checked in the main settlement. The result was that private initiative was ruined in Norfolk Island, and settlers from the marines and others returned to Sydney, where they might have a market.

The conflict between King and Grose was essentially one in which the military dominance was raised as a question demanding solution. The case had arisen on that island where King had had to take measures against the military for assault upon free people; his action was resented, and it was argued that the military could not be held accountable for injuries done to settlers. King promptly disbanded and disarmed the whole recalcitrant militia, raised a new body from ex-marines and others, and sent ten soldiers to Sydney charged with mutiny. His action was regarded by the officers at Sydney as an insult, and though the men were found guilty, provocation by the settlers was found in their favour. In an impertinent letter to King, Grose unequivocally stated the privileged position of the military in the colony. When the case

was referred to England, the Duke of Portland replied in a well-reasoned judgment on June 10, 1795, affirming the right of private farmers to sell their stores to the Government at a fair market price, reprehending Grose for his treatment of King and laying down the principle that as the civil and military departments were separate institutions, redress of grievances was possible to either party, by one through the magistrate to the governor and by the other to his military superior.[19]

In the third place, the assignment system, now considerably expanded, has to be considered from the convicts' point of view. Hitherto, every convict in private employ could be punished only through the intervention of a civil magistrate, and even the convict himself had the right of recourse to this authority. The principle was, of course, abused, but in this period when the civil magistracy was abolished the power of punishment was confined to the military body itself, except in certain instances when the criminal court was assembled. With such a body it was evident that summary justice would be more readily applied than under the previous system. One of Governor King's first actions was to regulate the power of inflicting punishment, confining it to the jurisdiction of magistrates, and this interference caused dissatisfaction among landholders who had become accustomed to punish their servants as they thought fit.

Between the departure of Phillip and the arrival of Hunter 405 convicts were sent to the colony; of these 303 were from Ireland. Among the whole number only one died in transport, and he was a consumptive before sailing. The improvement in transport from this time, with one exception, was remarkable. A change was made in England in the contracting system and on two voyages at least, it was arranged that a premium of £5 per head should be paid for each convict landed in good health.[20] It is certain that much of the satisfactory condition that eventuated was due to the supervision of surgeons. The *Bellona*, arriving in August 1793, carried the first free settlers and seventeen women convicts, all of whom arrived in good health. The *Boddingtons* followed. When that ship arrived at Cork, the Surgeon-Superintendent reported that a contingent of the Irish convicts were received on board from the coastal transport where they had lain in a state of fever and dysentery over a period of seven weeks, but after being "cleansed" they improved in health. The ship was crowded beyond its capacity and five convicts over the stipulated number had to be taken at the order of the Lord-Lieutenant, who wished to transport as many as possible. No particulars of their trials or sentences could be obtained and the Sheriff had to confess that, as they had been gathered from all parts of the kingdom, it was impossible to procure

H

the details.[21] The soldiers on board, enlisted for the corps, proved more recalcitrant than the prisoners, and, despite the encomiums paid deservedly to the contractor for the food and less deservedly for the supervision and sanitary arrangements on the ship, it is recorded that the surgeon had to call upon "the convicts themselves to preserve order, cleanliness and regularity".[22] When this well-conducted ship arrived on August 7, 1793, an unusual spectacle of cheerful and cheering convicts presented itself, but the effect was weakened by some of their number who promptly stole a boat and went off to find China. The complement on the *Sugar Cane*, however, were described as "a lawless body", and disorder prevailed among the 110 male and fifty female Irish prisoners, and equally among prospective members of the New South Wales Corps on board that ship. An alleged plot to seize the vessel was ruthlessly put down and one man was executed.[23] The *Surprize* carried eighty-three prisoners, among whom were four of the Scottish political offenders; the mutiny on board her has already been referred to. Generally, during the period the numbers of life-sentenced prisoners increased to a small extent, in conformity with a change in penal policy in 1792.[24]

The provisioning of the settlement continued to be capricious. From January to June 1793 provisions were ample, then rations had to be restricted and but for private consignments obtained from India the colony would have starved. Reductions in rations had to be made frequently during the following twelve months, despite small purchases made abroad or from American ships trading regularly with the colony. In November the stores were nearly expended, and in January 1794, but ten weeks' supply remained on a weekly ration of three pounds of meat to each convict. Collins described this and the following months as a period of greater famine than had ever been experienced before in the settlement. Only a fortnight's provisions were left; the hours of work were reduced, convicts being left free after 10 a.m. to fend for themselves; men wandered into the forests and returned emaciated, pleading that famine was the cause of their lack of discipline. A fear arose that the convicts would seize the officers' flocks. On February 10, when the doors of the stores had been closed, two ships arrived, with limited cargoes of meat but no wheat, and the convicts were put upon a diet of Indian corn and meat. It was deeply resented that the settlers to whom Government had given liberal supplies of seed-wheat refused either to restore the grant or to sell wheat, insisting on retaining it for the next harvest, and as a retribution Grose issued instructions that sixty-three settlers who had been victualled over the legal period of eighteen months should be struck off and made to support them-

selves. Famine was lifted in June 1794, when five store-ships arrived, and in view of the new but temporary affluence Grose refused to purchase wheat raised by settlers at Norfolk Island. From that date until May 1795 provisions were sufficient; but then, once again, ships had to be sent for supplies, and in July a further reduction of rations had to be made, as all salt meat had been used up and only a few casks remained for the privileged use of the military.[25] It was immediately noticed that the famine conditions produced a wave of serious crime. While it is evident that the food problem of the colony was not fully appreciated in England, it must be understood that the right of commerce between India and the colony was recognized in England and the Bills drawn on the Treasury for these purchases were not disputed.[26] Nevertheless, the irregularity of supplies created conditions in the colony which were disruptive of law and order.*

In these years discipline in the settlement had been considerably relaxed. The hours of government labour were immediately altered, in 1793, convicts being bound to work from five in the morning until nine, when they were free until four in the afternoon, and again after sunset. At Parramatta all convict labour was placed under the immediate control of John Macarthur, but the public farming which had been concentrated at that settlement was reduced and large numbers of prisoners were sent back to Sydney, where they were busily employed in the Petersham district in the sawmills and at the brickfields making bricks and carting them to Sydney Cove, where a feverish haste was manifested in building barracks for the accommodation of the military. Special rations of spirits were officially issued to convicts employed at this work as an incentive to industry. Superintendents increased slightly in number and their wages were increased. Generally speaking, public work was reduced to a minimum and the preference was given to private assignment.

The prisoner population now had many classes. The expirees had increased in numbers. Some of them settled in the country, where they were given the usual concessions to begin farming, and although no official returns were made of those who returned to

* For the year ending 1793 the deaths in New South Wales numbered two settlers, seven soldiers, seventy-eight male and twenty-six female convicts and twenty-nine children. One was executed and six were lost in the woods. (Cf. Collins's *Account*, I, 331.) At Norfolk Island crops had been plentiful and the people generally healthy. Between November 1791 and January 1794 deaths had amounted to sixty-three, comprising forty male and three female convicts and nineteen children. Meanwhile ninety-five children had been born there. In the year ending December 1795 the mortality was considerably lower, as the food supplies had been deficient for only a small portion of the year, and the new convicts arriving were in a much healthier state. The deaths were twenty-six in New South Wales, and included thirteen male and seven female convicts, and one executed. (Collins, *op. cit.*, I, 446.) In March 1795 the population, exclusive of the civil and military staffs and their dependants, was stated as 4334. The settlers were thirty-eight from free people and 190 from ex-convicts. The emancipated numbered twenty-eight, and the convicts 2056 men and 740 women. Six hundred and fourteen of these were at Norfolk Island. All children numbered 389. (*H.R.A.*, 1.1.493.) However, the returns sent by the Lieutenant-Governors were generally untrustworthy. The total population figure is approximately right; but the number of settlers is understated; Cf. *post*.

England casual references in Collins's *Account* make it clear that large numbers left the colony. Desertions from ships made it necessary for captains to employ labour from the settlement; hence passages were now more easily obtained, the only conditions being permission from the governor to return, the approval of captains and enough money to buy provisions for the journey. From December 1792 to the end of 1794 seventy-four definite departures are recorded, including that of a venturesome female expiree over eighty years of age. Taking into consideration the number of secret departures, Collins believed that the average of returning expirees amounted to three or four on every vessel that sailed from the colony, during a period when oversea commerce was frequent.[27]*

Among the convicts at the settlement the political "exiles" were few. To the Scottish politicals Grose acted generously, giving each of them a brick hut, so that they stated that conditions were not so bad as they had expected. Emancipations became less conditional on service and were more frequently granted. In 1793 fifty-three convicts were emancipated in order to enter the corps, most of them being ex-soldiers, and eight more, at least, were similarly favoured in the following year.[28] Grose pursued a policy of holding out emancipation as a reward to convicts, and it actually happened that five men were freed on condition of their becoming settlers.[29] To convicts employed at the public stores, emancipation was made an inducement for honesty over a stated period, and with good results, Collins writing in 1794 that it was gratifying to see so many withdrawing from evil society and attempting to make themselves worthy of emancipation. Nevertheless, the conduct of emancipated settlers was far from satisfactory in general and most of them fell under the devastating influence of alcohol, forfeiting their properties or losing interest in their work.[30]†

In this lax régime the influence of religion was not only neglected but discountenanced. The Rev. R. Johnson complained that

* An analysis of departures from the colony compiled by Jeremy Bentham from Collins's statements, from the beginning of the settlement to the end of 1795 (excluding eight cases early in the following year), shows that eighty-nine expirees had left with permission, one expiree without permission, and seventy-six convicts had successfully absconded. The totals are unreliable, and in five instances, relying on Collins, he had to be satisfied with such indefinite information as "some" or "several" had departed. Nevertheless, prior to this date it is certain that at least 166 had left the colony, and "several" in addition. Cf. Bentham's *Panopticon versus N.S.W.* (*Works,* Vol. IV, 193).

In evidence given before the Select Committee on Finance in 1798, Colquhoun stated that there was no precise information as to the number of convicts who had returned to England. However, not one of these, whom he knew of, was employed in any creditable pursuit; "all" of them had become notorious thieves and some had been executed for new offences. One man was hanged two months after returning. One of the greatest pickpockets that had ever existed had regrettably returned from Australia, and another was then a pedlar, using his trade as a means for committing new crimes. (Cf. 28th Report, S.C. on Finance, p. 382.)

† Collins seems to indicate that the former paragon, Ruse, grew tired of work, but his dissatisfaction was more against the fertility of the land originally granted. He and three others sold their properties to the military at prices ranging from £40 to £100. He resumed his work, and maintained his former good name later at Hawkesbury. (Collins's *Account,* I, 320.)

although the medical man had his hospital and the military his barracks, he had no building for a church; consequently, he was compelled to build one at his own expense, for which, and then only after a bitter correspondence, he was not compensated until 1797. In view of the personal quarrels between the Lieutenant-Governor and the clergyman one has to exercise care in subscribing to Johnson's outspoken recrimination. It is certain, however, that Grose disregarded religion as a means of reform, issuing a regulation that Sunday services were to be held at 6 a.m., and allowing the Sabbath to be interrupted by noisy, wilful gatherings of the military guard waiting impatiently outside the church. Johnson's efforts were powerless to check the officially-condoned interruptions of services, and when the less amenable Marsden had a party of abusive convict disturbers of the Sabbath imprisoned Grose promptly had them released. Orgies of drink and gambling became the feature of Sundays, and Johnson confessed, probably with some exaggeration, that only between twenty and forty convicts were made to attend his services.[31]

(b) The Penal and the Lesser Settlers

It would be unwise to pass lightly over such observations about the lack of a religious outlook in the people of this period, for the evidence has much significance, direct and indirect. The surprising features about this contemporary criticism of the decline of religion and morality are that it is made by men of all types and that it is urgent and apprehensive—as if these men were shocked by the general attitude of godlessness and irresponsibility and regarded it as being much more extensive than that which had existed in Phillip's time and increasing so rapidly that it threatened the security and sane-mindedness of society in the future.

The evidence, coming from different sections of the community, is naturally coloured by the self-interests of those who submitted it. The ecclesiastical section viewed it from the religious angle. The opinions of Grose and Macarthur, strongly emphasizing the facts of a moral and social degeneration, were based on the assumptions that the territory presented great opportunities to free men for unrestricted trade and agriculture and that the proposed exploitation of it by actual and freed prisoners must necessarily be wasteful and abortive. Although their views were economically sound, they were prejudiced. There is also the evidence of the smaller settlers themselves, who candidly recognize the fact of the extraordinary deterioration, but assign causes different from those of the other witnesses. Finally, there is the evidence of impartial and highly competent observers, whose opinions are

much in accord with those of the smaller settlers. These include such as P. G. King, who had known the settlement since its commencement and who later succeeded Hunter as Governor; David Collins, the contemporary historian whose judgments are always objective; and Governor Hunter, who at the end of 1795, had to face the situation which had arisen in the previous three years. These witnesses confirm the rapid moral and economic deterioration of the general community, but carefully attribute it to two causes, the incapacity of many of the smaller settlers and the restrictions exercised against these by the new group of speculators.

These opinions are noted in various places in this chapter, and those of Hunter will be seen in the following section which deals with his term of office. However, the opinions of two groups of them, the ecclesiastics and the settlers, merit a particular analysis now.

It was natural that the two clerics, Johnson and Marsden, should complain of the indifference to Sunday worship among officials and prisoners, because they chiefly concentrated on that aspect of religion. But, laxity in church attendance was in harmony with the general religious outlook of that age. In England itself there was but little practise of religion by any classes of the people, and it can be assumed that most of the transported prisoners had had no experience of it before leaving England. Moreover, official-dom had never manifested much interest in religion, either before or after the foundation of the Settlement. But it was now apparent that the indifference of officials towards Sunday observances and rest from work had developed into positive opposition. The religious attitude of the people had deteriorated since Phillip's time and continued to deteriorate to such an extent that large sections of the public were lacking in appreciation of even funda-mental moral values and elementary civic responsibilities.

Soon after his arrival Governor Hunter, who had been shocked by the change which had come upon the colony, requested the Rev. Samuel Marsden to report on "the state of immorality", as it had existed under the Lieutenant-Governors. Marsden submitted his report in June 1798.* It is important, as the evidence of an eye-witness of events. Speaking in his dual capacities as a clergyman and as a "principal magistrate", he states that the colony was "deluged in sin" until several months after Hunter's arrival. "No one could adequately describe the conditions of riot, dissipation and depravity that existed among the lowest class of the inhabitants. Drunkenness, murder and robbery had become common crimes." The majority of the convicts spend their Sabbath

---

* See Appendices to Bigge's Report, Box 12; pp. 105-115; also *H.R.A.*, I, 2, p. 185.

day in "cabals, labour, organizing, or drunkenness or robberies". He charges Lieutenant-Governor Grose with having no respect for the importance of religion in the colony; the desecration of the Sabbath had been deliberately condoned by Grose, and he had been actively supported by "Captain Macarthur, the Commanding Officer". "No other place in His Majesty's Dominions exhibits such disrespect to the clergy." Idleness, drink, prodigality among settlers and prisoners have contributed to the desecration of the Sabbath. In these circumstances he and his colleague, the Rev. R. Johnson, have little more to do than baptize children and bury the dead, and they have "little more than bare walls of the Church to preach in (to) on the Sabbath".

It would be wrong to doubt the accuracy of Marsden's observations, for he was a shrewd and capable man. But in that long report he remains strangely aloof from the problem; his nearest approach to seeing it as a problem was when he implicated Grose and Macarthur (and probably the little clique associated with Macarthur) as men who had helped to precipitate it. But he implicated them only in so far as they condoned desecration of the Sabbath, and did not hold them responsible for changing the social system to such an extent that it had created in New South Wales a condition, similar to that which was then existing in England, where the lack of social security for the underprivileged tended to breed crime and listlessness in that section of the community. This was characteristic of Marsden, who was typical of the contemporary English clergy described earlier in this book. Soon he would become a great land-owner, an expert breeder of sheep and an industrious and severe magistrate; but as a clergyman he never adopted an intelligent spiritually-reformative attitude towards the convict section of the Settlement. One might therefore be inclined to see a not obvious significance in the following item of the Report which he submitted in 1798: "It is not possible to exhibit a more convincing proof of the dissipation and immorality of this country than the beggary and ruin of this description of its inhabitants, who ought to be the strength and support of the Settlement." His use of the word "ought" could indicate a mental conflict in the writer. It could indicate that the settlers had been much impeded by forces outside themselves. It could also be interpreted as making many of them responsible for their own beggary and failure in citizenship. If Marsden, consciously or otherwise, suggested both these causes, he was justified. But he should also have made distinctions among the group, loosely called "settlers", noting that many could not have succeeded under any circumstances, and that others had the capacity to succeed but were denied direction, and even impeded, by public

maladministration. The opinions of the settlers on the condition of the Settlement should therefore be considered.

Governor Hunter arrived towards the end of 1795 and, after two years' observations and experience of frustration in his well intentioned efforts, provided an opportunity for the smaller settlers to narrate their own views on the problem. It was judicious of Hunter to allow these people to speak on their own behalf. It was possibly the first time in Australian history when the common people were allowed to express their views as a body. When they did so they handed down to posterity a valuable document,* and also began an embarrassing habit of making such protests.

In his letter to Marsden (February 19, 1798) Hunter said that he knew the settlers' grievances and had questioned them at the General Muster at Parramatta four days previously. He asked Marsden, as Magistrate, to go into the different districts and there assemble the settlers and allow them to state their grievances. Their evidence, recorded and signed by each in the presence of Thomas Arndell, the surgeon, was submitted by Marsden to the Governor. In the Bigge Transcripts that evidence covers about forty pages. Signatures are frequently attested marks made by illiterates, but as a whole the evidence reveals moderation and judiciousness in statement, candid comment and some constructive proposals for the solution of the problem. Out of the mass of specific charges and observations a few statements may be selected to illustrate the nature of the evidence.

Twenty-seven settlers in the district of Kissing Point stated that "the difficulties and impositions the farmers in general meets with in this colony are owing to the trading part meeting with great countenance and protection." As a result of this favouritism "the farmer in reality is no better off than an abject slave of the mercenary trader, whose only merit lies in extortion and chicanery". A farmer is "obliged by the forestallers from necessity to pay 400 per cent (above the original purchase price) for every article of consumption or to let his land go uncultivated".† They cited instances where

---

* Appendices to Bigge's Reports (Box 12, pp. 62-104: "State of Agriculture in N.S.W., and grievances of the Farmers. Causes of agricultural distress." See also *H.R.A.*, I, ii, 135-146.

† "Forestallers": officials, larger settlers and traders who enjoyed precedence at the Government Store, which was the only authorized market. A letter written by Mrs John Macarthur describes the system more or less as it existed in 1795: Thousands of persons are fed from the public stores, all of whom had previously been supplied with flour from England for bread. But because so many have recently cultivated land and raised grain, there is a great quantitiy of it. It is purchased by the Commissary at 10s. a bushel; and it is also issued by him for what are termed rations, or the proportionate quantity due to (eligible) persons instead of flour. In payment for grain received from settlers the Commissary issues an official receipt. These receipts pass current here as coin, and are accepted by Masters of ships and adventurers who come here with merchandise. When these receipts become accumulated in the hands of individuals, they are returned to the Commissary, who then gives a bill on the Treasury in England for them. These bills amount to thirty or forty thousand pounds per annum. . . . Pigs are bought on the same system, as would cattle and sheep also if there were sufficient to enable them to be killed for beef. Any horse is worth £100, but a good one is valued at £150. A cow is worth £80. "You will perceive that those persons who took early precautions to raise live stock have at present singular advantages." (Cf. Macarthur Onslow: *Early Records of the Macarthurs of Camden*, p. 50).

Williamson, the official in charge of the Government Store, countenanced this practice.

Also, they make constructive suggestions for reform. Settlers should be encouraged. Arrangements should be made for them to purchase directly a part of all cargoes of ships, and if the Governor requires security for such an enterprise they will make over to him all, or part, of their grain crops. Failing this, they ask that if cargoes must still be purchased by the rich dealers, the Governor should determine a just retail price for such goods.

Settlers from the Prospect and Toongabbie districts state that "exploitations by the dealers have tended to the destruction of many settlers and their families". "Under the present circumstances we can't long exist. Necessity will force us to sell our farms for the payment of our debts." In the same strain the Settlers from Concord and Liberty Plains describe their abject poverty. They cannot realize more than 3s. per bushel for their wheat.* They are unable to forestall the forestallers at the Stores for sale of grain, and consequently have to barter their products to purchase necessary implements and commodities. They give instances where farms have been seized for the payment of debts, and express the opinion that it is "beyond our strength to surmount our difficulties" unless the magnates and dealers are restrained.

Settlers from the Ponds district say that in this area there are only seventeen small farms, but two-thirds of these are now being worked by tenants, because the original settlers of those farms had been so embarrassed by debt that they had to relinquish their holdings. The present tenants of the farms are in great need, because as tenants they are ineligible for public rations but have to pay high wages for labour and high prices for commodities. Articles for sustenance and work are purchased by the rich, sold to agents at a profit of 200 per cent, and then retailed to the public at a price 500 per cent above the original cost. This group of settlers gave many instances of extortion and intimidation by dealers in order to force settlers into redeeming promissory notes or to forfeit securities associated with their debts.

Settlers in the Parramatta district gave numerous examples of trading in essential commodities at 400 to 500 per cent above the imported price. "The colony is infested with dealers, pedlars and extortioners." Not one man among them had brought with him a penny when he came to the country, but they are now in positions of eminence and wealth and are owners of store rooms. Is this property their own? the settlers ask; or is it the property of the richer men for whom these other men act as secondary

* In the letter quoted, *ante*, Mrs Macarthur stated that 10s. per bushel was customary; but Grose in 1793 said he had issued instructions to pay up to 5s. regarding this as a cheap purchase for the Government and an accommodating market for the settlers of convict origin. Cf. *H.R.A.*, I, i, p. 448.

agents? It is obvious that these agents have been vested with power by the officials of the Settlement and therefore can expect favour and precedence when crops are being sold to the Commissariat Stores. A few years ago, when provisions were being issued to labourers and such, it was customary for these dealers to wait at the store door with a portion of spirits in their hands. They would buy from the unfortunate labourer the corn allowance that had been made to him by Government authority, bartering in exchange for it spirits which had a fictitious quadrupled value. When they had collected many of these sustenance allowances of corn, they would sell the produce back to the Government Store.

It is obvious that these smaller settlers of the Parramatta district are not weaklings, for they candidly observe that this system of "ruin has been pending over our heads too long unperceived", and even more candidly they remind Hunter that despite his two years' control of the Settlement the ruinous system has been allowed to continue "for too long without redress".

Eighteen settlers from the northern district related similar experiences of having been excluded by "gentlemen and dealers" from the public stores when they attempted to sell their grain, with the result that they had to barter it or sell it cheaply in order to pay debts and purchase farming implements. Therefore, they were reluctant to raise new crops, despite their eagerness to do so, because of the uncertainty of being able to market their produce freely into the Government Store. They gave instances of the seizure of lands by creditors and named ten of the most officious "huxsters" who preyed on the people of the Settlement. At present, they said, they could see no prospect of being able to maintain their families unless restraint were exercised over the prevailing commercial activities. Like the Parramatta settlers, they suggested that the Governor should allow the settlers to appoint their own agents to purchase and retail imported goods, and expressed willingness to collect among themselves a sum of £300 which they would hand to the Governor as security for such purchases.

Those who gave this evidence numbered seventy-three settlers, and it would appear that twenty-one others from these districts were absent from the meetings. The judicious and constructive quality of the evidence makes a good impression, as might be expected because these settlers were men who had been carefully selected by Governor Phillip for rewards of land-grants. Marsden and Arndell's observations, when presenting this evidence, specially note their long and well-tried good character and indicate that this band of seventy-three are, more or less, the survivors of the "old settlers". "Their distress is more to be attributed to the hardships they labour under than their own imprudences." The

two investigators also add this important observation, which makes
the required differentiation among people described as settlers,
and also gives an indication of the relative proportions of good
and bad settlers. It is a contemporary judgment: "The settlers
are considered by many, who probably have never visited their
farms or impartially weighed the difficulties they labour under,
as idle worthless characters, and that their own imprudencies
(*sic*) are the cause of this misfortune. This, in some particular
instances, may be true; but it is our joint opinion that it is by no
means general. Many of the farmers are sober, industrious men."
When sending these Reports to England Hunter emphasized
how under the existing system the trading officers contrived, through
monopolies and high charges for necessary commodities, to "pocket
the whole produce of the labouring classes". He advised that,
in these circumstances the country could not become self-supporting
but must become increasingly a charge upon London for the
sustenance of people, who should be able to support themselves
to an appreciable degree. He was then adverting, not only to the
difficulties of self-maintenance and impeded sales of produce
experienced by the smaller settlers but also to a system, which
had grown up, of withdrawing convict labour from public farming
for the benefit of the settlement and diverting it into assigned labour
for the benefit of the newer and greater settlers.

It is impossible to estimate the number of the new settlers who
became such during the administrations of Grose and Paterson.
The official returns of land-grants made in that period, or preserved
from that period, are obviously deliberate understatements.
It seems probable that little supervision was exercised over the
selection of settlers. The inadequate returns* reveal that land was
given to officers, privates, marines, chaplains, prisoners whose
sentences had expired, emancipists,a nd prisoners whose sentences
had not expired. After twelve months in the Settlement Hunter
was able to make an assessment of what had happened in the
preceding three years and presented it in a Report to the Duke
of Portland.† He ascertained that "considerable numbers" of
convicts, some still in bondage and some emancipated, were
authorized to become settlers and to possess landed property.
The only official title which they received was a slip of paper,
signed by the commanding officer, that they had "my permission
to settle". Most of them had servants allowed to them from the
convict labourers on the public farms, so that when Hunter arrived
in September 1795 he "could scarcely call twenty for any public
purpose at Sydney". A practice had then prevailed, whereby any

* e.g. *H.R.A.*, I, i, 438, 472. Also see Grose and Paterson Returns, *H.R.A.*, I, i, 438, 493.
† *H.R.A.*, I, i, 667.

soldier wanting land could get twenty-five acres, almost wherever he wanted it. Therefore, many new settlers were mere speculators, who had no intention of farming, or if they attempted to farm did it indifferently, and readily sold their allotments or mortgaged them to the enterprising official group, who were eagerly seeking opportunities to extend their landed property. As a matter of fact many of such sales and purchases were illegal; for in 1793, Dundas, the Secretary of State for the Home Department, had stipulated that grants to expirees were conditional on residence and cultivation for five years, and that within that interval any sale or conveyance was void, and land, which was attempted to be conveyed, reverted to His Majesty.* An echo, arising out of this ruling and recalling the lax methods of approving settlers and granting land in this period, is discernible in the official returns of land-grants made by Governor Hunter between August 1796 and January 1800. That interesting list, which records the names and descriptions of about 350 of the early settlers, includes eighty grants which had been made originally by the Lieutenant-Governors and which, probably through defective title, had to be ratified subsequently by Hunter.†

A survey of settlers, according to their residential districts, made by Hunter in August 1796, differentiates classes among them thus: "some are good, some indifferent, many idle and worthless"; in one district "many are industrious"; "most are industrious" in another; but elsewhere "some are so bad as not to promise much benefit to the colony". The observation which he made shortly after assuming office relative to the types of men who had become settlers under the Lieutenant-Governors, is probably a just assessment of them: "our settlers have been ill-chosen; many of them are bad characters". That statement concedes the existence of a preponderance of irresponsibles but recognizes the worth of others, whose small ambitions were restrained by the greater ambitions and opportunities of an intruding class of settlers.

(c) The new Landed-proprietors and Traders

It now remains to attempt an estimate of the new farming and trading section of the community, which emerged out of the ranks of officialdom immediately after the departure of Phillip. Their place in Australian history has never been adequately described.

---

* Cf. *H.R.A.*, I, i, p. 441. (Perhaps it might be observed here that Controls over the Settlement were generally exercised by the British Colonial Office. But in 1782 colonial affairs were incorporated in the Home Office and exercised by a committee for trade and foreign plantations. With some changes the control of the Settlement remained with the Home Office, but reverted to the War and Colonial Departments in 1801. The latter was the controlling portfolio until 1854.)

† *H.R.A.*, I, 2, pp. 454-464.

In some cursory accounts of this period they have been described as an evil force which destroyed a noble conception of peasant proprietorship, which Phillip had attempted to establish in the Settlement. In other places they have been lauded as a fortunate and opportune phenomenon in a vast and rich country, which England had doomed to remain indefinitely as a gaol. It is a big subject and difficult because of the meagreness of reliable and unprejudiced documentation and the abundance of contradictory evidence, relative to it. But, because this change in the economy of the Settlement occurred so early and had permanent results, it must be esteemed as a foundation-stone upon which all Australian history has been built. The observations which follow make no pretence to discuss the subject fully, but are rather an attempt to wade among conflicting evidences and evaluations and to state the more important aspects of this economic change.

When Grose succeeded at the end of 1792, the practice arose of giving grants of land and assigned convict labour to the officers of the Settlement. It should be understood, however, that Grose's practice was not illegal. Many years previously Phillip had expressed the opinion that free enterprise was necessary for the advancement of the Settlement. He suggested that land-grants to settlers should be from 500 to 1000 acres, that each settler should be allowed twenty convict labourers, and that soldiers and officers should be encouraged by grants to settle on the land. After the privilege was accorded to the non-commissioned ranks, Phillip specifically requested that similar opportunities should be afforded to the officers. This concession was granted by the Home Secretary, but arrived after Phillip's departure, when it was immediately taken advantage of by Grose. It should be noted, however, that the conditions for granting lands to officers were more liberal than those applicable to other classes of the community. When Dundas authorized officers to receive land-grants he did not specify occupation and cultivation as conditions for such grants, as was the custom relative to all other settlers at that time. The sole restriction for making the grants was "provided the allotments are made not with a view to a temporary but an established settlement thereon"; he then interpreted this provision thus: "that is, comprehending such portions of land and in such situations as would be suitable for a *bona fide* settler, should it ever come into the hands of such a person."* It would appear, therefore, that the right of the officers to dispose of these lands at their departure was directly envisaged. The new regulation may be interpreted as an authoritative recognition of land speculation.†

* Cf. *H.R.N.S.W.*, Vol. I., part 2; however, it is interesting to observe that in Grose's first grant to Macarthur, 1793, a provision requiring residence and cultivation for five years was inserted.

† *H.R.A.*, I, i, pp. 125, 157, 316, 365, 383, 416, 442.

Within eight weeks of his assumption of office Grose reported that he had already "allotted to such officers, as have asked, one hundred acres of land, which with great spirit they, at their own expense, are clearing". He was unsure whether their industry was due to the novelty of the occupation or to the advantages which they hoped from it; but he was sure that if the present enthusiasm was maintained they would be cultivating within six months an area equal to a third of all the land cleared since the colony began. That casual observation might indicate much liberality in granting land and should be placed alongside the two official returns of land-grants, which he forwarded to England in 1793 and 1794.* In the first he listed only twenty-two grants, including five for newly arrived immigrants, five for ex-prisoners, and only nine for high officials of the permanent staff. The total acreage of the grants was only 1575, covering the period from December 31, 1792 to April 1, 1793. In the second return, covering the period of June 1, 1793 to April 1, 1794, he showed a total of 2693 acres, distributed among sixty-three people, who included thirty-four of the penal class and only fifteen senior ranking officials. Those returns, of course, were false, for as a result of Hunter's investigations the total acreage granted by the Lieutenant-Governors had to be increased to about 16,000 acres. However, this does not necessarily suggest that the twenty-four higher officials, listed in Grose's returns, should have great additions made to their numbers. (They were only twenty-two, because two were in both lists). It rather indicates that the lower executive staffs and the non-official and penal types of grantees were ever so many more than Grose had stated. This view can be supported by an analysis of the numerous ratifications of Grose's and Paterson's land-grants which Hunter had to make when he succeeded to the governor-ship.† That list enumerates ninety-six ratifications of grants made by the Lieutenant-Governors, but only two of these referred to members of the higher official staff of that period. Hunter's list, however, demonstrates how wide was the distribution of land among other grades, favouring convicts in all degrees of servitude, settlers, and minor officials such as superintendents.

It would seem, therefore, that Grose's identifications of the higher official grantees are fairly accurate. Some of those whom he named later became well-known members of a new landed arist-ocracy. Among the grantees were John Macarthur (with two grants of 100 acres); Johnson, the Chaplain; Captain Foveaux, who within five years had extensive land at Toongabbie and a flock of 1350

* H.R.A., I, i, pp. 438, and 472.

† H.R.A., I, 2, 472 seqq.

sheep; Surveyor Alt; Commissary Palmer; three surgeons and the Provost Marshal.

It is wrong to single out these years of the interregnum as the period in which enterprising free men gained a stranglehold over the land and production of the colony. Those years marked only the beginning of proprietorship on the grand scale. Because the new system came suddenly upon the country it has been said that it was not a natural development out of the traditions of the past, but there is abundant evidence showing that Phillip had contemplated and often recommended private farming on a fairly extensive scale, because it was economically unsound to settle a vast new territory by the industry of convicts in bondage and incompetent ex-convict settlers. If, in this light, the new system may be regarded as a development, the suddenness of its rise should also be appreciated as something that gave it a revolutionary quality. To these new men might be applied the brilliant tag which Edward Shann fastened, less aptly, upon Governor Macquarie: they were autocrats in a hurry. In the period of the Lieutenant-Governors they were not yet great proprietors, but they then managed to establish a principle of expansive private enterprise which no later Governor could curtail. They quickly attached to their numbers other ambitious and capable men and steadily increased their holdings into vast tracts of fertile and well chosen land. When the rise of the land-magnates is being considered it is essential to note the extent of the grants made to them in later years. It is illuminating to make an analysis of even those early grants which Governor Hunter made to them between 1796 and 1800, and which are listed in the Returns quoted above. Here may be seen the real and effective beginnings of the rise to wealth and property of many, who soon became great landed-proprietors in the Settlement.*

Therefore, too great an emphasis should not be placed on the allocations of land to a few officials in the period of the Lieutenant-Governors, so as to suggest that this distribution of land and the competition of a new private agricultural enterprise were the causes of distress in the colony. The emphasis should be placed rather on the entry of this official class into the domain of commerce. Here they were unscrupulous exploiters, controlling imports, enriching themselves and impoverishing multitudes by exorbitant charges for necessary commodities, and, by an abuse of power, preventing the general marketing of produce while they gave

* Hunter's grants prior to 1800: e.g., Surgeon Balmain 600 acres; Lt-Colonel Foveaux 1270; Edward Abbott 700; Nicholas Bayley 450. Other distributions either multiplied the earlier grants of the former official coterie or introduced new names into the land-seeking groups. After 1796 and before 1800 there appeared such well-known names as, Marsden and five other chaplains, Captain Johnson, D'Arcy Wentworth, John Piper, Judge Advocate Dore, and even Matthew Flinders and John Shortland. (Cf. H.R.A., I, 2, pp. 454-464).

precedence to their own. Under such circumstances they were able to extend their holdings by seizures of mortgaged properties and, what is more important, they accumulated sufficient wealth to buy then, and later, other landed properties and high-class stock from speculators who had no farming ambitions and expirees who had no farming ability. Many of them, therefore, were deliberate, unscrupulous exploiters, using trade and commerce as a long-range means towards the realization of their ambitions to become great landed-proprietors. In the case of John Macarthur, who was the outstanding figure of that group, unscrupulosity and a determination to reach his goal were evident characteristics —but the consummate genius of the man would allow him to earn for a quarter of a century unrivalled pastoral, trading and political prestige.

John Macarthur, now dead for a century and a quarter, still awaits his biographer. The volume, *Some Early Records of the Macarthurs of Camden*, is in large part an intimate family chronicle. It establishes Macarthur as a model father and husband of an equally remarkable wife and demonstrates him as a man with marked patriarchal instincts for setting up a Macarthur clan in Australia. But it does not adequately portray him as the supremely commanding figure of the Settlement up to 1809, and as a personality of vast importance, both political and pastoral, after his return to Sydney at the end of 1817, following eight years of enforced exile in London. The collected original documentation for his history occupies more than a hundred large bound volumes at the Mitchell Library.

He was born in Devonshire in 1767, well educated, and arrived at Sydney in 1790 as an officer of the New South Wales Corps. In June 1791 he was appointed Commandant in the populous Parramatta district. At first he was not well-disposed towards farming, being disillusioned by the numbers of failures in that activity and convinced that, although Parramatta had distinct advantages, there was little hope that officers would be authorized to engage freely in that work. Early in November 1791 he was removed to Sydney. Meanwhile, Phillip had sent his request to London that officers should be given rights to occupy land. The news of that concession arrived immediately after Phillip's departure in December 1792. Grose then gave Macarthur an appointment as supervisor of public works, and on February 25, 1793 made a grant to him of 100 acres on the river banks near Parramatta.*
On 1 April, 1794, a further grant of 100 acres was added. It is

---

* A facsimile of the first grant appears as an illustration in the *Macarthurs of Camden*, bearing the super-scription of Governor Macquarie to cancel it, as having been included in a new grant of 850 acres to John Macarthur. In the original grant Grose inserted a clause stipulating residence and cultivation for five years.

said that a further 50 acres were granted to him as the successful winner of a competition to clear and cultivate land.

The farming dexterity of Macarthur is demonstrated in a letter written by his wife on August 23, 1794, only sixteen months after the date of the original grant. His wife and family had been living on the property since November 1793. Meanwhile, he had a house of brick, sixty-eight feet long and eighteen feet wide, exclusive of kitchen and servants' quarters. In his farm of 250 acres, 100 acres were under cultivation and the remainder cleared. Produce valued at £400 had already been marketed, 1800 bushels of grain were in granaries, twenty acres were under wheat, and eighty acres were prepared for corn and potatoes. His stock amounted to two mares, two cows, 130 goats and 100 hogs, out of which only one cow had been a government benefaction.

Thirteen months later his wife stated that the farm had increased to "between 400 and 500 acres, with fifty head of cattle, a dozen horses and about 1000 sheep". Apropos of this inventory of stock she made the pertinent remark: "those persons who took early precautions to raise live stock have at present singular advantages". On this farm he was the first to introduce a plough pulled by horses or oxen, and thus departed from the practice of a man-manipulated hoe. He employed frequently as many as thirty or forty people, all of whom, except two, were paid and maintained from the Macarthur farm. That practice was in accord with Macarthur's suggestion that most of the convict population could be absorbed by private enterprise and supported without liability to the government.*

In this interval and in the immediately following years Macarthur extended his original grants of two hundred acres by purchases of adjoining blocks, which had recently been granted to Stewart, Williams, Cummings, Roberts and Richardson. Stewart was one of Phillip's grantees of February 1792, but sold his land to Cummings, who in turn sold it to Macarthur. Cummings, then an ensign, had been given two grants by Grose, 1792 and 1794, and sold both to Macarthur. The grants to Richardson (a private) and Roberts had been made by Lieutenant-Governor Paterson 1795, but were transferred by them to Cummings and then sold by him to Macarthur. Of these grantees only Cummings is noted in the official lists of grants which Grose sent to London. The whole of Macarthur's land at Parramatta, 850 acres, was consolidated by a covering deed, issued on October 8, 1806. Later Governor Macquarie cancelled all the original deeds and noted that they had been "included in a new grant of 850 acres to John Macarthur."

---

* Cf. *Macarthurs of Camden passim*; and letters between Hunter and Macarthur, *H.R.N.S.W.*, Vol. 3, pp. 70-71.

A deed of transfer, issued in 1801, shows that Macarthur purchased from Major Foveaux, who was then about to depart on official duty to Norfolk Island, 1770 acres at Toongabbie with the entire stock of 1350 sheep, for £2000. Macarthur described his total acreage at Toongabbie as being 3000 acres at this period. The greater grants to Macarthur came later however, beginning with 5000 acres in 1805, at which date it was stated that he already was in possession of 3500 acres.*

Macarthur's activities in the field of commerce should now be noticed. His enterprise was varied—importing and exporting, and trading within the colony as a first distributor of imported goods at exorbitant prices, and marketing his own produce to the Government Stores. He so contrived it that all these activities were co-related, and all together served the main end of increasing the Macarthur stature. He did nothing in a small way, and this was a novel and incomprehensible phenomenon in a penal settlement which was strictly committed by Government to doing things in a small way. Consequently, he came into conflict with Governors who endeavoured to restrain his power, and with his peers who resented his leaping away from them and his capacity for sharp-dealing. It is, therefore, advisable to expect a degree of prejudice in the hostile contemporary opinions that were expressed about him. Being so fore-warned we may select a few observations, out of hundreds of a similar type, made by Governors Hunter and King relative to the variety and extent of Macarthur's commercial activities in this early period of his Australian career.

In 1798 Hunter described him aptly as having a "restless, ambitious disposition"; he cited instances where Macarthur had misused his official authority to prevent, in his own interests, the receipt of general produce at the Government Stores, and stated that later, when he had resigned from the government service, he was busily engaged as an importer of varied cargoes which ranged from sugar to spirits. In 1801, while Macarthur was temporarily in England, his commercial history was angrily reviewed by Hunter's successor, King, who had had an intimate knowledge of Macarthur for many years. Macarthur, he said, had come to the Settlement in 1790 more than £500 in debt, but was worth £20,000 in 1801. That fortune and his "accumulating gains" allowed him to challenge authority with impunity. He had concentrated his energy on making a fortune for himself and on showing less capable officers how to do the same thing for themselves, through the importation and distribution of spirits and through cornering the market for the sales of their local produce. According

---

* Cf. *Macarthurs of Camden, passim*; also *Journal of R. A. Hist. Society*, Vol. XIX, p. 113; also Macarthur original Papers at Mitchell Library: (a) Correspondence and Papers, cont'd; (b) Official, land-grants etc. cont'd.

to King, Macarthur was the "great monopolist" of that group and a strong defender of the "huckster" agents who retailed the imports of the greater traders. He was a daring and shrewd speculator. Before his departure for Europe in 1801 he had offered the whole of his farms and stock to the government at a fixed price, but while the Governor was awaiting sanction from England to accept the offer Macarthur had busied himself, to within a few days of his departure, in acquiring other farms and flocks and cattle from individuals, which he then wanted to unload upon the government at the same fixed price.

There is, of course, much truth in these frequent observations by Governors who were not competent enough and possessed too little power to be able to cope with a determined and fast-moving man of the Macarthur type. For instance, Governor King well knew that he had missed a big opportunity when Macarthur offered his farms and flocks for government exploitation at the cost of £4000; but Macarthur was shrewd enough to realize later that he should avoid fulfilling such a contract, which had been made impetuously when he was about to leave Australia under arrest to face a court-martial for having fought a duel with his commanding officer. Coloured though they be by prejudice, these general expressions of contemporary opinion show how Macarthur contrived to make his varied commercial interests fit into the general pattern of building up his possessions, so that his pastoral ambitions might be ultimately achieved. He was still the monopolist giant of commerce seven or eight years later, when Governor Bligh came into conflict with him precisely over the issue of trading and was deposed from office, chiefly through the expert and determined intervention of Macarthur.*

The most important feature of Macarthur's work, however, was his scientific breeding and conservation of stock, particularly sheep. For a description of his methods we have the evidence which he gave before Commissioner Bigge in 1820. In 1794 he purchased from an officer sixty ewes and rams which had been imported from Calcutta and later two ewes and a ram imported from Ireland. With these he experimented in cross-breeding and produced a fleece of mingled hair and wool. "This circumstance originated the idea of producing fine wool in N.S.W.," he stated. In 1796 he was able to import four ewes and two rams of Merino breed from the Cape of Good Hope. Sixteen other sheep of this breed also came to N.S.W. at that time and were distributed among settlers, "who did not take the necessary precautions to preserve the breed pure" and consequently wasted their stock; but he

---

* For Macarthur during the Hunter and King periods see *H.R.A.*, I, Vol. 2, pp. 160-177; and Vol. 3, p. 274 *seqq.*, and pp. 321-325.

took care to preserve his own and began to accumulate a special flock of high quality. Shortly after that, as we have already observed, he purchased the large farm of Major Foveaux at Toongabbie, together with the flock of 1350 common Cape Merino sheep which was on it, for the sum of £2000. In 1804, previously to his being granted 5000 acres at the order of the English Government, he stated that his lands amounted to approximately 4000 acres.

The rest of Macarthur's extraordinary history does not come within the scope of this volume, which extends only to 1800. After the turn of the century the skill and determination of this enterprising settler established him in a position of such influence as would largely determine the subsequent political and economic history of Australia. His experiments in cross-breeding had produced fine wool in Australia prior to 1800, but he soon realized that with better stock and greater pastures enormous quantities of even finer wool could be produced. Consequently, at the end of the century and again in 1801 he went to London bearing samples of the wool that had been produced and, with such evidence in his hands, made urgent demands for improved breeding stock, rights to acquire large tracts of land for his farming, and a market for Australian wool produce. His case was presented at a time when English industry was embarrassed by the small quantity and unsatisfactory quality of fine wool imported from Spain. As a result, Macarthur's general plans were approved. He had asked for 10,000 acres but was given the right to choose 5000 wherever he wished. On his return he concentrated his pastoral interests in the Camden area, much to the disgust of Governor King who observed that the ambitions of this man could never be checked. Such a man, said King, could comfortably exist only as Governor, because already half of the settled land belonged to him and it would not be long before he owned the other half. But Macarthur had no ambition of becoming Governor; what he wanted was unrestrained freedom for his own enterprises, and later, when restraints became too exacting, he contrived to depose and deport a Governor.

The important consideration, arising out of this outline of Macarthur's character and work is that, as a result of the entry of the official groups into the farming industry of N.S.W. in 1792, Macarthur was enabled to demonstrate both the way in which farming should be attempted and the capacity of the colony to compete, almost immediately, in world commerce. His successful experimentation and business acumen soon led many other private adventurers to enter that field, most of whom were successful. It is certain that, under the conditions existing in 1792 and thereabouts, settlers from the penal ranks were incapable of

founding industry of that type and scale. It is equally certain that many of those smaller settlers suffered, and were denied opportunities for settlement, by the exploiting trading methods which accompanied, and to a larger extent made possible, the pastoral achievements which later developed out of the economic changes of 1792-94.

*   *   *   *   *

It is unsatisfactory to try to estimate the economic change made in the colony by the invasion of the official groups into agriculture and commerce. The official returns from 1792 to 1800 are much confused, sometimes differentiating the official group from other settlers, and more frequently combining both. The statistics of the period 1792 to 1794 are meagre as well as unsatisfactory. However, it is unscientific to expect that great changes in the productivity of the Settlement should be registered quickly, as a result of the officers' intervention into agriculture. The significance of their work becomes apparent after 1800, when larger numbers of them with larger acreages of land vastly increased pastoral production.

Such facts as the following may generally indicate the development which ensued. When Grose assumed office at the end of 1792, grants totalled 6000 acres; settlers were 170, but only sixty-eight of them were in the Sydney settlements; cultivated land was 1700 acres, of which 1100 acres were under public control.

In 1794, 3000 acres were cleared, of which 1000 were the work of the officer farmers. In 1795 the acreage under wheat was 2720 acres, seven-eighths of which was held by private settlers. In that year cattle numbered 176 and sheep 832.

In 1796, land in cultivation was 5419 acres; of that acreage 1700 belonged to the Government, 1172 to the officer groups, and 2547 to other settlers. Sheep numbered 1507, of which the officers held 1176.

From that period onwards the returns reveal a strong development in private enterprise. In 1798 individuals of all classes owned 5582 acres of all cultivated land, with 4209 acres under wheat, and had 3486 sheep. In the following year the acreage under cultivation rose to 8679 acres. The officers, however, then owned 3843 of the 4090 sheep in the Settlement, but the generalized class of settlers had 5000 acres of wheat, which was nearly five times that of the officer group. Leaping to 1804, the year before Macarthur returned to set the pastoral industry on the grand scale, we may see officers and settlers with 62,000 acres and 20,000 sheep, while the Crown possessed only 1200 sheep.*

*   *   *   *   *

After the departure of Grose in December 1794 the control of the colony devolved upon Captain William Paterson, as the next highest military officer. As the appointment of Governor Hunter had already been announced he made few changes.[32] Realizing that with the concentration of convict labour at Sydney and in private employment the Government had practically ceased to be a producer at all, he transferred as many prisoners as could be spared to the Parramatta district, where they and fifty other convicts hitherto unemployed were set to work at agriculture. The generally lax system, however, continued to prevail until the arrival of Hunter in September 1795.

---

* Cf. Various returns from *H.R.A.*, I, Vols. 1 and 2; and *H.R.N.S.W.*, Vols. 2, 3 and 4; *passim.*

THE SECOND GOVERNOR

(a) The Failure of Governor Hunter

The governorship of John Hunter has only one reason to justify its being included in a study of the foundation of the penal settlement. It marked the final defeat of the policy to make New South Wales primarily an oversea gaol. In theory the colonial idea had never been excluded from British policy, but in practice the penal policy predominated and would have continued but for the interregnum that occurred after Phillip's departure. Governor Hunter's failure was due to the fact that the changes made in that period were too well established to be adjusted except by force, which it was inadvisable to use for two reasons. The colony was absolutely dependent on the military power for its protection and greatly dependent on the progressive policy of this body for the support of the settlement. Hunter remarked truthfully that anyone visiting the settlement after an absence of a few years would scarcely have recognized it; formerly the governor had been able to inspect it without difficulty, but now it extended forty miles in one direction and included a chain of farms in the new district of the Hawkesbury, and the population comprised an ever increasing number of free and freed men. The Australian settlement had begun to serve a double purpose and to travel in two widely diverging directions—one towards colonial expansion with all the problems, constitutional and economic, necessarily connected with this change, and the other towards an adjustment of the transportation system in order to allow it to function in altered circumstances. Hunter's aims and duties fell under four headings: he had immediately to restore order and civil government; the traffic in spirits and the trading monopolies had to be checked; assignment had to be adjusted so as to satisfy the claims of Government to the use of the prisoners and at the same time subsidize the new and growing industry of settlers; and not the least of all obligations, he had to exercise discipline among the convicts and provide for those who had been liberated. This was an impossible task because it attempted to stabilize two contradictory systems in the one country, and whatever the nature of the reform it had to be subversive of the policy hitherto obtaining.

His first act was to call a muster of the inhabitants to ascertain where and how the convict population were placed. He restored

the civil magistracy within the colony and gathered together as many of the convicts as possible and set them to government work. To solve the other problems he had to compromise. He has been blamed for his weakness in constantly departing from regulations which he established at the commencement of his career, but the strength of the opposition against him must be considered. He had no police to enforce his orders and practically no officials upon whom he could rely to pursue a policy that was directly opposed to the views held by officialdom in the colony.

He attempted to cope with the liquor traffic in three progressive steps, two of which were compromises and the third a gesture which proved abortive. He first restricted the importation of liquor and then approved of licensed houses within a limited area, later extending this to the Hawkesbury and forbidding illicit distillation. Two parties had to be disciplined in the sale of liquor, one, the convict and ex-convict population who had become used to this luxury and would sell their "labour of 12 months" to get it, and the other, the military officers who throve on the commerce. In 1800 after five years of vain endeavour he had to admit that he was sufficiently experienced to know that "whilst the article sought after is in the harbour or, indeed, any other on this coast, it is impossible to counteract the designs of those who wish to have it. . . . To oppose its being landed will be vain for want of proper officers to execute such orders as I might see occasion to give". Consequently, in an attempt to control the traffic he sanctioned its importation and gave the rights of distribution to the officers.

He was equally unsuccessful in checking the monopoly in trading. Soon after arrival he called the smaller settlers together and asked them to define the causes of their ill success. We have already considered the observations which they then presented to the Governor in February 1798. They all declared that their poverty was due to the ring of monopolists from whom they had to purchase supplies imported at a huge profit by the officers. Hunter vainly suggested that they should eschew such luxuries as were imported and vaguely hinted at establishing a government importing trade, by which articles might be sold at a reasonable profit. This uneconomic venture was, however, left to his successor to set going in New South Wales. He defined the rate of wages at which labour might be employed and the number of convicts who could be assigned to the small settlers, but his orders were never enforced. At first he had described the monopolist trade as degrading to the office of a soldier, but later relented by issuing a General Order on June 25, 1798, in which the right of the officers to act "as agents for the general benefit of the whole colony" was recognized. This indiscreet act was made the occasion for his recall.

When Hunter arrived it was the recognized practice that the military settlers should be given as many as thirteen assigned labourers, supported at the government expense. Free settlers were allowed two and ex-convict settlers one. Pulled by divergent forces, one the Secretary of State, who refused to subsidize the military settlers to the extent of £260 annually, the cost of maintenance for thirteen convicts, and the other the military settlers on whose efforts Hunter was convinced the future prosperity of the colony depended, he again attempted compromise. He asked the settlers to release some of the convict labourers and to support "a few" of the others who were assigned to them. This they failed to do. On August 11, 1796, Portland demanded that a reduction should be made and that all but two should be supported privately. Even then the employers refused to comply, and in May 1798 Hunter had to issue a General Order limiting the number to be supported by Government, but making the concession that farm produce would be received as payment for the rations issued to these servants. This reduction of numbers was never carried out, and Hunter, when public works were pressing, was forced into the position of withdrawing temporarily from private employ one or two of the assigned servants for a few days' work in each week. Before leaving the country Hunter admitted the deceptions that had been practised against him, when large numbers continued to be employed at the Government expense and only a few settlers provided for their servants in excess of the two who were allowed to them by law. To the Select Committee of 1812 Colonel Johnston said that besides the two allowed to him as a military officer he had employed twenty-three convicts whom he victualled and housed at his own expense. In 1795 at Macarthur's farm between twenty and thirty expirees were employed at weekly wages, thirteen assigned labourers, besides women servants, were fed and clothed at his own expense, but only two were employed at the expense of the Crown. When recording these facts Mrs Macarthur added that there were settlers who contrived to employ twenty or more publicly-maintained servants, "which the Governor does not or will not notice".[1]

The economic advantages of this cheap labour were such that the employers resented any curtailments of the numbers assigned, and advances were privately made to the authorities in India for the sending out of convicts to supply additional assigned labour in the colony. Hunter was not disinclined to accept the proposal, feeling that it would release labour for Government work, but when submitting the matter to the Secretary of State he demanded that the prospective employers must be able to support the imported assigned servants.[2]

Throughout his administration Hunter, "a pleasant, sensible

old man", as a resident described him in 1798, was thwarted by a formidable opposition. His first conflict had been with Macarthur, who resigned his official position and then wrote to England graphically describing the low moral state and lack of industry among the inhabitants and emphasizing the value of free settlers, who alone could absorb convict labour profitably. This extraordinary but unscrupulous man was prepared to take 100 labourers himself and support them. Consequently, he blamed Hunter not only for interfering with industry but also for allowing the moral decline to continue in the settlement.[3] When the correspondence was forwarded to Hunter the Governor informed Portland that the prevailing immorality was in great measure due to Macarthur's associates and their nefarious methods of trade. The offer to take 100 convicts off the Government Store was not so patriotic as it seemed, he explained, for a two pounds daily ration of bread cost only five pence and a convict labourer's hire was worth five shillings.[4] Portland, however, failed to understand the position and, anxious to be relieved of the responsibility to support the prisoners, the Government allowed the regulations to fall into disuse. Hunter was asked to economize in expenditure, and Portland observed with "infinite surprise" that in the fifteen months ending August 31, 1797, the colony had cost more than £40,000, exclusive of civil and military establishment expenses and of supplies sent from England. Every convict then was costing more than £20 per annum, which was more than two-thirds of what their maintenance would have cost in English gaols. Portland was convinced that the expense arose from "not adverting to the original purpose for which this colony was established" and from the prodigal support given to private employers of labour.[5]

The necessity for subsidizing private industry at the beginning was never realized in England. When Hunter endeavoured to create a larger number of producers by reforming the deteriorated settlers he was unsupported by his superiors and opposed by the capitalists of the Settlement. On account of charges made against him by this body, whom he had aided and abetted by failing to enforce his restraining regulations, he was ignominiously recalled by the Secretary of State in 1799.

(b) The Penal System, 1796-1800

Conditions on the transports between January 1, 1796 and February 2, 1801, were an improvement on those existing in the earlier years. In that period 2282 convicts were sent from England and Ireland. Of these 1967 arrived in the colony. The wastage of 316 was mainly due to the loss of sixty-eight convicts who sailed on

the *Lady Shore* in February 1797 and were taken when that ship was seized by the military on board, eventually being sold as slaves to the Spaniards in South America; and to the deaths of ninety-five who were victims of fever on the *Hillsborough* in 1798. As the numbers sent in this period were comparatively few, only a brief reference need be made to the procedure of transport. The *Marquess Cornwallis*, arriving in February 1798, carried 160 male and seventy female Irish convicts, most of whom were political prisoners. At an enquiry held at Sydney it was stated that an attempt was made to seize the vessel and the women were charged with a plot to mix pulverized glass in the flour used for the seamen's puddings. Punishment was severe and many had not recovered when the vessel reached Sydney, but the captain was able to justify his severity and the existence of a plot was proved. Eleven perished on the passage. On the *Brittania*, arriving May 27, 1797, eleven deaths occurred among 188 Irish convicts, and as a result Dr Balmain sent recommendations from Sydney for better transport, which were favourably received in England. On the *Ganges*, which followed with 203 convicts, thirteen died, and at an enquiry the fact of mutinous conduct was proved, but the captain was censured for acting too harshly and without consulting the officers.* The *Barwell* brought some useful mechanics in its complement of 296 English convicts, eleven of whom had died. The *Brittania* carried a supply of breeding stock and ninety-four females who, in view of the shortage of women in the colony, were just as welcome as the cattle. The *Hillsborough*, arriving on July 26, 1799, was, however, an instance, fortunately isolated, which recalled the deplorable mortality on the Second Fleet. The ship had sailed with 300 male English convicts, some of whom already had typhus. Ninety-five of these died on board and six after landing, but it was a remarkable fact that the epidemic was prevented from spreading in the Settlement. Though the ship had been well fitted up, Hunter remarked that the prisoners had not been supplied with clothing and arrived naked in the colony, where they found the other convicts in the same state of neglect. Three ships carrying 490 Irish prisoners, mainly political transportees, lost only thirty-seven, and on other transports with 353 English convicts on board the deaths did not exceed forty-six.

Though the food supply was not so acute a problem during Hunter's administration as in the earlier years, only the year 1796 passed without anxiety and a reduction of rations. Supplies from England continued to be irregular, and the production within the Settlement, though providing a margin of safety, was insufficient

* According to Collins (*Account*, II, 38) there were Irish convicts on board this vessel, but it is included in all English returns as an English transport. It may have picked up Irish convicts *en route*, or have brought Irish from England.

for so large a number. In 1799 and 1800 the promising harvests failed. Throughout all these years fresh meat could not be procured, except an occasional supply of hog-flesh. Private commerce by American and Indian ships relieved the situation, but only at great cost to the smaller settlers. Rations were reduced and a compensation had to be made by adjusting the hours of labour to this necessity. In 1798 Hunter complained that sixteen months had elapsed since supplies had been received from England; but in that time the ship, *Lady Shore*, had been lost with its stores. The most pressing need was clothing for the prisoners. Hunter frequently called attention to this deficiency, but supplies were not sent until 1800. He remarked on the forbearance of gangs of from four to five hundred men who were forced to work in the fields "naked as they were born"; they resented this degradation, and as Hunter sympathized with their position he tried to relieve it by importing thin canvas from India to make temporary outfits.[6] There was, however among them a section who cared little about clothing and preferred to barter it for liquor. Hunter endeavoured to check this abuse by issuing a Public Order in April 1796, subjecting both buyer and seller to corporal punishment, but like every other order it was not obeyed.

The conditions of a prisoner's life differed according to his position and employment. Men and women, youths, political prisoners, assignees and government labourers were classes each of which had its own peculiarities. In August 1796 there were 2012 male and 922 female prisoners, 546 of whom were at Norfolk Island, where famine conditions were not so severe. The total of assigned servants victualled at government expense was 136, and large numbers of the remainder were privately assigned.

The assigned servant was probably better situated than the convict in government employment. Before the Committee of 1812 this matter was discussed, but many of the facts then stated referred to the period after 1801, when the assignment system had been placed on a legal basis by Governor King and the rights of employers and servants had been determined and subjected to a contractual agreement to infringe which was punishable. Johnston, an employer of this labour from the days of Grose, naturally spoke highly of it, but he admitted that the welfare of the convict depended on his employer. He said that the settlers in general had to take whatever convicts were assigned to them without any opportunity for selection, but Margarot maintained that the selection process depended largely on bribery and that the smaller settler received only the refuse left after the Government and the greater settlers had satisfied themselves.[7] Some masters, such as Johnston and Macarthur, gave their convict labourers a sound agricultural

training and assisted in their reformation by exacting strict discipline
under capable overseers. These, however, were few. The fate of
the man assigned to the small, and usually drunken and unreformed,
settler was worse from every point of view. He suffered from the
evil influence, the lack of industry and the complete absence of
supervision. Women servants were assigned, but in smaller numbers,
and as they lived in the houses of employers their chances of
reformation under immediate association with ex-convict settlers
were remote. In later years it was found that many of them married
into the families of the emancipists.

Among the hundreds whom Hunter described as political
prisoners, divisions were made. It is evident from Hunter's
despatches that the majority of them were treated as ordinary
convicts, being forced to work among criminal associates, over whom
they were able to exert a seditious influence. Holt, however,
discriminated among these prisoners and regarded only a few of
them in the category of political exiles. "Those transported for
rebellion were left at large, to act as they thought proper", he wrote.
The descriptions given in his *Memoirs* and in the writings of Palmer
and Muir show their peculiar position in this land of criminal
transportation. The exiles constituted an aristocracy of breeding
and learning, recognized by the criminals but despised by the new
gentry who had arisen on the spoils of the rum traffic and the trade
monopolies. There is the picture of the dignified Holt stepping off
the ship with his wife and family, spurning the convicts who wished
to transport his luggage, then relenting so as to bestow gratuities
in golden guineas and leaving but four pounds to support himself,
his wife and son. His party were received as guests in the home
of Margarot and his wife, which he left after being informed that
it was "the most seditious in the settlement". This interesting man
insisted on using his rights as a free, but banished, aristocrat
to bring a charge against the captain of the ship, but was disillusioned when the Judge-Advocate informed him that his rights
were no greater than those of a convict. In the townships the
political and educated prisoners lived where they wished, a mixed
crowd—priests, ministers, lawyers, doctors, men of letters, and
the notorious pickpocket and author, Barrington. It was a discon-
solate existence for the worthier among them. The Scottish political
prisoners, no less than the Irish, presented petitions for their release,
claiming that their banishment precluded them from returning to
England only. Hunter was sympathetic and sent their petitions to
England, strongly urging their release, but Dundas emphatically
ruled that the governor was bound to prevent their departure.
Meanwhile, Palmer's *Narratives* of his trial and voyage had been
published in London for an appreciative public who demanded a

second edition in 1797, and in the same year his *Letters from Sydney* further enlightened the British public concerning conditions in the settlement. Palmer eventually settled on the North Shore in contentment, and when in 1800 he was declared free bought a vessel with which he traded among the islands, disastrously, however, and died in 1802. Muir's remonstrances to England proved equally unsuccessful, and he settled down, temporarily, to varied occupations, including that of conducting the first Presbyterian service in the settlement and the compilation of two *Consolatory Epistles* written in verse and published in England in 1796. In these effusions, characterized by caustic banter, he described conditions in the settlement and in scarcely veiled allusions depicted his persecutors as occupying new positions in the Antipodes and the nether regions.*

Muir escaped in 1796. Gerrald died, a broken-hearted man, in 1796, and Skirving followed him in the same year. Margarot, turbulent and ostracized even by his compatriots, was involved in all the insurrections in the colony and was banished to Van Diemen's Land in 1805. He returned to England on the expiry of his sentence in 1807.

The activities of the Irish prisoners in the colony have been mentioned in the first section of this chapter, where their unfortunate position in being unable to obtain particulars of their sentences was emphasized. The stern measures taken against them came only partly within Hunter's administration and their open rebellion occurred in 1804, when the military were employed to suppress it. Just prior to Hunter's departure rumours were current that the Irish were preparing an insurrection, and information was given by one of the priests, Harold, that pikes were being made for weapons. This unfortunate priest, unlike his associates, was of a turbulent disposition. Before a magisterial enquiry he was unable, or refused, to prove his charges and was committed to gaol for prevarication. Most of the leading political prisoners were arraigned before the bench, but the evidence forthcoming, while proving the existence of a plot and the fact that seditious meetings had been held, did not substantiate the allegation that weapons were in readiness. Six men were found guilty of sedition, and among numerous others who were supposed to be implicated twelve particularly were mentioned, including Holt. Five were sentenced to receive 500 lashes and six, including Holt and the priest, to be banished. Harold, moreover, was compelled to stand at the

---

* Here, Barrington, in awful virtue stands,
The scales of justice trembling in his hands.
Here Palmer, rob'd in lawn, with reverence due,
Preaches pure doctrines to the convict crew;
And I'm appointed, you must own with reason,
The King's Lord Advocate to crush High Treason.

The sacred right of insurrection there
May drive old Satan from his regal chair;
And the same honest means may raise, per-
    chance,
A *France* in Hell, that raised a *Hell* in France.
(Excerpt, *The Telegraph*, by Thomas Muir.)

whipping-post as a culprit and thus partake of the punishment of the others.[8] The brutality which characterized these punishments has been described by Holt. The prisoners were tied tight against trees and uninterruptedly 300 lashes were inflicted by two men, alternately flogging. As it was unlawful to administer more than fifty lashes without a doctor's approval, the medical man examined the broken bodies after the legal number had been reached, ordering one lot on the shoulders, others on the back, then over the body until the final hundred were inflicted on the calves of the legs.[9] Others implicated in the plot, and also a few innocent of the charges, were imprisoned or transported to Norfolk Island. Holt, though patently innocent, was imprisoned and set to work as a convict, but was later released and restored to freedom. The Irish conspiracy happened in the concluding days of Hunter's administration. Scarcely had he left the colony when another plot was discovered, and after an enquiry the bench of magistrates on October 1, 1800, declared that although "no act and fact" could be established so as to warrant a capital conviction, the intentions of the insurgents "were in progress to effect a plan of the most wicked and dangerous tendency". For their intentions it was recommended that five persons should be punished with 1000 lashes each, four by 500 lashes and seven by 200 lashes. Eight of these prisoners were to be further punished by banishment with hard labour for the term of their natural lives.[10] King informed Portland that the punishments had been inflicted and the principals were lodged on board a hulk in irons "until they shew a peaceful disposition".[11]

Hunter endeavoured to bring order into the employment of convicts in government service. In 1795 he ordered that work should be done from daylight until ten, and from two until sunset. The order was modified in the following year when the hours were from sunrise to 8 a.m., from 9 a.m. to 11.30 a.m., and from 1 p.m. to sunset. The orders were not regularly enforced and it was found necessary to prevent overseers from diverting convict labour to private tasks in the afternoon. Hunter adopted the principle that the labourers should be free at certain times during the day so that they might hire themselves to private employers. Margarot, in evidence before the 1812 Committee, stated that practically all of them availed themselves of this privilege, and some of them earned up to £4 or £5 weekly. This was evidently an exaggeration, but the wage of a labourer averaged five or seven shillings daily. The amount of government work done by convicts was far below that which free men would have done: it was devoted spasmodically and unscientifically to farming, but was more productive in buildings and public roads. Hunter also attempted to segregate the convicts,

placing youths—he stated that there were a few children about twelve or thirteen years of age—at special and lighter tasks under overseers responsible for their conduct.[12] Women, however, were an insuperable problem. Most of them were unemployed, others were assigned, and some were set to government work mending clothing. In 1796 he begged that women should not again be sent to the colony as they were "generally worse characters than the men" and "at the bottom of every infamous transaction in the colony". In a general order he threatened to remove all the indulgences they enjoyed and to inflict corporal punishment upon the worst of them. Children of convicts, legitimate and illegitimate, were supported by the Government, but Hunter found it necessary to warn convicts that once they became free they must support their own families. In view of the high rate of illegitimate births he encouraged marriage and found that legitimate unions considerably increased. In general, however, the convict women lent themselves to the low standard of morality which the military and the prisoners had created in the settlement. Nevertheless, even though the Governor regarded them as debased he did not fail to realize their importance as mothers: "If we estimate their merits by the charming children with which they have filled the colony," he wrote, "they well deserve our care."[13]

Year by year the problem of managing convicts freed by servitude became more acute. As the numbers of expirees increased it was found necessary to appoint regular days, three or four times a year, on which these people could present themselves for certificates of liberation. The Governor related that it had become customary for captains of American trading vessels to take the freed men from the colony; rather naively he forbade the embarkations of "so many of His Majesty's subjects" on American ships when their country had great need of their services. During this war period when officers came from India to recruit soldiers among the convicts, Hunter at first withheld his sanction, believing that only the best would be selected and the worst left at the settlement; but in 1797 when expirees had multiplied and additional convicts had arrived, he consented to it and the arrangement was temporarily agreed to in England.[14] In June 1797 certificates were issued to more than a hundred who refused further contacts with government favour and control; the Governor estimated that from 1793 to 1800 a total of 1264 male convicts had been discharged. Despite regulations requiring masters of vessels to have a certificate of character from the Judge-Advocate for every ex-convict embarking, unauthorized departures continued. When Hunter's successor arrived it was found that many had departed before the expiration of their terms, and that in about 200 cases the official entries of sentences in the

Governor's office had been altered by clerks who had been bribed
to the extent of from £10 to £20 for each re-entry. In his evidence
before the Committee of 1812 Hunter stated that convicts had
departed in large numbers during his administration, and that
after his return to England some of these had come to him and
begged him to arrange for their return to Australia as free settlers.
This evidence was supported by Margarot and Richardson, two
ex-convicts of that period, Margarot remarking that only the sick
and the aged and the women were prevented from departing
without inconvenience. These facts have an important bearing
on the question of heredity and the influence of the convicts upon
the settlement.

The expirees who remained in the settlement, however, created
a difficult problem. Hunter stated that those who were liberated
in his term of office were more numerous than those who arrived,
and as most of the latter were men of seven years terms with only
twelve or eighteen months to serve, the policy of transporting them
merely "filled the country with vagabonds". The expirees who
refused to become settlers, he said, generally allied themselves with
low-class members of the community, preying on the Settlement
and consuming a large amount of provisions which could have
been more advantageously supplied to worthier people. Many of
them were re-convicted and transported to Norfolk Island.[15]
He suggested that they might be recruited for the navy and recommended that ships should be sent for that purpose.

At so early a date it would be impossible to estimate the worth
of the ex-convict in the community and to decide whether the
emancipation policy was successful or not. If the ex-convicts are
to be judged by the evidence of contemporary despatches and
narratives, they would have to be condemned as a worthless body.
However, this evidence could not fail to be partisan, either because
it hoped that the system would fail or because it expected too much
from it and within too limited a time.

The ex-convict has to be considered in the two states under
which freedom was enjoyed, as expiree or conditionally pardoned.
Both classes were virtually in the same position; the first, however,
was free to leave the country, and the other was usually emancipated
for some reason of worthiness. Both might become free settlers.

The expirees were a dangerous element in the community. Freed
from restraint, many of them merely awaited an opportunity to
leave the country, and it was said that they refused to work and
were responsible for much of the crime committed. Nevertheless,
in view of the fact that these men supplied much of the labour for
which high wages were paid, it must be assumed that not all of
them were idle and profligate. The emancipists and expirees who

I

became settlers were also generally condemned as a class who refused to farm their land, sowing the seed of a present crop over the stubble remaining from the previous harvest, which too frequently had been sold in exchange for spirits. At the Hawkesbury, where ex-convict farmers were settled in large numbers, they were described as "immersed in intoxication", and in 1796 Hunter learned, what he had long feared, that the smaller settlers in three districts were in debt to the extent of £5098, most of which had been incurred in purchasing spirits and luxuries from the military traders. Consequently, the civil court was kept busy in deciding numerous claims for debt, and the amazing spectacle arose in this primitive settlement of a special debtor's prison in which emancipist settlers and others were confined under conditions that existed more naturally in capitalist England. So litigious did the colony become that Hunter had to republish Phillip's order, which had been "worn out" in six years, that no convict might be sued for debt and that all credit given to him was at the creditor's risk. However, at the enquiry into the state of the farmers at the Hawkesbury in 1796 besides the worthless, there were found many settlers "industrious and thriving", and one man was particularized as having a flock of twenty-two sheep which he had raised from the pair that were given to him in 1792. "Other instances were found to corroborate this," wrote Collins.[16] It would be unreasonable, therefore, to judge the ex-convict settlers absolutely by the condemnatory despatches written by governors and officials who were harassed by the majority of them, who were unthrifty, irresponsible and unproductive.

When it is taken into account that the lax control of the colony and the harmful monopolies practised by the upholders of the law deliberately contributed to their downfall, it is not surprising that so many of the ex-convicts failed to avail themselves of the advantages offered to them. Moreover, the system of settling inexperienced ex-prisoners on the land was not long enough in existence to allow it to be judged as a method of reform. When he was questioned by the Select Committee of 1812, Hunter took a broader view of the prisoner settlers of his day, differentiating the "highly meritorious" from others "not so well". "There are many men who have been convicts and are now settlers there", he said, "who were as respectable as any people who have gone from this country. I have seen many families going from this country, who when they arrived there were found as bad as any of the convicts —some of the lowest of the people." Lieutenant-Colonel Johnston, one of the New South Wales Corps and a large employer of convict labour as a military settler, spoke on the same occasion from an experience of the colony that had begun with the First Fleet.

"Some of the people that were convicts and have been allowed to become settlers, he said, "are the best people we have there, and far superior in point of industry to some that come from England as free settlers".

In 1796 there were about 250 settlers of all types, official and penal, thrifty and useless,[17] but in 1800 the number had increased to 402.[18] Pardoned convicts were few; in 1796 they numbered 20 men and 9 women, and in 1799 there were 23 men and 27 women. But the privilege was often granted without due consideration. Army enlistment, formerly prevalent as a motive for emancipation, was discouraged at the end of the century. As it had been found that convict influence was harmful to discipline, an order from Whitehall in 1799 forbade the reception of convicts and ex-convicts into the corps except in cases where good behaviour justified a departure from the rule.[19]

Among these ex-convicts interesting characters existed. One of the witnesses before the 1812 Committee was Richardson, an ex-convict who had married a convict, and both he and his wife after the expiration of the sentences became schoolteachers in the settlement. Crossley, a convict in Hunter's time, was soon practising as an attorney. Michael Massey Robinson, an Oxford under-graduate with a weakness for poor verse, was transported for blackmail, won the approval of the Judge-Advocate who travelled in the same ship, and within a few days of his arrival was emancipated and appointed a clerk in the judge's office. Though his later career was marred by repeated forgeries and blackmail, he eventually won an undeserved prominence under Macquarie.

The morality of the colony was deplorable. This was more or less to be expected among such a people; it was inevitable in the lax state of discipline that prevailed. In the long list of crimes recorded by Collins it is evident that the traffic in alcohol was the immediate cause of this moral degradation. Conduct was decidedly worse than in the earlier years. Murders were frequent and robberies with violence made property insecure and life cheap. It would be idle to describe these offences, which, owing to the increasing number of expirees, it was found impossible to check. Perjured evidence made it difficult to obtain convictions. By frequent orders and regulations Hunter endeavoured to restore discipline among abandoned women and idle men. He instituted a system of passports which every convict had to show when travelling from one district to another; he restored the four divisions in Sydney, in each of which a principal inhabitant was made responsible for good order and three men were elected by popular vote to serve as watchmen. He also completed the gaol, a building of strong logs, with separate cells and surrounded by a wall.

In his evidence before the 1812 Committee Margarot stated that justice was unfairly administered, but his charge appears to have been unfounded when one considers the number of cases in which patently guilty convicts were acquitted because of insufficient evidence. Sentences, however, were unduly severe, aiming usually at being exemplary. Death was the usual punishment for burglary, but for other crimes floggings up to eight hundred lashes were ordered. The commutation of a death sentence was generally transportation to Norfolk Island with hard labour, and this sentence was much dreaded by the prisoners. The gaol-gang in which men worked in irons and were denied all concessions of liberty was a frequently imposed sentence and the labour accruing from it proved profitable to the colony. Novel punishments were introduced in this period, designed to impress the rest of the criminal population, which purpose they usually failed to achieve. One man was hanged in chains on an island in the harbour, where his body provoked amusement in the hardened whites and terror among the natives, who abandoned that hunting-ground for ever. For manslaughter the old English penalty of burning in the hand was invoked, and for perjury one man was put in the stocks with his ears nailed to his cage. Another, reprieved on the scaffold, where his coffin rested before his eyes, expressed regret that he had not been allowed to die when he felt most prepared for it. As a final example the case might be mentioned where a seaman, arrested on suspicion of murdering a soldier, was compelled to handle and bury the body, but as he manifested no perturbation and the body did not bleed at his touch he was acquitted.[20]

Like the settlers, if the prisoners are to be judged solely on contemporary evidence they must be condemned almost universally. The clergy were no less outspoken against them than the governors. Johnson and Marsden, and some missionaries recently arrived from Otaheite and now become settlers, had formed the opinion that the convicts were unreformable. As the Sunday continued to be desecrated by uncontrolled excesses, Hunter ordered all convicts to attend the services with their overseers, but within a few weeks of his order the church was burned down, evidently as a reprisal. Hunter vainly offered a reward for information and promised that the informer would be pardoned and shipped from the colony immediately. He had much satisfaction in ordering the worst convicts to build a new church on their free days, and transferred services immediately to an unoccupied building. It was admitted in 1812 that only those in the labour-gangs, who were under strict discipline, attended the services despite the orders and the compulsion. Punishment and forced religious observance were insecure controls. It does not seem that any one of these well-meaning men

realized that the fundamental cause of dissoluteness was the system itself, authorized by the English Government to function in the settlement without any suitable provisions being made for its effectiveness.

While it must be admitted that the majority of the convicts were a dissolute body, the exceptions were not noted by their contemporaries, who naturally were more concerned with controlling the bad than praising the good. In 1812 Hunter may be said to have altered his earlier views and exaggerated the virtue of the prisoners. He recalled with much satisfaction the orderly conduct of men who worked naked in the fields and stated that they were generally orderly in their hours of leisure. He admitted the prevalence of drunkenness among most of them, but distinguished "respectable men". There were convicts of all ages, he said, boys and girls of twelve and thirteen years old and men and women as old as seventy. Some of the boys reformed and became artificers, others were contaminated by evil associations and ended their lives on the gallows; but many of the girls were "led away" by their elders and became infamous. The Rev. R. Johnson, however, had not changed his opinion. When asked if his experience led him to believe that convicts were capable of reformation in the colony, he naively answered that if a clergyman "with a proper salary" had been sent to the colony moral reforms would have been greater. He admitted that convict mothers were regular in having their children baptized and he found the convicts with few exceptions, as contented as the people of the same class in England. Witnesses distinguished between man and man, indicating that a minority were industrious and that many of the majority were victims of the unfortunate conditions existing in the colony. Two incidents, however, may be quoted to illustrate the fact that the penal settlement had its better and brighter side. In 1796 some of the better class men and women convicts opened a playhouse in Sydney, with the Governor's approval. Tickets were sold at the value of one shilling, to be paid in flour, meat or rum. They produced two different plays within a month and bestowed the proceeds, £12, on a deserving widow. This petty incident may be taken as characteristic of the few, and the fact that other convicts plundered huts and houses while the better class attended the playhouse was typical of the majority. Hunter and King both saw the necessity for founding schools, and funds were collected to begin an orphan school for female children. In 1797, however, there were three private schools, and Collins described the satisfaction of Hunter in receiving 102 clean and decently-dressed children coming with their masters and mistresses to pay their respects to the Governor, who examined them and kept samples of their work so that he could estimate their progress

in the following year. There were then 300 children in Sydney and "only a very few of them were born in England". These children, the progeny of decent as well as "vicious" parents, afforded reasonable grounds for hope and confidence amidst sordid surroundings.

(c) Norfolk Island

At Norfolk Island conditions were better than at the main settlement. The small island was more easily controlled. On its fertile soil crops were successfully raised, and, fed on an indigenous fodder, large numbers of hogs were bred, from which a fine industry was begun and the population had the advantage of constant fresh meat. In 1798, however, production was lessened and want was experienced. King had established the foundations of a firm control on the island and particularly interested himself in the education of children. In 1796 there were three schools, at one of which female orphans were supported by fines imposed for breaches of the peace and by private subscriptions. With the departure of King the military control of the island increased during the administration of officers of the New South Wales Corps from 1796 to 1800, and the trade monopoly and the traffic in spirits caused much discontent among the settlers. Resenting profiteering to the extent of 500 per cent by the military traders, who also effectively prevented them from selling their produce to the government stores, they formed a "Fraternal Society" to protect themselves. In response to the complaints of the settlers Hunter suggested that a public store should be opened.

In 1800 when Foveaux was appointed lieutenant-governor an attempt was made to bring about reforms which were overdue. Foveaux was instructed to open a government store where imported articles might be purchased at a price that allowed for only a moderate profit. He was ordered to regulate the importation of spirits, to forbid its sale except to the military and deserving settlers, and absolutely to prohibit military traders from "disgracing His Majesty's service by entering into the traffic". In Phillip's time only forty-nine acres of land had been granted to settlers; under Grose 205 acres were distributed; but from 1795 to 1800, during which the military administrators held sway in the island, 3267 acres passed over to settlers.[21] In view of the abuses to which this privilege had been subjected by speculators and ex-convicts who had no serious intention of permanently settling, Foveaux was ordered to limit land grants only to the most industrious. As it had been found inconvenient to remit prisoners constantly to Sydney for major trials, the New South Wales Judicature Act

of 1787 was amended in 1794 and 1795 by special Acts (34 Geo. III, c. 45, and 35 Geo. III, c. 18) establishing a court of criminal judicature at Norfolk Island. The patent was sent to that island in 1796 and in the same year the first criminal court was assembled under a deputy judge-advocate appointed for that purpose. Procedure and punishments were similar to those in Sydney, and the adjacent rock called Phillip Island was used as a place of banishment and hard labour. Norfolk Island fulfilled three purposes; a place to which convicts were diverted from Sydney to serve their original sentences, a gaol for secondary offenders transported from Sydney and a settlement for free and ex-convict farmers and labourers. The island had been comparatively peaceful throughout three years, but in 1800, almost at the same time as the Irish insurrections on the mainland, a mutiny occurred and was sternly repressed. The present history of this island, however, had not long to run. In 1803 orders were issued to abandon it and to transfer its population of free men and convicts to the new settlement at Van Diemen's Land. It was finally discarded in 1808, and was not re-occupied for penal purposes until 1825.

(d) The Dismissal of Hunter

On February 26, 1799, Portland reproved Hunter because he had failed to curtail the illicit trading monopoly carried on by the military clique in the settlement. His administration had been unwarrantably expensive, £80,854 worth of bills having been drawn in the colony on the Treasury during four years. On November 5, 1799, he was ungraciously dismissed from his governorship. It was true that he had failed, but it was equally true that no governor could have succeeded in his circumstances against the consolidated power of the new capitalist aristocracy. Control was necessary, but that would have to emanate from England and not from within the colony itself. There was much truth in Hunter's gentle remonstrance to his superiors. "Had I, my Lord," he wrote, "been less an enemy to the wretched and disgraceful traffic carried on here, so much to the injury of this colony, disapproval would not have been expressed in Australia or in England."[22] His successor, Philip Gidley King, assumed office on September 25, 1800.

The colony of 1800 was very different from that which Phillip had left in 1792. New South Wales, excluding Norfolk Island, now had a population of nearly 5000, of whom 402 were "settlers holding lands" and 759 were children: land-grants totalled 43,786 acres. It was no longer a small settlement confined to Sydney and Parramatta, but extended considerably to the north and west,

with an increasing cluster of farms along the Hawkesbury. Exploration by sea had reached north to Port Stephens and south to Bass Strait. Merino sheep had been introduced from the Cape in 1797, and in 1800 the first shipment of coal was exported from the colony. This economic advance was largely due to the revolt of the militarist settlers against the system of penal control, and once begun it could not be retarded. The convict problem, however, continued indefinitely; the convicts were not reformed at all, and the system was altered only in minor details. Collected statistics, relative to the Settlement at this period, are given in a note at the end of this chapter.

*   *   *   *   *

The story of the foundation of Australia may seem to lend colour to Sir John Seeley's oft-quoted statement that "the British Empire was acquired in a fit of absence of mind", and indeed the growth of the colonial aspect of the New South Wales settlement was casual enough. Nevertheless, the true strength of British imperialism, which is the disinterested efforts of private patriots, was strongly exemplified in the work of Banks, Phillip, Hunter, King and others, who strove for the welfare of the colony, while the military settlers, pursuing their own private gain, were at the same time laying the foundations of a new economic empire of the south. Without the co-operation of both, the settlement might have remained purely penal, but trade followed the flag and the flag in return fostered trade, to the ultimate prosperity of the Australian peoples.

ADDENDUM

Statistics after the departure of Phillip were generally unsatisfactory. The military governors had good reason not to reveal the state of the country, and Hunter did not prove much more energetic. Portland had repeatedly to ask for returns; he had received nothing satisfactory since 1796, he said; and Under-Secretary King complained that the returns eventually sent by Hunter were incomplete. In the prevailing disorder it was impossible to muster the inhabitants, and as the Catholics did not have their children baptized publicly there was no full record of births. (*H.R.A.*, i, II, 937.) The following statistics are compiled from various returns:

RETURNS FOR N.S.W. (excluding Norfolk Island. They are from Hunter's return of 30.9.1800, *H.R.A.*, i, I, 679 *et seq.*; but they

were compiled July 18-August 15, 1800, *H.R.A.*, i, I, 615, and went through several amendments. In September 1800 the Civil Department numbered twenty-seven men, nine women and eight children. The Military Department included 442 men, sixty-nine women and 113 children. Total of officials and dependants, 668. Free settlers (including ex-convicts) victualled: eighty-two men, forty-one women, 111 children. Free people and settlers (not victualled): 1777 men, 200 women. Convicts were 1230 men and 328 women, and there were 493 children of convict stock, excluding thirty-four orphans. The total population of all the districts in N.S.W. was stated to be 4936 people, including 759 children, practically all of whom had been born in the colony.

It is interesting to compare the returns of 1800 with those of previous years. The phenomenon of a temporary decline in population is evident, due to the large number of returning convicts and the reduced numbers of the military. As early as the end of 1791 the population was 4059, including 3178 convicts. The 1800 figures (4936 in N.S.W. and 5900 in both settlements) merit comparison with those of the preceding year. (*H.R.A.*, i, II, 679 *et sqq.*; 30. vi. 1799.)

The 1799 returns give the total population of N.S.W. as 5485; the civil and military departments with their dependants numbered 740. All other residents amounted to 4745, including 1744 convicts (1244 men and 500 women); the total children were then 812, but 146 of these belonged to the military. Between the dates of the two returns only 557 convicts arrived. (From August 1799 to January 1800, forty-eight births and twenty-seven deaths were recorded in N.S.W.; *H.R.A.*, i, II, 466.) King, in 1802, accepted these statistics of Hunter's time, stating that in July 1800 the total population of N.S.W. was 4953, and in September of the same year it had dropped to 4827. A year later it had increased only by 720 (*H.R.N.S.W.*, iv, 936); but in that year 404 additional convicts had arrived.

RETURNS FOR NORFOLK ISLAND. Hunter was accused of taking little interest in this settlement. The return of November 6, 1800, appears to be the most satisfactory (*H.R.N.S.W.*, iv, 252). The Civil Department numbered seven with eight children; the Military Department were ninety-eight, with three women and three children; People not victualled: 205 men, sixty women and sixty-six children; Free people: fourteen and six children; Settlers: seven free men and twenty-two freed men; Emancipists: twenty-five; Convicts: 175 men and ninety-seven women; Children of convict stock, 183. Total on the Island was 953 (519 men and 434 women).

In the two settlements the total population was stated to be about 5900. (Hunter's totals differ slightly, however; cf. *H.R.A.*, i, II, 567, 617). Of these only 1830 were convicts (1405 men and 425 women). They were the residue from 6631 (5302 men and 1329 women), who had arrived from the beginning up to November 1800. (Cf. Appendix B.) All children at both settlements at that date numbered 1025.

According to Hunter's returns of 1800 (*H.R.A.*, i, II, 566) the total of land-grants between 1788 and 1800 was 47,307 acres, and 456 acres leased. Of this, 3521 acres of grants and 456 acres of leases were situated in Norfolk Island. To the general total at least 6000 acres (which are not included in the official returns of Phillip's time) should be added. In the military interregnum 15,639 acres (at least) were granted. The grants made by Hunter, following directions from London and due to increased population and termination of sentences, amounted to 28,279 acres.

The following figures give some idea of the grants made to convicts whose sentences had expired. Before November 1791 only fifty-seven of this class were given land (*H.R.A.*, i, I, 279 *et sqq.*), but, before the end of 1792, 112 ex-convicts were settled on the land at both settlements; from December 1792 to April 1794 (the military period) the incomplete returns show grants to forty-three expirees, and seven convicts whose terms had not expired (*H.R.A.*, i, I 438, 472). From 1796 to January 1800, Hunter made or ratified grants of land to 134 ex-convicts in N.S.W. and forty-two of the same class in Norfolk Island. Four grants were made to wives or children of convicts (*H.R.A.*, i, II, 454 *et sqq.*)

Maritime Trade and Commerce in this period is described in Appendix G.

CHAPTER VIII

THE FIRST REACTIONS OF ENGLISH PUBLIC OPINION

AFTER the departure of the First Fleet, the Government, as we have seen, seems promptly to have lost any direct interest in the new colony. The domestic political scene presented a much more absorbing spectacle than the fate of a thousand or so convicts and marines in the South Seas. February 1788 saw the beginning of Warren Hastings's seven years long trial, and at the end of the year George III's tottering brain lapsed into insanity, and a stiff fight over the Regency Bill developed between Pitt and Fox. 1788 also marked the beginning of Wilberforce's noble efforts to abolish the slave trade, and, before another year had passed, events were to happen on the other side of the Channel which diverted the English governing classes from the mild reformism represented by Blackstone and Eden to the unreasoning reactionary attitude of Eldon and Ellenborough. In the midst of these distractions even the influence of Sir Joseph Banks, who seems never to have given up hope of his original project for a free settlement, appears to have been unable to change the lethargic and culpably negligent policy of the Government.[1]

In March 1789 arrived the first news from New South Wales, and the Government began making plans to send provisions to the Settlement, together with 1300 more convicts. Within three months, Tench's and Phillip's accounts of the "voyage out" had been published and passed quickly through several editions, indicating that the general public, at least, was interested in the new enterprise.[2] * Howard, in his book on Continental prisons, published this year, referred to the "expensive, dangerous and destructive scheme of transportation", and Bentham, who was writing his *Principles of Penal Law* about this time, strongly disapproved of all penal colonies.[3]

The affairs of the colony appear first to have come before Parliament on February 9, 1791, when Sir Charles Bunbury, seconded by Mr Jekyll, called for an enquiry into the whole system.[4] He contended that New South Wales was not a fit place for a convict settlement on account of the sterility of the soil,

---

* Some rather fatuous suggestions by a Middle Temple barrister are in the "Chatham Papers", 344, under the title "Observes on Botany Bay", dated 13.iv.1789. He tells Pitt, for example, how easy it is to build huts if there is a forest in the vicinity, and how to kill bears and wolves with the aid of a mixture of quicklime and flour.

and that the sentence of transportation would be in vain if a proper place were not found. Twice as many convicts, he said, had been sentenced to death, and four times as many found guilty of single felonies in the past decade as during the previous twenty years. Mr Jekyll lamented the failure of the Blackstone-Eden penitentiary scheme and called for the suspension of the sailing of the Third Fleet until the allegations as to the unsuitability of Botany Bay had been disposed of. Pitt, in reply, denied the rumours of the unfitness of New South Wales to be a convict settlement, and refused to delay for one moment the departure of the Third Fleet with its 1850 convicts. From a purely financial point of view, he argued that as the main charges had already been met, it would be folly to scrap the work thus begun, and added that he hoped to see every county adopt the plan of pentitentiary houses for minor offenders. "It was," he said, "a necessary and essential point of policy to send some of the most incorrigible criminals out of the kingdom;" he thought transportation "a very fit punishment for incorrigible offenders", as he "saw no reason to hold out a prospect of luxury to exiles", and did not wish "that the effect of their conviction should be so described". In conclusion, he opined that "the condition of the felons who were sent to Botany Bay was far preferable to that which befell them under the former mode of transportation, previous to our loss of the colonies".

With this unimaginative answer the reformers had to be content for the moment. The columns of the Press, however, continued to show dissatisfaction with the situation. An indignant correspondent of *The Bee*, an Edinburgh weekly, wrote in October 1791 to complain of ministerial extravagance, saying that "the Botany Bay scheme is the most absurd, prodigal, and impracticable vision that ever intoxicated the mind of man", and avowing that "there is not an old woman in the three kingdoms who could not have suggested a better plan".[5] The writer was, however, misinformed as to the expenditure already incurred, alleging that £600,000 had been spent, when in fact the total cost of the Settlement to the end of 1791 was only about £420,000.* In December 1791 the *Dublin Chronicle* considered that a parliamentary committee was likely to be set up, owing to the return of expirees, the atrocious treatment of the Second Fleet convicts, and the lack of civil justice in the colony.[6] By May 1792 news of continued starvation and inability of the colony to support itself was coming

---

* Prof. Holland Rose makes a curious slip in the opposite direction on p. 441 of his *William Pitt and National Revival*, where he misquotes Bonwick's *First Twenty Years of Australia* to make the whole cost of the expedition and settlement up to October 1789 only £8632. Bonwick's figure was for the civil establishment only. The actual cost was about £220,000. (See Appendix E.) Owing to this error, Prof. Rose is driven to make elaborate excuses for Pitt's stinginess in Empire-building, while paying off £150,000 of the Prince of Wales's debts.

in, and the same newspaper seemed to think that a plan of Lord Dorchester, the Governor-General of Canada, for a penal settlement in Upper Canada was likely to be adopted instead.[7]

On May 31, 1793, Bunbury returned to the attack in the House of Commons, in the last parliamentary debate on New South Wales until Romilly began his campaign in May 1809.[8] His cogently argued speech showed signs of the influence of Bentham, not only in its advocacy of the Panopticon scheme, but also in its statement of aims. "His object," he said, "was to lessen the sum of human misery, and to prevent an unnecessary expenditure of the public treasure." Bunbury began by complaining of the conditions in which convicts were kept at Newgate and on the hulks prior to transportation, and estimated that at least two years of a seven years sentence were spent in idleness and bad company before arrival at Port Jackson. He also deprecated the recent practice of inflicting solitary confinement for slight offences. He reprobated the sending of felons, sentenced to transportation for as short a period as seven years, "to a barren spot in one of the remotest corners of the globe, at which, when they arrived, after much trouble and expense, they were to be preserved from perishing by famine, by corn and meat sent from England, the precarious arrival of which had subjected them to frequent alarms and distress".

These more corrigible offenders, Sir Charles continued, together with the very old, the very young, the crippled, the infirm and the penitent, might more advantageously be kept in a penitentiary, which had proved a most beneficial institution in those counties where it had been tried. The remainder of incorrigible criminals, he thought, if the United States still refused them admittance, should be sent to Hudson's Bay. In conclusion he specially commended the Panopticon, and then proposed six resolutions: (1) for the discontinuance of the hulks system; (2) against the promiscuous confinement of prospective transportees in gaols and hulks; (3) for a proper prison for the reception of prospective transportees; (4) that only life or fourteen years transportees should be sent to Botany Bay; (5) that North America should be reconsidered as a place for the disposal of convicts; and (6) that a space of at least two tons per person should be allowed on the transport vessels.

Dundas replied non-committally to the debate, but three months later we find the *Dublin Chronicle* reporting that owing to Phillip's unfavourable report (he returned to England just before the debate) and the great expense involved, ministers were considering abandoning the settlement,* and would in any case

* Abandonment of the settlement was proposed by Tench in his second book, published in 1793.

not send out any convicts sentenced for less than fourteen years.[9] Actually, between July 1792 and August 1796 only about 200 convicts were sent out from England (in February 1794 and October 1795), and among these the proportion with seven years sentences was considerably lower than before. In May 1794 an Act (34 Geo. III, c. 60) was passed continuing the transportation laws until 1799.*

The hulks, for the abolition of which Bunbury called, had now been in existence for nearly twenty years and had become a recognized part of the transportation system.† In the twelve years 1783 to 1795, 4775 convicts were put on board Duncan Campbell's hulks at Woolwich, and upwards of a thousand others found an uncomfortable prison at Plymouth and in Portsmouth and Langstone harbours.[10] The total sums paid to the hulks contractors during the first twenty years of the system amounted to £331,286.[11] Some interesting figures for the years 1789 to 1791 are contained in a parliamentary paper of March 1792, and relate to the *Justitia*, *Censor* and *Stanislaus* at Woolwich, the *Dunkirk* at Plymouth, the *Lion* at Portsmouth, and the *Ceres* and *Fortunée* in Langstone Harbour.[12] Quarterly censuses reveal an average population of just over two thousand convicts on these seven vessels,‡ until after the departure of the Third Fleet in 1791, when it dropped to about 900, the *Justitia*, *Ceres* and *Dunkirk* being then paid off. These convicts performed a total of 260,440 days' work in 1789-1791.

In December 1789 Henry Dundas, writing to Grenville about the latter's proposal to employ convicts in making a canal between Fort William and Fort George in the Highlands of Scotland, said: §

"I am not surprised you would wish to substitute something in the room of the hulks. I believe it a very mischievous institution, and produces many more crimes than it punishes. I believe you will find nothing so good as transportation, and I cannot see any good reason why in smaller offences, which are chiefly committed by boys or very young men, some plan might not be adopted to convert them into recruits for regiments situated in our colonies abroad, either east or west; and after being inured to exercise and military discipline for a few years, they are very likely to lay aside their idle dispositions, and become

---

* *Viz.*: 19 Geo. III, c. 74; parts of 24 Geo. III, c. 56, and 25 Geo. III, c. 46.

† Proposals for the reform of the hulks system, drawn up by William Richards, Jun., under date 3.vi.1788, and a later document comparing his plan with the existing practice, are in the "Chatham Papers", 311. In the same bundle is a plan for a model prison by a Mr Chamsley of 10 Plumtree street, Bloomsbury.

‡ Howard found about this number on the hulks on his visits in 1787 and 1788 (*Account of the Lazarettos*, 2nd Ed., 245).

§ *Dropmore Papers*, I, 555-6.

good subjects. If their crimes are of a nature not to give hopes of this, they are very proper objects for transportation. I had the same opinion as to the hulks that I now entertain when they were first proposed; but the plan was rather a popular one, and any objections to it were not listened to. Death, transportation and Bridewell are, in my judgment, the only variety of punishment that the manners of our country will admit of."

Grenville replied:*

"You will observe that if any of these people are to be kept in this country they must be maintained at the public expence, and, therefore, the applying their labour to any work of real advantage is, in fact, so much clear gain. The other idea which you mention, that of inlisting persons convicted of small offences is, I am convinced, quite impracticable, not from any real and considerable difficulty in the thing itself, but from insurmountable prejudices in those whose consent or acquiescence is necessary to its execution."

In place of the hulks, and as a receptacle for lesser criminals, Bunbury proposed the adoption of Bentham's Panopticon scheme, which had been especially designed by its author to supersede the existing methods of imprisonment and transportation. Bentham, as we have already seen, had originally become interested in prison reform through reading Howard's *State of the Prisons*, and in 1778 committed to paper his suggestions for the improvement of the Blackstone-Eden Penitentiary scheme in *A View of the Hard Labour Bill*. Seven years later he paid a visit to his brother Samuel, who was in South Russia undertaking some engineering work for Prince Potemkin, and found that he had devised a circular building to house the Russian peasants. Jeremy was greatly struck with the possibilities of the circular principle, applied not only to peasants, but to convicts, lunatics, schoolchildren, and even factory-workers. The fundamental idea of the Panopticon, as he named it, was that its circular shape enabled one or a few inspectors to watch all the prisoners or inmates at the same time. "To be incessantly under the eyes of the inspector is to lose in effect the power to do evil and almost the thought of wanting to do it." Moreover, by selling the produce of their labour the convicts could be made self-supporting, and so, unlike transported felons, would cost the nation nothing. By adopting the system of contract-management already employed in the hulk establishment, the three great rules of prison administration, lenity, or no suffering prejudicial to

* *Dropmore Papers*, I, 557.

health or life, severity, or less comfort than among the poorest class of free citizens, and economy would be assured.

The great scheme first saw the light in the form of letters addressed to Bentham's friend, George Wilson, from Russia in 1787, and was published at Dublin in 1791 at the instance of Sir John Parnell, Chancellor of the Irish Exchequer, as *Panopticon, or the Inspection-House*.[13] It at once attracted the attention of the small group of philanthropists and prison-reformers, who had previously supported the ill-fated Blackstone-Eden plan, and Parnell endeavoured, without success, to induce the Irish Parliament to adopt it.[14] The return of Samuel Bentham in 1790 and the death of his father, two years later, furnished Jeremy with both the skill and the money with which to prosecute his scheme. In March 1792, the month of his father's death, he approached Pitt and Dundas with an offer to take over a thousand convicts, but it was not until May 1793 that he was able to write to his brother that the two statesmen were coming to see his model, and that several people had been recommending it to them.[15]

Bentham also showed his plan to George Rose, then Clerk of the Parliaments, who told the philanthropist J. J. Angerstein that he had never in his life met such a taking proposition, and to Lord St Helens, ambassador to Madrid, who laid it before Sir Evan Nepean.[16] In August 1793 Jeremy wrote to Samuel that Nepean had told him that the Government was afraid to act under the Blackstone-Eden Penitentiary Act (19 Geo. III, c. 74), but would bring in a fresh Bill the next session.[17] Accordingly, 34 Geo. III, c. 84, was passed in 1794, reciting the previous Act, under which no action had been taken, and enjoining the Treasury to fix upon a piece of land and erect thereon a penitentiary house or houses. In June 1794 the Treasury made a grant of £823 10s. 5d. to William Blackburn, the architect of the Blackstone-Eden plan, "as a compensation for designing penitentiary houses intended to have been built at the public expense", and of £2000 to Jeremy Bentham, "to enable him to make preparations for the custody and care of the convicts proposed to be confined in the penitentiary houses".[18] Bentham was promised a total of £20,000, on the strength of which he spent £6000.[19]

The old difficulty of fixing on a site now cropped up again, and the objections of landowners and of George III had to be contended with, so that in spite of the support of Colquhoun in his *Police of the Metropolis*, published in 1795, we find Bentham complaining to Lord Lansdowne in March 1795, and to Wilberforce in August 1796, of official dilatoriness and obstruction.[20] The support of the Panopticon scheme by Colquhoun was continued when the magistrate came to give evidence before the Select Committee

on Finance, appointed in 1796.* There he stated that he had himself laid before the Home Secretary a plan of a "Village of Industry", but on becoming acquainted with the Panopticon at once recognized its superiority over all other prison plans he had seen. "Its immediate adoption," he thought, "would be a most important object to the Public, not only in a financial, but also in a moral point of view." Colquhoun, however, evidently considered the Panopticon as an alternative, not to New South Wales, but to the hulk establishment, which he condemned root and branch as a "complete seminary of vice and wickedness".[21]

Bentham himself was examined by the Committee and declared that he was in perfect readiness to do his part in the business. Tothill Fields, he added, was now proposed to be the site of the prison. A circumlocutory communication was sent by the Treasury to Abbot, declaring that certain "preliminary difficulties" were still holding the project up and enclosing a copy of the draft contract between the Lords Commissioners and Bentham.

In its report, the Committee discussed first the hulks. They found that there were still 1864 convicts under sentence of transportation in the country, of whom 1449 were in the hulks and 415 in the gaols. The Home Office had reported that the reason why this number was so great was that it had been found inexpedient to send more convicts out to New South Wales than had already been sent, until the colony had "attained a greater degree of cultivation". Such transportation, they added, had always been gradual, according to the advices from the settlement of its capability to receive them. From Portsmouth it had been reported "that a great number of convicts on the hulks were rejected as unfit to proceed to Botany Bay; and that many received from the gaols are so emaciated by long confinement and debility from former debaucheries, that they are unable to work". Though they concluded that there was little hope that convicts who had once been on the hulks, whether or no they completed their sentences in New South Wales, would ever again become useful citizens, they did not actually recommend the abolition of the hulk establishment. They did, however, call for immediate action by the Treasury to sign a contract with Bentham to erect a Panopticon as quickly as possible, in order to prevent the recidivism revealed by Colquhoun as prevalent in all convicts who had served their time on the hulks or at Botany Bay.

In considering the New South Wales settlement the Committee

---

* The monumental labours of Charles Abbot, later Speaker of the House of Commons and Lord Colchester, as chairman of this Committee, have been curiously neglected by historians. The Committee presented thirty-six reports, largely drawn up by Abbot himself, dealing with every aspect of the national administration of affairs, but the only concrete result seems to have been certain reforms in the keeping of the public accounts. They were reprinted in 1803 in a series of the more important parliamentary reports of the eighteenth century.

were principally concerned with the expense of the colony, which they estimated to the end of 1797 at £1,037,230.* After a trial of twelve years it seemed to them not too early to enquire whether its peculiar advantages were likely to compensate for its probable expense, a reduction in the rate of which did not seem likely in the near future, especially when the alternative Panopticon scheme, which was likely to yield an actual profit to the Government after the deaths of the two Benthams, was taken into consideration. The only prima facie advantage of a penal colony in the Antipodes was the difficulty of return for emancipated and escaped convicts, but Panopticon might render this advantage useless by showing how convicts could be entirely reformed, and in any case, as the settlement became stronger and more frequented, the facilities for ex-convicts to return would increase, and the prospect of being sent out there would become less terrible. A lugubrious catalogue of possible disasters to the settlement followed: failure of crops, mortality of livestock, attacks of the natives, rebellion of the convicts, or a piratical descent by a foreign power—presumably France, as Bonaparte was then in Egypt. The old mercantilist and depopulationist† delusions reappear in the Committee's statement that all convicts and settlers sent out represent so much labour lost to the mother country, for which no immediate recompense can be expected. Finally, the Committee called for the publication of more information on the state of the colony, none having been issued since 1792. That this request was not complied with until 1810, when the efforts of Romilly and his associates secured the publication of a parliamentary return of all convicts embarked since 1787, shows how neglected the affairs of New South Wales were by British statesmen at this period.

In conclusion, the Select Committee on Finance found that "our principal places of confinement and modes of punishment, so far from effecting the correction and reformation of the criminal, tend to send him forth, at the expiration of the period of his imprisonment, more confirmed in vice" and, therefore, recommended that "no time should be lost in taking the proper steps for carrying into effect [the Panopticon scheme], which seems to bid fairer than any other that was ever yet offered to the public, to diminish the public expenditure in this branch, and to produce a salutary reform in the objects of the proposed institution".

This, however, was the nearest that the Panopticon scheme ever came to supplanting the penal settlement of New South Wales,

---

* See Appendix E.

† It was only in this year that Malthus brought out his *Essay on Population*, announcing that unless the increase of population was artificially checked, it would soon outstrip the means of subsistence.

although a fresh Bill was drawn up, with the aid of Romilly, and the Act 39 Geo. III, c. 57 in 1799 continued the transportation laws, including the Panopticon Act of 1794, for a further period of three years. The Treasury kept on pretending that it was just about to sign the contract if only those troublesome landowners would agree,* and nothing at all was done until Bentham was compensated for his pains in 1811, and Millbank prison was erected on his site at the stupendous cost of three-quarters of a million pounds.[22]

For a good many years the only reliable information available to the public on conditions in New South Wales after the end of Phillip's governorship was contained in Collins's book, *An Account of the English Colony of New South Wales*, of which the first volume, considerably criticizing the attitude of the Government, appeared in 1798, and the second, carefully moderated because its author was out of a job, was published in 1802. The appearance of this second part gave the young Edinburgh Reviewers a chance to sharpen their teeth on the Government. The review appeared in April 1803 and is not signed, but it is usually attributed to Sydney Smith, whose flowing periods it would be impertinent to curtail:

Why we are to erect penitentiary houses and prisons at the distance of half the diameter of the globe, and to incur the enormous expence of feeding and transporting their inhabitants to, and at such a distance, it is extremely difficult to discover. Upon the foundation of a new colony, and especially one peopled by criminals, there is a disposition in Government (where any circumstance in the crime affords the least pretence for the commutation) to convert capital punishments into transportation; and by these means to hold forth a very dangerous, though certainly a very unintentional, encouragement to offences. And when the history of the colony had been attentively perused in the parish of St Giles, the ancient avocation of picking pockets will certainly not become more discreditable from the knowledge that it may eventually lead to the possession of a farm of 1000 acres on the River Hawkesbury. Since the benevolent Howard attacked our prisons, incarceration has become not only healthy, but elegant; and a county-jail is precisely the place to which any pauper might wish to retire to gratify his taste for magnificence, as well as for comfort. Upon the same principle, there is some risk that transportation will be considered as one of the surest roads to honour and to wealth; and that no felon will hear a verdict of "not

---

* Bentham himself always used to attribute his discomfiture to the personal animosity of George III.

guilty", without considering himself as cut off from the fairest career of prosperity. It is foolishly believed that the colony of Botany Bay unites our moral and commercial interests, and that we shall receive hereafter an ample equivalent, in bales of goods, for all the vices we export. Unfortunately, the expence we have incurred in founding the colony will not retard the natural progress of its emancipation, or prevent the attacks of other nations, who will be as desirous of reaping the fruit, as if they had sown the seed. It is a colony, besides, begun under every possible disadvantage; it is too distant to be long governed, or well defended: it is undertaken not by the voluntary association of individuals, but by Government, and by means of compulsory labour. A nation must, indeed, be redundant of capital, that will expend it where the hopes of a just return are so very small.

It may be a curious consideration to reflect what we are to do with this colony when it come to years of discretion. Are we to spend another 100,000,000 of money in discovering its strength, and to humble ourselves again before a fresh set of Washingtons and Franklins? The moment after we have suffered such serious mischief from the escape of the old tiger, we are breeding up a young cub, whom we cannot render less ferocious, or more secure. If we are gradually to manumit the colony, as it is more and more capable of protecting itself, the degrees of emancipation, and the periods at which they are to take place, will be judged of very differently by the two nations. But we confess ourselves not to be so sanguine as to suppose that a spirited and commercial people would, in spite of the example of America, ever consent to abandon their sovereignty over an important colony, without a struggle.[23]

Sydney Smith was well steeped in Paley, and represented a point of view very prevalent among the upper classes. The onslaught of the *Edinburgh Review* did not, however, alter the determination of the Government to let sleeping dogs lie. It did provoke at least one pamphlet,* whose anonymous author talked of the abandoned wretches in New South Wales who would not reform, even in England, "a country where the mildness of the laws" was renowned, and where scarcely a disease or a want either of body or of mind could not find a private or public institution to relieve it. Such a place of comfort New South Wales might become, he said, if only the convicts would reform.

Collins's work was relied on also by Bentham for the information on which he based two pamphlets written in 1802 and 1803 to further the waning cause of the Panopticon. These were *Panopticon*

---

* *A Concise History of the English Colony in New South Wales . . . with remarks on the treatment and behaviour of convicts and free settlers.* London (Harris), 1804.

versus New South Wales, consisting of two letters addressed to Lord Pelham, the Home Secretary, and dated November 2 and December 17, 1802, and *A Plea for the Constitution,* which was published in 1803.[24]

In *Panopticon versus New South Wales,* Bentham set out to show how superior his scheme was to the penal settlement as a means of disposing of convicts. The grounds, he stated, on which the Panopticon had been rejected were lapse of time, increased expense, alleged improvements in some of the existing gaols, and "the improved state of the colony of New South Wales". He then enunciated the five main objects of penal justice, viz. to deter others, to reform the criminals, to prevent recidivism, to compensate any injured party, and to do all this at the least possible cost to the public purse, and proceeded to demonstrate how much more effectively the Panopticon would achieve these aims than the existing penal settlement.

In so far as punishment should be exemplary, transportation removed the convicts to the Antipodes, right out of the ken of those on whose minds it is desirable to make an impression, he argued, whereas a penitentiary at home would be an ever-present reminder to potential criminals. Reformation he considered to be quite impossible in a penal settlement, because no efficient system of inspection could be introduced. Inspection, which he believed to be "the only effective instrument of reformative management", was, on the other hand, an inherent and characteristic feature of the penitentiary system. He particularly drew attention to the lack of official interest in religious instruction in the colony and was the first public man to complain of the injustice done to the Catholics in denying them a priest of their own persuasion. "If there be a difference, of all branches of the Christian religion, the Catholic is surely that in which the services of a consecrated minister are most strictly indispensable."[25] Especially he condemned the practice of allowing clergy transported for sedition to perform their pastoral functions in a population largely transported for similar offences. His thesis was buttressed by a host of citations from Collins to show the untruth of the improvement in the colony, which had been claimed by Pitt and Portland.

On the third head, prevention of recidivism, he claimed, supported by a copious analysis of Collins, that during the term of the sentence the Panopticon would be more effective in preventing escapes, but admitted that he could not be responsible for the convicts' actions after their sentence had expired. He severely reprobated the flogging of the expirees who had attempted to return home without obtaining the governor's permission. The

Panopticon scheme also, in Bentham's view, provided a means of compensating private injuries, which the Botany Bay scheme did not. On the score of expense, he claimed that whereas the New South Wales scheme had cost a round million pounds sterling to the end of 1797, and the average annual cost of keeping a convict there was about £40, under his system the average annual cost per convict would only be £18 10s. In conclusion, he admitted his opposition to the whole principle of colonization, and scouted the suggestion of Collins that New South Wales would form a valuable training-ground for soldiers and sailors for the East India service.

The *Second Letter to Lord Pelham*[26] consisted mainly of a comparison between the penitentiary system in the United States of America and the penal settlement of New South Wales, which was distinctly unfavourable to the latter. Bentham contrasted the industry and frugality in the New York and Philadelphia penitentiaries with the corruption, sloth and improvidence which Collins's book showed to be prevalent in New South Wales. Then followed a number of extracts from Collins, showing the "general depravity" in the colony, and a catalogue of particular instances of crimes of violence and incendiarism. Further, he complained that existing remedies, both spiritual and temporal had proved unavailing, that the officials were corrupt, and insobriety in the colony both endemic and incurable. Against this damning catalogue of iniquity, Bentham contrasted the sobriety and strictness of the American penitentiaries and the general reformation of the convicts resulting therefrom, as attested by several American investigators.

*A Plea for the Constitution** was mainly concerned with questions of constitutional law, its thesis being that the Act of 1787 which set up the criminal court in New South Wales did not empower the Governor to legislate for the colony, which had therefore been governed by illegal ordinances for the past fourteen years. Even in America, argued Bentham, the Crown had had no right to legislate without Parliament, and the Governor's Ordinances in New South Wales were null, both because there was no Assembly to consent to them and for want of a Court to try offences against them. He particularly protested against the instances of expirees being forcibly detained in the colony, and being kept in bondage while under such detention.

These two pamphlets represented Bentham's final attempt to

---

* Full title: *A Plea for the Constitution: shewing the enormities committed, to the oppression of British subjects, innocent as well as guilty; in breach of Magna Charta, the Petition of Right, the Habeas Corpus Act, and the Bill of Rights, as likewise of the several Transportation Acts, in and by the design, foundation and government of the penal colony of New South Wales: including an inquiry of the right of the Crown to legislate without Parliament in Trinidad, and other British colonies.* Its original title was more polemical: *The True Bastille, showing the outrages offered to law, justice and humanity by Mr Pitt and his associates in the foundation and management of the penal colony of New South Wales.*

persuade the powers that were, by a simple exposition of the reasonableness of his proposals. Thereafter, disillusioned and revolting from the tyranny of "Judge & Co.", he became a democrat and a radical, and passed out of Australian history, except as a critic with no hope of being able to influence events. His attitude at this time is well summed up when he "shows the complete and incurable repugnancy of the system of penal colonization to the several ends of penal justice, as contrasted with the degree of perfection in which the same objects are provided for under the Penitentiary system, kept in suspense for these eight years by corrupt influence, in contempt of an imperative law of Parliament, and a long train of engagements grounded on it".[27]

After Bentham's final manifesto in 1803, a veil of apathy as to the state of the colony descended on English public opinion, which was only partially lifted by the news of the deposition of Governor Bligh in the colony in 1808, and prevailed until the report of the 1812 Committee recalled England once more to a realization of her responsibilities.

CONCLUSION

EXPENDITURE on the transportation system between 1786 and 1800 amounted to about £1,300,000. An analysis of this is given in Appendix E. As the worth of the system to England and Ireland should be estimated by the 7947 prisoners who had been transported, rather than by the 7035 who arrived in New South Wales, it appears that the cost had been about £164 per head. In an ordinary business undertaking initial expenditure would be considerably offset by an accumulation of plant suitable for future production, but it was not so in the penal settlement. Despite the vast amount spent upon it the colony was little more than a collection of tents and hovels, and its production of food had only just commenced. Its very constitution limited its prospects for self-sufficiency, for convicts were unproductive, wasteful, devoid of a social sense and trained to a dependence on the public stores.

By 1800 it was clear that unless reforms were immediately made the penal system was destined to become a permanent failure. It had never been seriously investigated in England and, consequently, was neither understood nor supported. In some vague way it was hoped that the colony would soon become self-supporting by either public or private enterprise; therefore the dual system, colonial and penal, was allowed to carry on as best it could, without definition and lacking the most essential means of control. When he had to answer the charges which led to his recall, Hunter gave an accurate analysis of the situation. It had become necessary, he said, to countenance certain abuses in the colony, and only "men with deficient local knowledge" could blame him for failing to check the traffic in spirits which was working such havoc among the penal section of the community. While the military guards were themselves interested in the trade, "an angel from heaven possessing the omnissient [*sic*] attribute of the Divine Being wou'd not have been able, as a single individual, to prevent it", he wrote to Portland. In an endeavour to convince his superiors that "theoretical reasoning at a distance" differed widely from "practical experience on the spot", he stated that when he had formerly been employed at the settlement, private enterprise had not yet come into conflict with penal discipline. At that time "a Public Order answered every end proposed", but now the outlook of the settlement had completely changed.[1] Following English recommendations to commence agriculture, a powerful group had arisen and prospered to such an extent that they could afford to

ignore petty regulations that were suited only to a penal settlement and were unenforcible in a community where the forces of law and order were engaged in speculation.

This good advice, however, went unheeded and the English attempt at a solution was merely to change the Governor, giving to his successor the same effete Instructions which Phillip himself had found inadequate after a few months of practical experience. The effective remedies were simple enough. The penal and colonial purposes of the settlement should have been determined and separated; trade and commerce should have been liberated to meet the demands of a growing free population; adequate police and gaols should have been instituted to enforce the law; and to stop the use of rum as currency a metallic or paper money should have been provided.*

In September 1800, Philip Gidley King took over the governorship with the most optimistic ideas of reform. He found "vice, dissipation and a strange relaxation" pervading "every class and order of the people"; "the fiery poison" was accumulated by all, from "the better sort of the people to the blackest character among the convicts"; children were "abandoned to misery, prostitution and every vice of their parents"; and there were "1500 people unnecessarily victualled from the store". Doubtless, he exaggerated the position, not mentioning the few exceptions to the rule, but much of what he stated was true. Although he was certain that discontent would be general and that he would have to work without co-operation from officials, he was determined "that a change in the administration must take place immediately". "I shall have to begin everything anew," he wrote in 1800, "and have to contend with the interested and root up long established iniquity."[2] In such a frame of mind he set himself to regenerate the country, and "General Orders flowed from his pen like thunderbolts from high Olympus".[3] Without the power of enforcing them his orders remained generally abortive, and having been ostracized by the trading community the disillusioned Governor applied to be relieved of his position within three years. Characteristically, however, the Government allowed its unsuccessful representative to continue three years longer, and then sent out the martinet, Bligh, giving him the unchanged Commission and Instructions of his predecessors and ordering him to restore harmony between the two sections of the community.

---

* Hitherto, only £1000 worth of silver had been sent to the colony; in 1801 a ridiculous contribution of £2500 was sent out in the form of clumsy, ounce-weight pennies valued at twopence, which the Governor refused to accept as payment for bills drawn on London. This problem continued for many years; the system of promissory notes had many disadvantages and encouraged forgery among a community experienced in that art; the currency eventually was that of the world—dollars, dumps of dollars, johannas, ducats, mohurs, guilders, etc. Consequently, rum remained the most convenient and the favourite means of paymen

Within eighteen months Bligh was arrested and deposed by the disaffected military group. It is unnecessary to trespass further on later history, when the military power was broken by Governor Macquarie. It is impossible to judge this man in a paragraph; he may be called the greatest of Australian governors, or one of the worst. Whatever may be said of his attitude to the free settlers and to his superiors in England, it has to be admitted that this fine old Scotsman lifted the colony out of the slough of convictism and set it on the road to becoming a free nation. He assumed an autocratic control, raising the class of ex-convicts to an undue prominence, permitting those in servitude to act much as they pleased, obstructing the free settlers, discouraging free immigration, and so far acting on his own initiative that in 1819 the farcical position arose of the British Government's being at last compelled to send out a special Commissioner to find out what had been done in the colony, how far it had departed from its original purpose of acting as a penal settlement, and whether it was still possible to use it as such in the future. Only after this Enquiry were amendments made to the old system, which had dragged on without essential reforms since the days of Phillip.

The Australian penal experiment naturally attracted attention from political students throughout the world, who studied it both as a method of colonization and as a means for punishing and reforming criminals. As most of the judgments passed on it refer to the complete system that functioned for half a century, they are scarcely applicable to the limited period discussed in this book. The French were particularly interested in penal colonization procedure. Before the system was stopped in New South Wales, Jules de la Pilorgerie set himself to dissuade French statesmen from copying the Australian system in all its details, and to convince them that the exposures of it made by de Blosseville were not fictitious but true.[4] Towards the end of the nineteenth century the French economist, Paul Leroy-Beaulieu, extolled it as a successful experiment in colonization. Australian progress had been due, he wrote, not to chance or the natural resources of the country, but to the "excellent" colonizing policy adopted by Great Britain in the early years.[5]* The judgment was evidently based on insufficient evidence; it was certainly untrue of the years preceding 1800 and too sweeping a generalization over the whole period of transportation. Penal conditions after 1824 and until

* Quelle doit être la conclusion de cette étude? Malgré les fautes . . . il nous paraît incontestable que le régime anglais a donné d'excellents résultats. Des éléments viciés et nuisibles, éloignés du vieux monde . . . sont devenus des instruments utiles de travail et de production; un grand nombre se sont amendés. . . . Sans la déportation des condamnés, sans le système de l'assignement des convicts, l'Australie ne se fût pas peuplée . . . ; or, s'il est vrai que c'est un bienfait inappréciable pour l'humanité d'avoir créé, sur un continent inhabité, des sociétés florissantes et rapidement croissantes, d'avoir mis en rapport d'immenses richesses naturelles ignorées, ce bienfait, c'est à la déportation et à l'assignement des convicts que l'humanité en est redevable.

1838 were immeasurably worse than in the earlier years. It would be truer to say that permanent progress in Australia came about independently of penal colonization. Free men, whether immigrants or the offspring of the transportees, were the real founders of Australia.* Free immigration has been responsible for Australian industry as much as for Australian population. The English policy of free immigration, scientifically begun after 1830, affords but little scope for criticism. The penal colonizing policy of the eighteenth century, and as continued up to 1820 at least, however, was the most futile, wasteful and harmful example in modern British history. It might be expected that statesmen would have profited by the lesson of the American Revolt, but they remained singularly incompetent in their dealings with the new outpost of Empire which they then called into being. All that can be said in extenuation of this inept policy is that English statesmen had necessarily to be more concerned with the French wars, which were practically coeval with the years of indifference towards Australia.

From the purely penal point of view the system was equally a failure, though even from this aspect it has had apologists. A recent Lord Chancellor of England, Lord Birkenhead, expressed the opinion that "in a historical sense . . . the wisdom and justification of that system lay in the incontrovertible fact that it worked well".[6] The Select Committee of 1838, however, condemned it absolutely, declaring that the transportation system had failed as a punishment; to all intents and purposes it was slavery; by the herding of various classes of criminals it had prevented the reformation of individuals and exerted an evil influence upon the nation at large. The Committee recommended the immediate abolition of transportation, because "inefficiency for good and efficiency for evil" were "inherent in the system". The Report of this Committee generally referred to conditions existing

---

* Certain well-known documents of the Macquarie period may be cited in support of the emancipists. For example, Macquarie's letter to Bigge: "You already know that above nine-tenths of the population . . . are, or have been convicts . . . these are the people who have quietly submitted to the laws . . . who have built houses and ships . . . who have made wonderful efforts . . . in agriculture, in maritime speculation and in manufactures" (*H.R.A.*, i, X, 223, 224). Also, the Petition of the emancipist settlers in 1821, which states that they numbered 7556 with 5859 children. The other settlers numbered only 1558 with 878 children. The emancipists then had 29,000 acres in cultivation and nearly a quarter of a million acres in pasture, and their property was valued at £1,123,600 (*H.R.A.*, i, X, 549-556). The position and value of the emancipists at this date is a big question. It must be considered that Macquarie's evidence in their favour was that of a partisan who, in defending them, was defending himself. When replying to Bigge's *Report* he had to concede that it was only "too true" that "many men and a still greater proportion of women . . . are habitually vicious, idle and in every way depraved and incapable of reformation" (Reply of Macquarie to Bigge's Report; Unpublished Records, 1823, Box A, Mitchell Library, Sydney). The weight of evidence at the Bigge Enquiry was generally against them as a body, but admitted exceptions. This evidence, too, was often partisan from the opposite side, and was regarded by Bigge as such, as is evident from his marginal annotations. The wealth accrued by several of this body in commerce is not to be taken as an absolute argument of their worth, for much of it was accumulated by methods no less questionable than those which characterized the early military settlers. Certain individuals among them cannot be dismissed from the history of Australian development, but their most permanent contribution was their children, numbering nearly 6000 in 1821.

after 1800, but in the following passage it considered the foundation years particularly, when "the consequences of this strange assemblage [of transported felons] were vice, immorality, frightful disease, hunger, dreadful mortality among the settlers; the convicts were decimated by pestilence on the voyage, and again decimated by famine on their arrival". "Such," in the opinion of these eminent statesmen, "is the early history of New South Wales."[7]*

The story of the foundation of Australia, concerned as it has been with the flotsam and jetsam of Great Britain, has necessarily been full of sordid details. The gloomy background fortunately allows the contrast of later Australian development to stand out the more boldly and creditably. Even the earliest years had a few great characters and some presage of hope. Phillip was a nobler man than the statesmen who sent him to carry out an ignoble task. Hunter was well-meaning and honest, but weak. Though the ways by which the military group assumed their dominance in the land were base and demoralizing of the community, these men were the beginners of the economic history of Australia. Convicts could not be expected to overcome their natural disposition under a system which allowed them to starve and dragged them, and others of non-criminal histories, to the lowest depths. They, too, had their exceptions, who farmed the land and managed to retain respectability in a degrading atmosphere.

The greatest element of hope, however, lay in the native-born children. Hunter praised them. King manfully endeavoured to rescue and educate them. Despite the conditions under which they grew up, Commissioner Bigge in 1819 found the male portion of them, in particular, a race with marked dissimilarities from their parents—rebels against the system that attempted to enslave them, temperate because of their parents' intemperance, and refusing to be employed as police or government labourers because these positions had been an essential part of the system of convictism.† This phenomenon greatly pleased Sydney Smith, who remarked in 1823 that "everything is to be expected from these feelings. They convey to the mother country the first proof that the foundations of a mighty Empire are laid". The same tendency in the native-born was seen by Cunningham at about the same period, who remarked on the warm attachment of the "Currency Youths", as they were then known, to their native land. "Drunkenness is almost unknown with them; honesty proverbial," he wrote.

---

* The Select Committee included Sir William Molesworth, Lord John Russell, Sir George Grey, Lord Howick, Sir Thomas Fremantle, Sir Robert Peel, Francis Baring and Charles Buller.

† Cf. Bigge's First *Report*, p. 105: "The marriages of the native-born youths with female convicts are very rare; a circumstance that is attributable to the general disinclination to early marriage that is discernible among them, and partly to the abandoned and dissolute habits of the female convicts but chiefly to a sense of pride in the native-born youths, approaching to contempt for the vices and depravity of the convicts, even when manifested in the persons of their own parents".

His story of a simple "Currency Lass", who was afraid to visit England because "of the number of thieves there", has more significance than might appear at first sight.[9] She knew England only by those whom England transported.

These descriptions, of course, refer to a period a few years later than that treated in this book. However, at the end of the eighteenth century the greatest of all Australians was already born. This was William Charles Wentworth, the son of D'Arcy Wentworth, who, though not strictly an ex-convict, having chosen to banish himself from England in order to escape a reasonably certain sentence of transportation, was always regarded by the military gentry of the settlement as belonging to the emancipist class. He had first gone to Norfolk Island, where he acted as assistant surgeon, and in 1796 returned to Sydney, bringing with him his infant son, who had been born on that island, probably in 1793, and probably, also, of a convict mother. To the unfortunate Australian community of 1800 it could have been said with real truth: "a chield's amang you takin' notes, and faith he'll prent it".

On this Australian, more than on anyone else, the liberation of his country was destined to depend.*

* In 1813 he was a member of the first exploring party to cross the mountains and open the way to the rich plains of the West. In 1816 he went to London and subsequently began his studies a t the Inner Temple. In 1819 he learned for the first time, through the exposures of H. G. Bennet in the House of Commons, that he was practically of convict origin. Long before this revelation he had determined to oppose the penal system in Australia; now he pledged his life to the liberation of his country. "Cut to the quick by the discovery", he was ready "to spill the last drop of his blood" in obtaining satisfaction for his father. Letter after letter followed to his father, begging him to send him money to buy a library. "You may rely that I will not suffer myself to be outstripped by any competitor, and that I will finally create for myself a reputation which shall reflect a splendour on all who are related to me," he wrote. He was called to the Bar in 1822. When the first Constitution Bill was being discussed he attempted to direct opinion along safe lines: "I, an Australian myself," he said, "solicit as a boon that which the British Constitution teaches me to demand . . . not as a favour but as a right." He went to Cambridge for a few terms: "There is a good deal in the name of having been at college", he wrote; then he determined to return to the colony, where "a sufficient field" awaited his attention. "I will only return as a private individual; I have fully made up my mind to hold no situation under government. As a mere private person I feel that I might lead the country, but as a servant of the Governor I could only conform to his whims, which would neither suit my tastes nor principles" (Cf. A. C. V. Melbourne's *W. C. Wentworth*, 31 *et seq.*). He had, meanwhile, published his two-volume history of the settlement, in which he advocated free political institutions and free immigration. Returning to Australia he founded the first free newspaper, the *Australian*, carrying it on in the face of the most violent opposition. In 1827 he began the campaign for representative government; for years he directed the well-organized movement in Australia and England, and in 1837 assisted in founding the Australian Patriotic Association to agitate for the amendment of the limited constitution, already won, and the abolition of transportation. His later change of opinion, favouring a regulated system of convict labour, scarcely detracts from his earlier work. To him the Constitution Act of 1840 was in great measure due, but he aimed at greater concessions. He was responsible for the foundation of Sydney University in 1849-52. He finally directed the drafting of a constitution and went to England to guide the passage of the bill that conferred full constitutional government upon N.S.W. He died in 1872; he is buried in his own country, of which he is justly regarded as the Father.

APPENDICES, NOTES AND BIBLIOGRAPHY

APPENDIX A

A Selection of Crimes and Punishments under the Criminal Law in the seventeenth, eighteenth and nineteenth centuries.

(Taken from the compilation by P. Colquhoun in *A Treatise on the Police of the Metropolis*, 1795 [sixth edition, 1800, pp. 437-444], and supplemented by a section from G. B. Barton's *History of N.S.W. from the Records* [1889; pp. 449-451].)

I. Crimes punishable by the Deprivation of Life; and where, upon the Conviction of the Offenders the sentence of Death must be pronounced by the Judge. These, it has been stated on the authority of Sir William Blackstone, including all the various shades of the same offence, are about 160 in number. The principal are the following:

Treason, and Petty Treason; Under the former of these is included the Offence of Counterfeiting the gold and silver coin; Murder; Arson; Rape; Piracy, or robbing ships and vessels at sea, under which is included, the Offences of sailors forcibly hindering their captains from fighting; Forgery of deeds, bonds, bills, notes, public securities, etc., etc. Bankrupts not surrendering, or concealing their effects; Burglary, or house-breaking in the night-time; Highway-robbery; House-breaking in the day-time; Privately stealing or picking pockets above one shilling; Shop-lifting above five shillings; Stealing above 40s. in any House; Stealing above 40s. on a river; Stealing linen, &c., from bleaching grounds, etc., or destroying linen therein; Maiming or killing cattle maliciously (*see* the Black Act, 9 Geo. I, c. 22); Stealing horses, cattle or sheep; Shooting at a Revenue Officer, or at any other person (*see* the Black Act); Breaking down the head of a fish-pond, whereby fish may be lost (Black Act); Cutting down Trees in an avenue, garden, &c.; Cutting down river or sea banks; Cutting hop-binds; Setting fire to coal mines; Returning from Transportation; or being at large in the Kingdom after Sentence; Stabbing a Person unarmed, or not having a weapon drawn, if he die in six months; Concealing the death of a Bastard Child; Maliciously maiming or disfiguring any persons, etc., lying in wait for the purpose; Sending Threatening Letters (Black Act); Riots by twelve or more, and not dispersing in an hour after proclamation; Being accessories to Felonies deemed capital; Stealing woollen cloth from Tenter Grounds; Challenging Jurors above 20 in capital felonies, or standing mute; Deer-Stealing, second offence; or even first offence, under Black Act, not usually enforced; Uttering counterfeit Money, third offence; Prisoners under Insolvent Acts guilty of perjury; Destroying Silk or Velvet in the Loom; or the Tools for manufacturing thereof; or destroying Woollen Goods, Racks or Tools, or entering a House for that purpose; Servants purloining their Masters' Goods, value 40s.; Personating Bail, or acknowledging fines or judgments in another's name; Escape by breaking Prison, in certain cases; Attempting to kill Privy Counsellors, etc.; Sacrilege; Robbery of the Mail; Destroying Turnpikes or Bridges, Gates, Weighing Engines, Locks, Sluices, Engines for Draining Marshes, etc.; Mutiny, Desertion, etc.; (by the Martial and Statute Law) Soldiers or Sailors enlisting into Foreign Service.

II. The following is a list of offences, selected by G. B. Barton (*ut supra*), for which transportation was considered an appropriate punishment:

1. Quakers denying any oath to be lawful, or assembling themselves together under pretence of joining in religious worship—third offence.

2. Notorious thieves and spoil-takers—commonly called moss-troopers—in Northumberland and Cumberland.

3. Persons found guilty of stealing cloth from the rack, or "imbezzling" his Majesty's stores to the value of 20s.

4. Persons convicted of wilfully burning ricks of corn, hay, etc., or barns, etc., in the night-time.

5. Persons convicted of larceny and other offences, and entitled to benefit of clergy, except receivers and buyers of stolen goods: transportation for seven years; felons excluded from benefit of clergy, and receivers and buyers of stolen goods: fourteen years' transportation.

6. Persons convicted of entering into any park and killing or wounding any deer, without the consent of the owner.

7. Persons convicted of perjury or forgery, afterwards practising in any Court as attorneys, etc., might upon complaint to the Judge thereof, in a summary way be transported to the plantations for seven years.

8. Persons convicted of perjury or subornation.

9. Persons convicted of assaulting others with offensive weapons and a design to rob.

10. Persons convicted a second time of hunting and taking away deer out of unenclosed forests or chaces; or of coming into a forest with an intent to steal deer, and beating and wounding the keepers.

11. Vagrants or vagabonds escaping from house of correction, or from service in the Army or Navy.

12. Persons convicted of stealing any linen, etc., laid to be printed, bleached, etc.—death, or transportation for fourteen years.

13. Rebels returning from transportation without licence, or voluntarily going into France or Spain—death, without benefit of clergy.

14. Persons convicted of solemnizing matrimony without banns or licence.

15. Persons convicted of stealing fish in any water within a park, paddock, orchard, or yard, or receiving, aiding, and abetting.

III. Crimes denominated *Single Felonies*; punishable by Transportation, Whipping, Imprisonment, the Pillory, and Hard Labour in Houses of Correction, according to the Nature of the offence. The Principal of these are the following:

Grand Larceny, which comprehends every species of theft above the value of one shilling, not otherwise distinguished; Receiving or buying stolen goods; Stealing from furnished lodgings; Setting fire to underwood; Stealing letters or destroying a Letter; Petty Larcenies, or Thefts under one Shilling; Assaulting with intent to Rob; Aliens returning after being ordered out of the kingdom; Stealing fish from a pond or river; fishing in enclosed ponds; Stealing roots, Trees, or plants, of the value of 5s. or destroying them; Bigamy; Marriage, solemnizing clandestinely; Manslaughter, or killing another without malice, etc.; Cutting or stealing timber trees, etc., etc., etc.; Stealing a shroud out of a grave; Watermen carrying too many passengers in the Thames, if any drowned.

IV. Offences denominated Misdemeanors, punishable by Fine, Imprisonment, Whipping, and the Pillory. The principal of these are the following:

Perjury, or taking a false Oath in a judicial proceeding, etc., Frauds; Conspiracies; Assaults by striking or beating another person, etc.; Stealing dead bodies; Stealing cabbages, turnips, etc. growing; Robbing orchards and gardens; Stealing dogs; Setting fire to a house to defraud the Insurance Office; Making and selling fire-works and squibs; Throwing the same when on fire about the streets; Uttering base money; Combinations and conspiracies for raising the price of Wages, etc. (*see* stat. 39 Geo. III, c. 81); Keeping Bawdy Houses and other Disorderly Houses.

V. Idle and Disorderly Persons described by the Act of 17 Geo. II cap. 5, and subsequent Acts; punishable with One Month's Imprisonment—namely:

Persons threatening to run away and leave their wives and children on the Parish; Persons who tipple in ale-houses, and neglect their families, etc. as described in the 3d Geo. III. cap. 45; Persons who shall unlawfully return to the Parish or place from which they have been legally removed, without bringing a certificate; Persons, who not having wherewithal to maintain themselves, live idly without employment, and refuse to work for the usual wages; Persons begging in the streets, highways, etc.

VI. Rogues and Vagabonds described by the said Act of the 17th Geo. II cap. 5 and subsequent Acts; punishable by Six Months' Imprisonment—namely:

Fencers, Bearwards, Strolling Players of Interludes, or other Entertainments; Minstrels, (except those licensed by the Lord Dutton in Cheshire); Persons pretending to be, and wandering in the habit of, Gypseys Fortune-Tellers, pretending skill in physiognomy, palmistry, etc. or using any subtle craft to deceive and impose on others; Persons playing or betting at any unlawful games or plays; Persons who run away, and leave their wives and children upon the parish; Petty Chapmen and Pedlars wandering abroad without a Licence; Persons wandering abroad, and lodging in ale-houses, out-houses, or the open air, and not giving a good account of themselves, etc., etc.

The crimes mentioned in the first and third classes of the foregoing selection (except Petty Larceny) are always tried by the superior courts. The offences specified in the fourth class, as also Petty Larceny, and every species of misdemeanour and vagrancy, are generally tried (with some few exceptions) by the Justices in their General and Quarter Sessions, where, in certain cases in Middlesex, they act under a commission of Oyer and Terminer. The Magistrates in Petty Sessions, and in several instances a *single Magistrate*, have also the power of convicting in a summary way, for a variety of small misdemeanours, and acts of vagrancy: and of punishing the delinquents with fine and imprisonment.

(COLQUHOUN, op. cit., 445.)

APPENDIX B

THE NUMBER OF CONVICTS TRANSPORTED, 1787-1800

I. THE FIRST FLEET, 1787

There is abundant material in the Public Record Office in London for determining the actual number of convicts who were embarked in the First Fleet, but only a few returns, rather arbitrarily chosen, have been reprinted in the *Historical Records of New South Wales*. Most valuable are two complete registers of convicts embarked on the First Fleet, which are among the Home Office papers (H.O. 10/6 and 10/7) and are virtually identical, one being described as a copy of the contractor's own list. In both the total number of convicts embarked is 778, a number also found in a return from Phillip, at Teneriffe, to the Admiralty on June 6, 1787 (in C.O. 201/2), on p. 13 of Phillip's *Voyage*, in Navy Office returns of June 13, 1794 and March 27, 1798 (*H.R.N.S.W.*, II, 222, III, 376), and in Appendix O.2 of the Twenty-Eighth Report of the Select Committee on Finance in 1798. This register is the one printed in the Appendix of Phillip's *Voyage*, but there, possibly owing to a copyist's error, the number given is only 777. In view of these facts, it may seem but a sterile undertaking to devote so much space to elucidating the exact number of convicts who sailed, and who landed in New South Wales, but it should be remembered that these men and women were Australia's first colonists, and are therefore deserving of more attention than their immediate successors. In addition, so many divergent statements have been made in the past about the number of convicts who sailed and who landed, that it is worth while endeavouring to arrive at an exact and accurate calculation.

Another document in the Home Office records is H.O. 11/1, which is a list of the names and sentences of all convicts transported between 1787 and 1809. The returns for the First Fleet here are quite inaccurate, the *Friendship* and the *Charlotte* being omitted, and a total of 286 convicts listed, with a note that 607 others were also sent "in the spring of 1787", making a grand total of 893, or 115 too many. H.O. 11/1 was summarized in a parliamentary return in 1810 (*P.P.* 1810 (45) XIV, p. 487), which was copied in all subsequent official returns, with the unfortunate omission of the 607, leaving the even more inaccurate total of 286, or 492 too few.

A different class of documents is to be found among the papers of the Colonial Office. In C.O. 201/2, all the returns sent to the Home Office, prior to the sailing of the fleet, by Richards, the contractor, and Ross, the commandant of marines,

still exist in manuscript. From these, which cover the period March 13 to May 8, 1787, it appears that only 769 convicts had actually been embarked by the latter date, but the balance of nine probably arrived between then and the departure of the fleet on May 13, a period which is not covered by any returns, but during which we know that at least one more man was put on board. From this source, and from the Home Office registers, we learn that seventeen convicts died and two were pardoned before May 13, so that only 759 actually sailed.

The eight Orders in Council of December 6 and 22, 1786, February 12 and April 20, 1787, however, name 883 persons to be transported to Botany Bay, 105 more than were actually embarked. As, however, the names of forty-eight persons who were not convicted until 1787 are to be found in the Home Office registers, and 816 convicts were named in the December Orders, a considerable number of the 883 cannot have been embarked in the First Fleet; and must either have died in gaol or have been otherwise disposed of.

The first mention of specific numbers on the various vessels in the First Fleet is to be found in a letter from Captain Teer to Nepean on December 9, 1786, in another letter to Nepean on December 30 (*H.R.N.S.W.*, I, ii, 33, 42), and in a letter from the Navy Board to Thomas Steele, dated January 10, 1787.* These letters give the ships' complements as follows:

	Convicts		
Ship	*Male*	*Female*	*Total*
Alexander . . .	210	—	210
Charlotte . . .	100	24	124
Friendship . . .	80	24	104
Lady Penrhyn . . .	—	102	102
Prince of Wales† . .	—	30	30
Scarborough . . .	210	—	210
	600	180	780‡

These figures seem to have formed the official complement of convicts in the First Fleet until April 1787, though in the letter from the Navy Board to Steele on January 10, thirty marines' wives are mentioned on the *Prince of Wales*, and Richards' return of April 1 gives the complement of that ship as twenty-five female convicts and twenty-five convicts' wives. Bowes's *Journal*, which begins on April 5, is the first source to give fifty female convicts on the *Prince of Wales* (*H.R.N.S.W.*, II, 389), and the return of May 6 definitely gives a complement of fifty female convicts, which brings the complement of the fleet up to 800, and probably accounts for Hunter's figure (*Journal*, p. 4). The *Prince of Wales* eventually sailed with one male and forty-nine female convicts.

The first convicts were embarked in the *Alexander* and the *Lady Penrhyn* lying off Woolwich on January 6, 1787, and sailed round to the Solent with H.M.S. *Sirius*, anchoring at the Mother Bank on February 21. The *Lady Penrhyn* then seems to have taken on board some women from the hulks in Portsmouth and Langstone harbours, the men from which were put into the *Scarborough*. On March 13, Ross enumerated the convicts in these three vessels, and found that 209 men had been embarked in the *Alexander* (of whom eight had died and one had been pardoned§), 185 men in the *Scarborough*, and 100 women and five children‖ in the *Lady Penrhyn*. The *Friendship* and the *Charlotte* sailed from Plymouth on March 5, and were enumerated by Ross on March 21. On board the two ships were seventy-five men and twenty-one women, and 107 men and twenty women respectively, two women from the *Friendship* and twenty-one men from the *Charlotte* being subsequently transferred to the *Lady Penrhyn* and the *Scarborough*

* Also on p. xv of the anonymous *History of New Holland*, and at the end of the anonymous *History of Botany Bay.*

† Not in letter of December 9.

‡ All these figures will be found summarized in Appendix C.

§ The Home Office registers record only six or seven men as having died up to March 13. One man is stated to have died on March 13 in one register and on March 24 in the other.

‖ One child had already died on February 8. (See Log-book, *H.R.N.S.W.*, II, 406.)

respectively. Finally, six women were counted on the *Prince of Wales* on March 29, a note being added to the effect that three more arrived on April 9, and a fourth on April 12. Up to the end of March, 576 men, 147 women and six children appear to have been embarked.

These figures are exactly borne out by the contractor's return on April 1, which is identical with Ross's, except for the transfers mentioned above, and may be tabulated as follows:

	Alexander	Charlotte	Friendship	Lady Penrhyn	Prince of Wales	Scarborough
Ship						
Full Complement:						
Male . .	210	100	80	—	—	210
Female . .	—	24	24	102	25	—
On board (embarked):						
Male · ·	209	86	75	—	—	206
Female · ·	—	20	19	102	6	—

The next return was made by Ross on April 15 (*H.R.N.S.W.*, I, ii, 79), when he found 198 men on the *Alexander*, eighty-six men, twenty women and two children on the *Charlotte*, seventy-five men, nineteen women and three children on the *Friendship*, one man, 104 women and five children on the *Lady Penrhyn*, ten women and one child on the *Prince of Wales*, and 205 men on the *Scarborough*, eleven men having died and one been pardoned on the *Alexander*, and one woman having died on the *Lady Penrhyn* (see *H.R.N.S.W.*, II, 389). The deaths are corroborated by the Home Office registers. The other changes are accounted for by the four women already mentioned arriving on the *Prince of Wales*, by the transfer of John Irvine from the *Scarborough* to the *Lady Penrhyn* to act as assistant surgeon, and by the counting of three too many on the *Lady Penrhyn* and one too many on the *Alexander*.* The totals are now 564 men, 150 women, and eleven children on board, out of 576 men, 151 women, and twelve children embarked.

The next return is on April 22, when the only change is that one man has died on the *Alexander*, making a total of twelve dead on that ship since embarkation, and the arrival of one man, two women and two children on the *Friendship*, bringing the totals up to 564 men, 152 women, and fourteen children, out of 577 men, 153 women, and fifteen children embarked.† There is also a contractor's return on April 26, which differs only in that it gives the correct number (209) embarked on the *Alexander*, and only eleven dead on that ship. There is also a note to the effect that John Irvine is to be transferred to the *Prince of Wales*. A further return on April 29 records no change except one child dead on the *Lady Penrhyn*, leaving only five children on that ship, and a total of thirteen in the fleet.

The last full return was made on May 6, when there were 195 men on the *Alexander*, eighty-six men, twenty women and two children on the *Charlotte*, seventy-six men, twenty-one women and four children on the *Friendship*, one man, 101 women and five children on the *Lady Penrhyn*, two men, forty-seven women and two children of the *Prince of Wales*, and 205 men on the *Scarborough*, leaving a deficiency of thirty-five men and eleven women out of a complement of 600 men and 200 women. The changes since the last return are accounted for by the arrival of two men, thirty-seven women and one child on the *Prince of Wales* on May 3, the death of another convict on the *Alexander*, and of a child on the *Friendship*. Totals are now 565 men, 189 women and thirteen children on board, out of 579 men, 190 women and sixteen children embarked. After this, there is only a letter from Richards to Nepean on May 8, in which he says that the two men who arrived on May 3 have been put on the *Alexander* and that three men died on the same ship on May 6, bringing the total deaths there up

* See, for the error for the *Lady Penrhyn*, the letter from Ross to Nepean on April 12, and the return of April 22; for the *Alexander*, the returns of April 26 and May 6.

† Six children are counted on the *Lady Penrhyn*; one was born on April 13, which seems not to have been counted in the return of April 15. (See Log-book, *H.R.N.S.W.*, II, 406.)

to sixteen, and with another man pardoned on May 10 (see H.O. registers), the total on board to 193 out of 211 embarked.

The numbers on the fleet on May 13 now seem to be:

		Alex- ander	Char- lotte	Friend- ship	*Ship* Lady Penrhyn	Prince of Wales	Scar- borough
Embarked:							
Males	· ·	211	86	76	1	—	205
Females	·	—	20	21	102	47	—
Children	· ·	—	2	5	6	2	—
On board:							
Males	· ·	193	86	76	1	—	205
Females	·	—	20	21	101	47	—
Children	· ·	—	2	4	5	2	—

Totals are 561 men, 189 women and thirteen children on board out of 579 men, 190 women and fifteen children embarked. This leaves us seven men and two women short of the total of 586 men and 192 women given in both Home Office Registers and in Phillip's return from Teneriffe. Careful scrutiny of the Home Office registers shows that one man on the *Scarborough* was not convicted until April 21, 1787, and therefore cannot have been put on board until after that date. No record exists of such an embarkation, and it must therefore be assumed that he was embarked between May 8 and May 13, in which case the other six men and two women were probably embarked at the same time, to fill up last minute gaps.

There are slight differences between the two Home Office registers. H.O.10/6 and the Appendix to Phillip's *Voyage* give one convict's name as Mary Phyn, which in H.O. 10/7 is Mary Finn, and a certain Joshua Peck is put on the *Scarborough* in H.O. 10/6, but on the *Charlotte* in H.O. 10/7. Phillip's return from Teneriffe also differs slightly from the two registers. It gives the *Prince of Wales* fifty women, instead of the one man and forty-nine women of the registers. The one man is George Youngson, probably the husband or other relative of Elizabeth Youngson in the same ship. To balance this, the *Friendship* is given seventy-seven men and twenty women instead of seventy-six men and twenty-one women, as in the registers. Possibly, George Youngson was transferred to the *Friendship* in exchange for a female convict, but we cannot tell. Phillip's return also favours Joshua Peck's presence on the *Scarborough* rather than on the *Charlotte*.

To make up the total of 778, two men each appear to have been put on the *Alexander*, the *Scarborough*, and the *Charlotte*, and one man and two women on the *Prince of Wales*. John Irvine is counted as being on the *Scarborough*, as Phillip's return does not give him on the *Lady Penrhyn*. The position at the sailing on May 13 is now seen to be as under:

		Alexander	Charlotte	Friendship	*Ship* Lady Penrhyn	Prince of Wales	Scar- borough
Embarked:							
Males	· ·	213	88	76	—	1	208
Females	· ·	—	20	21	102	49	—
Sailed:							
Males	· ·	195	88	76	—	1	208
Females	· ·	—	20	21	101	49	—

This gives totals of 586 men and 192 women embarked, and 568 men and 191 women sailed, or added together, 759 convicts sailed out of 778 embarked. This compares with the figures of 756 given by Collins (*Account*, I, iii), 757 by Tench (*Narrative*, 6), and 752 by King (*Journal, H.R.N.S.W.*, II, 514), who may not have known of the late arrivals. Tench's other figure of 775 (*Narrative*, 46) is obviously embarkations, and Hunter's 800 (*Journal*, 4) is probably the complement, as amended by fifty women being allotted to the *Prince of Wales*. Surgeon Bowes of the *Lady Penrhyn* (*Journal. H.R.N.S.W.*, II, 389) has the figure of 772,

which must be intended for embarkations but is remarkable in giving 104 women for his own ship, the figure of the admittedly false return of April 15. Figures even more wide of the mark are 850 (600 men, 250 women) on p. vii of Phillip's *Voyage*, which thus gives three different figures, and 893 in the Home Office register (H.O. 11/1).

We have now to consider the returns sent in by Phillip and White from Teneriffe and Rio. According to White, on June 4 eight convicts had died since the fleet sailed, and by August 30 this number had risen to fifteen (*H.R.N.S.W.*, I, ii, 107, 111). By the Home Office registers, the deaths up to June 4 are only six, but as by August 30 (the last death recorded is on August 5) they agree with White at fifteen (twelve men, three women), and as the distribution of these fifteen deaths among the various ships is identical in both sources, it is permissible to assume that wrong dates were entered up in two cases in the Home Office registers. As sixteen men and one woman were dead and two men had been pardoned before sailing, and eight men and one woman died at sea up to and including June 10, there should have been 560 men and 190 women on the fleet on that date. Instead, we find Phillip giving a return of 558 men and 192 women. The figure of 192 women is palpably wrong, since by his own return of the total numbers embarked, which he also sent from Teneriffe, only 192 women embarked, and we know that two of them were already dead. The total of 750 convicts is, however, correct. Another error is the total of twenty-one convicts, stated by Phillip as having died since embarkation. We know that twenty-six convicts had died.*

At Rio, we find yet more serious discrepancies. The total dead since embarkation has now risen to twenty-nine men and three women, an increase of five men and one woman since Teneriffe, which means that 555 men and 189 women should be on board. Phillip, however, returns 552 men and 190 women on September 1, three men too few and one woman too many. These figures do not agree with his own at Teneriffe, for he returns six fewer men and two fewer women than on that date, whereas actually only five men and one woman had died. We leave the fleet, then, at Rio with 744 (or possibly 742) convicts still on board. There appears to have been no official return from the Cape. The *Annual Register* says that there had been twenty-one deaths up to this point, but marines and children are probably included. The best figure we have for the total number of deaths on the fleet is White's return on July 9, 1788, of thirty-six men and four women dead "from the time of embarkation to landing" (*H.R.A.*, I, i, 54). There is also Tench's statement that twenty-four convicts died on the voyage (*Narrative*, 46), and Collins's statement "that of the whole number of all descriptions of persons coming to form the new settlement, only thirty-two had died since their leaving England" (*Account* I, 2). Collins's figure includes two convict children, one marine, one marine's wife, and one marine's child. The discrepancies may be due to the reckoning of deaths between arrival in the colony and disembarkation. As White was surgeon, and thus more likely to know the facts, it seems safer to accept his return. It means that seven men and one woman died since Rio, and gives a figure of 736 convicts (548 men and 188 women) who actually reached their destination in Australia. There appears to be no authority for the statement in the *H.R.A.* (I, i, p. 712) that twenty-five convicts died between Rio and Port Jackson, which seems to have been arrived at by subtracting the fifteen convicts who died between sailing and Rio from the forty who died between embarkation and landing, and then ignoring those who died before sailing, thus assigning the whole twenty-five to the last part of the voyage.

* The figure for deaths on the first stage of the voyage are very contradictory. Phillip gives two figures: twenty-five since embarkation with his return of the total numbers who embarked, and twenty-one with his return of convicts actually on the Fleet at Teneriffe, both dated June 10. Twenty-one appears to be the figure for the *Alexander* alone, since all sources agree that sixteen died on that ship before May 13, and five between that date and Teneriffe. With regard to the other ships, Phillip's more accurate return agrees with the Home Office registers, probably because the latter were compiled from information supplied by Phillip. Whereas White gives one dead each on the *Charlotte*, the *Friendship* (this one is omitted in the reprint of the return in *H.R.N.S.W.*, I, ii, 107) and the *Lady Penrhyn* between May 13 and June 10, Phillip and the two registers give only two dead on the *Charlotte* up to June 10 (one died actually on that date), and one on the *Lady Penrhyn*, who had died on April 3.

The convicts' children present a rather simpler problem. Fifteen were embarked, one was born on board, three died before May 13, leaving thirteen who actually sailed. This figure is also given by Collins (*Account*, p. iii), but Tench (*Narrative*, p. 6) gives eighteen, and Appendix O.2 of the 1798 Report gives seventeen. Phillip's Teneriffe return also shows thirteen convicts' children on board, and three dead since embarkation. The log of the *Prince of Wales* (*H.R.N.S.W.*, II, 404) records a birth on July 1, bringing the total up to fourteen, which agrees with Phillip's return of seven girls and seven boys on September 1. White's return of July 9, 1788 gives two deaths of convict children on the voyage, and, if we can rely on the statement in the *H.R.A.* (I, i, 727), seventeen children were actually landed, so that five more children must have been born between Rio and Port Jackson. To sum up, fifteen children were embarked, seven were born on the passage, and five died between embarkation and landing, leaving seventeen who arrived.

The exact number of all classes of people who first landed in Australia is of relatively little importance, inasmuch as many of them stayed a comparatively short time. We have, however, Collins's statement that "every person belonging to the settlement being landed, the numbers amounted to 1030 persons" (*Account*, I, 6), and Phillip repeats this figure in a despatch to Lord Sydney two years later (*H.R.A.*, I, i, 144). These 1030 appear to be made up of 736 convicts, seventeen convicts' children, 211 marines and officers, twenty-seven marines' wives, nineteen marines' children, Phillip and his staff of nine, the Surveyor-General, the Chaplain and his wife, the Surgeon and four assistants, and two servants. The thirteen men drafted from the fleet into the service of the colony by Phillip appear not to have been counted on this occasion (*H.R.A.*, I, i, 727).

II. The Second Fleet, 1789

The first ship to leave England for New South Wales with convicts, after the departure of the First Fleet, was the transport *Lady Juliana*, which sailed from Plymouth on July 29, 1789, with a load of female convicts. 159 women were embarked in June (*H.R.A.*, I, i, 189)* and she sailed with 226 women and six children on board (*C.O.* 201/4; *H.R.N.S.W.*, I, ii, 386; II, 222, 755). At the Cape, where she arrived on March 1, 1790, the surgeon reported that five women had died, and seven children had been born (*H.R.N.S.W.*, I, ii, 323), and no more seem to have died between there and Port Jackson (*C.O.* 201/4, *H.R.N.S.W.*, I, ii, 386). Collins, however, says that 222 women arrived, five women and two children having died (*Account*, I, 118, 123). It seems fairly safe to say that 226 women and six children embarked, and 221 women and eleven children arrived.

The next vessel to leave was the supply ship *Guardian*, which sailed in September 1789 with twenty-five specially selected convict artificers. After calling at the Cape, she struck an iceberg on December 23, but managed to struggle back to port with twenty-one convicts still aboard. One of these died later, and the remaining twenty were sent on to the settlement when the Second Fleet called at the Cape, twelve on the *Neptune* and eight on the *Scarborough*.

The Second Fleet proper consisted of the *Neptune*, the *Scarborough* and the *Surprize*, in which 1017 convicts were embarked in December 1789.† The mortality on this fleet was the worst on record, as many as 267 convicts dying between embarkation and arrival. In the *Neptune*, 424 men and seventy-eight women were embarked, of whom three, probably men, were landed again before the fleet sailed, and 147 men and eleven women died on the voyage, eleven of whom had succumbed before the ship sailed. Only 353 convicts (286 men, sixty-seven women) eventually landed, including twelve men from the *Guardian*, who had been embarked at the Cape (*H.R.A.*, I, i, 189; *P.P.* 1731-1800, A. & P., xxxv, 1792, No. 751, p. 58). These are the figures supplied by Phillip and adopted by the Navy Board. A document in *C.O.* 201/4 seems to indicate that it was originally intended to send 442 men and eighty or ninety-five women,

---

* These are the only ones recorded in the 1810 returns.

† The figure of 1008 (930 men and seventy-eight women) mentioned by Grenville in a letter to Phillip on December 24 (*H.R.N.S.W.*, I, ii, 284) may allow for deaths before sailing. Cf. also 1005 in Navy Office Return of June 13, 1794 (*H.R.N.S.W.*, II, 222).

and the Rev. Richard Johnson writes from the colony that 520 convicts had been embarked (*H.R.N.S.W.*, I, ii, 387). Collins gives 151 men, eleven women and two children as having died (*Account*, I, 123) and Johnson gives 163 convicts dead. There is no record of any children having arrived.

The *Scarborough's* complement appears to have been 260, but only 259 men were embarked (252 according to Johnson), of whom six were disembarked before sailing and seventy-three died on the voyage. Six of the *Guardian's* men were taken on at the Cape. (The original of Phillip's return in *C.O.* 201/4 differs here from the version in *H.R.A.*, I, i, 189, which gives eight.) Only 186 landed. According to Johnson and Collins, sixty-eight died on the voyage. The *Surprize's* complement seems also to have been 260, but Phillip and the Navy Board show 256 men embarked (Johnson gives only 211), of whom two returned to shore before sailing, and thirty-six died on the way out, leaving 218 who landed. Johnson and Collins give forty-two dead. The totals of 939 men and seventy-eight women embarked, and 690 men and sixty-seven women arrived are the ones made out by Phillip and officially used by the Navy Board. Collins, however, who uses returns said to have been made by the masters of the vessels, gives 272 dead, and Johnson gives a total of 983 embarked and 273 dead. The only discrepancy in the official returns is that although twenty men from the *Guardian* are said to have been picked up, only eighteen are actually accounted for.

The 1017 convicts embarked on the Second Fleet, added to the twenty-five on the *Guardian* and the 226 on the *Lady Juliana* give a total of 1268 convicts embarked for Botany Bay in 1789. The Navy Office returns of June 13, 1794 and March 27, 1798 and the 1798 Report give 1251 convicts and 22 children. These figures, however, include only twenty on the *Guardian* and 1005 on the Second Fleet, which probably allows for deaths before sailing. The 1810 returns give 1242 and the 1819 and 1838 Reports give 1239. For the First and Second Fleets combined the 1791 *Accounts and Papers* give 2029 (i.e. 778+1251).

III. THE THIRD FLEET AND AFTER, 1791 to 1800

The statistics relating to the convicts who sailed on the Third and subsequent fleets are not nearly so disputable as those for 1787 and 1789. The main sources are the *Accounts and Papers* of 1792 (*P.P.* 1731-1800, A. & P. xxxv, No. 751), the official returns of 1798, 1810, 1812, 1819 and 1838, the various returns and despatches reprinted in the *H.R.A.* (I, i, 225, 274, 336, 365, 367, 397, 446, 454, 464, 494, 545, 570, 579; ii, 1, 106, 126, 376, 378, 436, 532, 563, 589, 697; iii, 4, 9, 15, 18, 115), and the *H.R.N.S.W.* (II, 222, III, 376), and the accounts of Collins and Hunter.

Of these, the Navy Office returns of June 13, 1794 and March 27, 1798 in the *H.R.N.S.W.* are identical, and the 1798 Report copies them as far as they go. The Third Fleet is dated 1790 because the contract was signed in that year, and Irish convicts embarked after 1792 are omitted. The 1810 returns, as has been said, are a reprint of H.O. 11/1 (convict embarkations 1787-1809), but err as to the First Fleet, and relate to Great Britain only. The returns attached to the 1812 Report are most useful, giving the arrivals in the colony and deaths at sea of both British and Irish convicts, but only start in 1795. The returns in the appendix of the Report of the Committee on Gaols in 1819 are very similar to those of 1810. The 1838 Committee's Report contains a list of transports, which gives only four for the First Fleet, a table of Irish convicts embarked since 1793, which is fairly accurate, and a reprint of the 1819 Committee's table of British convicts embarked. The Appendices to the Bigge Report also contain two returns similar to the 1819 ones (*C.O.* 201/130 L.4, 201/130 N.1.).

The Third Fleet sailed early in 1791. Figures are again conflicting, but as they substantially agree, it does not seem worth while discussing them in too great detail. So far as can be ascertained, 1889 male and 172 female convicts were embarked in the ten vessels of the Third Fleet, together with H.M.S. *Gorgon*, of whom 194 men and four women died on the way out, and 1696 men and 168 women arrived in Australia. Phillip, Collins and Hunter all agree as to the total arrivals and deaths, but their separate figures add up to a deficiency of twenty-one male deaths and a surplus of one male arrival. There is also a deficiency of twenty males embarked, but as the embarkation figures for some of the ships

have to be calculated by adding the deaths and arrivals, there is a possibility of error, and the totals given above include the missing twenty. The original complement of the *Queen*, the first Irish transport to go to New South Wales, was 175 male and twenty-five female convicts, but only 133 men and twenty-two women seem to have sailed, 126 men and twenty-one women arriving. Some ten to twelve children (one died on the way out) and six to eight convicts' wives and mistresses also landed from the Third Fleet. The *Pitt* sailed in July 1791, having threatened to be a very bad case of overcrowding, but, thanks to timely representations by the surgeons, many convicts were taken off just before she sailed. According to Collins 319 men, forty-nine women, five children, and seven free women, arrived, and Phillip's despatch of March 19, 1792 reported that twenty men and nine women had died.* This gives a grand total of 2229 male and 230 female convicts embarked during 1791.

The details of the remainder of the convict departures and arrivals until 1800 are more straightforward. The figures for all departures up to and including 1800, and for the corresponding arrivals will be found in the tables at the end of this Appendix. Altogether 7947 convicts (6387 men, 1560 women) were shipped off to New South Wales by the British and Irish Governments between 1787 and 1800, of whom 7035 (5595 men, 1440 women) actually landed in the colony. Most of the balance of 911 died at sea, except those lost by the mutiny of the *Lady Shore*. The Irish contingent was 1384 convicts embarked (1114 men, 270 women), and 1317 arrived (1048 men, 269 women). Although the population of Ireland at this time was nearly half that of Great Britain, the proportion of Irish convicts to all convicts transported in the period was only 17·4 per cent. Owing to the greater mortality on the English transports, the proportion rose to 18·72 per cent of those who arrived.

CONVICT EMBARKATIONS AND ARRIVALS

Great Britain and Ireland	Embarked			Arrived		
	Male	Female	Total	Male	Female	Total
1787	586	192	778	548	188	736
1789	964	304	1268	690	288	978
1791	2228	230	2458	2015	217	2232
1792	309	96	405	291	91	382
1793	235	71	306	233	71	304
1794	23	60	83	23	60	83
1795	164	203	367	153	201	354
1796	347	44	391	324	43	367
1797	298	66	364	287	—	287
1798	300	96	396	205	94	299
1799	440	103	543	403	100	503
1800	493	95	588	423	87	510
	6387	1560	7947	5595	1440	7035

Irish only						
1791	133	22	155	126	22	148
1792	—	14	14	—	14	14
1793	235	70	305	233	70	303
1795	163	70	233	152	70	222
1796	144	44	188	134	43	177
1799	440	50	490	403	50	453
	1115	270	1385	1048	269	1317

* One man escaped at the Cape and was brought in on the *Royal Admiral*.

CONVICT TRANSPORTS—1787 to 1800

Ship	Convicts Embarked			Sailed	Arrived Port Jackson	Convicts landed		
	Male	Female	Total			Male	Female	Total
Alexander . .	213	—	213	13.v.87	26.i.88			
Charlotte . .	88	20	108	13.v.87	26.i.88			
Friendship . .	76	21	97	13.v.87	26.i.88			
Lady Penrhyn .	—	102	102	13.v.87	26.i.88	548	188	736
Prince of Wales .	1	49	50	13.v.87	26.i.88			
Scarborough .	208	—	208	13.v.87	26.i.88			
Lady Juliana .	—	226	226	29.vii.89	3.vi.89	—	221	221
H.M.S. Guardian .	25	—	25	Sept. '89	(a)	—	—	—
Surprize .	256	—	256	19.i.90(b)	26.vi.90	218	—	218
Neptune .	424	78	502	19.i.90(b)	19.i.90(b)	286	67	353
Scarborough .	259	—	259	19.i.90(b)	28.vi.90	186	—	186
Mary Ann . .	—	150	150	16.ii.91	9.vii.91	—	141	141
H.M.S. Gorgon .	31	—	31	15.iii.91	21.ix.91	30	—	30
Matilda .	230	—	230	27.iii.91	1.viii.91	205	—	205
Atlantic .	220	—	220	27.iii.91	20.viii.91	202	—	202
Salamander .	160	—	160	21.iii.91	21.viii.91	155	—	155
William and Ann .	188	—	188	27.iii.91	28.viii.91	181	—	181
†Queen . .	133	22	155	Apr. '91	26.xi.91	126	22	148
Active . .	175	—	175	Apr. '91	26.ix.91	154	—	154
Albemarle .	282	—	282	Apr. '91	13.x.91	250	6(c)	256
Britannia .	150	—	150	Apr. '91	14.x.91	129	—	129
Admiral Barrington .	300	—	300	Apr. '91	16.x.91	264	—	264
Pitt . .	340	58	398	17.vii.91	14.ii.92	319	49	368
‡Kitty . .	10	30	40	Mar. '92	18.xi.92	2(d)	27	29
Royal Admiral	299	49	348	30.v.92	7.x.92	289	47	336
Bellona. .	—	17	17	8.viii.92	15.i.93	—	17	17
†Boddingtons .	125	20	145	15.ii.93	7.viii.93	124	20	144
†Sugar-Cane .	110	50	160	13.iv.93	17.ix.93	109	50	159
William .	—	1	1	1.vii.93	10.iii.94	—	1	1
Surprize .	23	60	83	2.v.94	25.x.94	23	60	83
†Marquess Cornwallis	163	70	233	9.viii.94	11.ii.96	152	70	222
Sovereign .	1	—	1	Jan. '95	5.xi.95	1(e)	—	1
Indispensable .	—	133	133	Oct. '95	30.iv.96	—	131	131
†Britannia .	144	44	188		27.v.97	134	43	177
Ganges .	203	—	203	Aug. '96	2.vi.97	190	—	190
Lady Shore .	2	66	68	Feb. '97	(f)	—	—	—
Barwell .	296	—	296	Sept. '97	18.v.98	287	—	287
Britannia .	—	96	96	Jan. '98	18.vii.98	—	94	94
Hillsborough .	300	—	300	Oct. '98	26.vii.99	205	—	205
†Minerva .	165	26	191		11.i.00	162	26	188
†Friendship .	133	—	133		16.ii.00	114	—	114
†Luz St Ann .	142	24	166	24.viii.99	16.ii.01	127	24	151
Speedy . .	—	53	53	Oct. '99	15.iv.00	—	50	50
Royal Admiral	300	—	300	23.v.00	20.xi.00	257	—	257
Earl Cornwallis	193	95	288	18.xi.00	12.vi.01	166	87	253

† Irish convicts.
‡ Some Irish convicts.
(a) Struck an iceberg 23.xii.89.
(b) Embarked December 1789.

(c) Probably transferred from the Mary Ann.
(d) Eight men escaped before sailing.
(e) Joseph Gerrald, the Scottish Martyr.
(f) Mutinied; convicts handed over to Spaniards.

APPENDIX C

SOURCES FOR ESTIMATING

Date	Source	Total	Convicts			Alexander			Charlotte		
			M.	F.	C.	M.	F.	C.	M.	F.	C.
	A. Official Sources										
9.xii.86	Teer to Nepean . .	750	600	150	—	210	—	—	100	24	—
30.xii.86	Nepean to Thomas .	780	600	180	—	210	—	—	100	24	—
10.i.87	Navy Board to Steele .	780	600	180	—	210	—	—	100	24	—
13 21 iii.87 29	Ross's First Enumerations	723	576	147	5	209	—	—	107	20	—
1.iv.87	Richards's Return . .	723	576	147	—	209	—	—	86	20	—
15.iv.87	Ross's Return. . .	718	565	153	11	198	—	—	86	20	—
22.iv.87	Ross's Return. . .	717	565	152	14	197	—	—	86	20	—
26.iv.87	Richards's Return .	717	565	152	13	197	—	—	86	20	—
29.iv.87	Ross's Return. . .	717	565	152	13	197	—	—	86	20	—
6.v.87	Ross's Return. . .	754	565	189	13	195	—	—	86	20	—
—	Home Office Registers .	778	586	192	—	213	—	—	88	20	—
10.vi.87	Phillip's Return . .	778	586	192	—	213	—	—	88	20	—
10.vi.87	Phillip's Return . .	750	558	192	13	—	—	—	—	—	—
1.ix.87	Phillip's Return . .	742	552	190	14	—	—	—	—	—	—
13.vi.94	Navy Office Return. .	778	—	—	—	—	—	—	—	—	—
27.iii.98	Navy Office Return. .	778	—	—	—	—	—	—	—	—	—
26.vii.98	28th Rep. of Select Comm. on Finance . . .	778	—	—	17	—	—	—	—	—	—
1810	Return of Transportees .	893	—	—	—	—	—	—	—	—	—
1819 and 1838	Select Comms. on Gaols and Transportation .	286	171	115	—	—	—	—	—	—	—
1846	Document in C.O. 201/61	750	—	—	—	—	—	—	—	—	—

	B. Unofficial Sources										
	1. Phillip's Voyage, p. vii	850	600	250	—	210	—	—	100	24	—
	,, ,, p. 13	778	586	192	—	213	—	—	88	20	—
	,, ,, p. lv	777	585	192	—	—	—	—	—	—	
	2. Collins's Account, p. iii	756	564	192	13	192	—	—	89	20	—
	3. King's Journal .	752	563	189	—	194	—	—	86	20	—
	4. Hunter's Journal, p. 4	800	600	200	—	—	—	—	—	—	—
	5. Tench's Narrative, p. 6	757	565	192	—	—	—	—	—	—	—
	,, ,, p. 46	775	—	—	—	—	—	—	—	—	—
	6. Bowes's Journal . .	772	—	—	8	210	—	—	78	20	—
	7. History of New Holland, p. xv . . . and History of Botany Bay	780	600	180	—	210	—	—	100	24	—

APPENDIX C

NUMBERS ON FIRST FLEET

Friendship			Lady Penrhyn			Prince of Wales			Scarborough			REMARKS
M.	F.	C.	M.	F.	C.	M.	F.	C.	M.	F.	C.	
80	24	—	—	102	—	—	—	—	210	—	—	First Estimate.
80	24	—	—	102	—	—	30	—	210	—	—	
80	24	—	—	102	—	—	30	—	210	—	—	Also gives estimate of marines.
75	21	—	—	100	5	—	6	—	185	—	—	Includes eight men dead and one pardoned on *Alexander*.
75	19	—	—	102	—	—	6	—	206	—	—	Ditto (nine dead).
75	19	3	1	104	5	—	10	1	205	—	—	Numbers actually on board.
76	21	5	1	101	6	—	10	1	205	—	—	Ditto.
76	21	5	1	101	5	—	10	1	205	—	—	Ditto.
76	21	5	1	101	5	—	10	1	205	—	—	Ditto.
76	21	4	1	101	5	2	47	2	205	—	—	Ditto.
76	21	—	—	102	—	1	49	—	208	—	—	Numbers embarked.
77	20	—	—	102	—	—	50	—	208	—	—	Ditto.
—	—	—	—	—	—	—	—	—	—	—	—	Numbers on board at Teneriffe.
—	—	—	—	—	—	—	—	—	—	—	—	Ditto at Rio.
—	—	—	—	—	—	—	—	—	—	—	—	(The 1810 Returns give "607 persons" in a note at the beginning, and two small batches of 264 and 22 in full at the end. The 1819 and 1838 Committees merely copied the latter figures, which are also to be found in documents L.4, and N.1, of the Bigge Appendices: C.O. 201/130.)
—	—	—	—	—	—	—	—	—	—	—	—	
—	—	—	—	—	—	—	—	—	—	—	—	
—	—	—	—	—	—	—	—	—	—	—	—	
—	—	—	—	—	—	—	—	—	—	—	—	
80	24	—	—	102	—	—	100	—	210	—	—	Estimate.
77	20	—	—	102	—	—	50	—	208	—	—	Including deaths and pardons.
—	—	—	—	—	—	—	—	—	—	—	—	
76	21	—	—	101	—	2	50	—	205	—	—	Numbers at sailing.
76	21	—	—	101	—	2	47	—	205	—	—	Ditto.
—	—	—	—	—	—	—	—	—	—	—	—	Ditto.
—	—	—	—	—	—	—	—	—	—	—	—	Ditto.
—	—	—	—	—	—	—	—	—	—	—	—	Numbers embarked.
100	(M.&F.)		—	104	8	—	50	—	210	—	—	
80	24	—	—	102	—	—	50	—	210	—	—	Estimate.

APPENDIX D

WARRANTS OF PARDONS

THE first paragraph in each document recited the powers and authority with which the Governor (or the Lieutenant-Governor in his absence or at his death) was vested, in virtue of the Commission given under the Great Seal on November 8, 1790, to remit either absolutely or conditionally the whole or any part of the sentences of those transported.

Absolute Pardon: "By virtue of the power and authority vested as aforesaid, I, Arthur Phillip, His Majesty's Governor of the Territory of New South Wales and the Islands thereto adjacent, taking into consideration the unremitting good conduct and the meritorious behaviour of John Irving and deeming him, the said John Irving, a proper subject of the Royal Mercy do hereby absolutely remit the remainder of the time or term which is yet unexpired of the original sentence or order of transportation passed on the said John Irving in the year of Our Lord One Thousand seven hundred and eighty-five.

"Given under my Hand and Seal of the Territory at Sydney in New South Wales, the Sixteenth day of December, in the year of Our Lord, One Thousand seven hundred and ninety-one.   "A. PHILLIP."

Conditional Pardon: To the above the following clause was added: "Provided and on condition that they continue to reside within the limits of this government and do not return and appear within any parts of the Kingdoms of Great Britain or Ireland during the terms or times specified in their several sentences of transportation."

(To both the above identification remarks were attached, detailing name, native place, trade or calling, age, height and complexion, etc. The warrants were registered in the Secretary's Office. Cf. *H.R.A.*, I, 1,325, 326, and *History of New South Wales from the Records*, Vol. II., (Britton), 336 *sqq.*)

Tickets-of-Leave, which were subsequently introduced, were in this form: "It is his Excellency the Governor's pleasure to dispense with the attendance at Government work of . . . , tried at . . . , convicted for . . . , arrived per ship . . . , . . . master, in the year . . . , and to permit . . . to employ . . . self (off the Government stores) in any lawful occupation, within the district of . . . , for . . . own advantage during good behaviour or until His Excellency's further pleasure shall be made known."

On March 15, 1806, Governor King amended the above by adding: "If he demands extortionate pay for his labour or transgresses any of the rules or orders of the colony, he will be recalled to government labour, and such other punishment be inflicted on him as the case shall merit or as the magistrates shall award, and of which all officers, settlers, cultivators, and every other individual is to take notice."

APPENDIX E

THE EXPENSES OF TRANSPORTATION TO 1800

An excerpt from an analysis of expenditure, from 1786 to 1817 (Bigge Appendix, *C.O.* 201/130, N.1). Figures are to the nearest pound.

Year	Trans- porting convicts	Victual- ling convicts	Tools, Clothing, etc.	Treasury Bills Provisions	Civil Estab- lishment	Military Estab- lishment	Marine Estab- lishment	Total
1786	28,339						7	28,346
1787	23,779		2099		2878		2586	31,341
1788	7393	261		4728	2878		2749	18,008
1789	39,558	21,125	12,853	891	2878	6847	3877	68,058
1790	8,203	1840	18,402	1341	4558	6576	3853	44,774
1791	47,356	25,682	25,603	13,064	4758	9946	2611	129,020
1792	34,234	17,261	31,139	2842	4726	10,110	4275	104,588
1793	21,411	19,762		11,411	4657	10,724	1996	69,962
1794	15,363	25,470	12,309	11,217	4795	10,228		79,382
1795	14,909	36,696	4392	3814	5241	10,228		75,281
1796	16,156	31,081	7931	10,020	5241	13,427		83,855
1797	7703	7092	4031	78,898	5524	16,906	220	120,372
1798	38,990	12,033	5169	26,407	6157	19,726	3032	111,514
1799	7672	6568	88	43,448	6017	16,481		80,274
1800	8276	13,834	11,796	50,707	6310	18,953	1107	110,985

£1,115,760

Notes on the above figures.—In 1786-1788 the expense of victualling is included under the first column. In the early years the following amounts have to be added: Service at N.S.W. of *Sirius*, £50,993; *Supply* Tender, £20,685; *Guardian*, £22,924; *Gorgon*, £17,113; hire of a Dutch vessel for the return of officers, etc., £4924; purchase of *Reliance* and *Supply* (1793) for service in the colony, £23,982; annual expense at £4 per man per month, £5720 (Captain Hunter's ship), the *Lady Nelson* sent on an expedition of discovery, £4700. Total to be added, including the last item, £151,041.

The total expenditure, as stated above, up to 1800, inclusive, was £1,306,801. The figures of the earliest years differ somewhat from those submitted on 5 June 1793, but the dispersal of items differs in both (cf. *H.R.N.S.W.*, II, 38-44). Incidentally, the expenditure up to 1817 amounted to £3,829,381 (this total being £120,000 in advance of that given by Bigge). In the following four years (1818-1821) a total of £1,423,105 was added to the above.

APPENDIX F*

THE ORIGINAL CIVIL AND CRIMINAL JURISDICTIONS, 1784-1800

Although the period of active challenge directed against the Criminal and Civil Jurisdictions of N.S.W. occurs after 1800, it is essential to recognize that the bases of the controversy are in the first legal provisions for establishing the Settlement. These, and the incidents arising out of the exercise of both jurisdictions prior to 1800, are discussed in several places in this book. The following points, however, may indicate at a glance why and how this major constitutional problem arose.

1. In 1784 the Act 24 Geo. III, c. 56 authorized the resumption of transportation and enabled the King in Council to determine when and where the resumption might be implemented (cf. p. 169).

2. On July 8, 1786, Lord Sydney announced that Botany Bay had been selected, and issued the "Heads of a Plan" in which it was forecasted that "the whole regulation and management of the settlement should be committed to a discreet officer and provision should be made in all cases, both civil and military, by special instructions under the Great Seal or otherwise, as may be thought proper" (*H.R.N.S.W.*, I, ii, 18). Phillip was selected, and it seems that all authority was to be vested in this single officer under the Crown.

3. On 12 October 1786, Phillip received his First Commission, authorizing him to be "Governor in and over our said territory" and to do all manner of things thereto belonging "according to the rules and discipline of war and . . . such orders and directions" as should be sent to him. (*H.R.N.S.W.*, I, ii, 24).

4. On December 6, 1786, the Privy Council made two orders relative to transporting convicts to N.S.W. "or some one or other of the islands adjacent". (cf. p. 130 of this book, and *H.R.N.S.W.*, I, ii, 30).

5. In a message to Parliament in January 1787, George III referred to the Plans already made for the new settlement of N.S.W. and asked for "such further measures as may become necessary for this purpose". There followed, on January 29, 1787, the Act of Parliament of 1787 (27 Geo. III, c. 2). This was "the only direct statutory authority dealing with the foundation of N.S.W.", and was the natural sequence out of the Act of 1784 and the Orders in Council of December 1786. (cf. p. 195 of this book.)

Note that on April 2, 1787, Phillip received his Second Commission appointing him "Captain-General and Governor in Chief" of the Territory and empowering him to appoint Justices of the Peace and officers for administering justice "for the better administration of justice and putting the law in execution"; to pardon, to issue warrants for payment of monies, to execute martial law, to grant lands, and to direct commerce. If an inference might be drawn from the restraints placed upon the spending of public funds, he was also commissioned to *raise* public monies "that all public monies which shall be raised be issued out by warrant from you and disposed of by you for the support of the Government or for such other purpose as shall be particularly directed and not otherwise" (cf. *H.R.N.S.W.*, I, ii, 61-67). Phillip's own interpretation of his authority was that the laws of England would be introduced into N.S.W. (*H.R.N.S.W.*, I, ii, 53).

6. The Act of 1787 (27 Geo. III, c. 2.) after citing the Act of 1784 and the Orders in Council of 1787, which had authorized sending prisoners to and holding prisoners at a place on the Eastern Coast of N.S.W. . . . . , forecasted that "it may be found necessary that a colony and civil government should be established" in that place, "under and by virtue of the said Act" and "the said two Orders in Council". In similar terms it forecasted that "a Court of Criminal Jurisdiction should also be established . . . with authority to proceed in a more summary way than issued within this realm, according to the known and established laws thereof", (cf. *H.R.N.S.W.*, I, ii, p. 69).

7. The Act (27 Geo. III, c. 2.) then proceeded to enact that "His Majesty may . . . authorise the person to be appointed Governor . . . to convene" a Court of Criminal Jurisdiction "for the trial and punishment of all such outrages and misbehaviours as, if committed within this realm, would be

* Cf. pp. 136, 138 of this volume.

deemed . . . according to the laws of this realm, to be treason or misprision thereof, felony or misdemeanour. . . .". The Act then set up the personnel and machinery of such a Criminal Court.

8. But that Act (27 Geo. III, c. 2.) failed to make any enactment relative to a Court of Civil Jurisdiction.

9. On April 2, 1787 Letters Patent were issued establishing Courts of both Civil and Criminal Jurisdictions (*H.R.N.S.W.*, I, ii, 74). Relative to Civil Jurisdiction the Letters Patent recited the pertinent statement of the Act (27 Geo. III, c. 2.) that "a colony and a civil government should be established and that provision should be made in N.S.W., for the recovery of debts and for determining personal causes". The Letters Patent then "purported to set up what was called 'a court of Civil Jurisdiction' ", and determined its composition and procedure and machinery for appeals to the Governor or the Privy Council. The Letters Patent also established and regulated the Courts of Criminal Jurisdiction, which, however, had already been specifically provided for by the Act (27 Geo. III, c. 2).

10. The difficulties experienced by Phillip and other Governors in regulating the administration of these Courts, which had been so inadequately constituted, are discussed elsewhere in this book.

Although the Criminal Jurisdiction was challenged as conflicting with the laws of England, its chief deficiencies were concerned with the incompetent and unwilling personnel of the Courts. The same problems existed on the Civil side also, but gradually, as the Settlement grew, the legality of the Civil Jurisdiction came to be questioned. In the complex situation of the Colony, with its military, free, freed and convict population and its trade and land-settlement, it became necessary for Governors to issue proclamations controlling the discipline and amenities of civil life. The pattern of English civil law could not always be followed, and to meet the situation the Governor became an uncontrolled legislator, exercising powers "as great as those which are the prerogative of parliament". Such were Phillip's regulations of town discipline in 1789, and other later regulations after Phillip's time, controlling prices, currency and the spirits-traffic. Some were notified to England and specifically approved by Ministerial or Departmental action; others were neither notified nor endorsed.

11. After the turn of the century protests began to be made against the practice of the N.S.W. civil jurisdiction on the grounds that the legislative power of making regulations belonged only to Parliament. It was contended that the Civil Jurisdiction in its entirety in the Colony was invalid; that the Governor had not power to issue Regulations and Orders; that the Civil Court lacked jurisdiction because, unlike the Criminal Court, it had not been set up by the Statute of 1787, but only by Letters Patent. (cf. the exhaustive discussion of the problem in Jeremy Bentham's *A Plea for a Constitution*, 1803, in which he argued against the Governors' "original Acts" and Acts which in England would not be deemed misdemeanours and contended that all Acts of legislation in N.S.W., are contrary to law. (*H.R.A.*, IV, I, 883, *sqq.*). In the course of years these arguments were invoked by Macarthur and others, who maintained that Governors' ordinances and regulations were void. The same argument was used against the subsequent creation, by Letters Patent, of the new Courts of Civil Jurisdiction in 1814.

Meanwhile, the British Government generally continued to ignore the controversy, sometimes validating such matters as Governors' pardons which had not been ratified by the Crown, or indemnifying Governors' levying of duties, but generally assuming that the original grants of civil jurisdiction had been and were adequate in the circumstances of a penal colony. In 1819 Earl Bathurst advised Commissioner Bigge that "not having been established with any view to territorial or commercial advantages", the settlements of New Holland "cannot be administered with the usual reference to those general principles of colonial policy which are applicable to other foreign possessions". Nevertheless, by that date, constitutional rights and determinations could no longer be delayed. The controversy was finalized by the Act of 1823 (4 Geo. IV, c. 96), when the legal defects of the past were rectified and a constitutional

position temporarily established. This was confirmed and elaborated by the Act of 1828 (9 Geo. IV, c. 83).

12. The subject is discussed in the Constitutional histories of E. V. Sweetman, A.C.V. Melbourne and F. L. W. Wood. But the most complete analysis of the original problem is that of Dr H. V. Evatt in the *Australian Law Journal* (vol. II, no. 10; 1938 at p. 409).

The significant points of Dr Evatt's exposition and argument appear to be these: The subject should be examined from the English point of view rather than from that of the Settlement. Then, the English Government was mainly interested in the removal of prisoners, while the Settlement (including Phillip) was much interested in its evolution towards free institutions. This would explain why there was a specific statutory creation of a criminal jurisdiction (which should be regarded as an automatic application to N.S.W. of the criminal law of England), and why there was only a non-statutory and insecure basis of the civil jurisdiction. Nevertheless, the omission from the Act of a specific Civil provision does not imply that no portion of English law was to be applied, for the Crown had the right to decide what part of English civil law should prevail in any territory. It is "an irresistible inference" from the Letters Patent, which set up a court of civil jurisdiction and the right of appeal to the Privy Council, "that *some* system of civil law should govern all personal actions and determine the lawfulness of matters therein litigated". Until the setting-up of a local legislature the Crown retained the power to "prescribe by ordinance or other appropriate legal instrument such modifications of English civil law as were deemed necessary for the good government of the Settlement". Hence, the Governor exercised absolute control over the two classes of the population (those compelled to remain in the Settlement and those choosing to do so) and his regulations and ordinances were essential parts of a disciplinary régime, and, in the earliest years, indispensable for the safety of all. Viewed in this light the Orders of the Governor did not lack legality, and the jurisdiction of the Civil Court must be justified in the same way. This Court had been established to execute the laws of England (when applicable) and the General Orders of the Governor and Superintendent-General of the penitentiary-settlement.

That line of legal-historical interpretation is given here not to suggest that it is necessarily final, but rather to indicate the nature and extent of the constitutional problem, which for about thirty years remained important in the Settlement, and which arose out of the original provisions made for the Penal Settlement in 1787.

APPENDIX G

N.S.W. TRADE AND COMMERCE, 1788-1800

Two features of trade and commerce in this initial period of the Settlement should be emphasized: (1) the official restrictions placed against oversea trading and (2) the beginnings of commerce—despite the restrictions.

The subject is surveyed in the three opening chapters of Professor John Ward's *British Policy in the South Pacific* (Sydney, 1948) and the American side of it in Professor G. Greenwood's *Early American-Australian Relations* (Melbourne Univ. Press, 1944).

The following are the essential facts up to 1800.

A very early English suggestion had been made that Phillip should obtain supplies, and even women, from Tahiti. He refused to adopt the human traffic, but Tahitian supplies, through the Vancouver expedition, were ordered for the Settlement in 1792. Tahitian trade, however, did not develop until 1801. Trade with the closely associated settlement at Norfolk Island was constant, as can be seen in this book.

Phillip's Instructions made it clear that the monopoly trading rights of the East India Company should not be jeopardized by the new foundation of a settlement in N.S.W. The Company's opposition to colonial development sought

to limit N.S.W. trading "to the bare minimum essential for the existence of a penal colony". Professor Ward remarks: "Apart from anti-colonialism and indifference the greatest obstacle in the way of development of British interests in the Pacific had been the monopoly of the Company. It was generally conceded that in view of the Company's rigid insistence on its rights, no Settlement in the South Pacific could build up a trade of its own". Therefore, "the whole basis of British policy . . . towards N.S.W. was bound up" in the questions, whether industries in N.S.W. should be restricted in order to preserve its penal purpose, and whether the Company's rights might be invaded by British ships outside the monopoly, and, if so, whether British or N.S.W. traders were to benefit by such a decision. (Cf. Ward, *op. cit*, 10; 14.) Phillip foresaw the problem in 1791 and asked for a ruling on his attitude towards American and British whaling enterprises, but, in view of this new and attractive field of commerce, London postponed its decision.

Despite the restrictions and indecision maritime trade soon manifested itself at the Settlement. Port Jackson became a convenient port of call for American traders; Professor Greenwood lists 15 such ships, mainly commercial, between 1792 and 1800. Commerce increased by the new sealing industry, 1791, which was largely centred in near-Australian waters; and after 1796, when war closed the Spanish-American ports against British ships, Port Jackson became more a settled base for British whalers.

As a result of these developments the monopoly rights of the East India Company in South Pacific Ocean waters were reduced by minor concessions to licensed British shipping during the last decade of the eighteenth century, and more effectively by Acts of 1802 and 1811. By 1813 the Company ceased to be of practical interest to N.S.W.

The monopoly rights of the Company militated particularly against the growth of localized economic development. A decision of 1792 that cargoes and convicts were to be sent out to N.S.W. only in the Company's ships (*H.R.N.S.W.*, I, ii, 623) restricted both imports and exports, and did this in a period when the Settlement was often in dire need of supplies through the curtailment of shipping.

Although maritime commerce was not of considerable magnitude prior to 1800, the fact that it began so early in the history of the settlement is one more evidence that the natural and economic evolution of a community, which allowed free men to function in it, could not be restrained permanently by the indeterminate plans of a penal settlement. From the desultory commerce of this period there emerged the more consolidated traffic that ensued at the beginning of the eighteenth century. The rise of commerce was evident to Governor Hunter, and it had to be recognized by Governors King and Bligh as an established and essential economic factor in the growth of the Settlement. After 1800, therefore, the official attitude develops towards a compromise between the facts of an established commerce and the determined, though ineffective, official policy of opposition to the monopolistic aspects of it.

This early emergence of maritime commerce, overseas and coastal, is significant, because it set a precedent for the near future, when under King and Bligh, the constitutional set-up of the Settlement would be challenged through the issue of the Citizens' rights to engage freely in trade and commerce.

NOTES

INTRODUCTION

[1] Census returns, 30 June 1947, gave the total population as 7,579, 358 including 38,800 non-British. Meanwhile, official activity for the migration of Britishers and Displaced European peoples have made rapid changes. Total population on 31 December, 1949 is estimated at 8,050,000, including about 160,000 non-British, who now are about 2 per cent of total. Future immigration of both classes may reach 200,000 *per annum*.

[2] J. D. LANG, *Freedom and Independence for the Golden Lands of Australia*, p. 304, and Ch. v, *passim*.

[3] G. W. RUSDEN, *History of Australia*, Vol. I (1883), 13-19.

[4] J. HOLLAND ROSE, *William Pitt and National Revival*, 437, 439, 440.

[5] Cf. Article, "Transportation," *Australian Encyclopaedia*.

[6] G. A. WOOD: cf. Article "Convicts", *Journal* of the R.A.H.S., Vol. VIII, Part IV, p. 178.

[7] *Cambridge History of the British Empire*, Vol. VII, Part I, p. 92.

[8] JAMES BRYCE, *Modern Democracies*, Vol. II, 183.

[9] T. A. COGHLAN, *Labour and Industry in Australia*, Vol. I, 561, 562; R. C. MILLS, *The Colonization of Australia*, p. 323.

[10] CHARLES MERCIER, *Crime and Criminals*, 225 *et seq*.

[11] Cf. *Edinburgh Review*, Feb. 1823, Vol. XXXVIII, Article 4, pp. 88-89.

[12] *Alphab. Lists*, Vol. I (1789-1825); Vol. II (1823-1825); C.O. 207. Cf. also *Returns of Convicts Transported* (1787-1809); H.O. 11/1.

[13] *Report, I*, 138, 139.

[14] F. WATSON, *The Beginnings of Government in Australia*, 3, 4.

[15] Cf. G. A. WOOD, article "Convicts", *Journal* R.A.H.Soc., Vol. VIII, Part IV, 191 *et sqq*.; also cf. *C.H.B.E.*, Vol. VII, Part I. p. 90.

[16] H.O. 10/7. (These are complete Registers of the Convicts embarked in 1787, giving names, place and date of conviction, sentences, ship and casualties. Total embarked: 586 males, 192 females.)

[17] Table of Sir S. T. Janssen (Aug. 1, 1772); reprinted as appendix to Howard's *State of the Prisons*.

[18] *State Calendar of Home Office Papers* (1773, 1774), 2/98; 420, 829.

[19] *H.R.N.S.W.*, Vol. II, 734-736.

[20] H.O. 26/1, p. 8.

[21] Quoted, Colquhoun: *Police of the Metropolis*, 448, (6th ed.)

[22] Op. cit., 446, 447.

[23] Op. cit., 444.

[24] *P.P.* 1819 (138), 22.iii.1819.

[25] ROMILLY, *Memoirs*, II, 397, 398.

[26] *Saunders' News Letter*, 4.ix.1795; *H.R.N.S.W.*, II, 818.

[27] *Dublin Chronicle*, 23.vii.1793; *H.R.N.S.W.*, II, 810.

[28] *Return of Criminals Transported*, P.P. (1810), 59.

[29] *Report of Select C'tee. on Finance* (Police, etc.), June 1798. *P.P.*, Reprinted Reports, 1803, Vol. XIII; also Appendix M to 28th Report (June 1798), 382, 383.

[30] Report of Select Committee of 1812, p. 11.

[31] ibid., 9, 10.

[32] ibid., Appendix, 77-78.

[33] Cf. *post* p. 187 *et seq*.

[34] *Dublin Chronicle*, 3.iii.1791; *H.R.N.S.W.*, II, 772.

[35] *P.P.* 1731-1800, A/cs. & Papers, XXIV (1790-91), No. 740 (8.iv.1791).

[36] Dublin: Rebellion Papers, 620/39, 187; loc. cit., 42a; 620/36, 85; also Irish "Official Papers" (described in Bibliography), where advice is asked by Government of grand juries re erecting penitentiaries in counties, Series 2, 17/4.

[37] Report of Select Committee of 1812, Appendix, **38,** 116.
[38] *P.P.* 1814-15 (354), XI, 215.

PART I

CHAPTER I

[1] *History of England in the Eighteenth Century,* VII, 347.
[2] Cf. Low, *The British Constitution,* pp. 52-55.
[3] Cf. H. BELLOC, *A Shorter History of England,* pp. 443-445.
[4] TURBERVILLE: op. cit., p. 483.
[5] SELLEY, *England in the Eighteenth Century,* 347.
[6] *P.H.,* XXV, 472.
[7] HOLLAND ROSE, *William Pitt and National Revival,* p. 242.
[8] LECKY, op. cit., II, 281.
[9] ibid., p. 286.
[10] ibid., p. 295.
[11] O'BRIEN, G., *Economic Hist. of Ireland in the Eighteenth Century,* pp. 10, 17.
[12] H. D. TRAILL, *Social England,* V, 507.
[13] A. TOYNBEE, *Lectures on the Indust. Revol.,* 8; Lecky makes a similar estimate, op. cit., VII, 258.
[14] *The Village Labourer* (1760-1832) (1920), pp. 9, 10.
[15] ibid., p. 17.
[16] HAMMOND, op. cit., pp. 12, 17, 58, 79, 81; Toynbee, op. cit., 40 *et sqq.;* cf. Toynbee's list of new landed gentry and their origins, pp. 40, 41.
[17] MACAULAY, *History of England,* Ch. iii, says 160,000; Toynbee, op. cit., 36.
[18] DEFOE, *Tour, etc.,* III, 144-46.
[19] *Northern Tour,* I, 124; II, 6, 427.
[20] WEBB, *Story of the Durham Miners,* quoted by Selley, *England in the Eighteenth Century,* p. 224.
[21] LIPSON, *Economic History of England,* Vol. II, p. 97.
[22] Cf. HAMMOND, *Town Labourer,* 145.
[23] HAMMOND, *Town Labourer,* 144.
[24] Royal Commission on Children's Employment, First Report 1842; quoted HAMMOND, op. cit., p. 173.
[25] HAMMOND, op. cit., 184.
[26] HANSARD, May 24, 1819.
[27] Cf. RICHARD BURNS's statement, quoted Eden, op. cit., I, 347.
[28] *The Farmer's Letters,* I, 302.
[29] *Wealth of Nations* (ed. Cannan, 1920), I, 142.
[30] Quoted: EDEN's *State of the Poor* (Rogers Edn.), p. 61.
[31] Report of Committee of Enquiry concerning Burglaries and Robberies, 10 April, 1770; *C.J.,* XXXII, 878.
[32] Quoted by EDEN, op. cit., p. 61.
[33] *P.P.* 1731-1800, Reports, IV, 31.
[34] *P.P.* 1731-1800, Reports, IV, 32.
[35] Cf. EDEN, op. cit. (Rogers), p. 72.
[36] "Chatham Papers" quoted by HOLLAND ROSE: *Pitt and Napoleon,* p. 80.
[37] EDEN, original edition, II, 581.
[38] TRAILL, op. cit., 492; and TOYNBEE, op. cit., 82.
[39] *The Village Labourer,* 98.
[40] *Parl. Hist.,* xxxii, 710.
[41] *Parl. Hist.,* xliv, 22; and EDEN, op. cit. (original), III ccclxiii-cccxxxviii.
[42] *The Village Labourer,* 118.
[43] *Selections from Political Works,* vi, 64.
[44] Cf. EDEN, *State of the Poor* (Rogers), p. 38.
[45] Op. cit., 85.
[46] Op. cit., 94.
[47] Op. cit., 100.
[48] *Police of the Metropolis,* 1806 edn., Chap. xiii, *passim.*
[49] *Speeches* of SIR ROBERT PEEL (ed. 1853, I, 560; Feb. 28, 1828).

L

[50] Dicey, *Law and Public Opinion*, p. 62.
[51] Wilson, *History of English Law*, pp. 157, 169.
[52] Leslie Stephen, *The English Utilitarians*, I, 37.
[53] Lecky, *History of England in the Eighteenth Century*, II, 600.

CHAPTER II

[1] *P.H.*, xxv, 888.
[2] Sir Walter Besant, *The Survey of London: London in the Eighteenth Century*, 475-562.
[3] P. Colquhoun, *Police of the Metropolis, passim*; Leslie Stephen, *The English Utilitarians*, I, 101-105.
[4] Sir Robert Peel's *Speeches* (ed. 1853), I, 401-402 (9.iii.1826), and *P.D.*, xiv, 1221.
[5] Sir James Fitzjames Stephen, *A History of the Criminal Law of England* (ed. 1883), I, 463.
[6] Sir R. K. Wilson, *History of Modern English Law*, 93-94.
[7] Sir J. F. Stephen, op. cit., 463, *et seq.*
[8] Sir W. Blackstone, *Commentaries* (17th ed.), Bk. IV, Ch. i, pp. 3, 18.
[9] W. T. Selley, *England in the Eighteenth Century*, 372.
[10] G. M. Trevelyan, *British History in the Nineteenth Century*, 31; J. Laurence, *A History of Capital Punishment*, 13.
[11] Sir J. F. Stephen, op. cit., 472.
[12] ibid., 470-471.
[13] *Fourth Report of the Criminal Law Commissioners* (8.iii.1839), App. V, p. 10-64; App. VI, p. 64-101.
[14] Sir J. F. Stephen, op. cit., 481.
[15] *Seventh Report of the Criminal Law Commissioners* (11.iii.1843) 100-103.
[16] Cf. Peel's *Speeches*, 243 (21.v.1823); 408 (9.iii.1826).
[17] Colquhoun, op. cit., 444.
[18] Paley, *Moral Philosophy* (12th ed.), II, 193-194.
[19] J. L. and B. Hammond, *The Town Labourer*, Ch. iv, "Justice".
[20] Leslie Stephen, op. cit., I, 27.
[21] G. M. Trevelyan, op. cit., 22-25.
[22] J. Holland Rose, *William Pitt and National Revival*, 15.
[23] Leslie Stephen, op. cit., I, 48.
[24] Peel's *Speeches*, 401 (9.iii.1826).
[25] Sir R. K. Wilson, op. cit., 110-12.
[26] Sir J. F. Stephen, op. cit., 284, *et seq.*
[27] Colquhoun, op. cit., 446, 448.
[28] Peel's *Speeches*, 403 (9.iii.1826).
[29] ibid., 403.
[30] J. H. Rose, op. cit., 433.
[31] Sir J. F. Stephen, op. cit., 478.
[32] H. D. Traill, *Social England*, V, 145-146; Sir W. Besant, op. cit., 546.
[33] J. Laurence, op. cit. 17, 18.
[34] H. D. Traill, op. cit., V, 529; G. B. Barton, *History of New South Wales from the Records*, 227-233.
[35] Jonas Hanway, *The Defects of Police the Cause of Immorality*, 3.
[36] *A Memoir of Elizabeth Fry*, I, 444; Blackstone's *Commentaries*, IV, xxii.
[37] *P.P.* 1731-1800, Reports IX, No. 97 (2.iv.1792).
[38] Cf. *Scots Magazine*, Sept. 1789: *H.R.N.S.W.* II, 749; see also *Dropmore Papers*, I, 516-524.
[39] Cf. *Dublin Chronicle*, 8.i.1791; *H.R.N.S.W.*, II, 770.
[40] *C.J.*, xl, 1161.
[41] Sir J. F. Stephen, *A General View of the Criminal Law of England*, 46-47.
[42] S. and B. Webb, *English Prisons under Local Government*, xxxiii.

CHAPTER III

[1] Montesquieu, *Lettres Persanes*, lettre lxxxi.
[2] Coleman Phillipson, *Three Criminal Law Reformers*, p. 53.   [p. 231.
[3] Voltaire, *Commentaire sur le livre des délits et des peines*, Œuvres, éd. 1819,

⁴ The summary of *Dei Delitti* which follows is largely based on Phillipson, op. cit., Pt. I, Ch. iii.
⁵ BECCARIA, *Dei Delitti e delle pene*, Ch. xix.
⁶ ibid., Ch. xlii.
⁷ BLACKSTONE, *Commentaries*, Bk. IV, Ch. i. p. 18.
⁸ LORD KAMES, *Historical Law Tracts; Criminal Law*, 1776. OLIVER GOLDSMITH, *Vicar of Wakefield*, Ch. xxvii; *Citizen of the World*, letter, lxxix. SAMUEL JOHNSON, *The Rambler*, No. 114 (1751).
⁹ FARRER, *Crimes and Punishments*, pp. 52-53.
¹⁰ ROMILLY, *Memoirs*, I, 65.
¹¹ PALEY, *Principles of Moral and Political Philosophy*, Bk. III, Ch. i.
¹² ibid., ed. 1785, p. 269.
¹³ FARRER, op. cit., p. 55.
¹⁴ PALEY, op. cit., ed. 1785, pp. 290-296.
¹⁵ WILLIAM EDEN, *Principles of Penal Law*, ed. 1775, pp. 6-28.
¹⁶ ibid., Ch. iv, pp. 50-52.
¹⁷ E. HALÉVY, *Growth of Philosophical Radicalism*, pp. 299-300.
¹⁸ ROMILLY, op. cit., I, 65.
¹⁹ ibid., p. 71.
²⁰ COMTE DE MIRABEAU, *Observations d'un Voyageur anglais sur la Maison de Force, appellée Bicêtre*, Œuvres, Tome III, éd. 1835, pp. 236-237.
²¹ ROMILLY, *Observations on a late publication intituled Thoughts on Executive Justice*, p. 87; quoted by C. G. OAKES, *Sir Samuel Romilly*, p. 63.
²² LESLIE STEPHEN, *English Thought in the Eighteenth Century*, ed. 1902, Vol. I, p. 126.
²³ HALÉVY, op. cit., p. 55.
²⁴ BENTHAM, *Works*, III, 169.
²⁵ ibid., I, 497 (*Principles of Penal Law*).

CHAPTER IV

¹ S. and B. WEBB, *English Prisons under Local Government*, Ch. I.
² WILLIAM Smith, M.D., *State of the Gaols in London, Westminister, etc.*, 1776, p. 9; quoted by Webb, op. cit., p. 19.
³ JOHN HOWARD, *State of the Prisons*, 4th ed., 1792, p. 9.
⁴ *C.J.*, XI (1697); XIII (15.v.1701).
⁵ See references in WEBB, op. cit., pp. 25 *et seq.*, and E. C. S. GIBSON's *John Howard*, p. 61.
⁶ *C.J.*, xxi, 237, 274, 376.
⁷ HOWARD, op. cit., Sect. III, VI and p. 86; W. E. H. LECKY, *History of England in the Eighteenth Century*, 1892 ed., vii, p. 331.
⁸ HOWARD, op. cit., p. 1.
⁹ ibid., pp. 4 *et seq.*
¹⁰ ibid., pp. 12 *et seq.*
¹¹ ibid. Section III, "Proposed Improvements in the Structure and Management of Prisons", pp. 19 *et seq.*
¹² *P.P.* 1731-1800, Bills, Vol. VII, No. 237.
¹³ *C.J.*, xxxiv, 138, 142, 288; Almon's *Debates*, Vol. viii, p. 215.
¹⁴ WEBB, op. cit., p. 36.
¹⁵ *C.J.*, xxxiv, 469, 535.
¹⁶ HOWARD, op. cit., p. 2.
¹⁷ SIR G. O. PAUL, *Proceedings of the Grand Juries, etc.*, Gloucester, 1808, p. 43.
¹⁸ HAKLUYT SOCIETY, *The Three Voyages of Martin Frobisher*, p. 118.
¹⁹ G. B. BARTON, *History of New South Wales from the Records*, Vol. I, pp. 12-13.
²⁰ BLACKSTONE, *Commentaries*, 17th ed., 1830, Bk. I, Ch. i, p. 137.
²¹ J. HANWAY, *The Defects of Police the Cause of Immorality, etc.*, 1775, p. 3.
²² 3rd ed. 1775, p. 31.
²³ G. IVES, *A History of Penal Methods*, Ch. iv.
²⁴ DOYLE, *History of America*, p. 45.
²⁵ BACON's Essay "Of Plantations" in *Works*, ed. 1878, Vol. VI, p. 457.
²⁶ BARTON, op. cit., p. 444; A. E. SMITH, *Transportation of Convicts to American Colonies in the Seventeenth Century; Amer. Hist. Rev.*, Vol. XXXIX, Jan. 1934.

[27] Acts of Privy Council, Colonial Series, Vol. I, p. 10.

[28] BARTON, op. cit., p. 444; MARGARET WILSON, The Crime of Punishment, p. 91.

[29] BARTON, op. cit., p. 456; J. D. BUTLER, British Convicts shipped to American Colonies; Amer. Hist. Rev., Vol. II, Oct. 1896.

[30] WILSON, op. cit., p. 93; see also J. C. HOTTEN, Original Lists of Emigrants, etc., who went from Great Britain to the American Plantations, 1600-1700.

[31] WILSON, op. cit., p. 92; H. E. BARNES, Art. "Transportation of Criminals", in Encyclopaedia of the Social Sciences.

[32] WILSON, op. cit., pp. 93-94.

[33] BARTON, op. cit., pp. 444, 449; BLACKSTONE, op. cit., Bk. IV, Ch. 31, p. 394; SMITH, loc. cit.

[34] 5 Geo. I, c. 28; 12 Geo. I, c. 29; 2 Geo. II, c. 25; 7 Geo. II, c. 21; 10 Geo. II, c. 32; 12 Geo. II, c. 21; 16 Geo. II, c. 15; 17 Geo. II, c. 5; 18 Geo. II, c. 27; 19 Geo. II, c. 38; 20 Geo. II, c. 46; 25 Geo. II, c. 10; 26 Geo. II, c. 19; 26 Geo. II, c. 33; 31 Geo. II, c. 42; 5 Geo. III, c. 14; BARTON, op. cit., p. 450.

[35] C.J., xxxvii, 306; April 1, 1779.

[36] BARTON, op. cit., p. 458.

[37] Ed. 1789, p. 6.

[38] H.R.N.S.W., Vol. I, Pt. II, p. 47.

[39] C.J., xxxvii, 306, April 1, 1779.

[40] Debate on the Committee stage of the Hulks Act, May 9, 1776; P.R., iv, 104.

[41] C.J., xxxvi, 926; April 15, 1778.

[42] P.P. 1731-1800, Vol. X, EDEN's Observations attached to Bill No. 315.

[43] BARTON, op. cit., p. 18.

[44] THOMAS JEFFERSON, Works, Vol. IX, p. 254; J. D. LANG, Transportation and Colonisation, 1837, p. 35.

[45] BUTLER, op. cit.; WILSON, op. cit., p. 97; BARNES, loc. cit.

[46] D. CAMPBELL's evidence: C.J., xxxvi, 926, April 15, 1778; C.J., xxxvii, 306, April 1, 1779.

[47] Second Report of Select Committee on the Working of 24 Geo. III, c. 56; July 28, 1785; C.J., xl, 1161.

[48] HOWARD, op. cit., pp. 17, 486.

[49] P.R., iii, 473.

[50] C.J., xxxv, 694; P.R., iv, 104; the Bill is printed as No. 286 in Vol. IX, P.P. 1731-1800; No. 288 is the Bill as amended.

[51] P.R., iv, 117.

[52] Report of Select Committee on the working of 16 Geo. III, c. 43, Evidence of Campbell and Howard, April 15, 1778; C.J., xxxvi, 926; HOWARD, State of the Prisons, 1st ed., 1777, p. 75.

[53] P.R., ix, 1, 4.

[54] P.H., xix, 970; P.R., ix, 83.

[55] C.J., xxxvi, 926.

[56] C.J., xxxvi, 952, 997.

[57] P.P., 1731-1800, Vol. X, EDEN's Observations attached to Bill No. 315.

[58] The returns are summarized in C.J., xxxvii, 307.

[59] P.R., xi, 283; C.J., xxxvii, 125.

[60] C.J., xxxvii, 306.

[61] C.J., xxxvii, 416.

[62] J. HANWAY, Distributive Justice and Mercy, London, 1781; letters xx-xxii.

[63] HOWARD, op. cit., pp. 465, 492.

[64] C.J., xxxix, 963, 968.

[65] P.H., xxiv, 755.

[66] P.H., xxv, 391, 430; P.R., xxxiv, 430.

[67] C.J., xl, 870, 954, 1161.

[68] P.R., xix, 329; C.J., xli, 823, 826.

[69] See A Letter to the . . . Marquis of Buckingham, etc., by SIR EDMUND CARRINGTON, 1818. The Tudor statutes were 23 Hen. VIII, c. 2; 33 Hen. VIII, c. 17; 37 Hen. VIII, c. 23; 1 Marv Sec. 2, c, 14; 5 Eliz., c. 24; 13 Eliz., c. 25.

[70] C.J., xx, 143 (18.ii.1722-23), 183 (29.iii.1723).

[71] HANWAY, The Defects of Police the Cause of Immorality . . . with various proposals for preventing hanging and transportation, etc., London, 1775.

72 *P.R.*, iv, 104 xi, 283; *P.P.*, 1731-1800, Vol. X, Bill No. 315.

73 *C.J.*, xxxv, 809; the Bill is printed as No. 287 in Vol. IX of *P.P.* 1731-1800.

74 *P.R.*, iv, 104.

75 P. COLQUHOUN, *A Treatise on the Police of the Metropolis*, 6th ed., 1800, pp. 355-356.

76 R. LESLIE-MELVILLE, *The Life and Work of Sir John Fielding*, p. 293.

77 HOWARD, op. cit., Section III.

78 *P.P.* 1731-1800, Vol. X, Bill No. 315; it was introduced into the House of Commons on May 11, 1778, by Sir Richard Sutton.

79 *Works*, iv, 1.

80 *P.R.*, xi, 283; *C.J.*, xxxvii, 125, 307.

81 *C.J.*, xxxvii, 199, 257, 445; *P.P.* 1731-1800, Vol. X, Bills 335-337.

82 *C.J.*, xxxvii, 306; *P.P.* 1731-1800, Vol. V, Report 37; Vol. VI, Report 56a.

83 *C.J.*, xxxvii, 334.

84 J. HANWAY, *A New Year's Gift to the People of Great Britain, pleading for the necessity of a more vigorous and consistent police, etc.*, London, 1784.

85 Most of the information in this paragraph is derived from the Report of the Select Committee of 1784; *C.J.*, xxxix, 1040; also HOWARD, *Account of the Principal Lazarettos, etc.*, 220-226.

86 *C.J.*, xxxix, 844, 982, 1040; a MS. copy of the Report is in the *Chatham Papers*, 363.

87 HOWARD, *Account of the Principal Lazarettos, etc.*; and WEBB, op. cit., Ch. vi.

PART II

CHAPTER I

1 *Calendar of Home Office Papers of the Reign of George III* (1773), No. 324.

2 J. HANWAY, *The Defects of Police the Cause of Immorality, etc.*, 3.

3 G. T. GRIFFITH, *Population of the Age of Malthus*, 90.

4 *C.H.B.E.*, I, 627.

5 *Terra Australis Incognita*, 3 vols., Edinburgh, 1766-68.

6 J. HANWAY, *Solitude in Imprisonment, etc.*, 6; *Distributive Justice and Mercy*, letter xxiv.

7 *Calendar of H.O. Papers* (1773), No. 39.

8 *P.R.*, iii, 473, iv, 104, ix, 83.

9 *P.R.*, iv, 104.

10 *P.H.*, xix, 970.

11 *C.J.*, xxxvi, 926.

12 *P.R.*, ix, 283.

13 *C.J.*, xxxvii, 306.

14 *C.J.*, xl, 954; *H.O.*, 13/1, 233, 273; *Gentleman's Magazine* (1783), liii, 800-802; G. B. BARTON, *History of N.S.W. from the Records*, I, 466; T. A. COGHLAN, *Labour and Industry in Australia*, I, 3; 28th Rep. of Select Comm. on Finance, 1798, App. L.1.

15 See *post*, p. 187 *et seq.*

16 Reprinted in *H.R.N.S.W.*, I, ii, 1; MS. copy, dated 6.iv.1784, in C.O. 201/1.

17 *B.M. Add. MSS* 33977 (206).

18 E. SMITH, *Life of Sir Joseph Banks*, 214-217; G. MACKANESS, *Sir Joseph Banks*, 20.

19 *H.R.N.S.W.*, I, ii, 6-8.

20 Howe to Sydney, 26.xii.1784; ibid., 10.

21 *C.J.*, xxxix, 963.

22 *P.H.*, xxiv, 755.

23 Matra to Nepean, *H.R.N.S.W.*, I, ii, 8.

24 ibid., 10; MS. and printed copies are in *C.O.* 201/1 and a MS. copy in *Chatham Papers*, 363.

25 BARTON, op. cit., 495.

26 *C.J.*, xl, 838; *P.C.* 2/130, pp. 75, 77, 90.

27 *P.H.*, xxv, 391; *P.R.*, xxxiv, 430.

28 *P.H.*, xxv, 430.

302 THE FOUNDATION OF AUSTRALIA

[29] BARTON, op. cit., 495; *C.J.*, xl, 870; *P.C.* 2/130, p. 156.
[30] *C.J.*, xl, 954.
[31] BARTON, op. cit., 495; *P.C.*, 2/130, pp. 219, 221.
[32] *C.J.*, xl, 1161.
[33] BARTON, op. cit., 494, official letter dated 28.viii.1785; La Pérouse sailed on Aug. 1; see also a letter from Pitt to Grenville, 2.x.1785, in *Dropmore Papers*, I, 256-257, and the anonymous *History of Botany Bay*.
[34] *H.R.N.S.W.*, II, 735.
[35] ibid., I, ii, 14.
[36] ibid., 20.
[37] *P.C.* 2/131, pp. 492, 505, 539, 540; the order of Dec. 6 is also in BARTON, op. cit., 451, and *H.R.N.S.W.*, I, ii, 30.
[38] *C.J.*, xlii, 278; *P.H.* xxvi, 211.
[39] *P.C.* 2/131.   [XI, 63.
[40] COGHLAN, op. cit., I, 4; see also MISS L. THOMAS in *Journal R.A.H.S.* (1925),
[41] A. C. V. MELBOURNE, *Early Constitutional History of Australia, New South Wales*, 1788-1856, 5-7.
[42] J. H. ROSE, *William Pitt and National Revival*, Ch. xix; see also E. SCOTT, *A Short History of Australia*, 42; *C.H.B.E.*, VII, i, 58.
[43] *C.H.B.E.*, VII, i, 59; J. H. ROSE, *Short Life of William Pitt*, 80.
[44] 21.xii.1785, quoted *H.R.N.S.W.*, II, 735.
[45] *Dropmore Papers*, I, 545-547.
[46] *Annual Register*, 1788, xxx, Chron., 223.
[47] *Dropmore Papers*, I, 539-555, 560.
[48] *H.R.N.S.W.*, II, 753.
[49] *Dropmore Papers*, I, 543.
[50] ibid., I, 567 (25.xi.1789).
[51] ibid., I, 482-483.
[52] ibid., I, 543.
[53] *Dublin Chronicle*, 18.ii.1790; *H.R.N.S.W.*, II, 752.
[54] ibid., 3 and 17.iii.1791; ibid., 772; also Appendix B.

CHAPTER II

[1] *C.O.* 201/2; *H.R.N.S.W.*, I, ii, 22.
[2] *H.R.N.S.W.*, I, ii, 6.
[3] Cf. W. S. CAMPBELL in *Journal R.A.H.S.*, XXI (1935), iv, 264.
[4] Phillip's 1st Commission: *H.R.N.S.W.*, I, ii, 24.
[5] Phillip's 2nd Commission: ibid., 61.
[6] A. C. V. MELBOURNE, *Early Constitutional Development in Australia: New South Wales*, 1788-1856, 5.
[7] *H.R.N.S.W.*, I, ii, 68.
[8] Phillip's Instructions, ibid., 87.
[9] *H.R.A.*, IV, i, 171 (Bathurst to Bent, 11.xii.1815).
[10] ibid., 46.
[11] Cf. *H.R.N.S.W.*, I, ii, 67; G. B. BARTON, *History of New South Wales from the Records*, 453.
[12] *H.R.N.S.W.*, I, ii, 70; *H.R.A.*, IV, i, 6.
[13] Phillip's Instructions, *H.R.N.S.W.*, I, ii, 85.
[14] Phillip's Additional Instructions, ibid., 256.
[15] ibid., 71.
[16] Camden to Pitt, 29.i.1787: quoted, J. HOLLAND ROSE, *William Pitt and National Revival*, 439.
[17] *H.R.N.S.W.*, I, ii, 73 *et seq.*
[18] A. C. V. MELBOURNE, op. cit., 10, 11.
[19] Phillip's 2nd Commission, *H.R.N.S.W.*, I, ii, 61.
[20] Phillip's Instructions, ibid., 85.
[21] Cf. Part II, Ch. i., 162-163; Mackaness, op. cit., p. 11.
[22] *H.R.N.S.W.*, I, ii, 18, 27, 42.
[23] *C.O.* 201/2.
[24] Heads of a Plan (18.viii.1786); *H.R.N.S.W.*, I, ii, 19.
[25] Collins's *Account*, p. i.

[26] King's *Journal*, *H.R.N.S.W.*, II, 514.
[27] *C.O.* 201/2.
[28] Heads of a Plan, *H.R.N.S.W.*, I, ii, 18.
[29] ibid., II, 739; TENCH's *Narrative*, 47.
[30] *H.R.N.S.W.*, II, 29; I, ii, 92 (2/3 of allowance made to troops serving in the West Indies).
[31] ibid., I, ii, 20.
[32] King's *Journal*, ibid., II, 514.
[33] ibid., I, ii, 34-36.
[34] ibid., 32, 34.
[35] Phillip to Nepean (11.i.1787), ibid., 46.
[36] WHITE's *Journal*, I, 2; KING's *Journal*; *H.R.N.S.W.*, II, 515.
[37] TENCH's *Narrative*, p. 1.
[38] Phillip to Nepean (1.iii.1787), *H.R.N.S.W.*, I, ii, 55.
[39] ibid., 50.
[40] ibid., 45.
[41] ibid., 46.
[42] ibid., 56.
[43] ibid., 58.
[44] ibid., 50.
[45] ibid., 57.
[46] ibid., 55.
[47] ibid., 58-59.
[48] ibid., 80.
[49] ibid., 91-92.
[50] TENCH's *Narrative*, 2-4.
[51] WHITE's *Journal*, 2-11.
[52] *H.R.N.S.W.*, I, ii, 55.
[53] BARTON, op. cit., 46.
[54] *H.R.N.S.W.*, I, ii, 82-83.
[55] ibid., II, 740.
[56] ibid., I, ii, 102, 104.
[57] *Australian Encyclopaedia*, article "First Fleet".
[58] *H.R.N.S.W.*, I, ii, 107-109.
[59] ibid., 111-115; Adm. 1/2308 (1785-89); Appendix B.
[60] PHILLIP's *Voyage*, 28.
[61] BOWES's *Journal*, *H.R.N.S.W.*, II, 390.
[62] COLLINS's *Account*, pp. 1, 2.
[63] TENCH's *Narrative*, 46.
[64] Banks to Richards, the contractor (16.viii.1791): quoted BARTON, op. cit., 96.

CHAPTER III

[1] Phillip to Sydney, *H.R.A.*, I, 1, 18.
[2] COLLINS, *Account, etc.*, 6; this does not include the thirteen drafted from the Fleet (*H.R.A.*, 1, 1, 727).
[3] E. SHANN, *Economic History of Australia*, 12.
[4] *P.P.* 1812 (341), II, 573.
[5] 59 Geo. III, c. 114.
[6] EARL GREY, *The Colonial Policy of Lord John Russell's Administration*, 6-8.
[7] BOWES's *Journal*, *H.R.N.S.W.*, II, 392; TENCH's *Narrative*, 62.
[8] BOWES's *Journal*, loc. cit., 393.
[9] COLLINS, op. cit., p. 8; and TENCH, op. cit., 63.
[10] BOWES's *Journal*, loc. cit., 392.
[11] See Appendix B.
[12] Phillip to King, *H.R.A.* I, I, 32-34; Phillip to Sydney, *H.R.A.* I, I, 20; (see note op. cit., 715); KING's *Journal*, *H.R.N.S.W.*, II, 548.
[13] SURGEON WHITE, *Journal*, 122.
[14] *H.R.A.*, 1, 1, 20.
[15] *H.R.A.*, 1, I, 54.
[16] Phillip to Nepean, *H.R.A.*, 1, 1, 55, 56.
[17] Phillip to Sydney (15/5/1788), *H.R.A.*, 1, 1, 22.

[18] TENCH, *Narrative*, etc., 132.
[19] TENCH, op. cit., 135.
[20] Phillip to Nepean, *H.R.A.*, I, 1, 44.
[21] TENCH, op. cit., 135.
[22] Phillip to Sydney, 16.v. and 9.vii.1788, *H.R.A.*, I, 1, 35, 56.
[23] COLLINS, *Account, etc.*, 54.
[24] TENCH, op. cit., 132.
[25] Phillip to Sydney, 1.ii.1790, *H.R.A.*, I, 1, 134.
[26] Phillip to Sydney, 1788, 1789, *H.R.A.*, I, 1, 34, 56, 108.
[27] Grenville to Phillip, 19.ii.1791, *H.R.A.*, I, 1, 214.
[28] COLLINS, op. cit., 9.
[29] Report of Select Committee of 1812, p. 7.
[30] COLLINS, op. cit., 25, 33 *et passim*.
[31] Phillip to Sydney and Nepean, May 15, 16, and July 9, 10, 1788, *H.R.A.*, I, 1, 32, 44, 47, 57, 65.
[32] Ross to Nepean, 18.vii.1788, *C.O.* 201/3.
[33] Cf. Adm. 1/3824; also BARTON, *History of N.S.W. from the Records*, 499 *et sqq*.
[34] *H.R.A.*, I, 1, 51, 57, 58.
[35] WHITE's *Journal*, 216.
[36] E. SHANN, *Economic History of Australia*, 12.
[37] *H.R.A.*, I, 1, 100, and note on p. 733.
[38] *H.R.A.*, I, 1, 103, 104.
[39] COLLINS, *Account, etc.*, 50.
[40] *H.R.A.*, I, 1, 156; TENCH, *Account of Port Jackson*, 25, 26.
[41] COLLINS, op. cit., 81.
[42] *H.R.A.*, I, 1, 138.
[43] *H.R.A.*, I, 1, 139.
[44] Phillip to Sydney, 1.ii.1790, *H.R.A.*, I, 1, 134.
[45] *H.R.A.*, I, 1, 144; 147, and note on p. 745; cf. also COLLINS, op. cit., 83.
[46] TENCH, *Account of Port Jackson*, 38; COLLINS, op. cit., 92.
[47] COLLINS, op. cit., 98, 99.
[48] *H.R.A.*, I, 1, 166.
[49] COLLINS's *Account*, I, 108.
[50] TENCH, *Account, etc.*, 50; *H.R.A.*, I, 1, 190.
[51] *H.R.A.*, I, 1, 172.
[52] TENCH, op. cit., 46; COLLINS, op. cit., 118.
[53] Cf. *Annual Register*, 1789, 256; *Gentleman's Magazine*, April 1789, p. 340.
[54] Sydney to Lords Comm. of Treasury (BARTON, *Hist. of N.S.W. from the Records*, 365 *et sqq.*).
[55] *H.R.A.*, I, 1, 120; and *Dropmore Papers*, I, 482.
[56] COLLINS, op. cit., 115.
[57] Phillip to Nepean, 16.vi.1790, *H.R.A.*, I, 1, 178.
[58] COLLINS, op. cit., 150.
[59] Cf. *Gentleman's Magazine*, March 1789, Vol. lix, 274; cf. also Grenville to Phillip, Dec. 24, 1789, *H.R.A.*, I, 1, 131-134.
[60] *H.R.A.*, I, 1, 134.
[61] *H.R.N.S.W.*, 1, I, 423.
[62] *P.P.* 1731-1800, A/cs. & Papers, XXXV (1792), No. 751 (10 and 26.iii.1792), 53, 70.
[63] ibid., 63, *passim*.
[64] COLLINS, op. cit., 123.
[65] TENCH, *Narrative*, 51; COLLINS, *Account, etc.*, 122 *et sqq.*; Johnson to Thornton, *H.R.N.S.W.*, I, ii, pp. 386 *et sqq.*; and *C.O.* 201/6.
[66] Phillip to Grenville, 13.vii.1790, *H.R.A.*, I, i, 188.
[67] Phillip to Grenville, 17.vii.1790, ibid., 197.
[68] See Appendix B.
[69] Letter of Phillip and Dundas, *H.R.A.*, I, i, 225, 275, 288, *et seq.*, 353.
[70] Phillip to Grenville, 5.xi.1791, ibid., 274.
[71] Dundas to Phillip, 10.i.1792, 15.v.1792, ibid., 331, 353.
[72] *P.P.* 1731-1900, A/cs. & Papers, XXXV, No. 751 (10 and 26.iii.1792), Report of Navy Commrs., p. 62.

73 ibid., 63 *et seq.*
74 ibid., 30.
75 ibid., 46, 47, 79, 80, 107, 108.
76 ibid., 30.
77 ibid., 30.
78 Phillip to Dundas, 19.iii.1792, *H.R.A.*, I.1.336.
79 Phillip to Dundas, 11.x.1792, ibid., 397.
80 *P.P.* 1731-1800, A/cs. & Papers, XXXV, No. 751, pp. 45, 46.
81 ibid., also Report of Select Comm. of 1812, pp. 17, 18, 28, 29.
82 Phillip to Nepean, 24.vii.1790, *H.R.A.*, I, i, 203.
83 Collins's *Account*, I, 194; Phillip to Grenville, *H.R.A.*, I, i, 274.
84 Phillip to Grenville, 15.xii.1791, ibid., 332.
85 Collins's *Account*, I, 210.
86 Phillip to Dundas, 2.x.1792, *H.R.A.*, I, 372.
87 ibid., 374, 377.

CHAPTER IV

1 Returns of Oct. 1792, *H.R.A.*, I, i, 399.
2 Cf. Evidence of W. Cox, Bigge Appendix, *C.O.*, 201/120, A.9, A.11.
3 *H.R.A.*, I, x, 368, 485; I, i, 203; *C.O.*, 201/118, A.3, A.25.
4 Cf. Hunter's Orders, 1796, *H.R.A.*, I, i, 678, 690.
5 ibid., 130, 131, 185, 186, 544, 589.
6 Evidence of Hunter, Bligh and others; Report of Select Committee on Transportation, 1812; *P.P.* 1812 (341), II, 573, *passim*, and pp. 19, 30.
7 *H.R.A.*, I, vii, 614; viii, 134; ix, 199, 200, 504, 857.
8 General Order, 21.vii.1796; ibid., I, i, 696; and 20.viii.1798; ibid., I, ii, 218.
9 ibid., I, ii, 585.
10 ibid., 214; T. A. Coghlan, *Labour and Industry in Australia*, I, 53.
11 *H.R.A.*, I, ii, 76.
12 *H.R.N.S.W.*, I, ii, 359.
13 Dundas to Phillip, 10.i.1792, *H.R.A.*, I, i, 328.
14 Grey, *Colonial Policy of Lord John Russell's Administration*, II, 6.
15 Report of Select Committee on Transportation, 1838; *P.P.* 1837-38 (669), XXII, 1, *passim*, and pp. vii, viii, ix.
16 Merivale, *Lectures on Colonisation and Colonies*, lect. xii, 349, 373.
17 Evidence of Hutchison, Bigge Appendix, *C.O.* 201/120, 173 *et seq.*
18 Collins's *Account*, I, 72, 112, 165 and *passim.*
19 Thompson's *Journal*, *H.R.N.S.W.*, II, 796.
20 *Dublin Chronicle*, 23.v. and 4.vi.1793, ibid., 800, 802, 809, 810; Collins's *Account*, I, 155, 218; *H.R.A.*, I, i, 269, 369, ii, 116, 712.
21 *Dublin Chronicle*, 13 and 17.xii.1791; *H.R.N.S.W.*, II, 791, 792.
22 Cf. ibid., 788, 791; Grenville to Phillip *H.R.A.*, I, i, 584; Portland to Phillip, ibid., I, ii, 25.
23 Collins's *Account*, I, 169, 253.
24 *H.R.A.*, I, i, 209.
25 Cf. Bigge's 1st Report, 118-119. 131-132.
26 ibid., 131.
27 Collins's *Account*, I, 93.
28 *H.O.* 13/1, p. 2; *P.C.* 2/131.
29 *H.R.A.*, I, i, 279-280.
30 *C.O.* 210/1, 201/5 (15.xii.1791).
31 Returns of 8.xii.1792; *C.O.* 201/1.
32 Tench's *Account*, 208.
33 Collins's *Account*, I, 258.
34 Phillip to Dundas (11.x.1792), *H.R.A.*, I, i, 398.
35 Returns of Oct. 1792, ibid., 399; Dec. 1792, *C.O.* 201/1.
36 Cf. *H.R.N.S.W.*, II, 38-44.
37 ibid., II, 818.

CHAPTER V

[1] *Parl. Hist.*, xxxii, 705-712 (1806).

[2] *Parl. Hist.*, XXX, 1298, 1308, 1449, 1460, 1486; XXXI, 263.

[3] HOWELL, *State Trials*, XXX, 766.

[4] Cf. HOLLAND ROSE, *Pitt and the Great War*, 183.

[5] G. M. TREVELYAN, *British History in the Nineteenth Century*, 71.

[6] *H.R.N.S.W.* (King to Grose, 26.iv.1794), Vol. II, 856, 879.

[7] Fremantle's, *England in the Nineteenth Century*, I, 291.

[8] CONRAD GILL, *The Naval Mutinies of 1797*, Ch. XXVI, 355 *et seq.*

[9] *P.P.*, *Returns of Criminals Transported* (15.ii.1810), pp. 36, 38.

[10] Cf. H. FURBER, *Henry Dundas*, p. 93.

[11] E. SCOTT, *A Short History of Australia*, 61.

[12] Dundas to Phillip, 14.vii.1792, *H.R.A.*, I, 1, 365.

[13] *H.R.A.*, I, 1, 438, 472-474.

[14] Op. cit., 414, and Phillip to Banks 13.iii.1794, cf. Mackaness, *Sir Joseph Banks*, 38.

[15] R. C. MILLS, *The Colonization of Australia*, 156.

[16] *H.R.A.* (Dundas to Grose), I, 1, 441.

[17] Cf. COLLINS, *Account, etc.*, 277, 377, *passim*.

[18] *H.R.A.*, I, 1: Dundas to Grose, 31.vi.93 [*sic*], p. 441; Portland to Hunter, 10.vi.95, p. 495.

[19] Portland to Hunter, *H.R.A.*, I, 1, 494 *sqq.*

[20] COLLINS, *Account, etc.*, 304.

[21] Surgeon Kent to Nepean, *H.R.N.S.W.*, II, 7.

[22] Kent to ———, 2.ix.93, *H.R.N.S.W.*, II, 61.

[23] Op. cit., 17; and COLLINS, op. cit., 311, 312.

[24] *H.R.N.S.W.*, II, 810, 816.

[25] Cf. COLLINS, op. cit., *passim*.

[26] *H.R.A.*, I, 1, 407.

[27] *H.R.N.S.W.*, II, 73; COLLINS, op. cit., 261, 272, *passim*.

[28] COLLINS, op. cit., 304, 317, 391.

[29] ibid., 391.

[30] ibid., 336, 425.

[31] For the religious disaffection see COLLINS, op. cit., 265; *H.R.N.S.W.*, II, 201; I, ii, 259; *H.R.A.*, I, 1, 441 *et seq.*; BONWICK's *Australia's First Preacher*.

[32] Dundas to Grose, 15.ii.1794, *H.R.A.*, I, i, 464.

CHAPTER VI

[1] *The Macarthur Papers*, 1.ix.1795, *H.R.N.S.W.*, II, 511.

[2] *H.R.A.*, I, 2, 476.

[3] Macarthur to Portland, *H.R.A.*, I, 2, 91.

[4] Hunter to Portland, *H.R.A.*, I, 2, 165.

[5] Portland to Hunter, *H.R.A.*, I, 2, 107.

[6] Cf. *H.R.A.*, I, 2, 152; COLLINS (Vol. II), 101, 142; Report of 1812 Committee, 20, 21.

[7] Report of 1812 Committee; cf. Evidence of HUNTER, p. 17, 47; MARGAROT, 52; RICHARDSON, 55; G. JOHNSTON, 72.

[8] Cf. the Report and Evidence of the Inquiry, Sept. 1800; *H.R.A.*, I, 2, 575-583.

[9] HOLT, *Memoirs*, Vol. I, 84, 112, 120-126.

[10] *H.R.A.*, I, 2, 650.

[11] *H.R.A.*, I, 2, 615.

[12] Report of the 1812 Committee; Evidence, 22.

[13] Hunter to Portland, 20.vi.1797, *H.R.A.*, I, 2, 24.

[14] *H.R.A.*, I, 1, 584; I, 2, 25.

[15] *H.R.A.*, I, 2, 32, 352, 564.

[16] COLLINS, op. cit., (I), 482.

[17] *H.R.A.*, I, i, 596.

[18] *H.R.A.*, I, 2, 617.
[19] *H.R.N.S.W.*, III, 649.
[20] COLLINS, op. cit. (II), 72.
[21] Returns, 25.ix.1800, *H.R.A.*, I, 2, 566.
[22] *H.R.A.*, I, ii, 440-450.

CHAPTER VII

[1] G. MACKANESS, *Sir Joseph Banks: His Relations with Australia*; G. B. BARTON, *History of New South Wales from the Records*, I, 78-85.
[2] TENCH, *A Narrative of the Voyage to Botany Bay*, London, 1789, reprinted twice in London and once in Dublin, and translated into French and Dutch in 1789; PHILLIP, *The Voyage of Governor Phillip to Botany Bay*, London, 1789, four further editions in 1790, translated into German in 1789 and into French in 1790; BARTON, op. cit., pp. 363, 580-581.
[3] HOWARD, *An Account of the Principal Lazarettos in Europe*, p. 147; BENTHAM, *Principles of Penal Law*, 490-498 (*Works*, I, 365).
[4] *P.H.*, xxviii, 1221.
[5] *H.R.N.S.W.*, II, 785.
[6] ibid., II, 792.
[7] ibid., II, 793.
[8] *P.H.*, xxx, 956.
[9] *H.R.N.S.W.*, II, 809, 810.
[10] COLQUHOUN, *Police of the Metropolis*, ed. 1800, p. 463.
[11] Twenty-Eighth Report of the Select Committee on Finance, 1798, App. L.
[12] *P.P.* 1731-1800, A/cs. & Papers, XXXV (1792), No. 751, 10 and 26.iii.1792.
[13] *Panopticon; or the Inspection House: containing the idea of a new principle of construction applicable to any sort of establishment, in which persons of any description are to be kept under inspection; and in particular to penitentiary-houses, prisons, houses of industry, workhouses, poor-houses, manufactories, mad-houses, lazarettos, hospitals and schools: with a plan of management adapted to the principle: in a series of letters written in the year 1787, from Crecheff in White Russia to a friend in England.* By Jeremy Bentham, of Lincoln's Inn, Esquire. Dublin and London, 1791.
[14] BENTHAM, *Panopticon*; *Works*, iv, 171.
[15] BENTHAM, *Works*, x, 291; xi, 99.
[16] ibid., x, 250.
[17] ibid., x, 294.
[18] *C.J.*, I, 231, 235.
[19] BENTHAM, *Works*, x, 301.
[20] ibid., iv, 171; x, 306; xi, 107, 113.
[21] *Reports from Committees of the House of Commons*: reprinted by Order of the House, 1803; Vol. XIII, 28th Report of the Select Committee on Finance, June 26, 1798, pp. 344-426.
[22] ibid., pp. 779, 800; BENTHAM, *Works*, x, 3230 xi, 101, 116.
[23] *Edinburgh Review*, Vol. II, April 1803, Art. ii, p. 30.
[24] BENTHAM, *Works*, iv, 173-248, 249-284.
[25] ibid., p. 176.
[26] ibid., pp. 212-248.
[27] ibid., xi, 129.

CONCLUSION

[1] Hunter to Portland, 15.xi.1799, *H.R.N.S.W.*, III, 741 *et seq.*
[2] P. G. King to Under-Sec. King, 3.v.1800, *H.R.N.S.W.*, IV. 83 *et seq.*
[3] E. SHANN, *An Economic History of Australia*, 35.
[4] J. DE LA PILORGERIE, *Historie de Botany Bay*, cf. Introduction.
[5] P. LEROY-BEAULIEU, *De la Colonisation chez les Peuples Modernes* (ed. 1891; cf. pp. 618-629).
[6] Cf. Introduction to *The Adventures of Ralph Rashleigh*, 1929.
[7] *Report from the Select Comm. on Transportation* (1838), iv.
[8] *Edinburgh Review*, Vol. XXXVIII, p. 101.
[9] P. CUNNINGHAM, *Two Years in New South Wales* (1827), I, 47, 51.

BIBLIOGRAPHY

THE following sources, except where otherwise stated, have been consulted in the preparation of this book. Generally they are confined to the eighteenth century; a few documents and books, published after that time but bearing on the foundation period, have been included.

PART I: MANUSCRIPT SOURCES

1. IN THE PUBLIC RECORD OFFICE, LONDON:

A. INDEXES AND GUIDES

> (i) GIUSEPPI, M. S. *A Guide to the MSS. preserved in the Public Record Office* (Vol. II, State Papers and Records of Public Depts., London, 1924).
> (ii) *List of Colonial Office Records, etc.* (36A): (*Lists and Indexes*, XXXVI).
> (iii) *List of Volumes of State Papers . . . including the Records of the Home Office, from 1782 to 1837*: (*Lists and Indexes*, XLIII).
> (iv) *List of Admiralty Records preserved in the P.R. Office*, Vol. I: (*Lists and Indexes*, XVIII).

B. COLONIAL OFFICE PAPERS

C.O. 201. Original Correspondence, Secretary of State (1-631; 1784-1900):
> 1-20 (1784-1801), comprise the Plans for the Settlement, Phillip's First Commission, Preparations, foundation of colony at Sydney and Norfolk Island, Despatches from Governors, etc., and Miscellaneous.
> 118-141, The unpublished Appendix to Bigge's Report. In the course of this Inquiry the collected evidence and statistics frequently refer to the earlier years of the system; cf., e.g.:
> 118, 119, Convicts, Docs. A. 1-93; especially 84 *et seq.*
> 120, Evidence, A. 1-33.
> 121, Police.
> 123, Agriculture.
> 125, Judicial.
> 130, Population and Colonial expenditure.
> 138, Returns of births, deaths and marriages.

C.O. 202. Entry Books (1-78; 1798-1873):
> 1. (1798-1801), Accounts of Provisions sent to N.S.W., etc.
> 2. (1800-1802), Précis of letters to Sec. of State.
> 5. (1786-1800), Letters and dispatches from Sec. of State, Commissions, Instructions.

C.O. 206. Blue Books, etc.:
> 61 contains a brief history of New South Wales, mainly from the military angle.

C.O. 207. Entry Books of Correspondence re Convicts (1-8; 1786-1867):
> 1. Alphabetical list of Convicts, 1788-1825.

C. HOME OFFICE PAPERS

H.O. 7. Convicts, Miscellaneous:
> 1. Minutes of H. of C. C'tee re transportation of convicts to Africa, 1785.

H.O. 10. Convicts, N.S.W. and V.D.L. (1-64; 1788-1869):
> 1. Register of Male Convicts, 1788-1819.
> 2. Register of Female Convicts, 1788-1819.
> 6 and 7. Registers of Convicts embarked in 1787.

H.O. 11. Convict Transportation Registers (1-21; 1787-1870):
> 1. Register of Convicts transported (from G.B.) 1787-1809.

H.O. 13. Convict Entry Books:
  1. Contains correspondence of 1783, re George Moore.

H.O. 28. Admiralty Correspondence (1-56; 1782-1840):
  5. (1785-87), letters re decision to found N.S.W.
  6-26, Correspondence to 1800.

H.O. 29. Entry Books of correspondence with Admiralty (1-7; 1779-1836):
  1-4 (1779-1800).

H.O. 30. Entry Books of correspondence with Colonial Office (1-5; 1794-1840).

D. ADMIRALTY PAPERS

  Adm. 1. Secretary's Dept. In Letters, Captains, alphabetically arranged:
    2308 (1785-1789), Phillip, equipment of fleet, directions for sailing, and some later letters from the colony.
    3824, Letters relating to the Colonies (N.S.W. 1787-1792).
    4152, Letters from Secs. of State (1786-1800); cf. 25, 31.
    4153-4183 (1788-1800).

  Adm. 106. Navy Board Letters (contain little of interest):
    1286-1300, In letters (1786-1800).
    2214-2226, Out letters (1787-1800).

E. PRIVY COUNCIL RECORDS

  P.C. 1. Unbound Papers:
    61-66, Miscellaneous papers relating to early period.

  P.C. 2. Privy Council Registers (Orders in Council):
    130-156 (1785-1800).

F. CHATHAM PAPERS (G.D. 8)

  The papers of the younger Pitt contain only a few references to the foundation of the settlement; cf. Vols. 311, 342, 344, 363.

2. IN THE BRITISH MUSEUM:

  (a) Letters and Log-book of Daniel Southwell, mate of H.M.S. Sirius, 1783-92 (Ref. 16, 381-3); (Partly reproduced in Appendix D of H.R.N.S.W., Vol. II).
  (b) The Banks Papers.

3. IN IRELAND:

The Irish Transportation Records were originally preserved in the Public Record Office and at the State Paper Office. During the insurrection of 1922 the Papers in the Public Record Office were destroyed. In *A Guide to the Records in the Public Record Office of Ireland* (Hubert Wood, Dublin, 1919), these papers are described. They included practically all the relevant documents of transportation prior to 1836.

In the State Paper Office at Dublin Castle a varied assortment of Papers is available, by which the history of the system after 1836 may be traced. The Papers comprise fifteen volumes of Transportation Indexes (1836-57); "Convicts Embarked" (1851-56); "Male Convict Register" (1842-47); "Returns from Clerk of Peace" (1848-56); the Diary of a Catholic Chaplain on the *Pestonjee Bonanjee* (1848-49); and various documents in "Country Letters", Warrant Books, and Civil Affairs Books. For the early period useful documents on the transportation system are few. Among many cartons of "Official Papers" (Series II, 1789-96; Chief Secretary), under the headings "Naval" and "Prisons," there are reports of grand juries, tenders for provisioning transport ships, and petitions from prisoners. The "Rebellion" (or "State of the Country") Papers (sixty-six cartons, 1790-1803), being reports from officials and private individuals throughout the country, describe the procedure of arrests and summary trials, and the eagerness of the Government to commute death sentences into penal transportation for life terms. The amount of directly relevant matter is, however, small.

4. IN AUSTRALIA, (*at the Mitchell Library, Sydney*):

    (*a*) *Unpublished documents:*

        I The Banks Papers; the Brabourne Collection (*passim*); also the Corres-
pondence of Sir Joseph Banks, and Letters from Governor Phillip to
Sir Joseph Banks.

        II *The following "Journals" and Letters mainly relate to the Voyage of the First
Fleet and to the earliest years of the Settlement:*
Journal of Arthur Bowes (Surgeon)
Journal of Lieut. Ralph Clark (1787-92)
Letter-book of Lieut. Ralph Clark
Journal of Lieut. W. Bradley (1786-92)
Letters of David Blackburn (re Norfolk Island)
Letters of Rev. Richard Johnson (First Chaplain)

        III Among other letters see the few of Major Francis Grose (mainly among
the King Papers). See also the first volume of the *Letters of D'Arcy
Wentworth* (1785-1808) re Norfolk Island and the Settlement.

        IV The voluminous Papers of P. G. King (later Governor) are much
concerned with the period after 1800, but throughout even these
constantly reflect back on the earlier period. Among the many King
volumes see: *Journal*, 1786-1790; *Remarks and Journal*, 1786-1790; *Journal*,
1791-1794 (Norfolk Island); *Letter-book*, 1788-99; *Norfolk Island General
Order Book*, 1791-1794; *Norfolk Island Victualling Book*, 1792-1796.
N.S.W. General Orders, Sept. 1798-Dec. 1799.
N.S.W. General Orders (Lt. Governor Patterson) Sept. 1795-Dec. 1797.

        V The "Bonwick Transcripts" of original documents preserved at *P.R.O.*
and elsewhere in London. (The originals were used in this book; Cf. Bib.
Part I, I, B.) The Transcripts of the Appendices to Bigge's three *Reports*
constantly refer to the period prior to 1800. Boxes 1 to 28 are relevant.
Of particular value is box 12, containing the Reports (submitted to
Hunter through Marsden in Feb. 1798) on the grievances of settlers
and the causes of agricultural distress (pp. 62 to 104). See also (box 12,
pp. 103 to 115). Marsden's observations on the population, June 1798.

        VI Government Orders (printed):

            N.S.W. Instructions for the Constables . . . (Govt. Press, Sydney, 1796).
N.S.W. Instructions to the Watchmen . . . (Govt. Press, Sydney, 1796).
N.S.W. General Orders, Conditions of Employment of Assigned
Servants . . . (Govt. Press, Sydney, 1800).

            For "Abridgement of General Orders, September 28, 1800 to October
8, 1801" (Govt. Press, Sydney) see Patterson to King, *H.R.A.*, III, 462.
Cf. also the first book printed in Australia: *General Standing Orders:*
selected from the General Orders issued . . . from February 11, 1791
to September 6, 1800, also General Orders . . . September 28, 1800
to September 30, 1802 (Govt. Press, Sydney, 1802).

PART II: PUBLISHED COLLECTIONS OF DOCUMENTS

(*a*) *The Dropmore Papers:* "The Manuscripts of J. B. Fortescue, Esq., preserved
at Dropmore", 7 vols. (1892-1910; Historical Manuscripts Commission;
especially vols. I—III.

(*b*) *The Historical Records of New South Wales*, published by the N.S.W. Government, 1889-1901. These volumes contain most of the earlier documents
preserved in the Public Records Office, as well as excerpts from contemporary
manuscripts and newspapers. (Volumes I, parts i and ii, II, III and IV
cover the period up to 1802.)

(c) *The Historical Records of Australia*, published by the Commonwealth of Australia, are in four series, and contain a fuller collection than the *H.R.N.S.W.*; but in some instances they need to be amended or supplemented by the original documents in the Public Record Office. Series I contains the dispatches between the Secretaries of State and Governors of the colony. The first three volumes cover the period of this book. Series III deals with the settlement and its colonies after this period. Series IV, only one volume, is confined to legal papers in connexion with the settlement.

PART III: PARLIAMENTARY SOURCES

Only Papers dealing with transportation and with the hulks and penitentiary schemes from 1776 to 1786, and with the New South Wales settlement up to 1800, are listed here, together with such later Papers as have a definite bearing on the early period.

The main sources of information are the collection of Parliamentary Papers (1731-1800), the *Parliamentary History* and the *Parliamentary Register* (for debates), the *Journals* of the two Houses and the collected Statutes of the Realm.

A. ACTS AND BILLS

(i) Act 16 Geo. III, c. 43, establishing hulks system; Royal Assent 23.v.1776; see Bill in *P.P.* 1731-1800, Vol. IX, Nos. 286, 288.

(ii) Penitentiary Bill, First Draft, 1776: *P.P.* 1731-1800, ix, 287; also *C.J.* xxxv, 809 (23.v.76).

(iii) Act 18 Geo. III, c. 62, continuing 16 Geo. III, c. 43, Royal Assent 28.v.78.

(iv) Penitentiary Bill, Second Draft, 1778, with Eden's *Observations* attached: *P.P.* 1731-1800, x, 315; also *C.J.* xxxvi, 970, 977.

(v) Act 19 Geo. III, c. 54, continuing 16 Geo. III, c. 43; Royal Assent 31.v.79.

(vi) Act 19 Geo. III, c. 74, authorizing construction of two penitentiaries, Royal Assent 30.vi.79; see Bill in *P.P.* 1731-1800, x, 340-342.

(vii) Act 24 Geo. III, sess. I, c. 12, continuing hulks and penitentiary schemes, Royal Assent 24.iii.84; see Bill in *P.P.* 1731-1800, xiv, 454.

(viii) Act 24 Geo. III, sess. 2, c. 56, re-establishing transportation system, Royal Assent 20.viii.84; see Bill in *P.P.* 1731-1800, xiv, 472.

(ix) Act 25 Geo. III, c. 46, extending 24 Geo. III, c. 56, to Scotland, Royal Assent 4.vii.85.

(x) Act 27 Geo. III, c. 2, establishing a Court of Criminal Judicature in N.S.W., Royal Assent 27.ii.87.

(xi) Act 28 Geo. III, c. 24, continuing hulks and transportation Acts, Royal Assent 2.vi.88.

(xii) Act 30 Geo. III, c. 47, empowering Governor to pardon convicts, Royal Assent 9.vi.90.

(xiii) Act 34 Geo. III, c. 45, establishing a Court of Criminal Judicature at Norfolk Island, Royal Assent 9.v.94.

(xiv) Act 34 Geo. III, c. 60, continuing hulks and transportation Acts, Royal Assent 23.v.94.

(xv) Act 34 Geo. III, c. 84, authorizing the erection of a Panopticon, Royal Assent 7.vii.94.

(xvi) Act 35 Geo. III, c. 18, repealing and amending 34 Geo. III, c. 45, Royal Assent 16.iii.95.

(xvii) Act 39 Geo. III, c. 51, continuing hulks and transportation Acts, Royal Assent 13.vi.99.

(xviii) Act 39 Geo. III, c. 52, continuing Penitentiary Act, Royal Assent 13.vi.99.

B. REPORTS

(See also Catalogue of Parliamentary Reports, 1696-1834, in *P.P.* 1834
(626), Vol. L, p. 1.)

    (i) Select Committee on Hulks, 15.iv.78: *C.J.*, xxxvi, 926.

    (ii) S.C. on Returns of Felons, 1.iv.79: *C.J.*, xxxvii, 306.

    (iii) S.C. on Penitentiary Act, 22.iii.84: *C.J.*, xxxix, 1040.

    (iv) S.C. on Transportation Act, 9.v.85: *C.J.*, xl, 954; and 28.vii.85,
C.J., xl, 1161.

    (v) Twenty-Eighth Report of S.C. on Finance (Police, including
Convict Establishments), 28.vi.98; in Vol. XIII of *Reports from
Committees of the House of Commons*, reprinted in 1803; also reprinted
in *P.P.* 1810 (348), iv, 375.

Information relative to 1787-1800 is also to be found in the evidence
and appendices of the following Reports:

    (vi) S.C. on Laws relating to Penitentiary Houses, 31.v.1811, *P.P.*
1810-11 (199), iii, 569; 10.vi.1811, *P.P.* 1810-11 (217), iii, 691;
27.vi.1812, *P.P.* 1812 (306), ii, 263.

    (vii) S.C. on Transportation, 10.vii.12: *P.P.* 1812 (341), ii, 573.

    (viii) S.C. on the State of Gaols, 19.vii.19: *P.P.* 1819 (579), vii, 1.

    (ix) J. T. Bigge's *Inquiry into the State of New South Wales*, 19.vi.22:
P.P. 1822 (448), xx, 539; 13.iii.23: *P.P.* 1823 (33), x, 515; 4.vii.23:
P.P. 1823 (136), x, 607.

    (x) S.C. on Transportation, 3.viii.1838: *P.P.* 1837-38 (669), xxii, 1.

    (xi) Parliamentary Reports in connexion with the Irish Rebellion:

        (a) Rept. from C'tee. of Secrecy of H. of C. (Ireland), 21.viii.1798
(printed Dublin and London, 1798); appendices iv to xxviii
describe the policing and punishment of the disaffected. This
Report contains:

        (b) Rept. from C'tee. of Secrecy of H. of L., 1793 (App. I).

        (c) Rept. from C'tee. of Secrecy of H. of C., 1797 (App. II).

        (d) Rept. from C'tee. of Secrecy of H. of L., 1797 (App. III).

        (e) Rept. C'tee. of Secrecy, H. of L. (Ireland), 30.viii.98; (London,
1798).

        (f) Rept. of C'tee. of Secrecy, H. of C. (Eng.), 15.iii.99; with
twenty-eight appendices, describing courts martial in the
navy and army, and the relationship existing between the
"United Irishmen" and the English and Scottish Radical
Societies. (The appendices to these reports have occasional
references to transportation of offenders.)

C. DEBATES IN PARLIAMENT

    (i) North's motion for leave to bring in Hulks Bill, 1.iv.76: *P.R.* iii,
473.

    (ii) Committee stage of Hulks Bill, 9.v.76: *P.R.*, iv, 104.

    (iii) Report stage of Hulks Bill, 13.v.76: *P.R.*, iv, 117.

    (iv) North's Budget Speech, 6.iii.78: *P.R.*, ix, 1, 4.

    (v) North's motion for a Bill to continue the Hulks Act, 23.iii.78:
P.H., xix, 970; *P.R.*, ix, 83.

    (vi) Debate on returns of felons, 5.ii.79: *P.R.*, ix, 283.

    (vii) Report stage of 24 Geo. III, c. 12, 11.iii.84: *P.H.*, xxiv, 755.

    (viii) Burke's motion on the state of convicts sentenced to transportation,
16.iii.85: *P.H.*, xxv, 391; *P.R.*, xvii, 430.

    (ix) Beauchamp's motion for information on the Government's policy
as to transportation, 11.iv.85: *P.H.*, xxv, 430.

    (x) Bastard's motion for returns of criminals, 7.iii.86: *P.R.*, xix, 329.

    (xi) King's speech and debates thereon, 23.i.87: *P.H.*, xxvi, 211.

    (xii) Bunbury's motion re convicts sent to N.S.W., 9.ii.91: *P.H.*, xxviii,
1221.

    (xiii) Bunbury's resolutions re transportation, 31.v.93: *P.H.*, xxx, 956.

    (xiv) Various motions respecting the Muir and Palmer trials, and

Palmer's petition, 24.ii.94: *P.H.*, xxx, 1449; 27.ii.94, *P.H.*, xxx, 1460; 10.iii.94, *P.H.*, xxx, 1486; 15.iv.94, *P.H.*, xxxi, 263.

D. Accounts, Estimates, Returns, Etc.:

These are too numerous and incidental to be listed in full, but the following is a selective list of references:

(i) Extracts of Letters, etc., and Accounts relative to the settlements in N.S.W. (8.iv.1791). (*P.P.* 1731-1800, xxiv, 1790-91, No. 740).

(ii) A/cs. and Papers relative to convicts on board the Hulks and those transported to N.S.W. (10 & 26.iii.92); also, Extracts of Letters, etc., from Governor Phillip relating to N.S.W. (21.v.92). (*P.P.* 1731-1800, xxxv, 1792, No. 751.)

(iii) Return of Criminals transported to N.S.W., 1787-1809: (15.ii.1810), *P.P.* 1810 (45), xiv, 487.

(iv) *C.J.*: xli (1786), 826; xlii (1787), 700, 702; xlv (1790), 364, 368; xlvi (1791), 552, 570, 572; xlvii (1792), 68, 70, 406, 470, 499; xlviii (1793), 292, 295; xlix (1794), 85, 88, 225, 312-315, 446; l (1795), 231, 234, 239, 242; li (1795-96), 179, 181, 610-11; liii (1797), 89, 90; liv (1798), 596; lv (1799), 162, 166; lvi (1800), 82, 729.

(v) *L.J.* (1794), 15, 123-26.

PART IV: GENERAL SOURCES

A. Contemporary Newspapers and Periodicals of Great Britain and Ireland, especially the *Gentleman's Magazine* and the *Annual Register.*

B. Bibliographies, Guides, Etc.

The *Australian Encyclopaedia*, 2 vols., Sydney, 1925-27.
The *Cambridge History of the British Empire*, Vol. VII, Part I, Australia, Cambridge, 1933.
Dictionary of National Biography.
MENNEL, P., *Dictionary of Australasian Biography*, 1892.
HEATON, J. H., *Australian Dictionary of Dates and Men of the Time*, 1879.
LECKY, W. E. H., *History of England in the Eighteenth Century* (7 vols., editions of 1878 and 1892), *History of Ireland in the Eighteenth Century* (5 vols., London, 1892).
ROYAL AUSTRALIAN HISTORICAL SOCIETY: *Journal and Proceedings*, Sydney, 1901——

PART V: SELECTIVE ENGLISH BIBLIOGRAPHY

Other books from this extensive literature are indicated in the text. Where not otherwise stated, the book was published in London.

A. Political, Social and Economic

ABBEY, C. J. and OVERTON, J. H., *The English Church in the Eighteenth Century*, 1896.
ANDREWS, A., *The Eighteenth Century*, 1856.
ASHTON, J., *The Dawn of the Nineteenth Century in England*, 1906.
BESANT, SIR WALTER, *London in the Eighteenth Century*, 1902 (the relevant volume in his series *The Survey of London*).
BURKE, EDMUND, *Works* (Rivington Ed., 1803; cf. Vol. III for "Speech at Bristol previous to the Election").
CLAPHAM, J. H., *Economic History of Modern Britain*, Vol. I, Cambridge, 1926.
COLE, G. D. H., *A Short History of the British Working Class Movement*, 1789-1927, 1932.
COUPLAND, R., *Wilberforce*, 1923.
DALTON, E. A., *History of Ireland*, 6 vols. n.d.

EDEN, SIR F. M., *The State of the Poor* (A History of the Labouring Classes in England), 3 vols., 1797; cf., also, an abridged edition by A. G. L. Rogers, 1928.
ERNLE, LORD, *English Farming—Past and Present*, 1917.
FREMANTLE, A. F., *England in the Nineteenth Century*, 2 vols., 1929.
GARNIFR, R. M., *History of the English Landed Interest (Its Customs, Laws and Agriculture)*, 1908; cf. Ch. xxii, Vol. II.
GRIFFITH, G. T., *Population Problems of the Age of Malthus*, Cambridge, 1926.
HALÉVY, ELIE, *Histoire du Peuple Anglais au XIXe Siècle*, Paris, 1924 (cf. Vol. I; an English translation exists).
HAMMOND, J. L. and B., *The Skilled Labourer*, 1760-1832, 1919.
—— *The Town Labourer*, 1760-1832, 1917.
—— *The Village Labourer*, 1760-1832, 1932.
KNOWLES, L. C. A., *The Industrial and Commercial Revolutions in the Nineteenth Century*, 1928.
LASKI, H. J., *Political Thought in England from Locke to Bentham*, ed. 1932.
LIPSON, E., *Economic History of England*, ed. 1934 (cf. Vols. II and III).
MADDEN, R. R., *The United Irishmen; their lives and times*, 4 vols., ed. 1842-46; 1857-60.
MALTHUS, T. R., *Essay on Population* (1798); ed. 1872.
MUSGRAVE, SIR R., *Memoirs of the Different Rebellions in Ireland*, Dublin, 1801.
NAMIER, L. B., *Structure of Politics at the Accession of George III.* 1929.
—— *Government of England at the Time of the American Revolution*, 1930.
NICHOLLS, SIR G., *History of the English Poor Law*, 3 vols., 1898 (cf. Vol. II, 1714-1853).
O'BRIEN, G., *Economic History of Ireland in the Eighteenth Century*, 1918.
O'CONNOR, SIR J., *History of Ireland*, 1798-1924, 2 vols., 1925.
PAINE, THOMAS, *The Rights of Man*, 1791-92.
POWER, EILEEN, *Select Bibliography of the Industrial Revolution*.
ROSE, J. HOLLAND, *William Pitt and National Revival*, 1911.
—— *William Pitt and the Great War*, 1911.
—— *Pitt and Napoleon*, 1912.
SCULLY, DENYS, *A Statement of the Penal Laws*, Dublin, 1812.
SMITH, ADAM, *Theory of Moral Sentiments* (1759), ed. 10th, 1804.
—— *Wealth of Nations* (1776); Everyman ed.
STRANGELAND, C. E., *The Pre-Malthusian Doctrines of Population*, 1904.
SYKES, N., *Church and State in the Eighteenth Century*, Cambridge, 1935.
TOYNBEE, ARTHUR, *Lectures on the Industrial Revolution of the Eighteenth Century in England*, ed. 1908.
TRAILL, H. D., *Social England* (5 vols., cf. Vol. V).
TREVELYAN, SIR G., *Early Life of C. J. Fox*, 1887.
TREVELYN, G. M., *British History in the Nineteenth Century*, 1922.
VULLIAMY, C. E., *John Wesley*, 1931.
WARNER, W. J., *The Wesleyan Movement in the Industrial Revolution*, 1930.
WILBERFORCE, R. and S., *Life of William Wilberforce*, 5 vols., 1838.
YOUNG, ARTHUR, *The Farmer's Letters to the People of England*, 1767.

B. CRIME, PUNISHMENT AND THE REFORMERS

(i) *Contemporary*

ANONYMOUS, *The Right method of maintaining security in person . . . a letter to a Member of Parliament*, 1751.
—— *Proposals for Employing convicts within this kingdom, instead of sending them to Botany Bay, etc.*, by G.R., 1787.
—— *A Serious Admonition to the Publick on the intended Thief Colony at Botany Bay*, with a letter from Alexander Dalrymple, 1786.
BECCARIA, CESARE, *Dei Delitti e delle Pene* (1764).
BENTHAM, JEREMY, *Collected Works*, edited by Bowring, 11 vols., Edinburgh, 1843. References to transportation in his Works.
(a) *A View of the Hard Labour Bill* (1778), IV, 1.
(b) *Introduction to the Principles of Morals and Legislation*, 1789, I, 1.

(c) *Panopticon, or the Inspection House*, 1791, IV, 37.
(d)*Panopticon versus N.S.W.* (two letters to Lord Pelham), 1802, IV, 173 *seqq.*
(e) *A Plea for the Constitution*, 1803, IV, 249.
(f) *Principles of Penal Law*, I, 365.

BLACKSTONE, SIR W., *Commentaries on the Laws of England*, 4 vols., 1765-69 (17th ed., 1830).
CALLANDER, *Terra Australis Incognita*, 3 vols., Edinburgh, 1768. (Vol. III recommends the settlement of this region for advantageous British commerce).
COLQUHOUN, P., *A Treatise on the Police of the Metropolis*, 1795 (eds. 1796 and 1800).
DALRYMPLE, A., *Historical Collection of the several Voyages and Discoveries in the S. Pacific Ocean*, 1770-71.
—— Cf. above, Anonymous: *A Serious Admonition*, etc.
EDEN, W. (1st Baron Auckland), *Principles of Penal Law*, 1771 (3rd ed. 1775).
—— *Preface to a Draught of a Bill*, 1778.
FIELDING, SIR J., *A Plan for preventing robberies within twenty miles of London*, 1755.
FIELDING, HENRY, *An enquiry into the causes of the late increase of robbers, etc.*, 1751.
HANWAY, JONAS, *Distributive Justice and Mercy: showing that a temporary real solitary imprisonment of convicts, supported by religious instruction and well-regulated labour is essential to their well-being and the safety, honour and reputation of the people* (1781).
—— *A New Year's Gift to the People of Great Britain, pleading for the necessity of a more vigorous qnd consistent police, etc.* (1784).
—— *The Defects of Police the cause of immorality . . . with various proposals for preventing hanging and transportation, etc.* (1775).
—— *Solitude in imprisonment, with profitable labour . . . the most humane . . . means of bringing malefactors who have forfeited their lives or are subject to transportation to a right sense of their condition, etc.* (1776).
HOME, HENRY (Lord Kames), *Historical Law Tracts: Criminal Law*, 1776; he disapproves of capital punishment.
HOWARD, JOHN. *The State of the Prisons in England and Wales*, 1777 (4th ed. 1792).
—— *Account of the Principal Lazarettos in Europe*, 1789.
MADAN, MARTIN, *Thoughts on Executive Justice with respect to our Criminal Laws, etc.*, 1785.
MIRABEAU, G. H., COMTE DE, *Observations d'un voyageur Anglais sur Bicêtre*, 1778 (*Oeuvres de Mirabeau*, Tome III, Paris, 1835).
MONTESQUIEU, BARON DE, *Esprit des Lois* (Tomes 3-6, Oeuvres, éd. Laboulaye Paris, 1876).
Lettres Persanes (Tome 2, Oeuvres, éd. Lahure, Paris, 1859).
PALEY, W., *The Principles of Moral and Political Philosophy*, 1785, 2 vols., 7th ed., 1790 (cf. Vol. II, Chapters vii, viii, ix).
PAUL, SIR G. O., *Proceedings of the Grand Juries . . . of Glocester . . . on executing a general reform . . . in prisons, etc.*, Glocester, 1808. (It contains his two works: *Considerations, etc.*, 1784, and *An Address, etc.*, 1783.)
—— *Thoughts on the alarming progress of the gaol fever, etc.*, Glocester, 1784.
PEEL, SIR R., *Speeches delivered in the House of Commons*, 4 vols., 1853; cf. Vol. I.
ROMILLY, SIR S., *Memoirs of the Life of, written by himself, with a selection from his correspondence, edited by his sons*, 2 vols., ed. 3rd, 1841.
—— *Observations on the Criminal Law of England*, 2nd ed., 1811.
—— *The Speeches of Sir S. Romilly*, 2 vols., 1820.
—— *Observations on a late publication*, 1786.
A STUDENT OF POLITICS, *Proposals to the Legislators for preventing the frequent executions and exportations of convicts, etc., in a letter to H. Pelham*, 1754.
VOLTAIRE, *Commentaire sur le livre des délits et des peines*, (Geneva, 1766). (Cf. *Oeuvres complètes*, Politique et Législation, Tome I, Paris, 1819.)
WEDDERBURN, A. (Lord Chancellor Loughborough), *Observations on the State of the English Prisons and the means of improving them*, 1793.

(ii) *Later Writers*

BARNES, H. E., Article: "Transportation of Criminals," in *Encyclopaedia of the Social Sciences*, 1930, Vol. XV.

BUTLER, J. D., "British Convicts shipped to American Colonies," *American Hist. Review*, II, Oct., 1896.

DICEY, A. V., *Lectures on the Relation between Law and Public Opinion in England during the Nineteenth Century*, 2nd ed. 1914.

FARRER, J. A., *Crimes and Punishments, including a new translation of Beccaria's "Dei Delitti, etc.,"* 1880.

FURBER, H., *Henry Dundas, First Viscount Melville*, 1931. (The third chapter deals with the Scottish martyrs and the Government attitude to Jacobinism.)

GIBSON, E. C., *John Howard*, 1905.

GILL, C., *The Naval Mutinies of* 1797, Manchester, 1913.

GILLESPIE, J. E., "The Transportation of English Convicts after 1783" (*Journal of Crim. Law and Criminology*, Vol. XIII, 3, Nov. 1922, Chicago).

GRIFFITHS, A., *Chronicles of Newgate*, 2 vols, 1884.

HALÉVY, ÉLIE, *La Formation du Radicalisme Philosophique*, 3 vols., Paris, 1901. Translated by Mary Morris, *The Growth of Philosophic Radicalism*, ed. 1934, London.

HOWELL, T. B., *State Trials*. Cf. Vol. XXIII re Scottish martyrs.

IVES, G., *A History of Penal Methods*, 1914.

LAURENCE, J., *A History of Capital Punishment in Great Britain*, London, n.d.

LESLIE-MELVILLE, R., *The Life and Work of Sir John Fielding*, 1934.

MACNEVIN, T., *The Leading State Trials in Ireland from* 1794 *to* 1803, Dublin, 1844.

MERCIER, C., *Crime and Criminals*, 1918.

OAKES, C. G., *Sir Samuel Romilly*, 1935.

PARTRIDGE, S. G., *Prisoner's Progress*, 1935.

PHILLIPSON, C., *Three Criminal Law Reformers: Beccaria, Bentham, Romilly*, 1923.

SMITH, A. E., "Transportation of Criminals to the American Colonies in the Seventeenth Century" (*American Hist. Review*, Vol. XXXIX, Jan. 1934).

STEPHEN, SIR J. F., *A General View of the Criminal Law of England*, 2nd ed., 1890
—— *A History of the Criminal Law of England*, 3 vols., 1883.

STEPHEN, SIR L., *The English Utilitarians*, 3 vols., 1900.
—— *English Thought in the Eighteenth Century* (2 vols., 3rd ed., 1902; cf. Vol. II, S. 84-140).

WEBB, S. and B., *English Prisons under Local Government*, 1922. (Bernard Shaw has an interesting preface to this book, in which a typically Shavian view of punishment is given.)

WILSON, M., *The Crime of Punishment*, 1931.

WILSON, SIR R. K., *History of Modern English Law*, 1875.

PART VI: WORKS RELATING TO THE SYSTEM IN AUSTRALIA

This section includes works written by, or about, contemporaries of the foundation period. Among numerous later works those are included which treat directly of the system in the eighteenth century; but a few useful works, which show how political and economic developments followed from the precedents established at the foundation, are mentioned here, and others are indicated in the text.

A. CONTEMPORARY

ANONYMOUS, *A Concise History of the English Colony in N.S.W. . . . from* 1788 *to May* 1803, etc., London, 1804. (A compilation based on Collins.)

—— An Historical Narrative of the Discovery of New Holland and N.S.W., etc., London, 1786. (Largely fictitious and political.)

—— History of New Holland from its discovery, London, 1787 (with an introductory discourse on banishment by William Eden). This work had been attributed to Eden and Barrington (cf. Part II, Ch. I of this volume): it was re-issued in various forms in 1787, as an appendix to Phillip's Voyage (2nd and 3rd ed.), and in 1808 when it was credited to Barrington.

—— Other anonymous pamphlets included: Copious Remarks on the Discovery of N.S.W., etc. (London, 1787); The History of Botany Bay, etc. (Bristol, 1787).

—— Observations on the Remonstrance of the Rev. Peter O'Neill (a protest against Cornwallis's pardons).

BARRINGTON, G., A Voyage to New South Wales, etc., 1793. (Probably Barrington had a hand in compiling this work. The numerous editions and the works attributed to him in later years were not genuine; they were based on Collins. Memoirs and Lives of this ex-convict were published in London, 1790, 1791, 1839, 1872.)

BOND, G., A Brief Account of the Colony etc., Southampton 1803, 18 pp.

COLLINS, D., Account of the English Colony in New South Wales. (This is the most important work on the history of the early settlement: the first volume, published 1798, narrates from personal knowledge the course of events to the end of 1796; his second volume (1802) was compiled from information sent to him in England.)

HOLT, J., Memoirs (edited by T. C. Croker), 2 vols., 1838.

HOWE, G., General Standing Orders: selected from the General Orders issued by former Governors. From 11 Feb. 1791 to 6 Sept. 1800, etc., Sydney, 1802.

HUNTER, J., An Historical Journal of the Transactions at Port Jackson and Norfolk Island, etc., London, 1793. (Another edition and translations into German and Swedish followed.)

—— "Biographical Memoirs of Captain John Hunter, late Governor of N.S.W." (Naval Journal, Vol. VI, London, 1801).

JOHNSON, REV. R., An Address to the inhabitants of the Colonies established in N.S.W. and Norfolk Island, written in 1792, London, 1794.

MACKENZIE, P., Life of Thomas Muir, Glasgow, 1837.

MARGAROT, M., Trial of, before the High Court . . . at Edinburgh, 13 and 14 Jan. 1794, etc. Printed for M.M.

MASSON, M., "Thomas Fysh Palmer, a Political Exile" (Scottish Hist. Review, Vol. XIII, Jan. 1916, Glasgow).

MASSON, M., and JAMIESON, J. F., "The Odyssey of Thomas Muir" (American Hist. Review, XXIX, Oct. 1923, N.Y.).

MUIR, T., The Telegraph, a Consolatory Epistle to the Hon. Henry Erskine, 1796.

—— The Telegraph Inverted (Lauderdale's Peep at the author and adherents of the Telegraph), 1796. (Edition published Edinburgh, 1825. Cf. also, Histoire de la tyrannie du Gouvernement Anglais exercée envers le célèbre Thomas Muir, etc., Paris, 1798.)

PALMER, REV. T., A narrative of the sufferings of T. F. Palmer during a voyage to N.S.W., 1794. (Two editions, Cambridge, 1797; the second contains letters to Governor Hunter, 1795.)

—— The Trial of the Rev T. F. Palmer at Perth, Sept. 12 and 13, 1793, London,

—— Two letters from Sydney, 1795, 1797 (n.d.).   [1793.

PHILLIP, A., Voyage to Botany Bay, etc., London, 1789 (with several subsequent editions and translations into French and German).

—— "Biographical Memoir of Arthur Phillip" (Naval Chronicle, Vol. XXVII, London, 1812).

REDESDALE, LORD, and FINGALL, EARL OF, Correspondence between (Aug. 22 to Sept. 26, 1803). (Concerns the clergy transported after the '98 Rebellion.) Dublin, 1804.

RIOU, LIEUT., Journal of proceedings on board H.M.S. Guardian . . . Dec. 22, 1789 to 15 Jan., 1790 (London, 1790).

SMITH, REV. SYDNEY, Review of Collins's Account (Edinburgh Review, Vol. II, April 1803, p. 30).

TENCH, WATKIN, *A Narrative of an Expedition to Botany Bay, with an account of N.S.W., its productions, inhabitants, etc.*, London 1789. (Subsequent editions and translations into Dutch, Swedish and French.)

—— *A Complete Account of the Settlement at Port Jackson in N.S.W., including an accurate description of the situation of the colony*, London, 1793. (These works are particularly valuable sources.)

THOMPSON, G., *Slavery and Famine.* (An account of N.S.W. and of the miserable state of the convicts, by George Thompson, who sailed in the *Royal Admiral*, May 1792 with some preliminary remarks, etc., 1792. The 1794 edition contains an "Extract from the Journal of G. Thompson".)

WATLING, T., *Letters from an Exile at Botany Bay to his Aunt at Dumfries, etc.*, Penrith, 1794, 28 pp.

WHITE, J., *Journal of a Voyage to N.S.W.*, London, 1790. (White was principal surgeon from the time of the First Fleet. This is an excellent source book. French translation, Paris, 1795.)

B. Selective Lists of Later Publications

BARTON, G. B., and BRITTON, A., *History of New South Wales from the Records*, 2 vols., N.S.W. Government publication, 1889, 1894.

BECKE, L., and JEFFERY, W., *The Naval Pioneers of Australia*, 1899.

BLOSSEVILLE, B. E. (Marquis de), *Histoire de la colonisation pénale et des établissements de l'Angleterre en Australie*, 2 vols., Evreux, 1859.

BONWICK, J., *First Twenty Years in Australia*, 1882.

—— *Australia's First Preacher*, 1898.

—— *Romance of the Wool Trade*, 1887.

COGHLAN, SIR T. A., *Labour and Industry in Australia*, 1788-1901. Oxford, 1918.

FORSYTH, W. D., *Governor Arthur's Convict System*, 1935. (An excellent study of convictism, though after 1824.)

JOHNSTONE, S. M., *Samuel Marsden*, Sydney, 1932.

JOSE, A. W., *History of Australia*, various editions.

LANG, REV. J. D., *Transportation and Colonisation: the Causes of the Comparative Failure of the Transportation System, etc.*, 1837.

—— *Historical and Statistical Account of N.S.W. as a Penal Settlement*, 1834 (ed. 1837).

—— *Freedom and Independence for the Golden Lands of Australia*, 1852. (One of the strongest apologies for the transportation system.)

LA PILORGERIE, JULES DE, *Histoire de Botany Bay*, Paris, 1836. (A scientific examination of the effects of transportation, written to induce the French not to copy the English system.)

LEE, IDA, *The Coming of the British to Australia*, 1788-1829, 1906.

LEROY-BEAULIEU, PAUL, *De la Colonisation chez les Peuples Modernes*, Paris, 1874 (éd. 1891). (He passes a favourable judgment on British penal colonization methods: his facts are based on Merivale.)

LUCAS, C. P., *Historical Geography of the British Colonies*, Oxford, 1907 (cf. Vol. VI).

MACARTHUR-ONSLOW, S., *Some Early Records of the Macarthurs of Camden*, Sydney, 1914. (An essential work from the point of view of the free settlers.)

MACKANESS, G., *Sir Joseph Banks*, Sydney, 1936.

MARSDEN, J. B., *Memoirs of the Life and Labours of the Rev Samuel Marsden*, London, 1858 (new ed. Christchurch, 1913).

MILLS, R. C., *The Colonisation of Australia*, 1915. (Though dealing with the period from 1829, has some valuable observations on the earlier systems of colonization.)

MELBOURNE, A. C. V., *Early Constitutional Development in Australia* (N.S.W., 1788-1856) 1934. (He treats the constitutional aspect authoritatively.)

MERIVALE, H., *Lectures on Colonization and Colonies*, 1861. (One of the best surveys of the assignment system.)

MILFORD, G. D., *Governor Phillip and the Early Settlement of N.S.W.*, Sydney, 1935.

MURDOCH, W., *The Making of Australia*, Melbourne, 1917.

O'HARA, J., *History of N.S.W.*, 1788-1812 (published anonymously 1817).

ROYAL AUST. HIST. SOCIETY, *Journal of*: cf. "The Establishment of N.S.W.", by L. Thomas, xi, Pt. 2, 63; "James Mario Matra," by J. H. Watson, xi, Pt. 3, 152; "The Plan of a Colony in N.S.W.," vi, Pt. 1, 36-68; and "Convicts," viii, Pt. 4, 107-208, articles by G. A. Wood.

ROBERTS, S. H., *History of Australian Land Settlement*, Melbourne, 1924. (A valuable work illustrating the legacy left from the Grose-Paterson régime.)

RUSDEN, G. W., *History of Australia*, 3 vols., London, 1883, Melbourne, 1897.

SCOTT, E., *Short History of Australia*, var. ed. (1920 quoted).

—— *Terre Napoléon* (1910). (Cf. also his *Lapérouse*.)

SHANN, E. G., *An Economic History of Australia*, Cambridge, 1930. (A masterly survey from a new point of view.)

WATSON, F., *The Beginnings of Government in Australia*, Sydney, 1913.

WOOD, G. A., *The Discovery of Australia* (1922). (Covers the period prior to settlement.)

WHITE, C., *Convict Life*, (Bathurst, 1889). (The first attempt at a penal history.)

RECENT PUBLICATIONS

MACKANESS, G., *Admiral Arthur Phillip*, Sydney, 1937.

FITZPATRICK, B., *British Imperialism and Australia*, (1783-1833) London, 1939.

WARD, J., *British Policy in the South Pacific*, (1796-1893) Sydney, 1948.

GREENWOOD, G., *Early American-Australian Relations*, Melbourne, 1944.

ELDERSHAW, M.B., *The Life and Times of Captain John Piper*, Sydney, 1939.

FERGUSON, J. A., and others: *The Howes and their Press*, Sydney, 1936.

RUMSEY, H., *The Pioneers of Sydney Cove*, Sydney, 1937.

RUTTER, O., *The First Fleet*, Sydney, 1937.

EVATT, H. V., "The Legal Foundations of N.S.W." (Article in *The Australian Law Digest*, Vol. II, No. 10; 1938).

FERGUSON, J. A., *Bibliography of Australia*, Vol. I, 1784-1830, Sydney, 1941. (This is an indispensable work of reference, precisely describing all publications, books, pamphlets, newspapers, which expressly refer to Australian history in that period.)

INDEX

D0899194